# Cognitive Systems and Signal Processing in Image Processing

Cognitive Data Science in Sustainable Computing

# Cognitive Systems and Signal Processing in Image Processing


Edited by

**Yu-Dong Zhang**

Professor, Department of Informatics, University of Leicester, Leicester, United Kingdom

**Arun Kumar Sangaiah**

School of Computer Science and Engineering, VIT University, Vellore, India

Series Editor

**Arun Kumar Sangaiah**

Academic Press is an imprint of Elsevier
125 London Wall, London EC2Y 5AS, United Kingdom
525 B Street, Suite 1650, San Diego, CA 92101, United States
50 Hampshire Street, 5th Floor, Cambridge, MA 02139, United States
The Boulevard, Langford Lane, Kidlington, Oxford OX5 1GB, United Kingdom



**Library of Congress Cataloging-in-Publication Data**
A catalog record for this book is available from the Library of Congress

**British Library Cataloguing-in-Publication Data**
A catalogue record for this book is available from the British Library

ISBN 978-0-12-824410-4

For information on all Academic Press publications
visit our website at https://www.elsevier.com/books-and-journals

*Publisher:* Mara Conner
*Acquisitions Editor:* Sonnini R. Yura
*Editorial Project Manager:* Mariana L. Kuhl
*Production Project Manager:* Swapna Srinivasan
*Cover Designer:* Matthew Limbert

Typeset by STRAIVE, India

# Contents

# Contributors

*Numbers in paraentheses indicate the pages on which the authors' contributions begin.*

**Vishesh Agarwal** (83), SCOPE, VIT University, Vellore, India

**Rangel Arthur** (1, 101), Faculty of Technology (FT), State University of Campinas (UNICAMP), Limeira, São Paulo, Brazil

**K.R. Anu Bama** (253), Anna University Regional Campus-Tirunelveli, Tirunelveli, TN, India

**P. Darsana** (163), Department of Electronics and Communication Engineering, Amal Jyothi College of Engineering, Kottayam, Kerala

**D. Deepa** (277, 319), Department of CSE, Sathyabama Institute of Science and Technology, Chennai, India

**Dejey** (293), Department of Computer Science and Engineering, Anna University Regional Campus—Tirunelveli, Tirunelveli, Tamil Nadu, India

**M. Kaviya Elakkiya** (293), Department of Computer Science and Engineering, Anna University Regional Campus—Tirunelveli, Tirunelveli, Tamil Nadu, India

**Reinaldo Padilha França** (1, 101), School of Electrical and Computer Engineering (FEEC), State University of Campinas (UNICAMP), Campinas, São Paulo, Brazil

**K. Gopalakrishnan** (337), Department of Electronics and Communication Engineering, Mepco Schlenk Engineering College, Sivakasi, Tamilnadu, India

**Zhilin Hu** (47), Department of Informatics, University of Leicester, Leicester, United Kingdom

**Yuzo Iano** (1, 101), School of Electrical and Computer Engineering (FEEC), State University of Campinas (UNICAMP), Campinas, São Paulo, Brazil

**V. Kakulapati** (359), Sreenidhi Institute of Science and Technology, Hyderabad, Telangana, India

**Grace Prince Kanmani** (277), Sathyabama Institute of Science and Technology, Chennai, India

**B. Vijaya Kumari** (337), Department of Electronics and Communication Engineering, Mepco Schlenk Engineering College, Sivakasi, Tamilnadu, India

**Xiang Li** (145), College of Computer Science and Technology, Henan Polytechnic University, Jiaozuo, People's Republic of China

**Ana Carolina Borges Monteiro** (1, 101), School of Electrical and Computer Engineering (FEEC), State University of Campinas (UNICAMP), Campinas, São Paulo, Brazil

**Mahalakshmi Murugan** (27), School of Computer Science and Engineering, Vellore Institute of Technology, Vellore, Tamil Nadu, India

**Sureshkumar Nagarajan** (27, 129), School of Computer Science and Engineering, Vellore Institute of Technology, Vellore, Tamil Nadu, India

**S. Selva Nidhyananthan** (337), Department of Electronics and Communication Engineering, Mepco Schlenk Engineering College, Sivakasi, Tamilnadu, India

**Nimisha Anns Oommen** (163), Department of Electronics and Communication Engineering, Amal Jyothi College of Engineering, Kottayam, Kerala

**S. Poonguzhali** (319), Department of ECE, Sathyabama Institute of Science and Technology, Chennai, India

**G. Boopathi Raja** (223), Department of ECE, Velalar College of Engineering and Technology, Erode, Tamil Nadu, India

**Immanuel Rajkumar** (319), Department of ECE, Sathyabama Institute of Science and Technology, Chennai, India

**Rahul Raman** (83), IIITDM, Kancheepuram, Chennai, India

**Rohini Selvaraj** (27, 129), School of Computer Science and Engineering, Vellore Institute of Technology, Vellore, Tamil Nadu, India

**R. Newlin Shebiah** (337), Department of Electronics and Communication Engineering, Mepco Schlenk Engineering College, Sivakasi, Tamilnadu, India

**Sindhu** (227), Sathyabama Institute of Science and Technology, Chennai, India

**A. Sivasangari** (277, 319), Department of IT, Sathyabama Institute of Science and Technology, Chennai, India

**Kishore Sonti** (277), Sathyabama Institute of Science and Technology, Chennai, India

**R. Subhashini** (319), Department of IT, Sathyabama Institute of Science and Technology, Chennai, India

**S. Suja Priyadharsini** (253), Anna University Regional Campus-Tirunelveli, Tirunelveli, TN, India

**Junding Sun** (145), College of Computer Science and Technology, Henan Polytechnic University, Jiaozuo, People's Republic of China

**J.S. Vimali** (319), Department of IT, Sathyabama Institute of Science and Technology, Chennai, India

**Chong Yao** (203), School of Computer Science and Technology, Henan Polytechnic University, Jiaozuo, Henan, People's Republic of China

Chapter 1

# A cognitive approach to digital health based on deep learning focused on classification and recognition of white blood cells

Ana Carolina Borges Monteiro[a], Reinaldo Padilha França[a], Rangel Arthur[b], and Yuzo Iano[a]

*[a]School of Electrical and Computer Engineering (FEEC), State University of Campinas (UNICAMP), Campinas, São Paulo, Brazil, [b]Faculty of Technology (FT), State University of Campinas (UNICAMP), Limeira, São Paulo, Brazil*

## 1 Introduction

Cognitive computing (CC) brings together the concepts of artificial intelligence (AI) technology and machine learning (ML) technology, consisting of technologies that work in a complementary way, being the most advanced resources to have the generation of insights, making technology capable of processing information similar to the way the human brain does. Evaluating the great prominence of the technology applied in the support of doctors in the diagnosis and treatment of diseases through image analysis, for example [1].

Cognitive systems are taught not to consume information to deliver responses but to analyze complex situations, taking into account the context of each one, the environment, and the intention. The idea is that all decisions are made following the same reasoning as a person. In this sense, AI can learn, decide, and self-correct, being able to program so that it learns pattern recognition, identifying anomalies among other applications parallel to CC [2].

CC and AI have in common the resources they use to perform their tasks, highlighting ML and strands, such as an artificial neural network (ANN) and deep learning (DL), which can be applied to solve a problem, identify patterns between data, and relate them, which makes it able to handle only one dataset and indicate solutions that have been fed into the system. Considering the CC

**Cognitive Systems and Signal Processing in Image Processing. http://doi.org/10.1016/B978-0-12-824410-4.00016-7**

resources, this is directed at systems taught to think, simulating human lines of reasoning with algorithms, which makes them capable of dealing with complex demands that are not always related [3].

This is the great advantage of CC over other computer technologies, given its properties of imitating the functioning of the human brain, cognitive systems are able to adapt themselves to any unforeseen event occurring during the process, not requiring the intervention of human hands during the operation. It fits with DL emulating how the human brain operates, so machines can be trained to treat problems and ill-defined issues, which incorporates neural networks in consecutive layers learning from data iteratively, encompassing a system in which neurons organize themselves in "hidden" layers below the surface of the ANN, that is, it is especially useful to learn unstructured data patterns DL complex [4].

The challenge and the research problem is related to the recognition of medical digital images in the detection and classification of nonpathological leukocytes present in human blood smear fields. This is associated with the difficulty in the accuracy of this type of approach due to this type of medical image having several and different cell types present in it, which increases the degree of complexity in the differentiation, identification, and classification of the correct cell subtypes.

In this context, employing the Jupyter Notebook together with Python programming language, a dataset was utilized comprising 12,500 medical images of human blood smear fields of nonpathological leukocytes and achieving an accuracy from a respective cognitive approach at 84.19%, which demonstrates the high reliability of the proposal developed.

The major contribution and findings of the research are on the framework developed achieving high accuracy in the detection and classification of nonpathological leukocytes present in medical images of human blood smear fields. This framework can help diagnose and confirm medical suspicion related to infection and more serious cases, like leukemia, allowing for early diagnosis, given the possibility of measuring the quantity and types of white blood cells (WBCs).

The motivation of this chapter is related to the development of a framework based on a neural network (metaheuristics), which is a CC approach, consisting of the processing of a dataset of digital images for classifying leukocyte types (healthcare), through technology DL (branch of AI that deals with soft computing) employing Python, and achieving a high performance of accuracy.

So, it is worth highlighting the potential in developing tools (i.e., why this kind of research work is needed) that facilitate the obtaining of medical diagnostics with low cost and reliability, still pondering the inaccessible reality to populations of underdeveloped and developing countries concerning laboratory medical exams that generally present inapproachable costs. The importance of this study derives from factors like these, in line with the contributions of this research; it is necessary to use and employ knowledge and academic values for the development of frameworks for this purpose. Therefore, the cognitive approach is considered a reliable and inexpensive method that can be implemented as a third practicable procedure for blood count in often underprivileged countries.

In Section 2, the CC concept for understanding the research is presented. In Section 3, cognitive systems in medical image processing are discussed. In Section 4, neural networks concepts are presented. In Section 5, the metaheuristic algorithm proposal (digital image processing cognitive) is explained. In Section 6, the results are discussed. In Section 7, the conclusions are highlighted. Finally, the chapter ends with direction for future research.

## 2 Literature review

CC is derived from self-learning systems employing techniques to accomplish particular human tasks intelligently, in addition to being commonly associated with this conjunction between AI and CC. This method improves and extends the range of actions/processes that are generally correlated to the performance of the human thought process and traditional analysis. The growth of such innovations has been exponential as the applications of technology become more sophisticated [1, 5].

The ability of CC, including ML, DL, natural language processing, and even data mining, is applied against dense data sets assisting in finding known and unknown indicators and insights. Given the progression over time relating to using a huge volume of internal and external pieces of information and data from institutions, however, conventional methods of analysis have become unable to deal with that volume of data. Instead, cognitive analysis quickly takes advantage of unstructured data and reduces subjectivity in decision making [6].

CC affects all areas of society, from travel, sports, and entertainment to fitness, health, and well-being, including human health. This is an evolution of programmable computing (traditional), given that these systems aim to expand the limits of human cognition. This technology is not intended to replace or replicate how the human brain operates; it is about expanding your capabilities [7].

The human capacity to analyze and process a large amount of data, unstructured and structured, is naturally weak. Therefore, the main role of CC is to combine the forces of humans and machines in a collaborative way [8, 9].

The demands orientated by Big Data and the requirement for complex evidence-based decisions are beyond the previous (traditional) rule and the logical approach to evolved computing. In this context, CC refers to systems that learn at scale, interact with human beings naturally, and instead of being explicitly programmed, learns and reasons digitally with their interactions and experiences with the environment [8, 9].

CC finds insights blocked in the amount of data, serving to evolve the human experience with intelligent systems that reason about issues like a human. CC can help physicians do a lot of preliminary research and analysis, diagnosing a patient with unusual symptoms, by searching a vast amount of information to arrive at an appropriate diagnosis [10, 11].

In essence, CC can contextualize the data that professionals deal with daily, generating real value from it. CC uses the machine's potency to "simulate" human thought in a computer model. As CC mimics human thinking, the quality of the algorithms and models used are enhanced with ML throughout the learning and training process [10, 11].

## 2.1 Cognitive systems concepts

The explosion of data in recent years, mainly unstructured data, has led to the development of cognitive systems, which unlike programmable systems are not focused on making quick calculations on a large volume of data through software but are focused on exploring the data and finding correlations and the context in those pieces of information and data providing new solutions [11].

Cognitive systems rely on the premise to expand the limits of human cognition instead of replicating or even replacing the way the human brain operates by analyzing this huge amount of data quickly, identifying patterns of development, and predicting or projecting what is likely to happen in the near future [12].

A key element of cognitive systems is that it has properties to continuously learn and increase productivity by providing the ability to view and use, more effectively, a large volume of data, processed, and analyzed by a single task and a user. Another key element is a natural interaction between humans and machines, combining the ability of learning and adapting over time [12, 13].

Cognitive systems employ techniques like data mining, ML, natural language processing, and pattern recognition to mimic the functioning of the human brain. These systems have ideal characteristics for interacting with an increasingly complex world, such as the modern one. This method has several main characteristics, such as searching for a large volume of data, combining different pieces of information, and establishing connections and relationships between that data [13].

The advantages of this system are in making sufficient analyzations to extract key elements, understanding the issue that the human being is trying to resolve, and bringing information and data for this. The objective is for a human being to easily take advantage of the data provided and allow the evidence to be explored and utilize the insight to make decisions from it or to solve a particular issue [14].

The first advantage is in the more natural interaction and involvement between computers and human beings. Evaluating from a historical point of view, humans were required to interact with machines, adapting to the way they worked on the computer interface, which used to be inflexible. Exemplifying speech recognition technology allows users to interact digitally with the device using voice commands [5, 15].

Another advantage is the use of ML, expanding the learning potential and the ability to adapt over time with use. Therefore, a cognitive system captures the results of this interaction (man-machine) and learns from the resulting interaction, evolving automatically throughout it, improving its performance [5, 15].

In this way, cognitive systems "digitally comprehending" digital images, natural language, and even other unstructured data, like human beings, are operationalizing practically all data (structured and unstructured). It can also reason, form hypotheses, understand underlying concepts, and extract ideas. And still learn from each data interaction and result, developing and increasing the experience, and continue to learn and adapt [16].

In this sense, it is worth mentioning that information systems are deterministic, while cognitive systems are probabilistic. In other words, this generates not only answers to hypotheses but also numerical problems, arguments, and even recommendations for complex and significant data bodies [5, 16].

## 3 Cognitive systems in medical image processing

In practice, models of cognitive systems are based on DL and different techniques and concepts, such as computer vision and computer learning through ANNs. Since they are cheaper approaches compared to doctors and specialists and their superiority is demonstrated, they can be much more cost-effective, allowing diagnostic access to several regions with scarce resources [17].

To assess the potential of cognitive systems in supporting the diagnosis of medical images, it is possible to mention eye scanning (background examination, retinoscopy), given that a cognitive algorithm can identify data from the retina (through image tests) that are used to detect risks of cardiovascular disease and other perceptible diseases through eye changes. Through cognitive systems, this type of retinal analysis can gain greater reach and practicality, especially when an institution has a retinoscope but does not have a specialist (ophthalmologists) to interpret the images, mainly for normality screening [18, 19].

Naturally, the use of digital image processing techniques is responsible for attributing greater speed and reliability to medical analysis, especially when this process involves the quantification of human cells. It is important to note that activities normally performed by human beings tend to be flawed since health professionals are subject to tiredness, stress, and long work shifts, which consequently cause the attention and commitment in a cell quantification activity to be compromised. This error negatively impacts both the patient's life and those of health professionals [20–25].

Thus, combining cognitive systems with digital medical image processing methods can help a specialist detect rare cases and peculiarities that are sometimes not easily visible to the naked eye. Furthermore, when the possible diagnoses present very similar images or have extreme variability, the cognitive systems can provide greater security for professionals [26].

Cognitive systems have great potential in the area of radiology, since the specialty is based on the analysis of images of different modalities, supplementing and helping the clinical diagnosis. However, often the professional can only differentiate diagnoses that are equally possible based on additional information. Cognitive systems also make it possible to combine several sources of information, in addition to the image, to obtain more precise and specific diagnoses [19, 27].

Cognitive systems aimed at medical image processing are consistent for areas that present complex exams, such as tomography, MRI, and nuclear images, or even in more difficult diagnostic organs, such as lungs, breasts, and brain, and certain specialties such as mastology and oncology, are those that benefit from advances in this technology. This type of approach replaces invasive and high-risk actions such as brain biopsies, for example, or even confirming the diagnosis of bone fractures and other simpler exams [28].

Other advantages of cognitive systems and digital image processing methods in relation to imaging exams are increased productivity and better management of these exams, as specialist professionals will be able to focus on cases with abnormalities, thus optimizing their demands and identifying cases that require more time, care, and attention. A quick diagnosis of cases that require immediate treatment would be possible, prioritizing the analysis of images with anomalies previously identified by cognitive systems and preventing the progress of tumors and other serious diseases. This would mean greater security for the diagnosis, considering the used image banks containing an incomparably greater number of details than medical books and manuals, and greater certainty of the results to the specialist professionals [29–32].

## 3.1 Cognitive systems in the context of predictive analytics

In the health area, predictive analysis through cognitive systems can, for example, build the health profile of patients, map regions with a higher incidence of certain pathologies, predict the costs of exams and hospitalizations, predict bed occupancy rates, and inform how to apply preventive medicine to prevent potential infections and diseases [10, 32].

By identifying patterns using tools such as ML, DL, time series, data mining, forecasting, neural networks, among other techniques, making it possible to generate insights for more effective and assertive decision making. With this information, it is still possible to simulate new scenarios in a practical and fast way without the costs resulting from prototypes, for example [12, 32].

Predictive analysis is a technique that uses patterns observed in cognitive systems that occurred in the past, determining probabilities of future events. In this process, in general, methodologies such as ML and strands are used to analyze a vast amount of health data, for example, discovering the probabilities of a certain patient having a spine surgery 1 year before a clinical diagnosis [11, 32].

With the development of more accurate and powerful cognitive algorithms, predictive analysis becomes increasingly reliable, creating cognitive models in conjunction with physicians and obtaining gains in scale due to predictive analyses being processed with existing computational power. Predictive analysis using cognitive models can study the layout of hospital facilities and their influence on the level of care, creating an analytical profile for the proper functioning of the institution through predictive evaluation and interpretation of results. It can also perform predictive analysis on the supply and demand of services from a demographic, epidemiological, or even institutional point of view, minimizing the costs resulting from misdiagnosis and the disorder generated to the patient [33].

It is important to mention the possibility of identifying an event, even before it occurs, making the performance of health agents much more effective. The applicability of predictive analysis tools using data to predict a given scenario and identify a specific trend, such as COVID-19, has become essential in fighting disease outbreaks. Thus, predictive analysis with cognitive systems, in turn, filter data about people to determine the chances of disease occurrence, mapping, and prevention in an attempt to avoid an unfavorable outcome, thus taking a new look at the health sector [34].

The predictive analysis process with cognitive systems takes into account the volume of information for the creation of statistically robust and accurate predictive models that determine, without any guesswork or futurology, what will actually happen. In this context, from the patient's perspective, it is possible to outline their health profile, which can even prevent potential future diseases and improve the level of service provided. An example of this context would be the previous detection of individuals whose behavior indicates a high probability of infarction in a matter of months [10, 11, 34].

It is worth noting that for good efficiency of a predictive model, a considerable and consistent volume of historical data is required. In this sense, it is possible, for cognitive systems to map out what information and indicators are needed for the case studies as a fundamental step for the success of the predictive evaluation. A model's capacity to deal with data, interpret the information contained therein, and in turn, be independent of the human being is fundamental [10, 11, 34].

## 4 Neural networks concepts

Neural networks are computational algorithms with interlinked nodes that function like human neurons; this has been transforming the way users and companies interact with intelligent systems, solving problems, and making better decisions, and even better predictions. This is able to identify hidden patterns and correlations in volume data, with the ability to group and classify it, and continually improve learning [35].

ANNs are computational techniques that can have thousands of digital processing units acquiring knowledge through experience, presenting a mathematical model oriented by the neural structure (brain functioning) of intelligent organisms [36].

Taking into account that a simple ANN, including an input layer, an output layer, and among them, a hidden layer. The layers are linked through nodes, and these links form a "neural network" of interlinked nodes, making operations only on their local data. The operation of which is quite simple, usually connected and associated with a weight, since the "intelligent behavior" is from interactions between these digital processing units [37].

It is also worth mentioning that usually the layers in ANNs are categorized into input layer (inserted patterns to the neural network), hidden layers (processing, weighted connections, extraction of characteristics); and output layer (result is presented) [38].

Defining terminology with respect to the neural network, an artificial neuron is capable of single processing and each input receives only one type of signal or information. In that sense, given that a neuron can have several inputs, then it can perceive different signals. Or even connect several similar neurons in a network, making the system able to process more information and offer more results. Thus, signals are presented at the input; each one is multiplied by a value or weight indicating its influence on the output of the layer, given that neural architectures are typically organized in layers, with units that can be connected to the units of the posterior layer, responsible for perceiving a certain type of signal. In sequence, the weighted sum of the signals that produce an activity level is made; and if this level of activity exceeds a threshold, the layer produces a certain output response. In this regard, generally, ANN models have some type of training, that is, weights of connections are adjusted according to the standards of data, meaning they learn through examples (dataset) [39].

Analogously with human brain biology, an artificial node is modeled after the behavior of a human neuron, activating when there are inputs. This specific activation spreads through the ANN, responding to the stimulus, that is, a result. Likewise, the links between these neurons act as synapses, causing signals transmitted from one to the other. There is also signaling between layers as it transits from the input layer (first) to the output layer, that is, the result layer, performing information processing along the way. There are also artificial neural architectures that have a body of processors responsible for a feedback system that modifies its own programming depending on the input and output data. Finally, they have a binary output to display the answer "yes/1" or "no/0," depending on the result of the processing [40].

Given a problem to be solved, artificial neurons perform mathematical calculations to decide if there is sufficient data to be sent to the next neuron. Evaluating a simpler model of a neural network, the inputs are added and the artificial neuron transmits the information and activates the neurons connected to it. At the same time, as the number of hidden layers within an ANN increase,

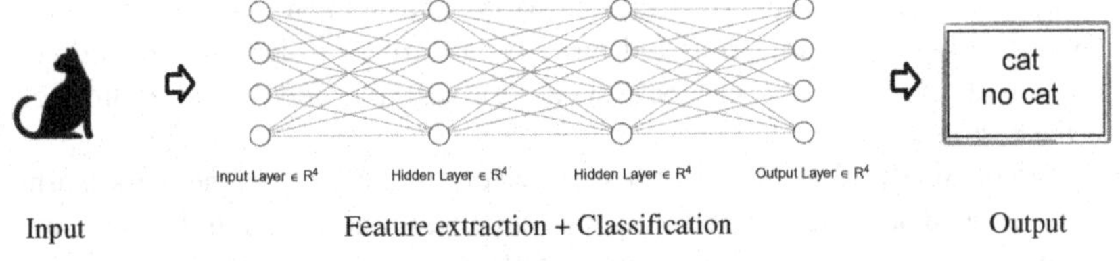


**FIG. 1** Deep learning.

deep neural networks are formed. This factor is characteristic of DL architectures taking simple ANN to another level (Fig. 1). Through this technology, it is possible that a trained neural network can accurately recognize patterns in many layers of processing, making predictions and obtaining insights. It is worth noting that an ANN is specified for its topology, the properties of the nodes, and the training rules [41].

In Fig. 1 a scheme exemplifying the operation of a logic based on DL is observed. With the input of the image (figure of a cat), the digital neurons transmit the information and connect to each other. There is an increase in layers and subsequent pattern recognition resulting in a classification of objects of interest; in this case, it classifies whether the input image is of a cat or not.

Through the panorama of neural networks with hidden layers, the data are inserted (input layer), communicating (hidden layers) and performing the processing through weighted connections. The nodes in these hidden layers match the data (input layer) with a set of coefficients evaluating different weights to the inputs. The results of these evaluated entries are then added up. The sum goes through the function of activating a node, determining the path that this signal must follow in the neural network to effectuate the final result. Thus, the hidden layers connect to the output layer, expressing the results (Fig. 2) [42].

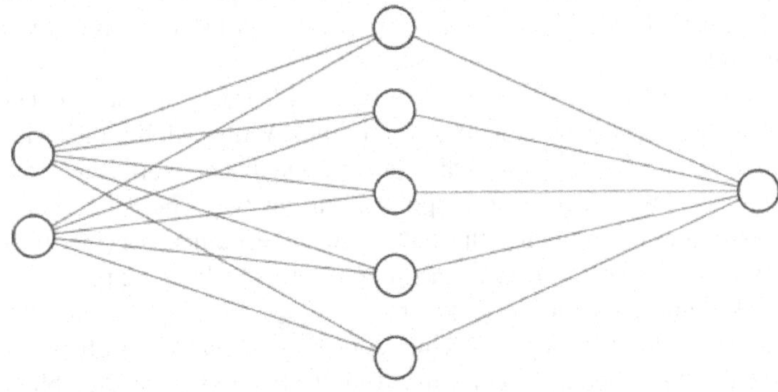


**FIG. 2** Neural networks.

In Fig. 2 an illustration of neural networks with hidden layers is observed, demonstrating communication and processing through weighted connections. There is a sum of the input coefficients, through the nodes, and expression of the results.

The great advantage of this is that to perform tasks, a neural network learns what needs to be done and performs the function, without having to store command instructions and logically execute them, as in a traditional computer. Thus, if this is enabled with the necessary artificial neurons, it is able to perform several different functions, regardless of memory space [43].

The applicability of neural networks is ideally directed to assist humans to resolve complex issues in different situations in real life. This can make inferences and even generalizations, reveal hidden patterns, and make predictions. This also models highly volatile data (financial time series data) and variances predicting events (fraud detection)—including fraud detection on credit cards and healthcare; recognition of characters and elements in medical images for medical diagnoses; identification of chemical compounds; or even computer vision for interpreting untreated photos and videos, such as obtaining medical images and facial recognition [18, 44].

From the characteristic of an iterative adjustment process applied to your weight (training), occurring when reaching a generalized solution for a class of problems. This is consistent with the most important characteristics of ANN that are directed at learning from its environment and thereby improving its performance. In terms of terminology, intelligent learning is a set of well-defined rules. There are types of particular learning for certain models of ANN, differing mainly on how network weights modify [45].

It is also important to note that there are learning paradigms, that is, how a neural network relates to the environment. In supervised learning, an external agent is used indicating the desired response to the input pattern to the network. Or still, unsupervised learning (self-organization) is directed when no external agent is indicating the desired response to the entry patterns; reinforcement learning is directed when an external critic evaluates the response provided by the network [46].

The main characteristic of the existing types of learning is when the neural network tests the object's perception several times. With each hit, the artificial neurons involved in the processing earn "points" and that network is reinforced. With each error, these neurons lose "points." In this way, the neural network creates the routine of following the path with more points, considering that the more attempts, the better it gets, reaching the end of a learning process, performing tasks almost without any error [47].

This health-oriented technology achieves predictive diagnostics, biomedical imaging, and patient health monitoring. Neural networks have the ability to identify anomalies in medical datasets. Offering doctors a second opinion, confirming a cancer diagnosis, or saying what the patient's problem is through an intelligent digital opinion faster and with greater precision [18, 47].

## 4.1 Convolutional neural network

Convolutional neural networks (CNNs) popularize image classification and object detection, usually containing five types of layers: input, convolution, grouping, completely connected (classifications), and output. Each having a specific purpose, such as summary, connection, or activation. This is a class of ML models widely used in problems in which data is organized in a grid, such as time series, text analysis, and image recognition. The way the structure of a CNN is constructed, that is, the number of convolution layers alternating with the grouping layers depends on the application [48].

A CNN can also be divided into two parts: feature extraction (convolution, padding, ReLU, pooling) and a traditional neural network. In this sense, convolution is a linear mathematical operation that from two functions, generates a third (feature map), since applied in the context of images, this process is understood as a filter/kernel transforming an input image [44].

Just as many convolutions impact CNN's assertiveness if the image size is very small, since bypassing this, padding is normally used. Padding is a process in which some pixels are added around the image before the convolution operation, maintaining the dimensionality in the resulting image during the operation [49].

ReLU is an activation function that makes a model linear, since most complex problems are not linear, and thus, to add nonlinearity to the neural network, activation functions are used.

The CNN input layer is an image of any color scheme, consequently, the deconvolution layer of each neuron is associated with a kernel window (composed of the values of the artificial neuron binding weights) that will be converted into the input image. The kernel in the image produces a filtered output for the next layer, that is, that output from each location through which the kernel passes forms a pixel of the map representing the image, which is then passed on to the next layer. This operation represented by a slide of a parameter grid through the image is that of convolution [44, 49].

After the convolution layer, it is common to apply a layer of pooling of pixels, given the importance of this step to be related to the reduction in the dimensionality of the characteristic maps, accelerating the time that is necessary for training the network. Usually, with a medium or maximum grouping, the grouping layer also has a kernel, which passes through the image by computing the grouping function. This is a downsampling process, basically, this digital transformation is understandable as a reduction in the image size [48, 49].

Max pooling removes the largest element of a given region of the image matrix, taking into account the size of the applied pool. Then, a slip is made considering a stride parameter (similar to the convolution operation) to apply a new operation. Dropout is used to prevent certain parts of the ANN from being too responsible/overloaded and being very sensitive to small changes, this is generally not a specificity of a CNN [39, 49].

Flatten basically operates a transformation in the image matrix, changing its format to an array, used in the division of the two parts of CNN: the part of the extraction of characteristics and the part of the traditional neural network [40, 49].

Generally, in a CNN, layers of convolution and pooling alternate, and after extraction of characteristics from the original image, there is a dense layer that consists of a conventional neural network for classification. The architecture of these neural networks uses multiple layers allowing the extraction of several characteristics of the image from the layers of convolutions, recognizing borders, circles, lines, textures, among other elements, due to the values of the filters (kernel) applied in these layers, which are result of the backpropagation of the training stage. In addition to reducing the number of parameters, CNN structures in such a way as to induce a priori knowledge that the data are in a grid format, as is the case with digital images [40, 41, 49].

Thus, CNN detects patterns in digital images, being able to learn the digital invariance in the dataset, increasing the representative power of the neural network, by adding convolutional layers or one or more dense hidden layers, and consequently detecting the pattern, regardless of the position of a desired element in the digital image, since the kernel passes through the entire image (Fig. 3). Therefore, a CNN through an image in the input layer of the neural network produces a refined and deep characteristic map as an output (Fig. 4) [40, 41, 49].

## 4.2 Deep learning

DL is a subcategory of ML that has become one of the most studied fields within modern computer science, which concerns the use of neural networks imitating the behavior of the human brain to understand the information that the system

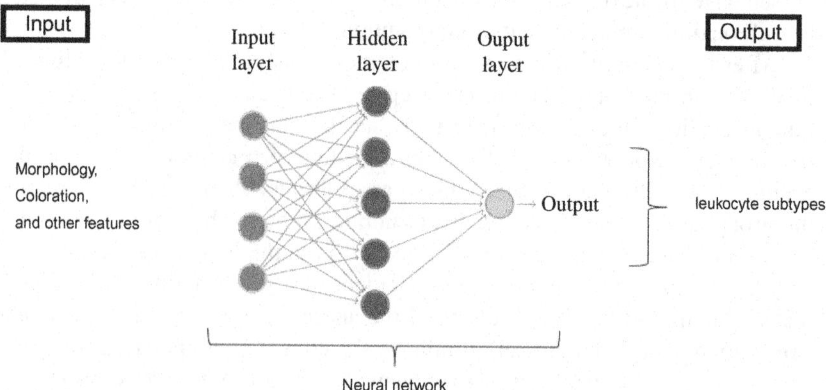


**FIG. 3** Scheme showing the logic of operation and recognition used by the deep learning technique.

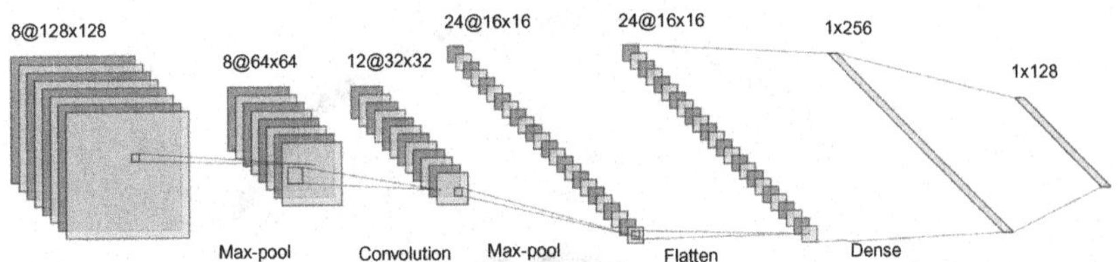


**FIG. 4** Illustration of the functioning of convolutional neural networks.

captures. Given that neural networks are chain layers that act hierarchically in the processing of information, allowing a larger and more complex analysis of each data, generating dynamic results with this data, with respect to speech recognition, computer vision, and natural language processing [50].

DL is the base technology for tools with a huge amount of computational power, making AI really intelligent and applicable, making machines able to recognize objects and translate voice in real-time. Technically, DL trains a computational model so that it can decipher the natural language, for example, making this model relate terms and words to infer meaning since it is fed with large amounts of data [51].

It is worth mentioning that the quality of the algorithms depends on the representation of the data in certain characteristics (features) since in the scope of image analysis, it is common to do the preprocessing with edge detection algorithms (edges) to facilitate the identification of objects. However, DL algorithms dispense with much of this preprocessing and automatically generate invariant properties in their hierarchical representation layers, using several layers of nonlinear data processing (image pixels) and managing to obtain a complex and abstract representation of the data in a hierarchical way [52].

Some of the main applications of DL used today are classification of medical diseases, such as technologies that assist ophthalmologists in medical examinations to identify retinas affected by diabetes through the analysis of digital images, reduce errors of cancer diagnoses, and assist in the identification of cancer cells through digital lymph node images. The healthcare industry has benefited greatly from digital image diagnoses in which diseases are identified much more quickly and efficiently, using the comparison of images in an updated database [53].

One of the main technologies that go hand in hand with the concept of DL is ML; both are closely linked to AI but are not synonymous. To understand these subtle differences, it is essential to understand that one has evolved from the other. It all started with AI, a branch of computer science in which research is developed to find solutions that simulate human reasoning ability (in which DL and ML are included) (Fig. 5) [42].

ML is the use of algorithms to make machines able to organize data, identify patterns, and through variations of inputs, learn from these models without necessarily having to preprogram. DL is a deeper level, with high-level algorithms,

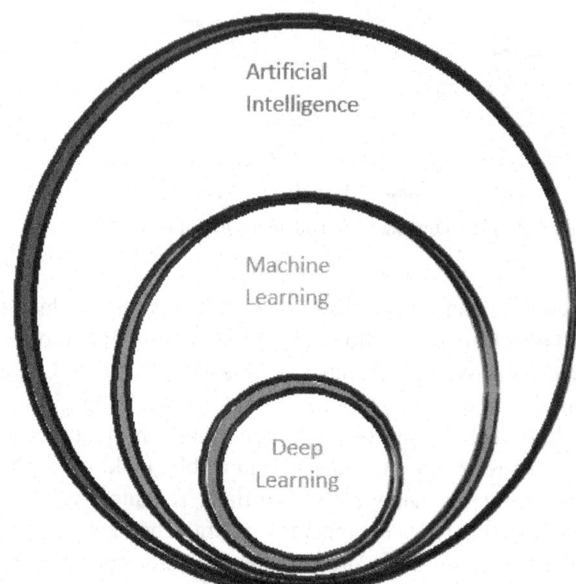


**FIG. 5** Artificial learning technologies.

making the machines start to act in a similar way to the neural network of the human brain. This assumes that the data are submitted to several layers of nonlinear processing, as occurs in the network of neurons, and are capable of recognizing images and speech in order to perform extremely complex tasks without human intervention in the process [54].

It is also worth noting that the database of an AI needs to be large, in addition to being fed uninterruptedly, for it to be able to develop. In practice, DL is an evolution of ML, since it is based on neural networks, while ML is linear. Because it is linear, machines learn from data without programming but do not have the digital capacity to assimilate it. DL is capable of assimilation since it recognizes and performs several tasks simultaneously from the data it captures. It also brings data capable of improving learning functions, recognizing and processing insights that make technologies continue to evolve independently (Fig. 6) [55].

## 5 Metaheuristic algorithm proposal (experiment)

A dataset [56] with 12,500 digital images related to blood cells was employed for implementing the algorithm of CNN, qualifying 4 morphological cell types (with dimensions of 320 × 240 px) as monocytes, neutrophils, eosinophils, and lymphocytes and taking into consideration the implementation of a denial logic for basophil morphological cell type categorization (Fig. 7). Further established was a class 2400 digital images (with dimensions of 320 × 240 px)

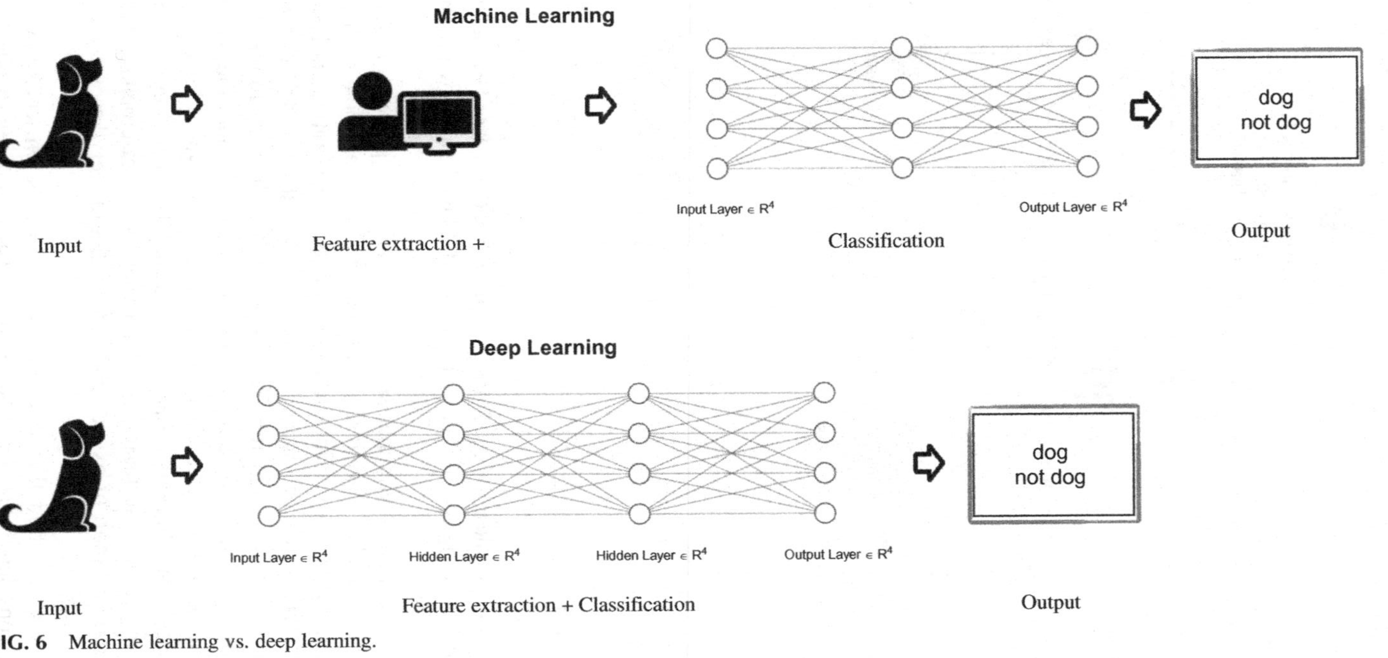


**FIG. 6** Machine learning vs. deep learning.

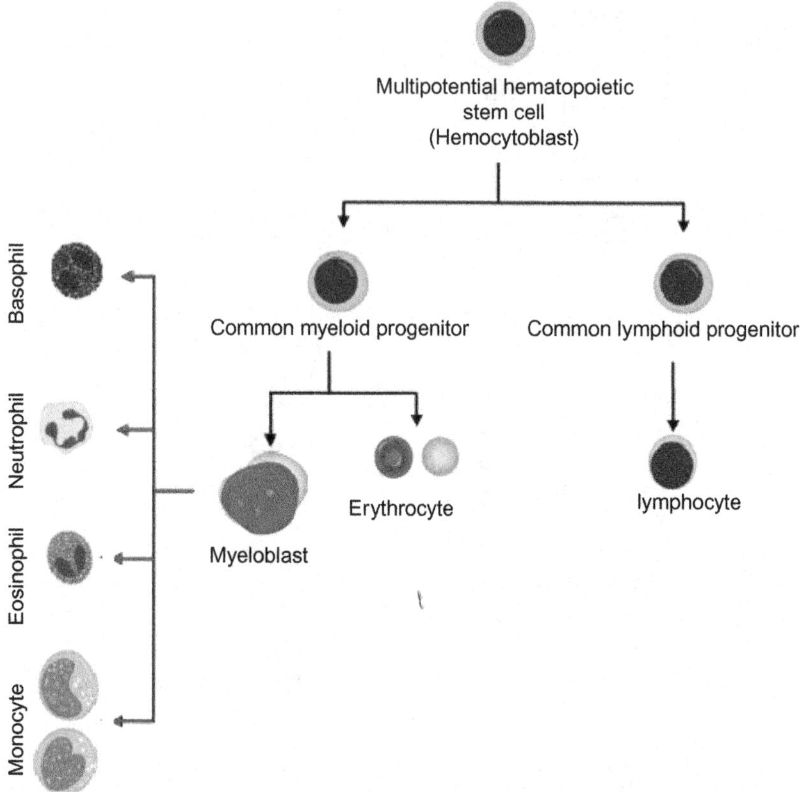


**FIG. 7** Blood cell morphological types.

corresponding to the training of implemented CNN (Figs. 8 and 9) and the application of 4 more classes utilizing 600 blood cell digital images (with dimensions of 640 × 480 px) to test the elaborate neural network.

Fig. 7 shows an erythropoiesis scheme, that is, the process of synthesis of blood cells that takes place inside the bone marrow of long bones. This process is performed from intrauterine life and goes through maturation until adulthood. For this, there is a dependence on cytokines, interleukins, and factors that stimulate the mutilation and maturation of blood cells, which are formed by means of a stem cell. The result is the release of mature cells into the bloodstream, which play the role of defending the body (leukocytes) against infections caused by viruses (lymphocytes), bacteria (neutrophils), parasites (eosinophils), chronic infections, and tissue repair (monocytes and macrophages), allergies (basophils), transport of oxygen and carbon dioxide (erythrocytes) and blood clotting (platelets).

Figs. 8 and 9 show the modeling proposed by the present study, where it must be considered that blood is a liquid tissue composed of plasma (water,

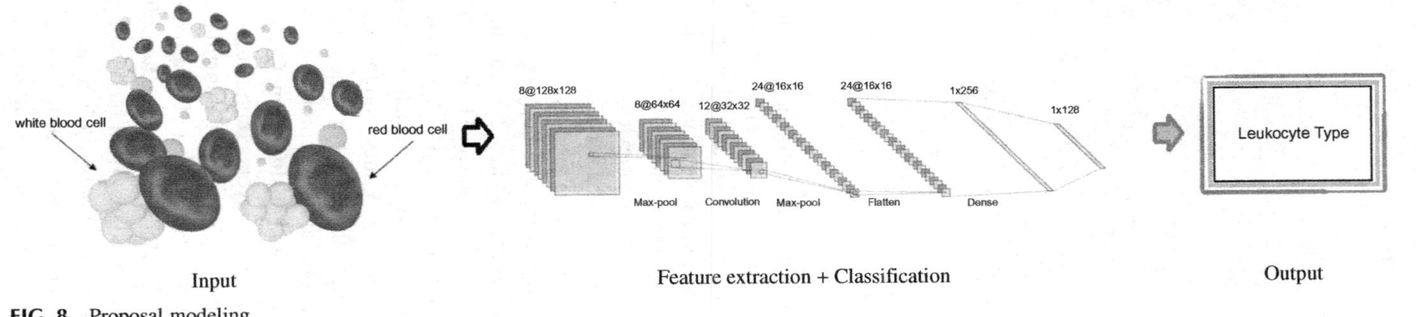


**FIG. 8** Proposal modeling.

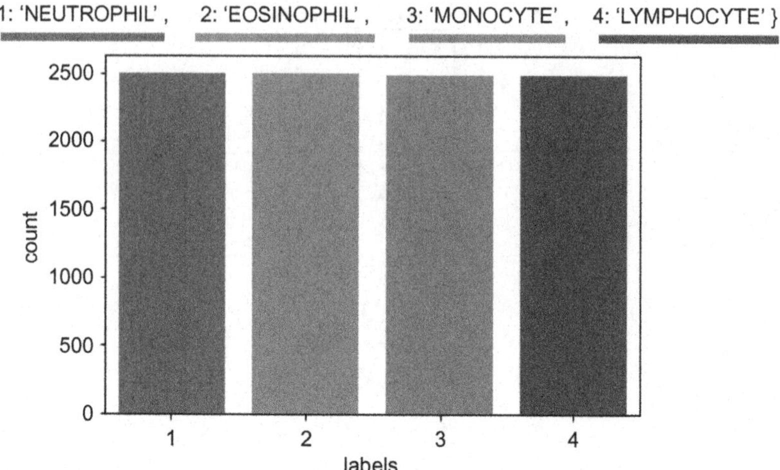


**FIG. 9** Leukocyte classes.

salts, hormones, antibodies, among others) and a solid part composed of blood cells (red blood cells, leukocytes, and platelets). As previously presented, each cell group performs its specific function and the increase in the synthesis of each of these elements is a strong indication of the presence of pathology. Based on this, the proposed modeling focuses on the identification of four groups of leukocytes: neutrophils, eosinophils, monocytes, and lymphocytes, which indicate the presence of diseases caused by bacteria, allergens, and viruses, which are extremely common in the medical laboratory routine.

The CNN was conceived using the Jupyter Notebook software (version 0.35.4), with Kera's open-source library for training a neural network, that is, DL API written in Python 3.7 language. The execution of the CNN algorithm was measured on a hardware Intel Core i3 with 4 GB RAM. The size of the dataset images was reduced to $60 \times 80 \times 3$, which favors the training of the neural network and avoids dimensionality issues, and the images were then loaded as numerical arrays. These were the employed methods and objects for dataset processing through Kera's libraries for preprocessing digital images. Thus, for blood image classification and qualification, CNN summarizes a set of convolution layers and feed-forward layers combined.

Regarding the dataset, it is composed of colorful blood cell images inserted in the structure of the neural network by a 3D matrix, that is, from an additive color system summarized by RGB (red, green, and blue) tones. In this sense, CNN extracts resources (from edges) from blood cell images, shaping convolution operations. A simple neural network is unable to learn those composite features present in a blood cell or even qualify these existing resources in each cell type in a dataset; they are laborious operations. So, CNN's logical architecture is illustrated in the flowchart related to Fig. 10.

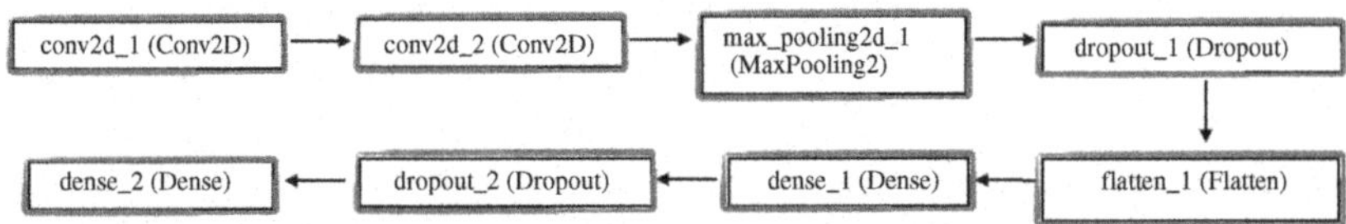


**FIG. 10** CNN architecture.

## 6 Results and discussion

The CNN algorithm was executed with 44 epochs on a physical machine, as previously mentioned, achieving an accuracy of 84.19% (Fig. 11), representing a significant result due to the complexity of the neural network developed in view of the heterogeneity relative to the different cell morphologies.

The research evaluation metric is related to parameter *Accuracy*, derived from the Keras library for Python, which is a metric for evaluating DL models for classifying digital images. As a standard, the logic used is derived through the parameter "*model.fit_generator*" with the training of 44 epochs, still performing model validation through the parameter "*validation_data*."

In this sense, Figs. 11 and 12 prove that trained CNN classified and qualified a cell type of leukocyte, particularly monocyte (Fig. 13), indicating the accuracy

```
A: 34s - loss: 0.2863 - acc: 0.89 - ETA: 33s - loss: 0.2865 - acc: 0.89 - ETA: 32s - loss: 0.2863 - acc: 0.89 - ETA: 32s
- loss: 0.2864 - acc: 0.89 - ETA: 31s - loss: 0.2867 - acc: 0.89 - ETA: 30s - loss: 0.2867 - acc: 0.89 - ETA: 29s - loss:
0.2866 - acc: 0.89 - ETA: 29s - loss: 0.2864 - acc: 0.89 - ETA: 28s - loss: 0.2861 - acc: 0.89 - ETA: 27s - loss: 0.2866
- acc: 0.89 - ETA: 26s - loss: 0.2862 - acc: 0.89 - ETA: 26s - loss: 0.2869 - acc: 0.89 - ETA: 25s - loss: 0.2875 - acc:
0.89 - ETA: 24s - loss: 0.2873 - acc: 0.89 - ETA: 23s - loss: 0.2877 - acc: 0.89 - ETA: 22s - loss: 0.2878 - acc: 0.89 -
ETA: 22s - loss: 0.2873 - acc: 0.89 - ETA: 21s - loss: 0.2870 - acc: 0.89 - ETA: 20s - loss: 0.2869 - acc: 0.89 - ETA: 19
s - loss: 0.2864 - acc: 0.89 - ETA: 19s - loss: 0.2859 - acc: 0.89 - ETA: 18s - loss: 0.2852 - acc: 0.89 - ETA: 17s - los
s: 0.2848 - acc: 0.89 - ETA: 16s - loss: 0.2846 - acc: 0.89 - ETA: 16s - loss: 0.2851 - acc: 0.89 - ETA: 15s - loss: 0.28
47 - acc: 0.89 - ETA: 14s - loss: 0.2850 - acc: 0.89 - ETA: 13s - loss: 0.2851 - acc: 0.89 - ETA: 13s - loss: 0.2854 - ac
c: 0.89 - ETA: 12s - loss: 0.2849 - acc: 0.89 - ETA: 11s - loss: 0.2848 - acc: 0.89 - ETA: 10s - loss: 0.2857 - acc: 0.89
- ETA: 9s - loss: 0.2860 - acc: 0.8930 - ETA: 9s - loss: 0.2856 - acc: 0.893 - ETA: 8s - loss: 0.2861 - acc: 0.893 - ETA:
7s - loss: 0.2861 - acc: 0.892 - ETA: 6s - loss: 0.2858 - acc: 0.893 - ETA: 6s - loss: 0.2858 - acc: 0.892 - ETA: 5s - lo
ss: 0.2860 - acc: 0.892 - ETA: 4s - loss: 0.2859 - acc: 0.892 - ETA: 3s - loss: 0.2854 - acc: 0.892 - ETA: 3s - loss: 0.2
853 - acc: 0.892 - ETA: 2s - loss: 0.2852 - acc: 0.892 - ETA: 1s - loss: 0.2846 - acc: 0.892 - ETA: 0s - loss: 0.2846 - a
cc: 0.892 - ETA: 0s - loss: 0.2847 - acc: 0.892 - 318s 1s/step - loss: 0.2844 - acc: 0.8929 - val_loss: 0.4900 - val_acc:
0.8420

Keras CNN #1C - accuracy: 0.8419782871887489
```

**FIG. 11** CNN accuracy result.

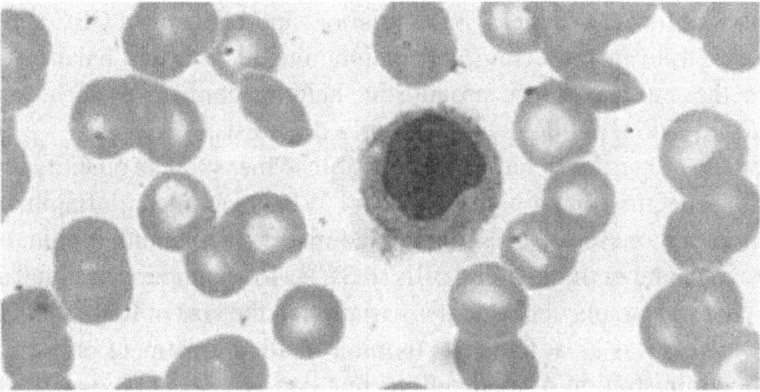

**FIG. 12** Monocyte.

```
In [42]: preds = model.predict_classes(xi)
         print(preds)

         [3]
```

**FIG. 13** CNN monocyte classification.

of the implemented neural network structure and the validity of the DL technique with respect to cell biology learning. Monocytes are cells with large diameter, spherical shape, and nuclear invagination, belonging to the class of agranulocyte neutrophils, that is, they do not have granules dispersed by the cytoplasm that prevent the nucleus from being visualized.

The significance of recognition and classification of human blood cell biology is that is allows for a greater understanding of the functioning of the human organism, deducing from the study of the structure, interaction, and functioning between it. In the same sense, this research contributes to an advance in the most diverse areas related to medicine, such as biomedicine, molecular biology, and even immunology—that is, this study integrates with other branches of knowledge.

Over the years, through digital electron microscopy image technology, it was possible to contribute to the detection of structures not revealed by the optical microscope, given the capacity limit of the eyes of human specialists. In this context, the type of technology presented in this research has the potential to improve human capacity further in the field of medical microscopy, given the constant technological evolution of cell biology.

A complete blood count (CBC) is a complimentary exam required in medical consultations and analyses, often taken as a starting point for most medical investigations. This exam is a very useful screening for valuable information about the patient, mainly due to quantitatively and qualitatively evaluating the cellular elements of the blood, that is, part of the analysis necessary for any routine exam or check-up.

Abnormal results from this type of examination signals the possible presence of a variety of conditions that counterbalance the individual's health, including anemias, infections, and even leukemia, among others.

In cases of fever, weakness, inflammation, and bleeding, a CBC test plays a fundamental role in protecting and maintaining the body's balance, helping diagnose the cause of these prognostic, helping confirm medical suspicion related to infection, and allowing for early diagnosis.

Given the properties of blood, it is possible to measure the quantity and types of WBCs, reflecting that a high number of WBCs can mean inflammation, an infection, or a more serious case like leukemia. Or from another point of view, related to the number of red blood cells (RBC), a low number can signal anemia; in these cases, there may be a greater variation in the size of RBC. That is, from all these factors it is clear that tests monitor medical treatment or even accompany the administration of medications that can affect the blood cell count.

Therefore, the classification of these elements (cell types) through CNN, that is, DL, makes it possible to evaluate a patient's clinical condition regarding the identification of diseases, following the progression of any adverse medical condition, and even to evaluate whether the medical treatment is having the expected effect. Digital medical imaging exams associated with DL techniques lead to lower health costs while also being safe, fast, and inexpensive. AI increases accuracy, enables the early diagnosis of various diseases, and improves certainty of diagnosis. Thus, DL is a technology directed to the progress of the modern world, including medical practices, given the diversity of technology-assisted exams that have enabled precise techniques for medical human specialists.

DL automates operational activities, standardizes diagnoses of serious and frequent diseases that can be analyzed by imaging, and facilitates the assistance of medical experience. DL assists in the decision making of the specialist clinical staff and increases the chances of a promising treatment.

Pondering the entire framework presented and linking the results achieved in this study, this is promising for medical areas, especially when considering the global presence of blood disorders. Those who live in situations of extreme poverty, with incompatible income, or even with little or no government assistance can be cured of illnesses when discovered in the early stages using this type of research.

Using a metaheuristic classification methodology in this research, that is, using cognitive approaches and methods of segmentation of types of WBCs, according to Ref. [57] showed a Naïve Bayes classifier for classifying types of WBCs with 83.2% accuracy, Ref. [58] presented a method generating 80.88% accuracy, and Ref. [59] showed a neural network without a principal component analysis classifier working with a rate of 65% accuracy based on the rotated training set. So, this demonstrates that the framework developed in this study shows superior results with other previous works. This adds value to the scientific community derived from improved accuracy with respect to this type of comparative study presented.

From this panorama, this framework can solve issues of confirmation of exams or accuracy in diagnoses for blood tests, providing a focus on the patient and greater productivity. Given the current reality present in medical institutions, which are dependent on high-cost hematological equipment or even specific reagents restricting purchasing from resellers, a computational device can produce higher quality, lower cost, and faster blood cell exam results using the framework presented.

## 7 Conclusions

It is worth mentioning that around the planet, the whole preparation of blood collected for analysis is the sole responsibility of professional humans, which is especially challenging in underdeveloped and developing countries. This procedure is naturally subject to errors when it is associated with long working hours, psychological and physical exhaustion, inadequate remuneration, and lack of motivation. However, factors associated with dissatisfaction tend to interfere in the performance of professional humans comprising critical vectors against the confidence of blood tests realized manually.

The proposed framework is also useful for populations with better economic conditions, employing this as a confirmatory tool validating the results of exams that are outside the reference values, decreasing the possibility of false-positive and false-negative results in medical routines.

In this sense, it is highlighted that the CNN achieved 84.19% accuracy, which is a significant performance due to the complexity of the studied problem. From this, it can be concluded that the framework modeling parameters enabled the respective satisfactory distinctiveness of the classification between blood subtypes. It is also possible to observe the positive exploration of CNN characteristics, enabling computational processing with respect to image interpreting regarding maintaining the spatial characteristics, such as width, height, and even colors.

In this context, we must consider that, in addition to the traditional manual and low cyst methodology, high-quality automated hematological equipment is available on the market but with costs incompatible with economically less privileged populations. Thus, the results presented in this study can be considered the first step toward the development of software for counting and recognizing blood cells, which presents as low cost, high accuracy, and high speed. These characteristics are important, as they facilitate implementation in the health area and increase the reliability of doctors and patients regarding the results obtained.

## 8 Future research directions

This study has its continuity concerning identification, classification, and recognition of WBCs, due to wide applicability aligned with the constant requirement for advances in the medical field optimizing cell qualification and classification, refining the level of related detail differentiation of T-lymphocyte and B-lymphocyte in digital smear blood.

Techniques such as generative adverse networks (GANs) perform recognition and classifying pathological blood cells of leukocyte subtypes. GANs are a new training paradigm for neural networks although mathematically complex, based on game theory, creating new instances of data resembling the training data, and modeling condition of strategic interactions. Due to this technique deriving from a field of applied mathematics (game theory), it has the characteristics of achieving realism learning distinguishing between real and counterfeit data, differentiating the generator output from true data.

## References

[1] D.S. Modha, et al., Cognitive computing, Commun. ACM 54 (8) (2011) 62–71.

[2] J.E. Kelly III, S. Hamm, Smart Machines: IBM's Watson and The Era of Cognitive Computing, Columbia University Press, 2013.

[3] J.O. Gutierrez-Garcia, E. López-Neri, Cognitive computing: a brief survey and open research challenges, in: 2015 3rd International Conference on Applied Computing and Information Technology/2nd International Conference on Computational Science and Intelligence, IEEE, 2015.

[4] M. Chen, F. Herrera, K. Hwang, Cognitive computing: architecture, technologies and intelligent applications, IEEE Access 6 (2018) 19774–19783.

[5] Y. Wang, D. Zhang, W. Kinsner (Eds.), Advances in Cognitive Informatics and Cognitive Computing, vol. 323, Springer, 2010.

[6] Y. Wang, et al., Cognitive intelligence: deep learning, thinking, and reasoning by brain-inspired systems, Int. J. Cogn. Inform. Nat. Intell. 10 (4) (2016) 1–20.

[7] M. Tarafdar, C.M. Beath, J.W. Ross, Enterprise cognitive computing applications: opportunities and challenges, IT Prof. 19 (4) (2017) 21–27.

[8] R.P. França, et al., Big data and cloud computing: a technological and literary background, in: Advanced Deep Learning Applications in Big Data Analytics, IGI Global, 2020, pp. 29–50.

[9] R.P. França, Y. Iano, A.C.B. Monteiro, R. Arthur, V.V. Estrela, A proposal based on discrete events for improvement of the transmission channels in cloud environments and Big Data, in: Big Data, IoT, and Machine Learning, CRC Press, 2020, pp. 185–204.

[10] J. Hurwitz, et al., Cognitive Computing and Big Data Analytics, Wiley, Indianapolis, 2015.

[11] S. Gupta, et al., Big data with cognitive computing: a review for the future, Int. J. Inf. Manag. 42 (2018) 78–89.

[12] W. Meng, Cognitive Computing: Theory and Applications, Elsevier, 2017.

[13] H. Demirkan, S. Earley, R.R. Harmon, Cognitive computing, IT Prof. 19 (4) (2017) 16–20.

[14] V.N. Gudivada, et al., Cognitive computing systems: their potential and the future, Computer 52 (5) (2019) 13–18.

[15] V.V. Raghavan, et al., Cognitive Computing: Theory and Applications, Elsevier, 2016.

[16] S. Skansi, Introduction to Deep Learning: From Logical Calculus to Artificial Intelligence, Springer, 2018.

[17] S.A. Bini, Artificial intelligence, machine learning, deep learning, and cognitive computing: what do these terms mean and how will they impact health care? J. Arthroplast. 33 (8) (2018) 2358–2361.

[18] N. Mehta, M.V. Devarakonda, Machine learning, natural language programming, and electronic health records: the next step in the artificial intelligence journey? J. Allergy Clin. Immunol. 141 (6) (2018) 2019–2021.

[19] R.K. Behera, P.K. Bala, A. Dhir, The emerging role of cognitive computing in healthcare: a systematic literature review, Int. J. Med. Inform. 129 (2019) 154–166.

[20] A.C.B. Monteiro, Y. Iano, R.P. França, Detecting and counting of blood cells using watershed transform: an improved methodology, in: Brazilian Technology Symposium, Springer, Cham, 2017.

[21] A.C.B. Monteiro, et al., A comparative study between methodologies based on the Hough transform and watershed transform on the blood cell count, in: Brazilian Technology Symposium, Springer, Cham, 2018.

[22] A.C.B. Monteiro, Y. Iano, R.P. França, An improved and fast methodology for automatic detecting and counting of red and white blood cells using watershed transform, in: VIII Simpósio de Instrumentação e Imagens Médicas (SIIM)/VII Simpósio de Processamento de Sinais da UNICAMP, 2017.

[23] A.C.B. Monteiro, et al., Development of Digital Image Processing Methodology WT-MO: An Algorithm of High Accuracy in Detection and Counting of Erythrocytes, Leucocytes, Blasts, 2019.

[24] A.C.B. Monteiro, et al., Methodology of high accuracy, sensitivity and specificity in the counts of erythrocytes and leukocytes in blood smear images, in: Brazilian Technology Symposium, Springer, Cham, 2018.

[25] A.C.B. Monteiro, et al., Development of a laboratory medical algorithm for simultaneous detection and counting of erythrocytes and leukocytes in digital images of a blood smear, in: Deep Learning Techniques for Biomedical and Health Informatics, Academic Press, 2020, pp. 165–186.

[26] A.C.B. Monteiro, Proposta de uma metodologia de segmentação de imagens para detecção e contagem de hemácias e leucócitos através do algoritmo WT-MO, 2019.

[27] M. Chen, et al., Edge cognitive computing-based smart healthcare system, Future Gener. Comput. Syst. 86 (2018) 403–411.

[28] F.C. Ghesu, et al., An artificial agent for anatomical landmark detection in medical images, in: International Conference on Medical Image Computing and Computer-Assisted Intervention, Springer, Cham, 2016.

[29] A.C.B. Monteiro, Y. Iano, R.P. França, R. Arthur, Medical-laboratory algorithm WTH-MO for segmentation of digital images of blood cells: a new methodology for making hemograms, Int. J. Simul. Syst. Sci. Technol. 20 (suppl 1) (2019) 19.1.

[30] A.C.B. Monteiro, et al., WT-MO algorithm: automated hematological software based on the watershed transform for blood cell count, in: Applications of Image Processing and Soft Computing Systems in Agriculture, IGI Global, 2019, pp. 39–79.

[31] A.C.B. Monteiro, Y. Iano, R.P. França, Proposal of a medical algorithm based on the application of digital image processing and visual communication techniques, SET Int. J. Broadcast Eng. 4 (2019) 9.

[32] A.C.B. Monteiro, et al., Hematology and digital image processing: watershed transform-based methodology for blood cell counting using the WT-MO algorithm, Med. Technol. J. 4 (2020) 576.

[33] V.V. Estrela, et al., Health 4.0: applications, management, technologies and review, Med. Technol. J. 2 (4) (2018) 262–276.

[34] C.L. Chowdhary, A. Darwish, A.E. Hassanien, Cognitive deep learning: future direction in intelligent retrieval, in: Handbook of Research on Deep Learning Innovations and Trends, IGI Global, 2019, pp. 220–231.

[35] B.M. Wilamowski, Neural networks learning, in: Intelligent Systems, CRC Press, 2018. 11–1.

[36] D.S. Levine, Introduction to Neural and Cognitive Modeling, Routledge, 2018.

[37] R. Stengel, Introduction to Neural Networks! Robotics and Intelligent Systems, MAE, 2017, p. 345. http://www.stengel.mycpanel.princeton.edu/MAE345Lecture18.pdf.

[38] E.P. Frady, D. Kleyko, F.T. Sommer, A theory of sequence indexing and working memory in recurrent neural networks, Neural Comput. 30 (6) (2018) 1449–1513.

[39] M. Flasiński, Introduction to Artificial Intelligence, Springer, 2016.

[40] P.C. Jackson, Introduction to Artificial Intelligence, Courier Dover Publications, 2019.

[41] P. Gambus, S.L. Shafer, Artificial intelligence for everyone, Anesthesiology 128 (3) (2018) 431–433.

[42] E. Charniak, Introduction to Deep Learning, The MIT Press, 2019.
[43] C. Steger, M. Ulrich, C. Wiedemann, Machine Vision Algorithms and Applications, John Wiley & Sons, 2018.
[44] V.-E. Neagoe, A.-D. Ciotec, G.-S. Cucu, Deep convolutional neural networks versus multilayer perceptron for financial prediction, in: 2018 International Conference on Communications (COMM), IEEE, 2018.
[45] S. Walczak, Artificial neural networks, in: Advanced Methodologies and Technologies in Artificial Intelligence, Computer Simulation, and Human-Computer Interaction, IGI Global, 2019, pp. 40–53.
[46] E. Alpaydin, Introduction to Machine Learning, MIT Press, 2020.
[47] R.E. Neapolitan, X. Jiang, Artificial Intelligence: With an Introduction to Machine Learning, CRC Press, 2018.
[48] J. Wu, Introduction to Convolutional Neural Networks, vol. 5, National Key Lab for Novel Software Technology, Nanjing University, China, 2017, p. 23.
[49] G. Yao, T. Lei, J. Zhong, A review of convolutional-neural-network-based action recognition, Pattern Recogn. Lett. 118 (2019) 14–22.
[50] K.G. Kim, Book review: Deep learning, Healthc. Inform. Res. 22 (4) (2016) 351–354.
[51] J.D. Kelleher, Deep Learning, MIT Press, 2019.
[52] R. Zhang, W. Li, T. Mo, Review of Deep Learning, arXiv preprint arXiv:1804.01653, 2018.
[53] I. Goodfellow, et al., Deep Learning, vol. 1, MIT Press, Cambridge, 2016.
[54] D. Cielen, A. Meysman, M. Ali, Introducing Data Science: Big Data, Machine Learning, and More, Using Python tools, Manning Publications Co., 2016.
[55] F. Hutter, L. Kotthoff, J. Vanschoren, Automated Machine Learning: Methods, Systems, Challenges, Springer Nature, 2019.
[56] GitHub—Shenggan/BCCD_Dataset: BCCD Dataset is a Small-Scale Dataset for Blood Cells Detection. BCCD Dataset is Under MIT License, 2018. (Online). Available from: https://github.com/Shenggan/BCCD_Dataset.
[57] M. Ghosh, D. Das, S. Mandal, et al., Statistical pattern analysis of white blood cell nuclei morphometry, in: Proceedings of the IEEE Students' Technology Symposium (TechSym '10), April 2010, pp. 59–66.
[58] A. Gautam, P. Singh, B. Raman, H. Bhadauria, Automatic classification of leukocytes using morphological features and naive Bayes classifier, in: IEEE Region 10 Conference (TENCON), 2016.
[59] S. Nazlibilek, et al., Automatic segmentation, counting, size determination and classification of white blood cells, Measurement 55 (2014) 58–65.

Chapter 2

# Assessment of land use land cover change detection in multitemporal satellite images using machine learning algorithms

**Mahalakshmi Murugan, Rohini Selvaraj, and Sureshkumar Nagarajan**
*School of Computer Science and Engineering, Vellore Institute of Technology, Vellore, Tamil Nadu, India*

## 1 Introduction

Human activities influence the environmental constraints of the Earth's surface. The rapid expansion of urban centers, the fast growth of population, scarcity of land, the demand for more production, and changing technologies are among the many drivers of land use land cover (LULC) in the world today [1]. LULC has become one of the major studies of researchers and decision-makers around the world today. Monitoring and tracking the changes are noted as change detection [2]. Change detection is useful in several applications related to LULC changes, such as landscape changes [3], forest fire [3], wetland change [3], shifting cultivation [2], environmental change [3], green cover [4], land degradation [3], disaster management [5], coastal change [6], habitat fragmentation, landslide mapping [7], snow cover mapping [8], urban landscape pattern change [9], climate change [10], deforestation [3], and other cumulative changes.

Recent improvements in geographic information systems (GIS) and remote sensing (RS) tools and techniques allow researchers to create and prognosticate urban expansion more effectively than traditional strategies. Urban expansion is a well-known aspect in most countries across the world, even the proportion of growth changes. Recently, these are the significant aspects that have to be examined and observed for efficient LULC administration. Numerous modeling strategies have also been promoted to model and

**Cognitive Systems and Signal Processing in Image Processing. https://doi.org/10.1016/B978-0-12-824410-4.00006-4**

determine the dynamic urban characteristics. In emerging countries, the sources, such as water, agricultural areas, and forests, are decreasing notably. However, knowledge concerning the frequency of compression is frequently lacking. Accurate land cover change details are required to acknowledge the principal purposes and the costs of environmental variations. Furthermore, interpreting the driving energies producing LULC change map is required to concede the modern variations to determine later modifications. Land cover change analysis using machine learning and RS approaches gives a chance to get less time-consuming results with low costs, good accuracy, and GIS permit updating new data whenever available. The LULC change has become a centerpiece in current strategies for tracking environmental changes and managing natural resources. Various change detection approaches were utilized for decades.

## 2 Related works

One study presented multitemporal land cover change analysis using the integrated hybrid classification technique, following a robust multisensor satellite image calibration strategy in western India [11].

Another study reviewed novel aspects of automated change detection using supervised classification, such as an artificial neural network and a structural phase congruency histogram (SPCH) [3] in RS images. They had excellent AUC values of 98.4375% and a kappa value of 0.97 over synthetic-aperture radar (SAR) images when compared with GLCM, PCA, SSND, CVA, IRMAD, and SSFA.

One study analyzed green cover change detection in northwestern India to identify vegetation change. They achieved an average testing accuracy of 97.8%, with an error percentage of around 1.48% [12]. The analyzed results show that the modified adaptive ensemble of extreme learning machines (mAEELM) has better accuracy than the extreme learning machine (ELM), NMF-ELM, maximum likelihood, support vector machine, naive Bayes, and back propagation.

Both supervised and unsupervised techniques were used to analyze drainage, landfilling, an excessive quantity of recreational, agricultural, municipal, and industrial water use on Turkish lakes [7]. This research permits dynamic tracking of quantity and quality of lake water, which can also be used for other resources. This enables a well-timed and productive development of preventative and alleviative measures. This study also used multiple nonlinear regression and correlation matrix models.

The nonsubsampling contourlet transform (NSCT) and k-means clustering algorithm were incorporated in one study to obtain good results and feature information [13]. It has more accuracy and stability against speckle noise and Gaussian than the traditional techniques (PCA-KMEANS algorithm). Change detection in satellite images using convolutional neural networks

(CNNs) [14], difference image generation algorithm, and gradient descent algorithm to detect changes like human-made objects (buildings and roads) urban areas, and parking with an accuracy up to 91.2%.

Unlike unsupervised classification, many scientists [2] have applied supervised classification in their studies. They obtained maximum classification accuracies in LULC classification by using the MLC decision rule. MLC along with the normalized difference vegetation index (NDVI) [15], and principal component analysis (PCA) [6] were used to analyze land cover [10], land surface temperature [15], and urban expansions [6]. MLC with classes such as built-up land, crop land, orchards, construction sites, water areas, and forests (China) with accuracy ranges from 84% [10] to 90.67% [6], and Kappa index was 0.89.

The primary purpose of this work is to identify the current and previous LULC classes and to monitor the changes over 2013–2019 in the study area. The leading theory is that the study region encounters dynamic changes because of the urban expansion over the agricultural fields and water bodies. RS software, ArcGIS 10.7 (ESRI), and Earth Resources Data Analysis System (ERDAS) version 15.1 Imagine were used to process, classify, analyze, and display the satellite data.

### 2.1 Gaps identified in existing works

Recent studies cover more change detection of urban expansion than the other classes, such as forestry, agriculture, and water bodies. Also, there are only a few studies of LULC changes that provide an integrated assessment of the land rehabilitation and land degradation processes. Extra effort is required for the accuracy assessment for LULC change detection of multitemporal (long-time sequence) satellite data, especially when the ground truth/reference data is inadequate or difficult to obtain.

## 3 Proposed work

### 3.1 Study area

Madurai (Fig. 1) is situated at 78.12°E 9.93°N, with 101 m of average elevation. The Madurai lies on the plane and productive plains of the Vaigai River, which runs through the city from the northwest to the southeast, almost dividing it into two halves. The north and west of the city include Sirumalai and Nagamalai hills. Madurai contains several mountain spurs since it lies in the southeast of the western ghats. The Madurai region is primarily employed for farming activities, which is enriched by the Vaigai River and the Periyar dam. Paddy, oilseeds, millets, pulses, sugarcane, and cotton are the main crops farmed in Madurai.

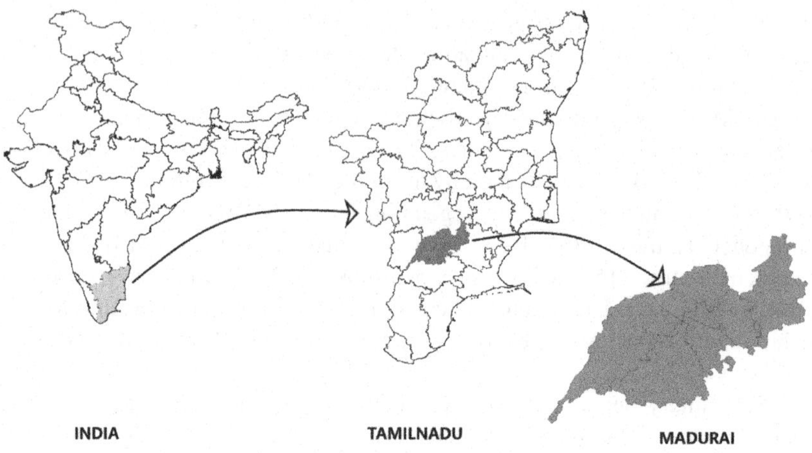


**FIG. 1** Map of the study area location, Madurai.

## 3.2 Data collection

In this research, we have utilized least-clouded high resolution (Landsat 8) multitemporal satellite data for the years 2013, 2015, 2017, and 2019. The satellite data were collected from the United States Geological Survey (https://landsatlook.usgs.gov/) website. Properties of the satellite data used were displayed in Table 1. Undesirable shade and cloud-free were set as standard during image selection. The cloud cover of the collected data was <5% to ignore atmospheric rectification that may alter the accuracy of classification. In this study, the overall cloud coverage of the study area is <1% (Fig. 2).

# 4 Methodology

Initially, multitemporal satellite data were collected, and then the data was preprocessed with radiometric correction. LULC maps were classified using MLC and NDVI in RS software. Preparation of LULC change detection map and matrix of change was analyzed. The accuracy of the calculated matrix was verified, and the final output maps were shown. The preprocessing process involved the allocation of the coordinates, layer stacking the dataset bands, and subsetting the boundary maps of the study region (Fig. 3).

Step-by-step procedure:

1. Read the multitemporal satellite data (11 bands from the multitemporal data of study region).
2. Composite the dataset bands into a single image (or layer stack).
3. Intersect the resulted natural-color image with the boundary file (study area).
4. Perform radiometric corrections, such as noise removal, haze removal, and more, for better classification accuracy.

**TABLE 1** Detailed information about multitemporal satellite data of the study area, Madurai.

| Imagery date | Scene identifier | Sensor identifier | Path/row | No. of bands | Spatial resolution (m) | Data format | Cloud cover (%) |
|---|---|---|---|---|---|---|---|
| 24/May/2013 | LC81430532013144LGN02 | L8 OLI/TIRS | 143/53 | 11 | 30 | GeoTIFF | 4 |
| 23/Feb/2015 | LC81430532015054LGN02 | L8 OLI/TIRS | 143/53 | 11 | 30 | GeoTIFF | 0 |
| 04/June/2017 | LC81430532017155LGN00 | L8 OLI/TIRS | 143/53 | 11 | 30 | GeoTIFF | 5 |
| 06/Mar/2019 | LC81430532019065LGN00 | L8 OLI/TIRS | 143/53 | 11 | 30 | GeoTIFF | 0 |

**FIG. 2** Subset of Landsat 8 image of the study area, Madurai over the period 2015.

Data Collection
Satellite Images

Landsat 8 OLI/TIRS 2013
Landsat 8 OLI/TIRS 2015
Landsat 8 OLI/TIRS 2017
Landsat 8 OLI/TIRS 2019

Data Preprocessing
&
Radiometric Correction

Georeferencing
& Area Subsetting

Maximum Likelihood
Classification

NDVI using
ERDAS IMAGINE

Preparation of
Land use & Land cover
Change Detection Map

Change Matrix Analysis

Accuracy Calculation

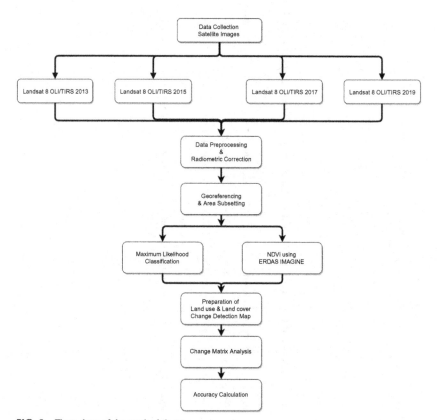

**FIG. 3** Flow chart of the methodology.

## 4.1 Maximum likelihood classification

The MLC algorithm is famous and frequently used efficiently in analyzing satellite data. It is a supervised approach based on Bayes theorem and pixel-based approach that specifies each pixel to the particular class with the maximum likelihood value and the data perform the multivariate Gaussian distribution.

$$MLC, L_{k=} P\left(\frac{k}{X}\right) = P(k) * P\left(\frac{X}{k}\right) / \sum P(i) * P\left(\frac{X}{i}\right) \tag{1}$$

where

$P\ (k)$: probability of class k.
$P\left(\frac{X}{k}\right)$: conditional probability or probability density function to observe $X$ from class $k$.

Usually, $P(k)$ is assumed to be equal to each other, and $P(i) * P\left(\frac{X}{i}\right)$ is also common to all classes. Therefore, $L_k$ depends on $P\left(\frac{X}{k}\right)$ or the probability density function.

In the case of normal distributions, the likelihood can be expressed as follows:

$$L_{k=} \frac{1}{(2\pi)^{\frac{n}{2}} |\Sigma_k|^{\frac{1}{2}}} \exp\left| -\frac{1}{2}(X - \mu_k) \sum\nolimits_k^{-1} (X - \mu_k)^t \right| \tag{2}$$

where

$n$: number of bands
$X$: image data of n bands
$L_k(X)$: likelihood of $X$ belongs to class $k$
$\mu_k$: mean vector of class $k$
$\sum_k$ : variance-covariance matrix of class $k$
$|\sum_k|$: the determinant of class $\sum_k$

For each LULC class, the change in magnitude was determined by differencing the coverage area for the next year and the previous (initial) year.

$$\text{Change\%} = \text{change in magnitude} * 100 / \text{initial year} \tag{3}$$

For each LULC class, the annual change rate is acquired by subtracting the first year to last year, which is divided by the number of years, that is, 2013–2015 (2 years), 2015–2017 (2 years), and 2017–2019 (2 years), respectively.

The NDVI is standard for recognizing the vegetated area and its properties. NDVI is determined by the proportion between infrared and red bands for each geographic location [2].

The NDVI is calculated by dividing the difference between NIR and R by the summation of NIR and R. In Landsat 8, NIR = Near Infra-Red (Band 5); R = Red (Band 4).

Step-by-step procedure:

1. Read the satellite data (multitemporal satellite bands 4 and 5 of the study region).
2. Initiate and adjust the preprocessing threshold value.
3. Calculate the NDVI value as in the formula; NDVI = (Band 5 – Band 4) / (Band 5 + Band 4).
4. Classify the image (NDVI) by changing the threshold value between 0.002 and 0.016(z-score).
5. Vegetation class has a z-score value lesser than the NDVI value, so assign 1, otherwise 0 for the nonvegetation class.
6. To calculate change detection, perform logical XOR between NDVI images.
7. No change area pixel value is represented as 0 and changing area as 1.
8. The resolution of the pixel determined the vegetation and the nonvegetation regions.
9. Measure the area of change between classes.

$$CD = \sum_{i=1}^{n} \frac{|NDVI_t{}^1{}_i - NDVI_t{}^2{}_i|}{|NDVI_t{}^1{}_i| + |NDVI_t{}^2{}_i|} \tag{4}$$

# 5 Results and discussions

## 5.1 Maximum likelihood classification

MLC, the most popular supervised classification approach, was applied [2, 15]. Six land cover classes using MLC were represented: waterbody, agricultural area, scrubland, dense forest, uncultivated/barren land, and urban built-up land. Diverse training samples were represented in each LULC class, which is validated using the ground truth points and depends on the visual interpretation. Signature files carrying the various statistics of each land cover class were created, which act as input for the MLC.

### *5.1.1 Change detection based on MLC maps*

The finalized MLC classified maps are shown in Fig. 4. The LULC change matrix between change in area with the specified period is displayed in Table 3. Change detection results were utilized to compute the agricultural deprivation over the past six years, the urban expansion over the farming area, and the decrease in forest and uncultivated areas. Agricultural lands were gradually changed to barren land over the period from 2013 to 2019 (Fig. 5).

Results show that forest area influences the land cover classes in the study region (35.5%, 1320 km$^2$; and 37%, 1371 km$^2$) in 2013 and 2015, respectively. The urban area influences the land cover classes in the study region (40%, 1497 km$^2$; and 47.5%, 1765 km$^2$) in 2017 and 2019, respectively (Fig. 6). This

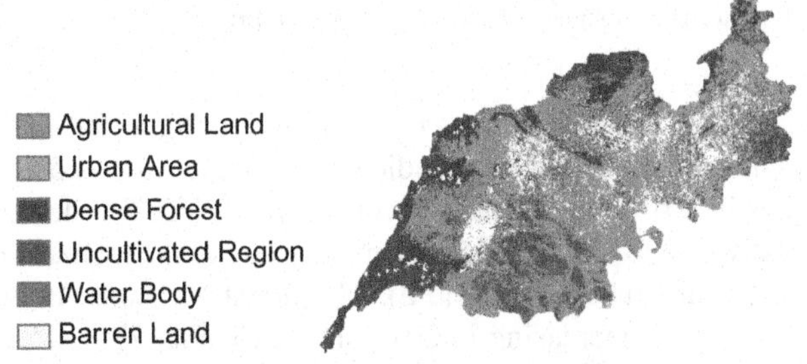


**FIG. 4** The maximum likelihood classified map of the study area—Madurai over the period 2019.

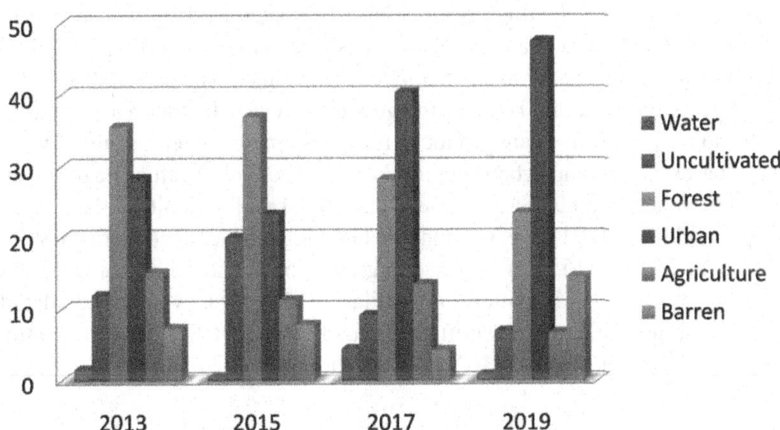


**FIG. 5** Bar chart indicates the land use land cover class values based on MLC in the study area, Madurai.

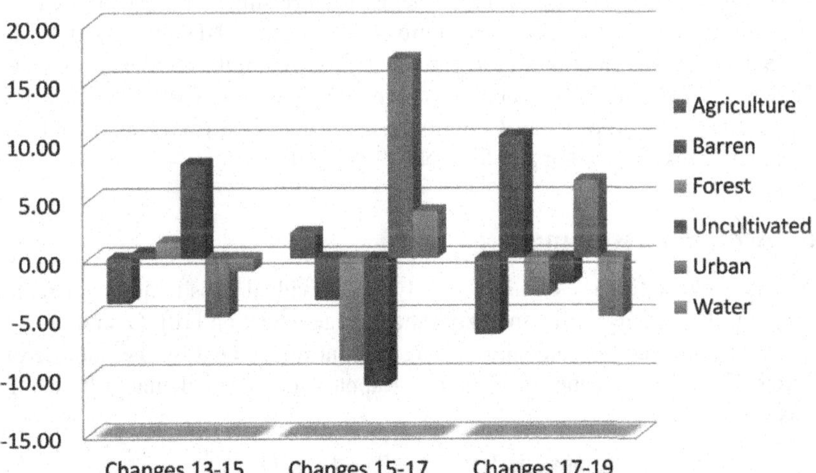


**FIG. 6** Bar chart indicates land use land cover changes between maximum likelihood classified maps of the study area, Madurai.

was primarily due to urban enlargement (rural-urban migration) that had happened in the study region. Water class indicates that there was ~4.5% (166 km$^2$) of water bodies in 2017 and decreases over the years. The 5% decrease in the urban sector between 2013 and 2015 was mainly due to the increase in vegetation (trees) in the urban sector (Table 2). The forest area and cultivated land classes were gradually decreasing in 2017 and 2019 (Fig. 7).

## 5.2 Normalized difference vegetative index classification

The NDVI was one of the extensively applied change detection approaches used predominantly for cultivating regions. NDVI is calculated by the proportion between two bands, which are extremely sensitive to the vegetation. The NDVI output is a grayscale raster map with indexes varying between 1 and − 1. The NDVI values greater than 0 denote the vegetation class. In contrast, the values near 0 and negative values are produced mainly from nonvegetated areas, water bodies, barren areas, and urban sectors (Fig. 8). The NDVI values near one are allotted to vegetation classes, such as dense forest and agricultural land.

The results of NDVI show the nonvegetated regions declined from 48.8% to 47.9% over 2013–2015 then increased again to 56% and 58.8% in 2017 and 2019, respectively. This pattern is similar to the MLC values calculated. Fig. 9 illustrates the spatial configuration of nonvegetation and vegetation change in classified maps of NDVI for the three specified periods.

### 5.2.1 *Change detection based on NDVI classified maps*

The change detection using the NDVI approach indicated that in 2017–2019, ~21% of the study region was shifted from vegetation class to nonvegetation class and vice-versa (Table 3). The brighter sectors, which denote a variation in vegetation class, were the outcome of the expansion of urban or barren region shifts. Differencing the NDVI is essential in distinguishing the urban regions by examining the variations in the vegetation cover. But this NDVI failed to determine the exact distribution of the nonvegetation area in the study region since there was a high density of vegetation (vegetation in urban areas), NDVI is lacking in classifying urban areas. Commonly, the result of MLC is more reliable in accuracy assessment comparable to NDVI (Fig. 10).

## 6 Accuracy assessment

Accuracy evaluation is essential to verify the individual classification when the resultant data are useful in analyzing the change detection [10]. Overall accuracy was calculated by the sum of diagonal entries divided by the number of pixels analyzed from the error matrix. Kappa value was calculated by using Eqs. (5)–(7).

$$\text{Kappa coefficient} = (P_o - P_c)/(1 - P_c) \tag{5}$$

**TABLE 2** The LULC change matrix based on the MLC in the study area, Madurai over the periods 2013–2015, 2015–2017, and 2017–2019.

| | | Agriculture | | Barren | | Forest | | Uncultivated | | Urban | | Water | | Total | |
|---|---|---|---|---|---|---|---|---|---|---|---|---|---|---|---|
| | | $Km^2$ | % | $km^2$ | % | $km^2$ | % | $km^2$ | % | $km^2$ | % | $km^2$ | % | $km^2$ | % |
| LULC 2015 | LULC 2013 | | | | | | | | | | | | | | |
| | Agricultural | 139.36 | 3.75 | 38.69 | 1.04 | 143.13 | 3.86 | 22.73 | 0.61 | 65.66 | 1.77 | 11.04 | 0.30 | 420.61 | 11.33 |
| | Barren | 58.54 | 1.58 | 93.17 | 2.51 | 66.30 | 1.79 | 6.90 | 0.19 | 60.83 | 1.64 | 5.72 | 0.15 | 291.45 | 7.85 |
| | Forest | 239.26 | 6.44 | 35.19 | 0.95 | 806.44 | 21.72 | 51.24 | 1.38 | 226.04 | 6.09 | 13.20 | 0.36 | 1371.37 | 36.94 |
| | Uncultivated | 33.20 | 0.89 | 10.87 | 0.29 | 157.25 | 4.24 | 337.53 | 9.09 | 196.54 | 5.29 | 9.09 | 0.24 | 744.49 | 20.05 |
| | Urban | 87.96 | 2.37 | 93.21 | 2.51 | 141.88 | 3.82 | 26.56 | 0.72 | 500.26 | 13.47 | 16.33 | 0.44 | 866.18 | 23.33 |
| | Water Body | 3.35 | 0.09 | 3.09 | 0.08 | 5.70 | 0.15 | 0.20 | 0.01 | 3.12 | 0.08 | 3.02 | 0.08 | 18.48 | 0.50 |
| | Total | **561.68** | **15.13** | **274.22** | **7.39** | **1320.69** | **35.57** | **445.15** | **11.99** | **1052.46** | **28.35** | **58.41** | **1.57** | **3712.59** | **100.00** |
| | Changes | **−141.07** | **−3.80** | **17.24** | **0.46** | **50.68** | **1.37** | **299.34** | **8.06** | **−186.27** | **−5.02** | **−39.93** | **−1.08** | | |
| LULC2017 | LULC 2015 | | | | | | | | | | | | | | |
| | Agricultural | 149.99 | 4.04 | 54.94 | 1.48 | 154.72 | 4.17 | 46.46 | 1.25 | 90.93 | 2.45 | 4.06 | 0.11 | 501.10 | 13.50 |
| | Barren | 16.62 | 0.45 | 50.05 | 1.35 | 27.86 | 0.75 | 5.31 | 0.14 | 58.46 | 1.57 | 0.82 | 0.02 | 159.13 | 4.29 |
| | Forest | 116.48 | 3.14 | 50.38 | 1.36 | 699.33 | 18.84 | 88.54 | 2.38 | 88.83 | 2.39 | 3.44 | 0.09 | 1047.00 | 28.20 |
| | Uncultivated | 19.06 | 0.51 | 4.05 | 0.11 | 77.60 | 2.09 | 218.71 | 5.89 | 22.01 | 0.59 | 0.26 | 0.01 | 341.68 | 9.20 |
| | Urban | 103.81 | 2.80 | 124.30 | 3.35 | 378.80 | 10.20 | 294.12 | 7.92 | 589.00 | 15.86 | 7.20 | 0.19 | 1497.23 | 40.33 |
| | Water Body | 14.64 | 0.39 | 7.73 | 0.21 | 33.07 | 0.89 | 91.33 | 2.46 | 16.96 | 0.46 | 2.70 | 0.07 | 166.44 | 4.48 |
| | Total | **420.61** | **11.33** | **291.45** | **7.85** | **1371.37** | **36.94** | **744.48** | **20.05** | **866.19** | **23.33** | **18.48** | **0.50** | **3712.58** | **100.00** |
| | Changes | **80.49** | **2.17** | **−132.32** | **−3.56** | **−324.37** | **−8.74** | **−402.80** | **−10.85** | **631.04** | **17.00** | **147.96** | **3.99** | | |

*Continued*

**TABLE 2** The LULC change matrix based on the MLC in the study area, Madurai over the periods 2013–2015, 2015–2017, and 2017–2019—cont'd

| | | Agriculture | | Barren | | Forest | | Uncultivated | | Urban | | Water | | Total | |
|---|---|---|---|---|---|---|---|---|---|---|---|---|---|---|---|
| | | *Km²* | % | *km²* | % | *km²* | % | *km²* | % | *km²* | % | *km²* | % | *km²* | % |
| LULC2019 | LULC 2017 | | | | | | | | | | | | | | |
| | Agricultural | 114.35 | 3.08 | 4.69 | 0.13 | 70.19 | 1.89 | 3.00 | 0.08 | 50.93 | 1.37 | 15.04 | 0.41 | 264.74 | 6.95 |
| | Barren | 102.26 | 2.75 | 29.85 | 0.80 | 91.43 | 2.46 | 48.63 | 1.31 | 205.07 | 5.52 | 68.07 | 1.83 | 558.17 | 14.69 |
| | Forest | 100.12 | 2.70 | 15.29 | 0.41 | 627.79 | 16.91 | 3.74 | 0.10 | 126.69 | 3.41 | 50.54 | 1.36 | 947.71 | 24.89 |
| | Uncultivated | 6.52 | 0.18 | 0.21 | 0.01 | 23.28 | 0.63 | 145.37 | 3.92 | 32.18 | 0.87 | 31.85 | 0.86 | 244.99 | 6.45 |
| | Urban | 176.54 | 4.76 | 108.43 | 2.92 | 230.13 | 6.20 | 120.36 | 3.24 | 1073.80 | 28.92 | 27.64 | 0.74 | 1782.94 | 46.78 |
| | Water Body | 0.73 | 0.02 | 0.27 | 0.01 | 0.78 | 0.02 | 0.00 | 0.00 | 4.70 | 0.13 | 2.04 | 0.05 | 8.70 | 0.23 |
| | Total | **500.53** | **13.48** | **158.73** | **4.28** | **1043.60** | **28.11** | **321.10** | **8.65** | **1493.37** | **40.22** | **195.19** | **5.26** | **3807.26** | **100.00** |
| | Changes | **−235.79** | **−6.53** | **399.44** | **10.41** | **−95.88** | **−3.22** | **−76.11** | **−2.20** | **289.57** | **6.56** | **−186.49** | **−5.03** | | |

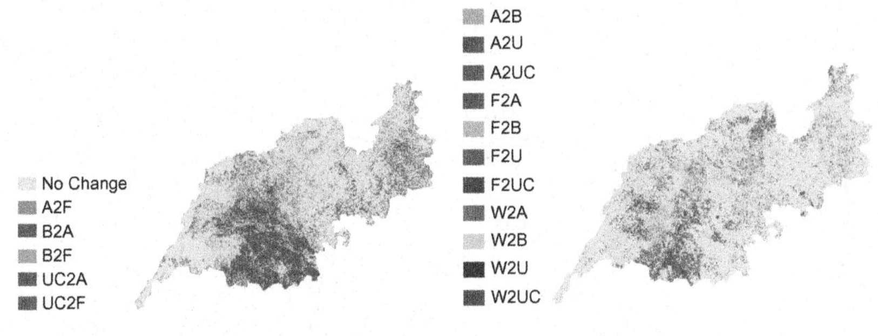


**FIG. 7** The spatial distribution of LULC changes from one class to another class in the study area, Madurai. UC, uncultivated land; W, water body; A, agricultural land; F, dense forest; B, barren land; U, urban built-up land.

**FIG. 8** The NDVI classified map of the study area, Madurai over the period 2019.

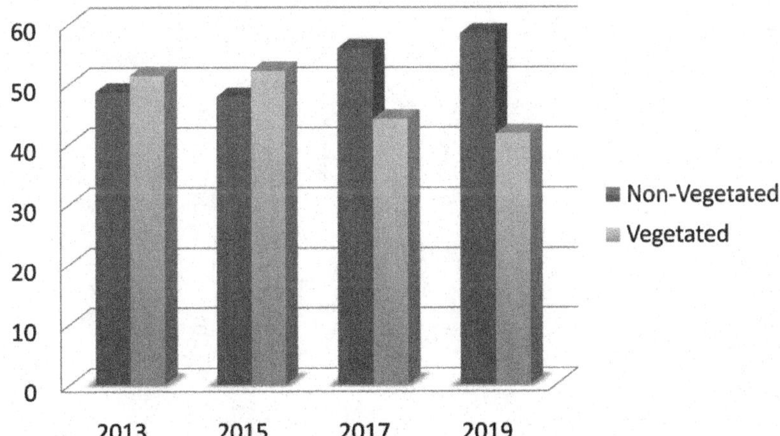


**FIG. 9** Bar chart indicates the land use land cover class values based on NDVI in the study area, Madurai.

**TABLE 3** The LULC change matrix based on the NDVI in the study area, Madurai over the periods: 2013–2015, 2015–2017, and 2017–2019.

| | | Nonvegetated | | Vegetated | | Total | |
|---|---|---|---|---|---|---|---|
| | | *Area* | % | *Area* | % | *Area* | % |
| NDVI 2013 | NDVI 2015 | | | | | | |
| | Nonvegetated | 1337.34 | 36.28 | 462.74 | 12.55 | 1836.36 | 48.83 |
| | Vegetated | 431.17 | 11.70 | 1455.22 | 39.47 | 1898.09 | 51.17 |
| | Total | 1768.50 | 47.98 | 1917.97 | 52.02 | 3734.45 | 100.00 |
| | Changes | 67.86 | 0.85 | −19.88 | −0.85 | | |
| NDVI 2015 | NDVI 2017 | | | | | | |
| | Nonvegetated | 1429.31 | 38.77 | 339.18 | 9.20 | 1807.26 | 47.97 |
| | Vegetated | 646.33 | 17.53 | 1271.55 | 34.49 | 1935.40 | 52.02 |
| | Total | 2075.64 | 56.30 | 1610.73 | 43.69 | 3742.66 | 99.99 |
| | Changes | −268.38 | −8.33 | 324.68 | 8.33 | | |
| NDVI 2017 | NDVI 2019 | | | | | | |
| | Nonvegetated | 1729.19 | 46.91 | 346.63 | 9.40 | 2122.73 | 56.31 |
| | Vegetated | 438.37 | 11.89 | 1172.34 | 31.80 | 1622.60 | 43.69 |
| | Total | 2167.56 | 58.80 | 1518.97 | 41.20 | 3745.33 | 100.00 |
| | Changes | −44.83 | −2.49 | 103.63 | 2.49 | | |

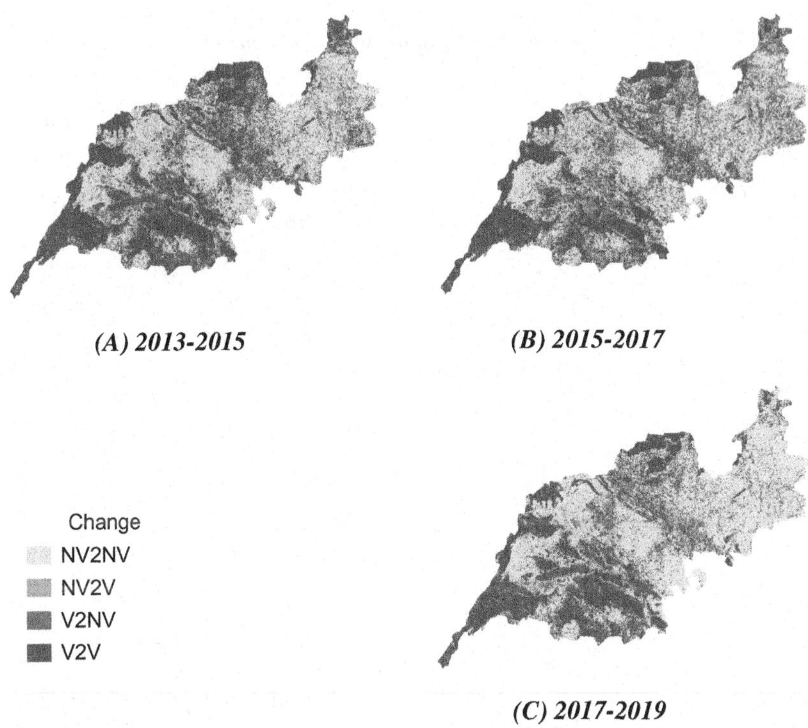


**NV-Non-Vegetation

**FIG. 10** The change between nonvegetation and vegetation classes in the study area, Madurai over the periods: 2013–2015, 2015–2017, and 2017–2019. NV, nonvegetation cover; V, vegetation cover.

$$P_o = \sum_{i=1}^{r} P_{\mathrm{ii}} \tag{6}$$

$$P_c = \sum_{i=1}^{r} (P_{\mathrm{i+}} {*} P_{\mathrm{+i}}) \tag{7}$$

Here

$r$ = total rows of error matrix
$P_{\mathrm{ii}}$ = pixel proportion of $i$th row and $i$th column
$P_{i+}$ = total marginal proportion of $i$th row
$P_{\mathrm{+i}}$ = total marginal proportion of $i$th column.

Error matrix classification is one of the most effective and widely used assessment techniques. Some alternative techniques are also used in recent years for analyzing and assessing the LULC change detection. It is often challenging, if

**TABLE 4** Error matrices for maximum likelihood classified maps of the study area, Madurai.

| Reference data | | | | | | | Total | PA (%) | UA (%) |
|---|---|---|---|---|---|---|---|---|---|
| **Classified data** | **AL** | **BL** | **DF** | **UCL** | **UA** | **WB** | | | |
| AL | 10 | | | | | | 10 | 100 | 100 |
| BL | | 15 | | | 3 | | 18 | 88.24 | 83.33 |
| DF | | 1 | 25 | 1 | 2 | 2 | 31 | 100 | 80.65 |
| UCL | | | | 34 | | | 34 | 97.14 | 100 |
| UA | | 1 | | | 16 | | 17 | 76.19 | 94.12 |
| WB | | | | | | 9 | 9 | 81.82 | 100 |
| Total | 10 | 17 | 25 | 35 | 21 | 11 | 119 | | |
| Overall accuracy = 91% | | Kappa coefficient = 0.89 | | | | | | | |

not impossible, to obtain reliable multitemporal ground truth points. Moreover, extra effort is required for the accurate assessment of change detection of long-time sequence images, especially when the ground truth data are inadequate or difficult to obtain.

Accuracy assessment of the classified maps was performed for the period 2019 to verify its reliability. Ground truth points (119) were collected in March 2019 to represent different LULC classes in the study area. The results indicate error matrices that decide the producer's and the user's accuracy, after differentiating the reference data and the classified data. Besides, a nonparametric kappa test was executed. The accuracy of land cover mapping using satellite data is greater than 80%, with no single class lesser than 70%. The classified maps of MLC and NDVI with accuracies >90% and kappa values >0.89 for all classified data (Tables 4 and 5).

## 7 Conclusion

This study explains the importance of integrating machine learning and RS for tracking the changes in land cover in Madurai, Tamil Nadu, India. In this study, we utilized the two most common classification approaches: MLC and NDVI. The accuracy of the classified maps was analyzed, and the NDVI maps were better than the MLC maps. The land cover change detection depends on MLC classified images provides essential information regarding the nature

**TABLE 5 Error matrices for NDVI classified maps of the study area, Madurai.**

| Reference data | | | Total | PA (%) | UA (%) |
|---|---|---|---|---|---|
| Classified data | NV | V | | | |
| NV | 25 | 1 | 26 | 92.59 | 96.15 |
| V | 2 | 37 | 39 | 97 | 94.87 |
| Total | 27 | 38 | 65 | | |
| Overall accuracy = 92% | | Kappa coefficient = 0.90 | | | |

of LULC changes besides the spatial distribution. Based on this study, MLC was witnessed to be an excellent classifier with an accuracy of up to 90%. The inference of multitemporal satellite images assisted in preparing an urban sprawl map of the study area. The agricultural or scrub sector declined due to urban sprawl or discontinuance of farming activities. The barren area increases as agrarian areas are abandoned with the discontinuance of farming owing to seasonal changes and lack of irrigation facilities, despite the government recovering old cultivated land and new areas in the study area, which is threatened by urban expansion. Agriculture is a significant economic activity; enhancing agricultural activities and enlarging its productivity can increase the well-being of the farmers in the study area. We need additional research to study the water distribution and to analyze the farming and drinking water needs in the study area.

## References

[1] S. Tamilenthi, Urban sprawl change, DEM, and TIN model of Madurai corporation area in Tamilnadu State (India) from 1980 to 2015 Using Remote Sensing and GIS, Amer. J. Geophys. Geochem. Geosyst. 1 (2) (2015) 52–65.

[2] M. Allam, N. Bakr, W. Elbably, Multi-temporal assessment of land use/land cover change in the arid region based on Landsat satellite imagery: a case study in Fayoum region, Egypt, Remote Sens. Appl.: Soc. Environ. 14 (January) (2019) 8–19, https://doi.org/10.1016/j.rsase.2019.02.002.

[3] C.P. Dalmiya, N. Santhi, B. Sathyabama, A novel feature descriptor for automatic change detection in remote sensing images, Egypt. J. Remote Sens. Space Sci. 22 (2) (2019) 183–192,-https://doi.org/10.1016/j.ejrs.2018.03.005.

[4] Y. Hu, Y. Dong, Batunacun, An automatic approach for land-change detection and land updates based on integrated NDVI timing analysis and the CVAPS method with GEE support, ISPRS J. Photogramm. Remote Sens. 146 (February) (2018) 347–359, https://doi.org/10.1016/j.isprsjprs.2018.10.008.

[5] L.A. Jude, A. Suruliandi, Performance evaluation of land cover change detection algorithms using remotely sensed data, in: 2014 International Conference on Circuits, Power and

Computing Technologies, ICCPCT 2014, 2014, pp. 1409–1415, https://doi.org/10.1109/ICCPCT.2014.7055027.

[6] P. Group, S. Analysis, F. Juelich, Pixel-based and object-oriented change detection analysis using high-resolution imagery, 2009.

[7] L.T. Ngo, D.S. Mai, W. Pedrycz, Semi-supervising interval type-2 fuzzy C-means clustering with spatial information for multi-spectral satellite image classification and change detection, Comput. Geosci. 83 (2015) 1–16, https://doi.org/10.1016/j.cageo.2015.06.011.

[8] S. Sahoo, A. Dhar, N. Kayet, A. Kar, Detecting water stress scenario by land use/land cover changes in an agricultural command area, Spat. Inf. Res. 25 (1) (2017) 11–21, https://doi.org/10.1007/s41324-016-0073-3.

[9] D. Qin, X. Zhou, W. Zhou, G. Huang, Y. Ren, B. Horan, N. Kito, MSIM: a change detection framework for damage assessment in natural disasters, Expert Syst. Appl. 97 (2018) 372–383, https://doi.org/10.1016/j.eswa.2017.12.038.

[10] T.G. Andualem, G. Belay, A. Guadie, Land use change detection using remote sensing technology, Journal of Earth Science & Climatic Change 9 (10) (2018), https://doi.org/10.4172/2157-7617.1000496.

[11] A. Roy, A.B. Inamdar, Multi-temporal land use land cover (LULC) change analysis of a dry semi-arid river basin in western India following a robust multi-sensor satellite image calibration strategy, Heliyon 5 (4) (2019), https://doi.org/10.1016/j.heliyon.2019.e01478, e01478.

[12] M. Khurana, V. Saxena, Green cover change detection using a modified adaptive ensemble of extreme learning machines for North-Western India, J. King Saud Univ. - Comp. Inform. Sci. (2018), https://doi.org/10.1016/j.jksuci.2018.09.008.

[13] J.S. Deng, K. Wang, J. Li, Y.H. Deng, Urban land use change detection using multisensor satellite images project supported by the National Natural Science Foundation of China (NSFC) (no. 30571112), Pedosphere 19 (1) (2009) 96–103, https://doi.org/10.1016/S1002-0160(08)60088-0.

[14] K.L. De Jong, A. Sergeevna Bosman, Unsupervised change detection in satellite images using convolutional neural networks, in: Proceedings of the International Joint Conference on Neural Networks, July 2019, 2019, https://doi.org/10.1109/IJCNN.2019.8851762.

[15] O.S. Babalola, A.A. Akinsanola, Change detection in land surface temperature and land use land cover over Lagos Metropolis, Nigeria, J. Remote Sens. GIS 5 (3) (2016), https://doi.org/10.4172/2469-4134.1000171.

## Further reading

P. Lu, Y. Qin, Z. Li, A.C. Mondini, N. Casagli, Landslide mapping from multi-sensor data through improved change detection-based Markov random field, Remote Sens. Environ. 231 (June) (2019) 111235, https://doi.org/10.1016/j.rse.2019.111235.

F. Song, Z. Yang, X. Gao, T. Dan, Y. Yang, W. Zhao, R. Yu, Multi-scale feature-based land cover change detection in mountainous terrain using multi-temporal and multi-sensor remote sensing images, IEEE Access 6 (c) (2018) 77494–77508, https://doi.org/10.1109/ACCESS.2018.2883254.

A. Muhuri, D. Ratha, A. Bhattacharya, Seasonal snow cover change detection over the Indian Himalayas using polarimetric SAR images, IEEE Geosci. Remote Sens. Lett. 14 (12) (2017) 2340–2344, https://doi.org/10.1109/LGRS.2017.2764123.

S.H. Khan, X. He, F. Porikli, M. Bennamoun, Forest change detection in incomplete satellite images with deep neural networks, IEEE Trans. Geosci. Remote Sens. 55 (9) (2017) 5407–5423, https://doi.org/10.1109/TGRS.2017.2707528.

F. Durmaz, N. Karakaya, F. Evrendilek, Spatiotemporal change detection analysis of the Turkish lake water surface area in response to anthropogenic ecosystem disturbances using long-term Landsat TM/ETM + data, J. Ecosyst. Ecogr. 6 (2) (2016), https://doi.org/10.4172/2157-7625.1000188.

W. Cui, Z. Jia, X. Qin, J. Yang, Y. Hu, Multi-temporal satellite images change detection algorithm based on NSCT, Procedia Engineering 24 (2011) 252–256, https://doi.org/10.1016/j.proeng.2011.11.2636.

S. Tamilenthi, P. Arul, K. Chandramohan, Detection of urban change and urban sprawl of Madurai City, Tamilnadu using GIS and RS, J. Environ. Protect. Sustain. Develop. 1 (3) (2015) 107–120.

J. Ghosh, Remote sensing and GIS technique enable to assess and predict landuse changes in Vellore district, Tamil Nadu, India, Int. J. Appl. Eng. Res. 12 (12) (2017) 3474–3482 (ISSN 0973-4562).

G. Ecology, S. Afonso, R. Mucova, W.L. Filho, U.M. Azeiteiro, Assessment of land use and land cover changes from 1979 to 2017 and biodiversity & land management approach in Quirimbas National Park, northern Mozambique, Africa (October) (2018), https://doi.org/10.1016/j.gecco.2018.e00447.

Chapter 3

# A web application for crowd counting by building parallel and direct connection-based CNN architectures

**Zhilin Hu**
*Department of Informatics, University of Leicester, Leicester, United Kingdom*

## 1 Introduction

A crowd-counting web application based on the convolutional neural network (CNN) model can quickly solve the user's crowd-counting problem, while increasing the user's understanding of the crowd density in the image, reducing the time to count the number of people and avoiding safety hazards. For example, when a company organizes an employee party, due to the large number of participants taking photos, the photos can be uploaded to the network application for crowd counting to avoid employee accidents caused by counting errors.

The application of CNNs in crowd counting is one of the research directions of CNN models, and crowd density is one of the indicators of safety in public places. CNNs are robust to image processing and classification, and the convolution operation is the main difference between CNNs and traditional neural networks [1].

In the processing and passing of parameters, CNN applies a parameter-sharing mechanism, which greatly reduces the number of parameters in the neural network, speeds up the training efficiency of the neural network, and to some extent avoids the overfitting state in the test. In the operation of the matrix, the CNN applies sparse connections of image units to avoid the deviation of the model for the image recognition. In contrast, traditional neural networks apply full connections, which will affect the recognition performance of the whole network if one of the image units is faulty.

CNNs have undergone dramatic changes in computational methods, application areas, and development models compared to traditional neural networks.

**Cognitive Systems and Signal Processing in Image Processing. https://doi.org/10.1016/B978-0-12-824410-4.00012-X**

Since AlexNet [2] won the image recognition and classification leaderboard at 2012, the academic exploration of CNN models has entered a feverish phase.

A large number of researchers have investigated CNN models for image recognition and classification in terms of depth of convolutional layer, size of convolution kernel, gradient optimization of back propagation, study of residual networks, and more, and the efficiency of CNN models for image recognition and classification has rapidly increased and the error has been decreasing.

This chapter deeply investigates the influence of the depth and width of the model architecture on learning model features from the CNN model architecture. With limited computing resources, optimization experiments are carried out according to the weighting factors that affect model learning, and an attempt is made to find a local optimal model for a specific data set with a fixed architecture. The purpose of this chapter is to provide a research and optimization idea for the study of a CNN model and combine it with the application direction when obtaining the local optimal model, so that the entire model research has more practical application value.

The structure of a CNN [3] generally consists of these layers: input layer, convolutional layer, excitation layer, pooling layer, and fully connected layer. The role of each layer is unique. As one of the development directions of network applications, it is the embodiment of the idea of object-oriented development [4].

## 2 Background

The emergence of neural networks has given humans a new way of thinking to solve current problems that cannot be solved through humans themselves by simulating the ability of human eyes to see and feedback the shape and characteristics of objects through the cooperation of related organs to further solve what human eyes can see but cannot quickly analyze. A modern neural network is a nonlinear tool for modeling statistical data [5, 6]. A typical neural network has the following three components:

1. Architecture: The structure specifies the variables in the network and their topological relationships [7]. For example, the variables in a neural network can be the weights of the neuronal connections (weights) and the excitation values of the neurons (activity of the neurons).
2. Activation values: Most neural network models have a short timescale dynamic rule that defines how a neuron changes its excitation value based on the activity of other neurons [8]. In general, the excitation function depends on the weights in the network (i.e., the parameters of the network).
3. Learning rules: Learning rules define how the weights in the network adjust as time progresses [9]. This is generally viewed as a long timescale dynamic rule. In general, a learning rule relies on the incentive value of the neuron.

It may also depend on the value of the target and current weights provided by the supervisor.

# 3 CNN algorithmic model

According to the analysis of the VGG network model structure, it can be seen that multiple small convolution kernels are used for feature extraction. The advantage of the VGG model structure is that the depth of the convolutions layers is increased to achieve the same perceptual field as that of the large convolution kernel without considering the number of feature parameters. However, this is also its most obvious disadvantage. Through relevant experimental verification, when increasing the number of convolutions layers beyond a certain critical number of layers, the feature learning ability of the VGG network model gradually decreases. For the ResNet model, the advantage is that the study is no longer limited by the increase in the number of convolutions layers, which is helpful for studying the effect of the width and depth of convolutions layers on the model learning, but the disadvantage is that at a certain level of network depth, the error arose, the effect becomes worse, the gradient disappearance phenomenon becomes more obvious, the backward propagation cannot feed the gradient to the previous network layers, and the previous network parameters cannot be updated, resulting in poor training. In this chapter, the problem is studied in two directions: (1) the traditional direct-connected method, which investigates the effect of depth on model learning by increasing the number of convolutions layers; and (2) the parallel method, which investigates the effect of network width on model learning by widening the height of convolutions layers. While studying this problem, an attempt is made to propose a systematic optimization method to explore the local optimum of the model, and multiple sets of control experiments will be conducted.

## 3.1 Data process

This project uses the Shanghai Science and Technology dataset as the main dataset [8] for training the ADCCNet model. Before training, the image data information needs to be processed and saved as a .h5 type file for the supervised learning model. The dataset is mainly divided into two parts: partA and partB. The main difference is the crowd density size: partA is the high-density crowd picture, and partB is the low-density crowd picture. The content of the file includes the original picture and label information, such as the location of the people, the number of people in the picture, and so on.

### *3.1.1 Gaussian blur algorithms*

This chapter validates the experimental findings by training the ShangHaiTech dataset. For the analysis of the dataset, it can be found that the picture has more disturbing factors, such as trees, tall buildings, and eaves, in addition to the characteristics of the number of people to be learned. The many interfering factors are not conducive to evaluating the true learning ability of the model, and based on this shortcoming, this chapter uses a Gaussian fuzzy algorithm to smooth the images and blur out the excess interfering factors to ensure the reliability of the results.

The Gaussian filtering algorithm is a filtering method that uses a Gaussian mask to perform convolution operations on the input signal, and the resulting filtered effect is also known as a Gaussian fuzzy algorithm [5, 6].

*scipy.ndimage.gaussian_filter(input, sigma, order = 0, output = None, mode = 'reflect', optinal(cval = 0.0, truncate = 4.0)).*

After processing the image with this function, a density map is generated, the input is the input array, and sigma is defined as the standard deviation of the Gaussian kernel, which acts as the same distance from the processed axes. Mode fills the past input edges with the given cval scalar value. The return value is a matrix with the same shape as the input. The relevant theoretical formula is based on Eq. (1):

$$f(x) = \frac{1}{\sqrt{2\prod\delta^2}} e^{\frac{-(x-\mu)^2}{2\delta^2}} \tag{1}$$

where *f(x)* is a one-dimensional Gaussian distribution formula whose values represent probabilities. The parameter $\mu$ is the mean, meaning the position parameter, and $\delta$ is the variance, whose expression determines the image shape, that is, height and width.

According to the one-dimensional Gaussian distribution function, it can be observed that the coordinate points are distributed in a manner related to the parameters $\mu$ and $\xi$. The parameter $\mu$ is related to the x-axis, and the parameter $\xi$ is related to the shape of the distribution function. Take the origin as an example, that is, set $\mu = 0$ to derive a two-dimensional Gaussian distribution function.

$$g(x_i, y_j) = \frac{1}{2\prod\delta^2} e^{\frac{-(x_i^2 + y_j^2)}{2\delta^2}} \tag{2}$$

Based on a one-dimensional Gaussian distribution, the formula for a two-dimensional Gaussian distribution is derived.

### 3.1.2 Binary space partitioning architecture

The random forest rule algorithm is a branch of the binary space partitioning architecture and is one of the important algorithms in machine learning. The algorithm was proposed by Leo Bremen and is an important processing method for datasets. It is based on the principle that k samples are taken from the original dataset by bootstrap resampling count and put back into the original dataset to form new training samples. Then k classification trees consisting of random forests are generated based on the set of self-help samples. The classification results of the new data form the score of the classification tree based on the number of votes. It is essentially an improvement on the decision tree algorithm, where multiple decision trees are combined, each tree generation relies on independently drawn samples, each tree in the forest has the same distribution, and the classification error depends on the classification ability of each tree and the correlation between them. Feature selection uses a stochastic method to split each node and then compare the errors generated in different cases.

A study of the algorithm reveals the use of K-D (decision tree), which is a tree structure (can be binary or nonbinary) [10, 11]. Each of its nonleaf nodes represents a test of a characteristic attribute, each branch represents the output of that characteristic attribute of the value domain, and each leaf node stores a category. The process of decision making using a decision tree is to test the corresponding feature attribute of the item to be categorized, starting from the root node, and select the output branch based on its value until it reaches the leaf node, where the category deposited by the leaf node is used as the result of the decision. There is no relationship between each decision tree in the random forest.

In this chapter, different decision trees are constructed using random forest rule, random variables are introduced, and Gaussian fusion is performed to reduce the negative effects of image noise on model learning. During the processing, the random forest rule does not require feature selection of image information, which reduces the loss of information in the dataset and can process the dataset well.

## 3.2 Core model structure

A neural network is a vector of instance features passed into the input layer, which, after a hidden layer and a series of calculations, can be used to obtain the output layer [9]. Each layer after the input layer can be obtained by a weighted summation of the previous layer, followed by a nonlinear equation transformation.

The process of weighted summation is that there are several lines between the units of the previous layer and the next layer, each line corresponds to a weight, the units of the previous layer and the corresponding weights multiplied and then added, and finally through the nonlinear equation transformation can be obtained the unit value of each layer [7]. The output of each layer is the input of the next layer. Since the equations computed after the weighted summation are nonlinear, they are theoretically powerful and can be used to simulate any equation as long as the training set is large enough and has enough hidden layers, so neural networks can be used for both classification and regression problems. Neural networks are powerful predecessor extensions to deep learning because the amount of computation increases dramatically as the dataset gets larger and larger [3]. Neural networks are powerful in that more hidden layers can be used to simulate more equations, but the downside is that the dataset and computational power increase dramatically [4].

With the continuous improvement of recognition algorithms, many neural network models have been developed. In the field of image recognition, the most applied one is deep learning, which is divided into different models according to the direction of application, that is, feedforward neural network (DNN), CNN, recurrent neural network (RNN) [12], and so on. Using different network model structures, the focus of model learning is inconsistent.

In the study of different models in deep learning, it is first necessary to analyze the common fundamental part of the model: the artificial neurons in deep learning. Similar to the neurons in biology, the artificial neurons in deep learning can be seen as a mathematical model; multiple neurons are connected together to form a neural network. DNN is a simpler type of neural network, each neuron belongs to a different layer, each neuron connects to all neurons in the upper layer, and the signal propagates unidirectionally from the input layer to the output layer. The input of DNN is in the form of a vector, which does not take into account the planar structure information, which is an essential position in the field of image and natural language processing. For planar structure information, the CNN model handles it better than the DNN model. The input and output lengths of both DNN and CNN are fixed, while the length of statements in natural language processing is usually variable, so DNN and CNN are inefficient in handling such problems and cannot handle time-dependent sequences.

CNN is a feedforward neural network computed by convolution, which is proposed by the biological sensory field mechanism, has flip invariance, and uses convolution kernels to maximize the application of local information and preserve planar structural information.

The input to the RNN model is sequential data, and the core idea is that the processing problem is decomposed into a series of identical "units" in chronological order, that the unit neural network can be extended in chronological order, and that all cyclic units are connected in chains that can pass the results of the previous moment to the next moment. However, the RNN model suffers from long-term dependency, that is, the farther a node is from the current node, the less impact it has on the processing of the current node. After gaining a better understanding of the differences between RNN, CNN and DNN, the design and study of the CNN model was chosen as a solution in line with this chapter.

### 3.2.1 *Transfer learning*

In the structural design of the model, transfer learning [13, 14] is used, that is, the pretraining part of the VGG [15] model is used. As an important application area of machine learning, transfer learning is widely accepted in the field of model learning development [16, 17]. The core idea is to facilitate the reuse of pretrained models in new tasks as a way to speed up the learning time of the models. Deep learning, as one of the methods to implement machine learning, has made users' lives easier in the era of iterative development techniques [18, 19].

Select the source model: Select a pretrained source model from the available models. Many research institutions have published models based on very large datasets that can be used as alternatives to the source model.

Reuse the model: The selected pretrained model can be used as a learning starting point for the model used for the second task. This may involve using and training all or part of the model, depending on the model training technique used.

Adjust the model: The model can be selectively fine-tuned to the input/output pairs in the target dataset to adapt it to the target task.

### *3.2.2 Activation function*

The essence of the activation function is the activation of a threshold, which operates the input value as an output value when it is greater than (or equal to) the threshold. Conversely, when the value is less than the threshold, no output operation is performed, i.e., the input value is discarded [20].

For activation functions, the first step is to discuss the question of linear or nonlinear transformations. For linear transformation functions, the formula for the distance from each point to a straight line, for example, the K-neighbor algorithm only yields a stiff fit to a small number of values [21].

For the nonlinear transformation function, it is possible to fit most points by adjusting the parameters of the nonlinear function and the power exponents of the variables. By comparison, it can be concluded that the nonlinear transformation function is better at receiving data than the linear function [22].

In the second step, the selection or discarding of feature points is discussed, i.e., the classical biclassical problem. In order to accomplish the task of dividing the feature points into two or more copies for screening whether certain data are needed, the first step is that the data are linearly divisible, that is, the data can be separated by a straight line. For example, in Fig. 1, a suitable linear equation needs to be found by some machine learning method, such as a perceptron learning algorithm.

For large amounts of data with complex data features, the feature point data is not linearly separable. For the following data, a second set of feature data requires a nonlinear function to differentiate the data. From this revelation, a function needs to be created to classify the multiple feature values and select a number of features for learning (Fig. 2).

In the process of learning of images, the model is selective for the learning of features of the image, for example, the selection of contour features, the selection of architectural features or the selection of head features. Features that are

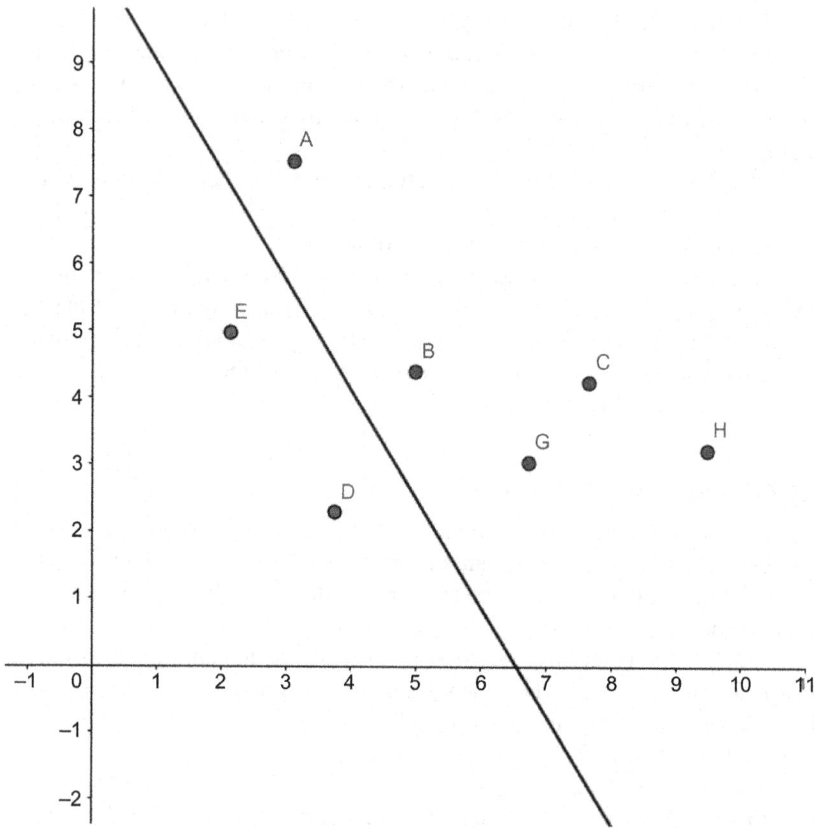


**FIG. 1** The ability to classify linear functions for different points.

not part of the target features to be learned by the model need to be blocked by a mechanism (Table 1). This is the meaning of the activation function (Fig. 3).

The activation function should have the following properties:

- Minimizability: This property is necessary when the optimization method is based on a gradient.
- Monotonicity: When the activation function is monotonic, the single-layer network is guaranteed to be a convex function.

### 3.2.3 *Batch normalization*

Batch normalization is a routine operation in the construction of neural network models, which not only speeds up the convergence of the model to some extent but also plays the most important role in solving the gradient dispersion problem in the network, i.e., the phenomenon of unstable gradient variation [23]. If normalization is not used, the distribution of data obtained by the model after

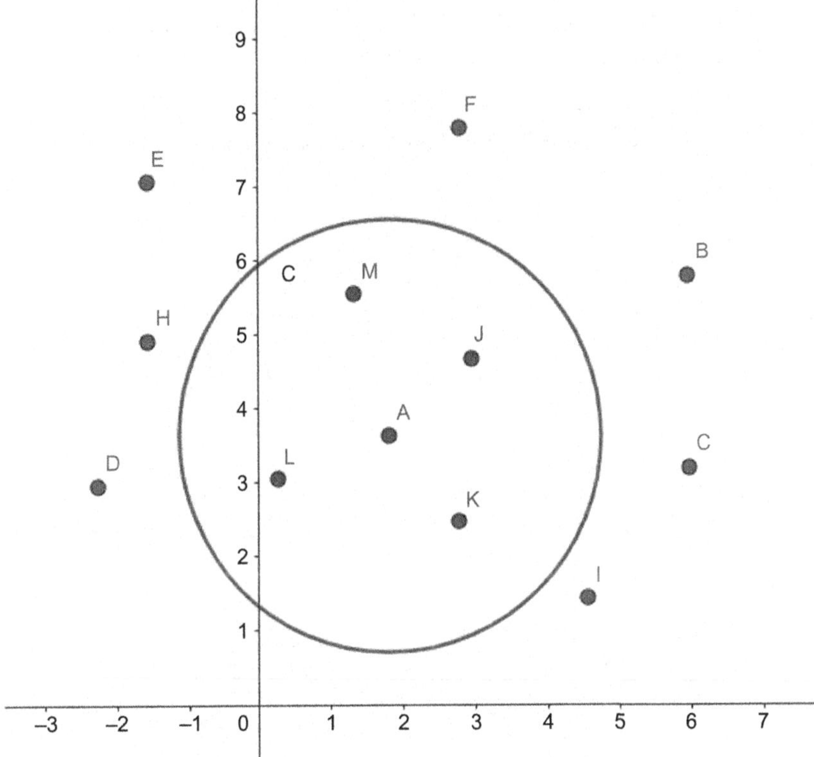


**FIG. 2** The ability to classify nonlinear functions for different points.

training at each layer has differences [24], and the computational volume of the model network will increase for different data processing, causing the network model to be more complex, and thus prone to overfitting and slower convergence of the model [25].

For the ADCCNet model in the residual unit, using the advantages of the normalization operation. The normalization operation is applied several times to ensure the nonlinear expression of the model fully, that is, the essence of normalization is to make the model acquired picture feature data more reasonable, optimize the learning ability of the model, improve the generalization ability of the model, and improve the counting ability.

## 3.3 ADCCNet model

According to the basic idea of building a CNN model, the input layer, the convolution layer, the pooling layer, the activation function layer, and the output layer are built [23].

**TABLE 1 The process by which the acquired image features are assigned weights and processed by the activation function.**

| |
|---|
| f = var 1 * w1 + var 2 * w2 + var 3 + gb |
| Notice: var1,var2,var3 are eigenvector set, b is bias |
| G = *a*(f) |
| α is represented activation function |

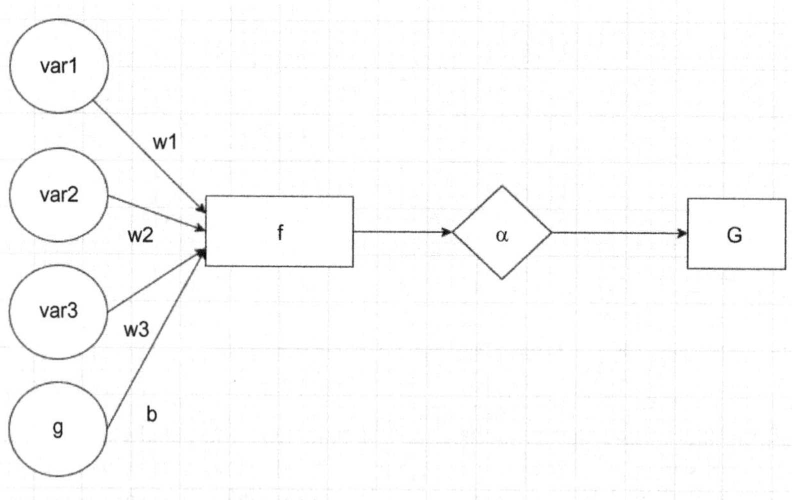


**FIG. 3** The position of the excitation function during neuronal transfer.

The image input layer is 224 × 224 × 3, the input image size is 224 × 224, and the image depth is 3, i.e., RGB (red, green, blue). The role of the convolution layer is to extract image features by setting the convolution nucleus for the image convolution operation, the resulting feature map. In essence, it is similar to the traditional image processing filtering operation, and the Gaussian filtering operation previously mentioned has the same essential significance [26]. A convolution layer is equivalent to using a filter to process the image. Convolution kernels are essentially set matrices, commonly 3 × 3, 5 × 5, or 7 × 7.

During the study, it was found that the size of the convolution kernel affects the size of the receptive field in the CNN, i.e., the larger the convolution kernel, the larger the receptive field and the greater the number of image features acquired in a single pass.

However, it is a sufficient condition that the larger the sensory field, the larger the convolutional nucleus may not be, and that a larger field of view and convolutional nucleus can be achieved by increasing the number of convolutional nuclei (Table 2).

It can be calculated that the number of parameters using two 3*3 convolution kernels is less than the number of 5*5 parameters. A computational comparison shows that using multiple small convolutional cores is preferable to using a single large convolutional core.

The pooling layer is an essential layer of matrix processing operations in the ADCCNet model. The introduction of the pooling layer mimics the process of biovision downscaling and abstracting of the input image. Pooling is essentially formal downsampling, and there are several line trial nonlinear pooling functions, the common ones being "average pooling" and "maximum pooling." The "maximum pooling" for the image feature extraction capability is more efficient than the "average pooling"; it is the matrix image after the previous layer of processing, divided into a number of rectangular regions, for each subregion of the output maximum. As the pooling layer reduces the size of the data space, the number of image feature parameters and the amount of computation decreases, suppressing the overfitting of the model to some extent. It has the following properties:

Feature invariant: The integration operation makes the model more concerned with the presence or absence of certain features than with the specific location of the features, that is, the a priori function, making feature learning fault-tolerant and tolerant of shifting changes in feature smiles.

**TABLE 2 Performance calculations for different sized convolutional cores.**

| |
|---|
| For example, input a 64*64 size picture, set the stride =1, padding =0 |
| Apply the function, size is output size, |
| *size* = (*picture_size* – kernel_size + 2Padding)/*Stride* + 1 |
| Kernel_size: 3*3 |
| Step 1, size = (64–3)/1 + 1 = 62 |
| Step 2, size = (62–3)/1 + 1 = 60 |
| Kernel_size: 5*5 |
| Step 1, size = (64–5)/1 + 1 = 60 |
| It can be calculated that two 3*3 convolution kernels can replace one 5*5 convolution kernel. |
| Parameters number: |
| Assuming bias exists and the value is 1 |
| Kernel_size = 3*3, parameter number = (3*3 + bias)*2 = 20 |
| Kernel_size = 5*5, parameter number = 5*5 + bias = 26 |

Feature downscaling: Due to the downsampling effect of the integration operation, an element in the integration result corresponds to a subregion of the original input data, so the integration operation is equivalent to a spatially dimensional reduction, which allows the model to learn more features.

The activation function is used to filter the features of the upper input image. The activation functions, such as rectified linear unit (ReLU), parametic ReLU (PReLU), and so on, are used to efficiently obtain the feature points of the image and reduce the computational effort as previously described [27].

The role of the input layer is to alternate through operations such as convolution and pooling. The learned model adaptation capabilities, such as feature parameters, hyperparameters, weight values, and more, are stored in the form of a matrix.

The first part is to load the first 11 layers of the pretrained VGG model for extracting image features [6, 28]. The second part is to build multiple residual-like network structures, the third part is the regular convolution operation layer, and the fourth part is the output convolution layer.

The ADCCNet model was developed to essentially mimic the conduction process of biological visual nerves. Based on the in-depth study of CNNs, five conjectures are proposed. The first one is to broaden the network structure by adding a parallel image data processing process similar to "binocular" on the basis of transfer learning. The second is to shorten the network on the basis of the first model, with the aim of maintaining the richness of the eigenvalues. The third is to add parallel channels on the basis of the second model, with the aim of cross-validating the feature matrix, which further amplifies the model-sensitive feature values and facilitates the extraction of feature points by the model. The fourth one is to further widen the network channel on the basis of the third model and introduce the idea of residual network to further screen out the model-sensitive feature points [23]. The fifth one is to deepen and enrich the convolutional layer of the model on the basis of the mainstream CNN model.

**Conjectures 1:**

See Figs. 4 and 5

**Conjectures 2:**

See Figs. 6 and 7.

**Conjectures 3:**

See Fig. 8

**Conjectures 4:**

See Figs. 9 and 10.

**Conjectures 5**:

See Fig. 11.

*Description VGG model architecture:* The VGG model uses multiple 3 × 3 convolution kernels instead of large convolution kernels for feature extraction, which reduces the number of parameters without affecting the receptive field, and reduces the amount of computation. At the same time, the increase in the number of convolution kernels enhances the nonlinear mapping capability of

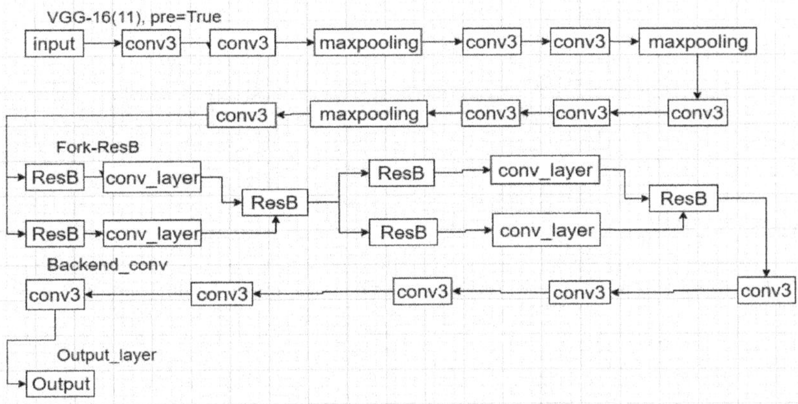


**FIG. 4** Build a parallel network model of CNNs, add on-the-fly processing of features, and broaden the model.

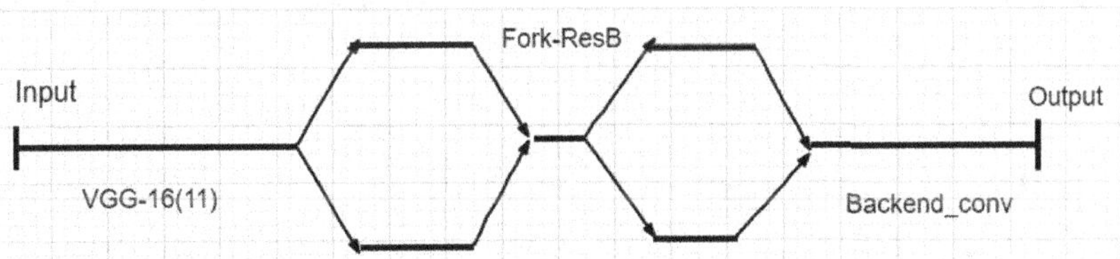


**FIG. 5** A description of the conduction process of the parallel CNN model flowchart. It corresponds to a core structure diagram of the flowchart in Fig. 4, which clearly shows the conduction process in the parallel model construction.

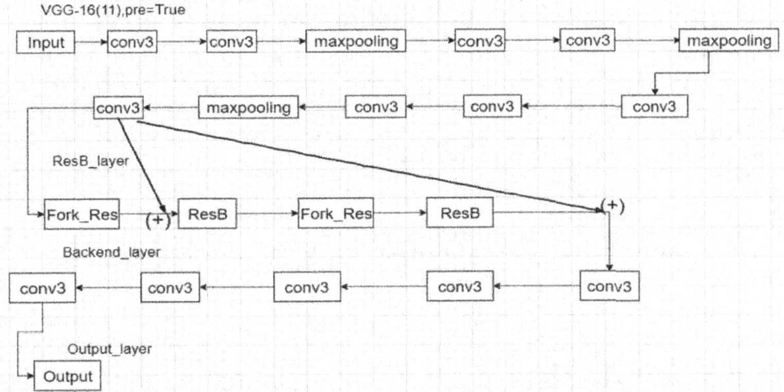


**FIG. 6** Add two short connections to the first model. It is described to further broaden the height of the network model and enrich the extraction of features in order to increase the complexity of the model and avoid the overfitting phenomenon of the model caused by regular learning of model features.

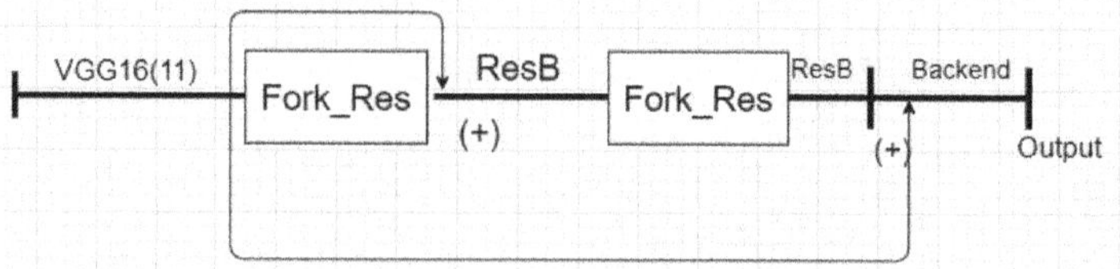

**FIG. 7** Described is an architectural diagram of the flowchart of Fig. 6, which further describes Conjecture 2.

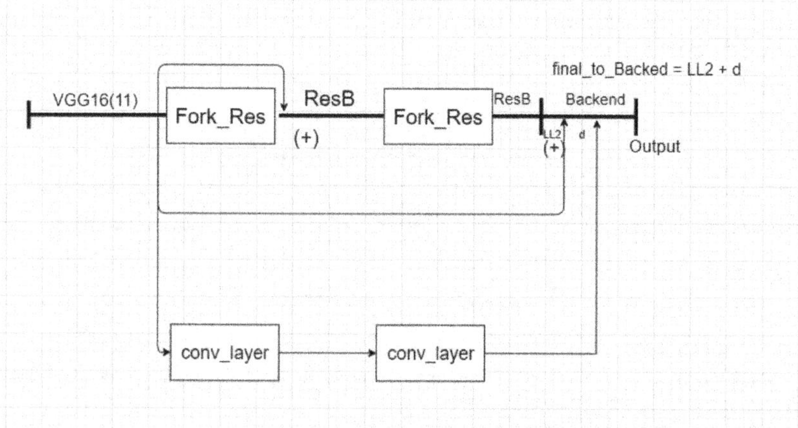


**FIG. 8** Conjectures 3 implements a dual pathway, with the added second pathway being the normal convolutional layer and the feature matrix summing before entering the back end.

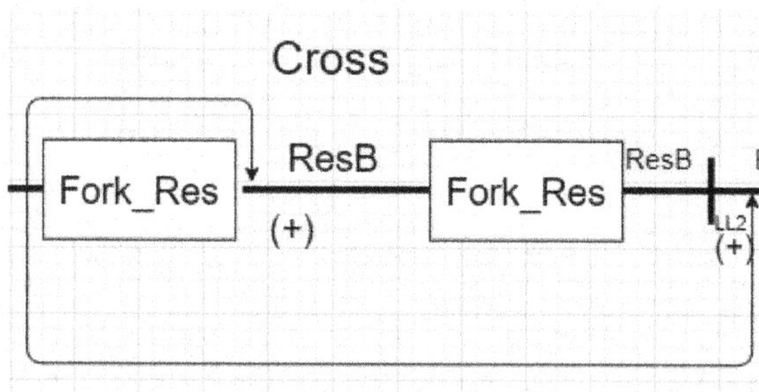


**FIG. 9** Conjectures 4 implements two pathways, with the same structure for both pathways and a single pathway.

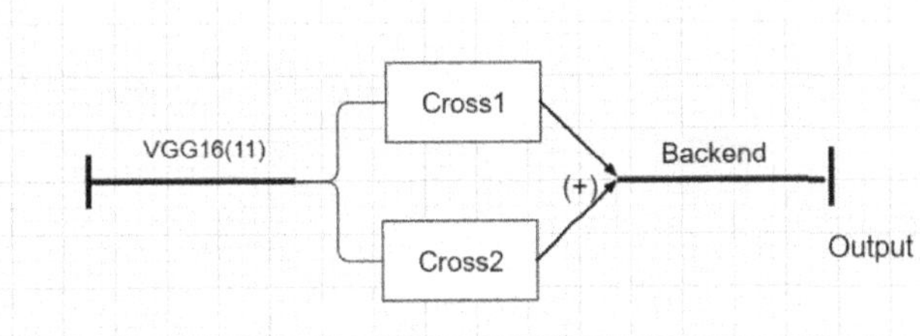


**FIG. 10** Conjectures 4 implements two pathways, both of which have the same structure and are represented by flow diagrams.

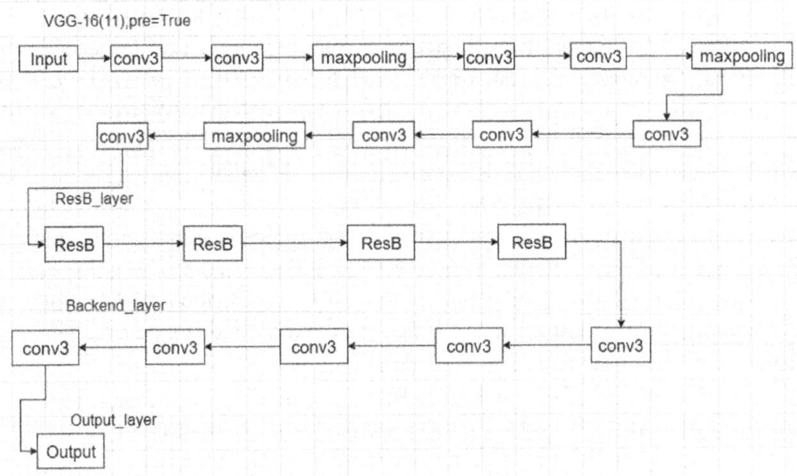


**FIG. 11** Flowchart of the CNN model used in this chapter.

the model, which increases the network depth and the network fitting capability to a certain extent under the condition that the receptive field remains unchanged.

The VGG model has a simple structure, and the same convolution kernel size and maximum pooling size are used for the whole network, which gives the VGG model a greater advantage for extracting image features under the increasing number of channels, allowing more image information to be extracted [28]. Due to the advantages of the VGG model, this project uses the first 11 layers of the VGG network (Fig. 12).

Description residual thought in model: In the second part, a residue-like block structure is used to further process the images and extract image features [29]. According to the study, it was found that for a single network model, consistently increasing the network depth can lead to gradient diffusion or gradient explosion, i.e., the model is unable to learn the image features properly due to the excessive computation.

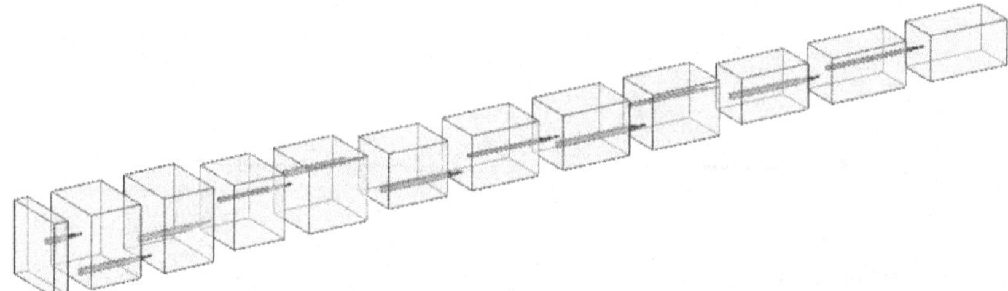

**FIG. 12** Schematic diagram of the model structure of the first 11 layers in the VGG-16 model.

The advent of the regularization algorithm alleviates this problem to some extent, but even if the regularized stochastic optimization algorithm is added to the model, the model will face degradation, that is, as the number of network layers increases, the accuracy of the model no longer changes or even decreases during the training process. This situation is opposed to the overfitting problem, which occurs when the model is extremely accurate on the training set but poor at extracting features on the validation set, that is, the essence is that the model loses its generalization ability during the learning process with too many parameters of the nonlinear function. Network degradation is the problem that occurs on the training set. Introducing the structure of the residual block does not simply increase the depth of the network but at the same time changes the learning structure of the network to some extent (Fig. 13).

The introduction of residual units allows the model network to express the hierarchy of features at a higher level. By observing the structure of the residual units, it is clear that the final output is the matrix output of the two-way features, combined with the valid features derived from the filtering of the activation function. On the one hand, it increases the nonuniqueness of the model features, and on the other hand, it reduces the loss of important image features when retraining the model through the direct connection of shortcut. For the whole model, the introduction of too many single-structure convolution layers can, to some extent, play a negative role in causing excessive computation, especially when doing back-propagation gradient calculations, which can affect the model performance. Replacing the single-structure convolutional layer with a residual unit, on the one hand, maintains the depth of the network structure so that the model can give full play to its performance, and on the other hand, reduces the pressure on the model during the gradient computation, and replaces the loss of image features caused by the introduction of pooling operations in the overall model performance.

*Description activation function in ADCCNet:* The application of the activation function in the model should be based on the actual situation of the model. The common sigmoid and tanh activation functions, that is, saturated functions, are often used in classification problems, that is, "0" and "1" problems.

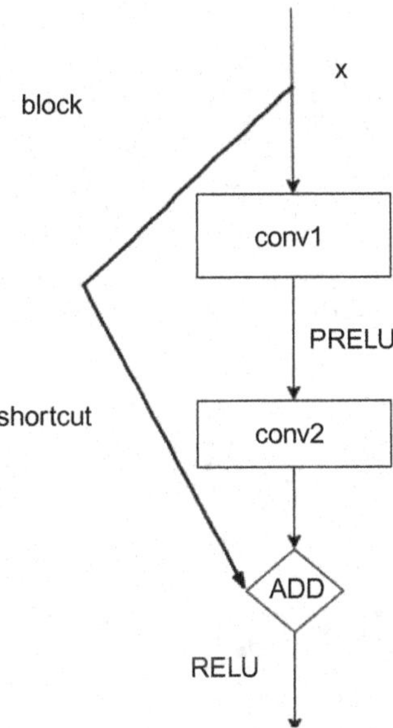


**FIG. 13** A flowchart of residual thoughts.

According to its function image and function properties, the threshold of the tanh function is (−1.1), the range of variation in a fixed interval, that is, beyond a fixed interval outside the variable, the function value will not change, for the acquisition of image features and the number of calculations on the problem more prominent disadvantages. Similarly, the sigmoid activation function is not applicable to the feature counting problem in this model for small variations and high function complexity.

The opposite activation function is an activation function such as ReLU, which functions to correct the linear unit, that is, rectify the linear unit. By looking at the definition of the ReLU function, it can be found that the model does not saturate in the region where $x > 0$ [30]. The complexity of the function is low, and only a threshold value is needed to pass through the ReLU activation function to get the activation value. It has been experimentally observed that the model using the ReLU function as an activation function converges faster than sigmoid and tanh. When using ReLU as an activation function to solve the saturation problem, it can be found that it chooses to discard neurons with negative variables, i.e., when doing gradient calculations, the gradient of the corresponding neuron is 0, and the parameters are no longer updated. There is uncertainty about the effect on feature extraction, i.e., whether the features obtained from neurons that are no longer activated have a negative impact on model learning.

In the continued research on this issue, the negative impact of the previous functions on the model can be compensated by using a segmented linear activation function, i.e., a PReLU [19] activation function [30].

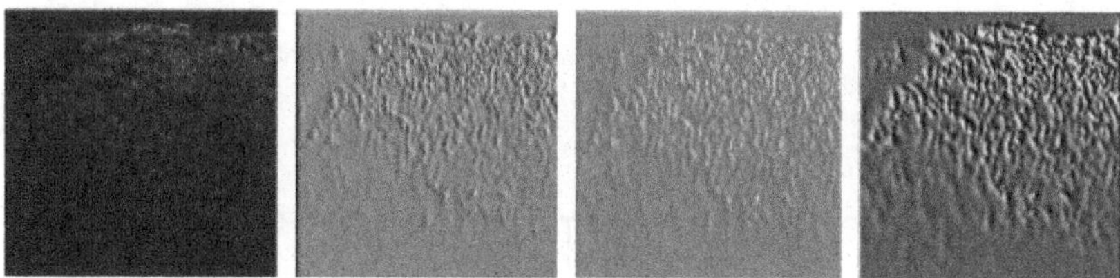

**FIG. 14** Under supervised learning based, the model learns only the given information. The feature maps are generated by processing conv1, conv2, and conv3 in the VGG model, respectively.

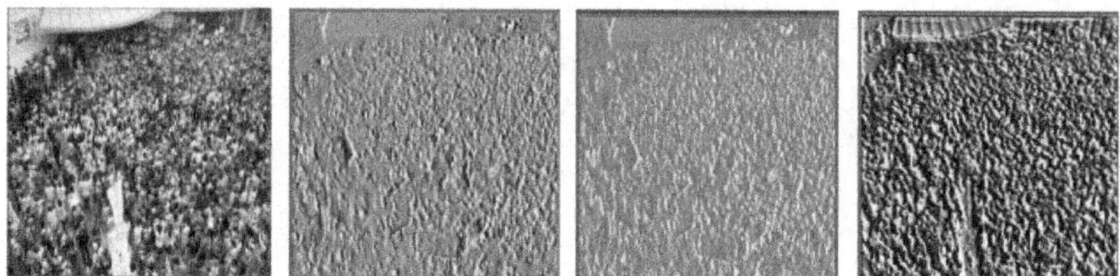

**FIG. 15** Based on the unsupervised learning case, the model learns features for the same picture. The feature maps are generated by processing conv1, conv2, and conv3 in the VGG model, respectively.

The ability of the model to learn by using the MAE [8] for different activation functions is evaluated by the degree to which they match the task the model is trying to accomplish.

*Description convolutional operation:* For understanding the convolution operations of the convolution layers, which is an important step in building the model, the data is entered into the model and the feature maps generated by the first, second, and third layer convolution operations are observed.

A comparison of the two sets of images shows that the features obtained are not consistent for the different training data used in model training. The first set of images (Figs. 14 and 15) feature acquisition of head position information and feature acquisition of original image information. In the head feature map, the model extracts the features of the "point" during learning, including the outline of the point, but no other information is extracted. In the original image, in addition to the crowd, there is additional information, such as buildings and objects in the hands of the crowd, and the outlines of the buildings and the outlines of the additional objects are extracted by convolutional layer processing and learned as features. For this model, the ultimate goal is to count people, not to identify objects, so the additional features are redundant, which increases the amount of computation and changes the learning direction of the model.

The second set of images (Figs. 16 and 17) are the original images for feature acquisition of head position information and crowd information. In the first picture, the model learns the features of the "dots," while the second picture learns the outline of the person, including redundant features such as height, which

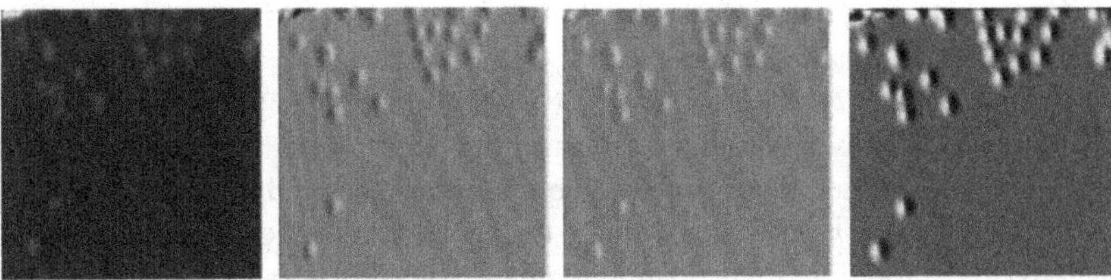

**FIG. 16** Under supervised learning based, the model learns only the given information. The feature maps are generated by processing conv1, conv2, and conv3 in the VGG model, respectively.

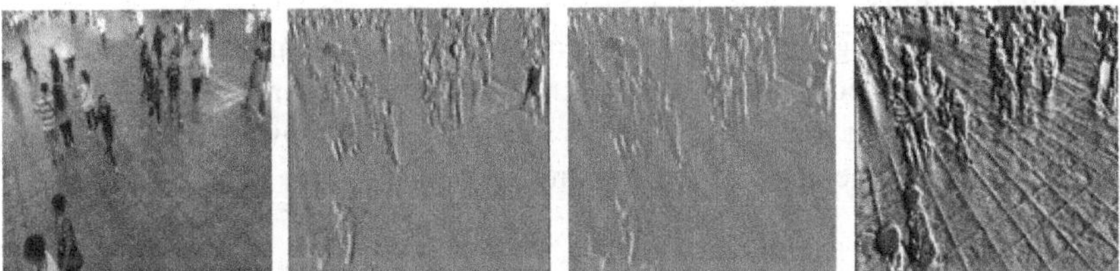

**FIG. 17** Based on the unsupervised learning case, the model learns features for the same picture. The feature maps are generated by processing conv1, conv2, and conv3 in the VGG model, respectively.

increases the complexity of the model learning but reduces the negative impact of the model on the population size.

## 3.4 Train model by learning data

### *3.4.1 Data enhancement*

For the training of the model, data is one of the factors that affect the model's ability to learn. The amount of data is too small; in one case, the model is unable to grasp the accurate extraction of data features, which affects the accuracy of model recognition [31, 32]; in another case, the model repeatedly learns a small amount of data, which will lead to overfitting phenomenon, resulting in poor generalization ability of the model. For CNN references in different directions, the acquisition of data sets is different. For example, for the characterization of medical images, the number of samples is not sufficient for the model to learn adequately, and data enhancement is invoked to obtain more sample data. Data augmentation is used to reduce the overfitting phenomenon that occurs when training the network model, and by varying the data set, the network model acquires more data features and enhances the generalization ability of the network model to better adapt to the application direction to which the model is applicable. The essence of this is to obtain more equivalent data for the training of network models with finite datasets through processing, such as cropping, scaling, and flipping.

Commonly used data enhancements fall into two categories, addressing different data and situations, respectively.

*Offline enhancement:* Direct quantity transformation of the dataset, where the number of datasets is the set enhancement factor and the amount of data in the original dataset, that is, it is suitable for cases where the dataset is small.

*Online enhancement:* When training the network model, data enhancements such as image rotation, image panning, image backsliding, and other enhancement operations are performed on the acquired batch_size data when loading the training set data. Due to the limitations of the dataset, e.g., the dataset does not support direct changes at the linear level, online enhancement is applicable for larger datasets.

The model is augmented by image cropping in a way that allows the dataset to be fully expanded through random cropping. The deeper network model is prone to overfitting for datasets with fewer images, as shown by the fact that the gap between the error of the training set and the error of the validator is too large.

### 3.4.2 Criterion

The mean absolute error (MAE) is commonly used as a method of error calculation to calculate the overall error of the model. Compared to the root mean square error (RMSE), MAE focuses on measuring the overall error and is less sensitive to outliers than RMSE, and this difference can be seen through its formula. The preferred error calculation function is inconsistent for different model applications, and can be applied according to the purpose of the network model application.

### 3.4.3 Gradient optimization

For the CNN network model, the optimization algorithm is one of the methods to adjust the learning ability of the network model, which is expressed in maximizing or minimizing the loss function M. The M function is used to calculate the degree of deviation of the predicted value P from the true value T in the test set, i.e., the model evaluation function.

Optimization algorithms are divided into two main categories

*First-order (bias-guided) optimization algorithm:* This algorithm is implemented by using the gradient values of each parameter to maximize or minimize the loss function M. A common optimization algorithm is gradient descent. The gradient describes the instantaneous rate of change of the independent variable concerning the variable by deriving the function. For multivariate functions, that is, the partial derivative of the variable is sought and passed as a gradient, and conversely, for univariate functions, the derivative value is used instead of the gradient.

*Second-order (bias derivative) optimization algorithm:* The heart of the method is that it is based on a first-order derivative, the Hessian method, and then a second derivative. However, due to the large number of parameters of some models, the use of second-order derivatives increases the computational volume of the model substantially, and the computational cost is too high.

## 3.5 Analyze error

### 3.5.1 Underfitting and overfitting

For the actual development of this project, one of the problems encountered is the overfitting and underfitting of the model. This is manifested in the following:

(1) The MAE of the training set is too low and the MAE of the test set is too high when the model is trained.
(2) The MAE value of the training set changes smoothly during model training and does not differ much from the MAE value of the model during initial training.

First, the principles of the two phenomena should be analyzed. The root cause of the underfitting problem is the acquisition of too few image feature dimensions, which results in the learning of the model that cannot be adapted to the entire training set [33]. The root cause of the overfitting problem is too many acquired image features, i.e., overfitting the information of the loaded data, resulting in the uniqueness of the loaded data and the exclusion or neglect of the feature information of the validation set data, i.e., the model becomes the only rigid model in the training set with poor generalization ability. To solve the problem of overfitting, ADCCNet adopts a partial VGG network and a residual block in the residual network to avoid the rigid learning of the model. For the underfitting problem, the depth of the network model should be deepened to obtain more feature dimensions to solve the problem.

### 3.5.2 Loss value

The loss value reflects the error between the predicted and true values in the ADCCNet model. The visualization of the loss value is one of the ways to observe the learning ability of the model, to judge the model's ability to fit the training set by whether the loss value converges, and to judge the degree of training of the model by observing its downward trend. Adding the Tensorboard package and writing the related visualization code, after the model has been trained, you can enter the command to get the relevant information.

### 3.5.3 Training epochs

Epoch plays a nonnegligible role in the model's ability to learn. When the epoch is too little, the learning ability of the model is not fully reflected, and there will be a decreasing trend in the loss value, which can be seen by observing the image of the loss value; when the epoch value is increased and visualized by the Tensorboard, a clear moderating trend can be seen. By comparing and examining the MAE data, from the training and validation sets, it is concluded that the epoch model with more training is better at learning than the model with fewer epochs.

The adequacy of image feature acquisition is one of the factors that directly affect the learning ability of the model, and with too little epoch, the model does not fully acquire the important features of the image. The model parameter values do not reach the optimal value, which is reflected in the count of the crowd in a picture, and there will be a large gap with the true value and is one of the reasons for the underfitting of the model. When increasing the value of epoch, it can be found that the accuracy of the count is improving and no longer changes when a certain value is reached, and if the epoch continues to increase at this time, the overfitting phenomenon will occur. Therefore, in the training of the model, adjusting the size of the epoch parameter is a factor that affects the learning ability of the model.

### 3.5.4 Learning rate

The setting of the model learning rate is one of the methods to assist the model in finding the optimal solution. The deeper reason is that the gradient cannot follow the regular gradient trend down under the influence of a learning rate that is too large and misses too many local optimal values [34, 35].

The training process of the model is reflected in the decreasing gradient and the reverse iteration of the parameters. It can cause noise in the learning process of the model, i.e., invalid edge parameters, and can even cause negative effects, reflected intuitively in the violent oscillation of the loss value, which cannot converge.

## 3.6 Verify web applications

This section describes the core module demonstrations for developing related web applications based on the CNN model, including code demonstrations and pages.

### 3.6.1 Login and register module

The development of the registration module is essentially an authorization function that allows the user to use more functions only after they have gained access to the web page. According to the actual requirements of this project, users need to gain access to image information pages, comment pages, and other pages before they can access them. For example, the ability to post comments in the comment section of the question page requires the user's mobile phone number and password to be verified before it can be used.

The final web application is oriented to tools, so the login or registration page does not require much information. Unlike recommended web applications, tools are not intended to benefit the website by obtaining user information, so the simple application can increase user stickiness, i.e., user's dependence on the application of the project.

From the user's point of view, user information that has already been registered should be given a reminder to the user when re-registering, so that the user can log indirectly. In the registration process, the password uses the operation of two inputs to check each other, and if the first and second user input password is not the same, the user should be prompted to reset the password. For the page jump, under the flask framework, use redirect function to set the jump destination page, after the user registration is complete, jump directly to the login page, enter the information registered, click the login button to get user rights.

The jump of the login page should be in line with the security of the website and the operation habits of the users when the user uses the function that needs special permission, and it should jump to the login page to remind the user. For example, if the user is not logged in when using the comment function in the comment section, the login page should be redirected to the login page.

For the form of the password stored in the database during registration, from the security point of view, if it is stored in plain code, that is, by directly recording the information entered by the user, and the website suffers a malicious attack and the database is invaded, any information of the user will be leaked, which is contrary to the most basic security principles of the website. Passwords should be set to the form of hash string to save user information. Therefore, even if the website is maliciously attacked, the user's information will not be threatened.

### 3.6.2 Display module

The design of the web page should be centered around the timeliness of the information and user habits. Introductory and clear features are important principles of web application development, and good interactivity is one of the criteria for measuring front-end and backend design. For the design of the display page, taking into account the visual habits of users, users want to see the original image, the effect of the processed image, and the relevant information about the crowd count, so it is necessary to mark the important information on the image, direct display.

KISS (keep it simple, stupid) is a design principle that was proposed in 1960 and has been well implemented in current web applications. The basic core point is that what can be achieved should not be made complex.

Users do not care how complex the design or the latest technology is used in the development of the website, and users are concerned about whether the functions developed are convenient and useful to them. Based on this design criterion, the logic of developing a display page is to get the processed image locally and upload it to the front page so that users can see the desired result directly.

When uploading the image, base64 encoding is used to convert the image format and output it as a string instead of an image address. The base64 encoding can improve the performance of the web application to a certain extent, and it is necessary to send a request to the server for the display of images on the web. In order to reduce the user request operation, that is, to reduce the server exchange operation, base64 encoding can be used (Fig. 18).

### 3.6.3 Solve picture module

The module that handles images is the core module of this project's application. The web terminal inputs the image, the server receives it for use and sends it to the backend, and the backend performs the image processing operations, including image address acquisition, model loading, and model parameters loading after training. Use plt.savefig to merge, rename, and export the images locally. Use plt.title to label images, plt.figure to merge multiple images, and plt.subplot to adjust the position of images.

For the loading of a model, parameters are one of the key operations of the whole web application, because this project is a web application tool developed based on crowd counting, accuracy is the only indicator to measure its performance.

From an interaction point of view, when the user uses this module, the web page should give a response, that is, return a description or logo of the information that the processing is completed.

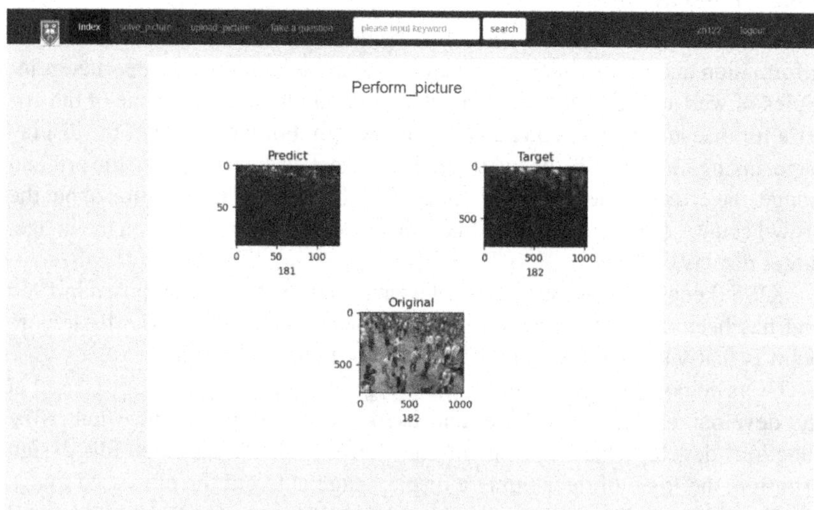


FIG. 18 The model-identified feature page is shown.

### 3.6.4 Take a question module

This module is a companion module to this project and is designed to solve problems related to the use of this application by users. From the user's point of view, users encounter problems with web applications, counting principles, and more. The user can submit the sorting problem in the form of title and content on the web page. Other users see the related problems and have their own answers and can comment to solve the doubts of other users who encounter similar problems. At the same time, this module can be used as a scientific area, and for some basic knowledge, administrators can post to this module in the form of title plus content, and users can enter keywords in the search box to find answers.

## 4 Experimental results

Whether or not the pretraining parameters of VGG16 are imported into the training model affects the model's ability to learn from the dataset. As the pretrained model has been trained many times (> > 400 or 1800), it has sufficient learning and feature extraction ability to the image; the learning parameters of each structure block are mutually influenced, and the parameter update is dynamic with high efficiency (Figs. 19 and 20; Table 3).

After the experimental validation of the need to import pretrained model parameters, the design of the model was divided into two main directions. The first (Conjectures 1) is the parallel network architecture idea, and the second (Conjectures 5) is the application mainstream development architecture idea. In order to ensure sufficient learning capacity, two sets of experiments were conducted (remaining conditions were the same, learning_rate = 7e-7, activation_fun = PReLU (process) + ReLU (forward) with epoch = 400 and epoch = 1800, respectively.

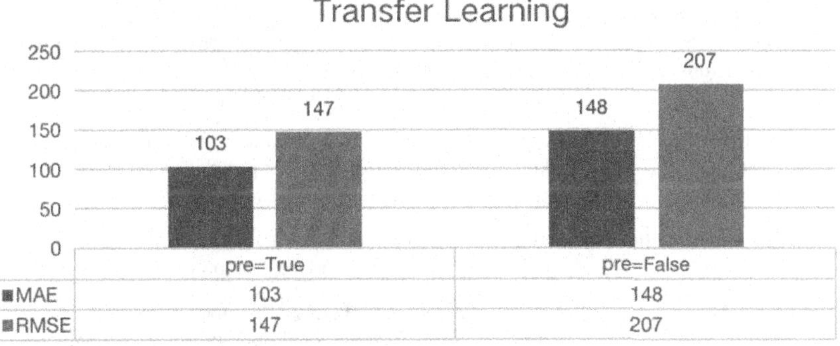


**FIG. 19** Experimental comparison 1.

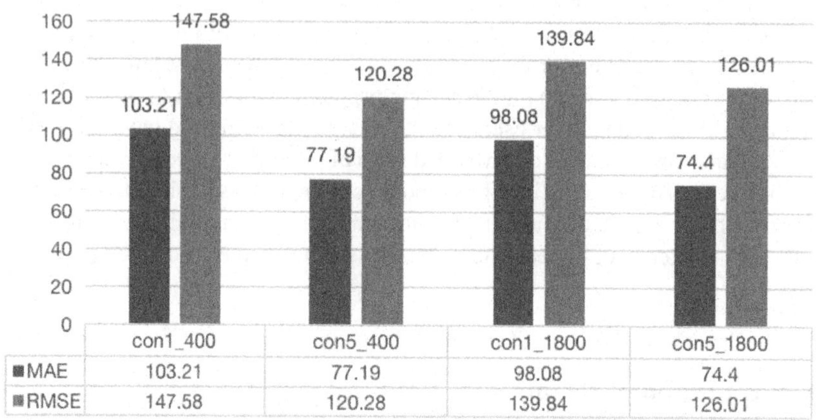


**FIG. 20** Experimental comparison 2.

**TABLE 3 Experimental description and purpose of the different experiments.**

| Experiment | Aim |
|---|---|
| 1. Transfer learning | The advantages of migration learning are derived by comparing whether the model is loaded with pretrained parameters. |
| 2. Effects of model Architecture_1 | The network model analyzes the characteristics of the models built in different directions by comparing the two broad directions of parallel and direct connections. |
| 3. Effects of model Architecture_2 | Based on Experiment 2, the parallel connections are further refined to compare the effects of parallel and direct connections on the model's ability to learn. |
| 4. Effects of ResB layers | Based on Experiment 3, the parallel connections are further refined to compare the effects of parallel and direct connections on the model's ability to learn. |
| 5. Effects of activation | Observe the effect of different activation functions on the model's ability to learn and further optimize the model. |
| 6. Effects of learning rate | By adjusting the learning rate of the model training, experimental data on the local optimum of the model are obtained. |

By observing the experimental results, the learning ability of the parallel multichannel CNN model is quite different relative to the mainstream structure for the Shanghai Tech dataset (Fig. 21).

Based on the considerations of Experiment 2, an in-depth analysis of the parallel network model raises two questions. Question 1, whether cross-connecting parallel networks can improve the model's ability to extract features from images without increasing the network depth. Question 2, based on Question 1, we continue to increase the parallel lines of the model to investigate the impact of parallel networks on the model.

From the previous problems, the model experiments of Con2_400, Con3_400, Con4_400 were carried out, respectively, which then solved Problem 1 and Problem 2. Through Experiment 3, it can be observed that Con2_400 has a positive effect on Con1_400, and Problem 1 was solved, that is, cross-connecting parallel networks can improve the feature extraction ability of the model for the pictures. Con3_400 and Con4_400 experiments can illustrate that continuing to increase the width of the parallel network has a negative effect on the model based on Con2_400, and Problem 2 is solved, that is, the model's feature extraction ability decreases if the parallel lines of the model continue to be increased based on Problem 1.

Looking at the results of the whole experiment, it can be seen that Con_5 has the best results. Through the analysis of the experimental data, starting from Con2_400, the learning parameters of the model increases exponentially, and the learning parameters generated by Con4_400 are twice as much as Con3_400 (RTX 2080 TI, GPU 11 g can no longer be analyzed, and RTX TITAN X, GPU 24 g is needed), which has a huge impact on the application direction of the model. Impact, increasing the training and application costs of the model. All things considered, the model of Con5_400 is chosen (Fig. 22).

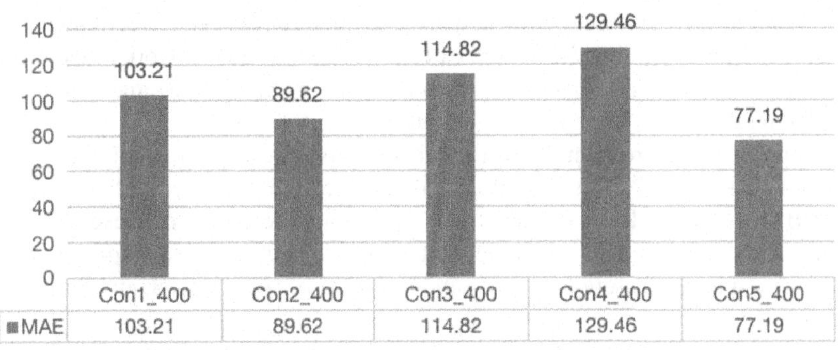


**FIG. 21** Experimental comparison 3.

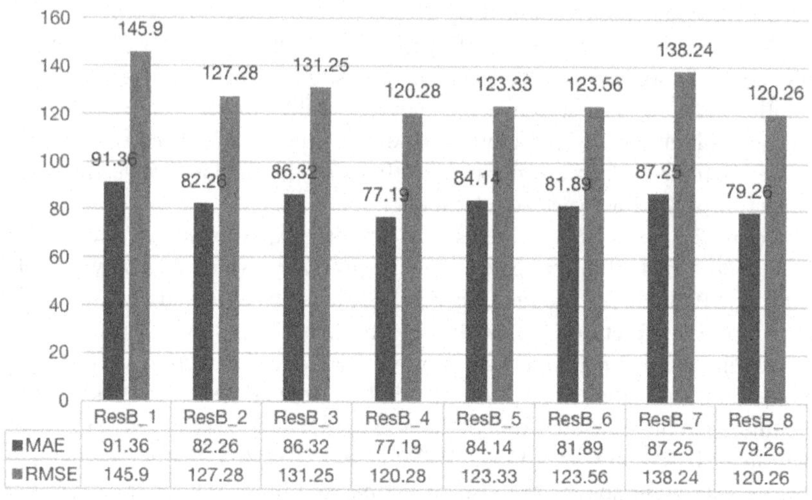


| | ResB_1 | ResB_2 | ResB_3 | ResB_4 | ResB_5 | ResB_6 | ResB_7 | ResB_8 |
|---|---|---|---|---|---|---|---|---|
| MAE | 91.36 | 82.26 | 86.32 | 77.19 | 84.14 | 81.89 | 87.25 | 79.26 |
| RMSE | 145.9 | 127.28 | 131.25 | 120.28 | 123.33 | 123.56 | 138.24 | 120.26 |

**FIG. 22** Experimental comparison 4.

Based on Experiment 3, the overall architecture of the model continues to be explored. After choosing the mainstream research architecture, the depth of the ResB is considered. Question 1 asks whether the deeper the network model depth, i.e., the more layers of the ResB, the better the learning ability of the model and the higher the accuracy for crowd counting. Question 2, whether the parity of the number of ResB layers affects the network's feature extraction ability. A deeper investigation is conducted through Experiment 4 to investigate the 8 layers of ResB.

After observing the experimental data, no obvious positive effect of the deeper layers on improving the feature extraction ability of the network model was found, i.e., Problem 1, the deeper the number of layers of ResB, the better the learning ability of the network is not necessarily true.

Investigating Problem 2 and further observing the experimental data, it is found that ResB_2, ResB_4, ResB_6, and ResB_8 are overall better than ResB_1, ResB_3, ResB_5, and ResB_7, that is, the parity of ResB affects the feature extraction ability of the model. In this experiment, ResB of the even layer has a better feature extraction ability for the network model, and Problem 2 is solved.

After comprehensive observation of the experimental data, the four-layer ResB is chosen as the optimal model architecture for this model based on the selected experimental data (Fig. 23).

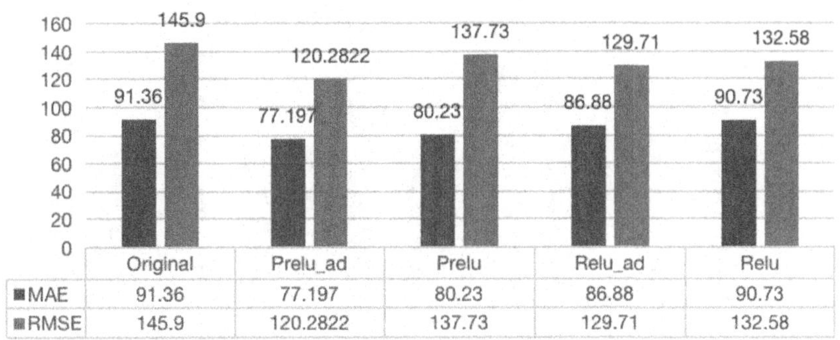


**FIG. 23** Experimental comparison 5.

Based on Experiment 4, the activation functions are selected according to the importance of the network model elements, and different activation functions match the model to different degrees, that is, the activation functions are not good or bad.

In order to avoid experimental chance, learning rate elements were added for control trials (the original was the comparative observation group). The question is posed whether the ReLU function, which is widely used, is a better fit to this model than the PReLU function. Conduct two sets of controlled experiments to fully derive the experimental results.

By observing Experiment 5, PReLU_ad and ReLU_ad, PReLU and ReLU, two sets of experiments, demonstrate that the PReLU activation function matches this model to a greater extent than the ReLU function. Thus, the proposed problem is solved, and the present model chooses to use the PReLU activation function, based on the architecture of Experiment 4, as a model pair feature filter (Fig. 24; Table 4).

Based on Experiment 5, the basic architecture of the model has been completed, and the training of the model is a critical and final step for CNN to complete the building of the model.

The choice of learning rate will affect the learning ability of the model to some extent [3]. A learning rate that is too large will result in missing the local optimum; a learning rate that is too small will find the local optimum and take too long to train.

Through the study of learning rate theory, it is divided into two parts: fixed learning rate and adjusted learning rate. It was experimentally demonstrated that by choosing learn4, the model reached the optimal value in five experiments.

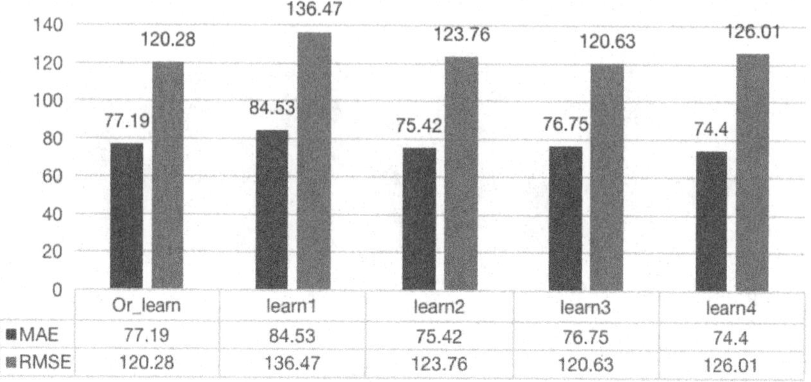


**FIG. 24** Experimental comparison 6.

**TABLE 4** Description of the learning rate from Experiment 6.

| | Learning rate | Decrease rate |
|---|---|---|
| 1. Or_learn | 8e-6 | NULL |
| 2. learn1 | 5e-7 | NULL |
| 3. learn2 | 5e-6 | 0.9 |
| 4. learn3 | 5e-6 | 0.5 |
| 5. learn4 | 5e-6 | 0.8 |

## 5 Future research directions

The variation of the model for depth and width is evident during model building, and it is worth exploring and studying how to find the patterns of variation. The drawbacks can be seen for the image processing of the dataset. Based on the consideration of the previous issues, I believe that the exploration of the correlation between depth and width of CNN will dominate the future research direction of population counting and the processing method of the dataset images will be further improved. Based on these reflections, I make the following observations:

1. There is a need for more accurate image processing algorithms for datasets, considering the quality of the images trained and how processing the original images can result in greater access to more feature points for the model. The current methods that exist for converting image densities are subject to large errors. For the depth of the picture scenario, overlap and other phenomena are not well solved.
2. CNN models need more explicit depth and width correlation consistency, and the current build of CNNs is in a position to continually improve and enhance the experimental results of other researchers. The ever-increasing number of parameters and the amount of computations put a heavier burden on the currently available computational resources. However, this is not a problem that can be solved by mathematical computation, which requires a large number of researchers to perform experiments, generalize, and find patterns.

## 6 Conclusion

This chapter focuses on the effects of width and depth on the CNN model in the process of building the model, and the more superior model is derived by a scientific method on limited computational resources. Of course, the experimental methods constructed for different lines of research are different, and this chapter cannot cover all the methods of investigation of the data. The point of this chapter is that it is more effective to increase the network depth than to widen the network width for a limited network structure.

## Appendices

### A An example of ShangHaiTech dataset .mat file

See Fig. 25.

### B Verify web applications feature showcase

See Figs. 26–31.


## Acknowledgment

This work was supported by the University of Leicester Library.

Variables - image_info{1, 1}.location

image_info | image_info{1, 1} | image_info{1, 1}.location

image_info{1, 1}.location

| | 1 | 2 | 3 | 4 | 5 | 6 |
|---|---|---|---|---|---|---|
| 1 | 86.0747 | 735.8438 | | | | |
| 2 | 31.9690 | 675.7263 | | | | |
| 3 | 39.4837 | 481.8477 | | | | |
| 4 | 12.4308 | 430.7479 | | | | |
| 5 | 236.3682 | 528.4387 | | | | |
| 6 | 337.0649 | 507.3976 | | | | |
| 7 | 356.6030 | 391.6715 | | | | |
| 8 | 433.2528 | 378.1451 | | | | |
| 9 | 585.0492 | 481.8477 | | | | |
| 10 | 676.7283 | 444.2743 | | | | |
| 11 | 930.7244 | 293.9807 | | | | |
| 12 | 978.8183 | 227.8516 | | | | |

**FIG. 25** The location of each person in the picture; the number represented is a two-dimensional coordinate representation. For example, person A is represented by the coordinates (86.0474,735.8438).

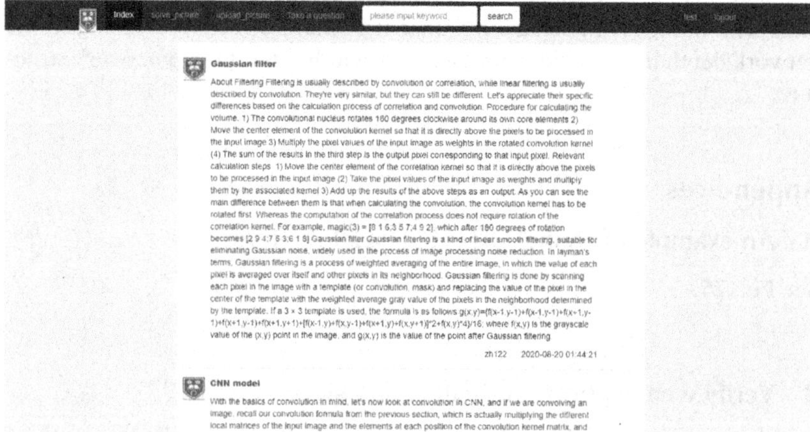


**FIG. 26** Demonstrate the full functionality of a web application developed with flask. As shown in the figure, there are five functions distributed on the navigation bar; from the basic web login and registration functions, solve_picture, upload_picture, and Take a question are the three core functions. They are the functions to solve the problem of the image name entered by the user, the image information returned by the processed image and the user's access to the CNN model or related background knowledge and to ask questions.

**FIG. 27** The registration module is one of the most basic but inaccessible features of this web application. Because the core functionality of the web application requires further permissions, users can only use it after registration. On the one hand, it attracts users, and on the other hand, it protects their privacy and security to some extent. The password settings are stored in the database using a hash string, which greatly improves the security of user information.

**FIG. 28** The login function is one of the basic functions of this web application, but it is worth noting that the password entered by the user is converted to a hash string code in the backend for database comparison.

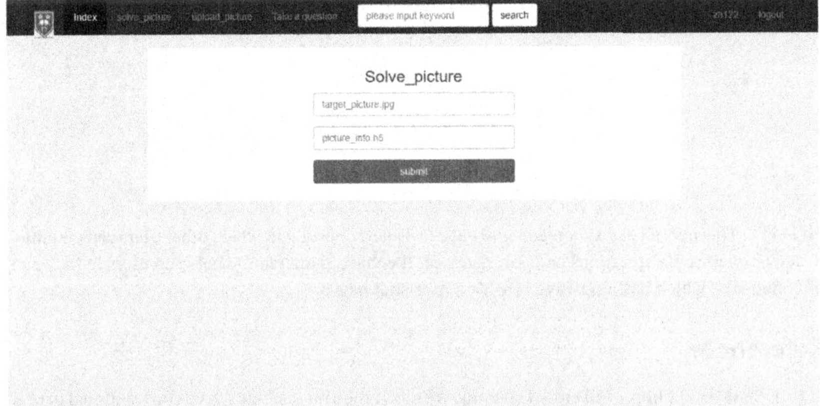


**FIG. 29** This module is based on the input image of the Gaussian fuzzy processing to generate .h5 format file, extract the file in the real number of people, and after the module, deal with the image generated by the predicted number of people to merge processing and extract the original image. The three images after plt.figure function are combined into one and saved in the local folder. This module is the core module of the whole web application, which is responsible for the information transfer to the upload_picture module.

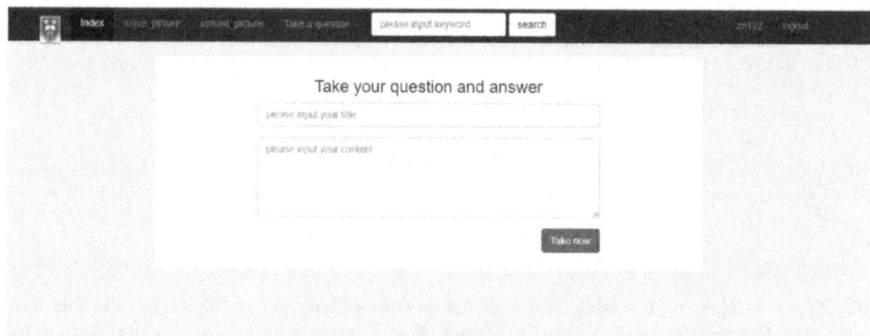


**FIG. 30** This module is a complementary module to the crowd-counting web application and is designed to address various issues encountered by users, such as operational issues, technical issues, display issues, and other issues of most concern to users. Administrators or other users can solve related problems or provide technical answers in the form of headings and content.

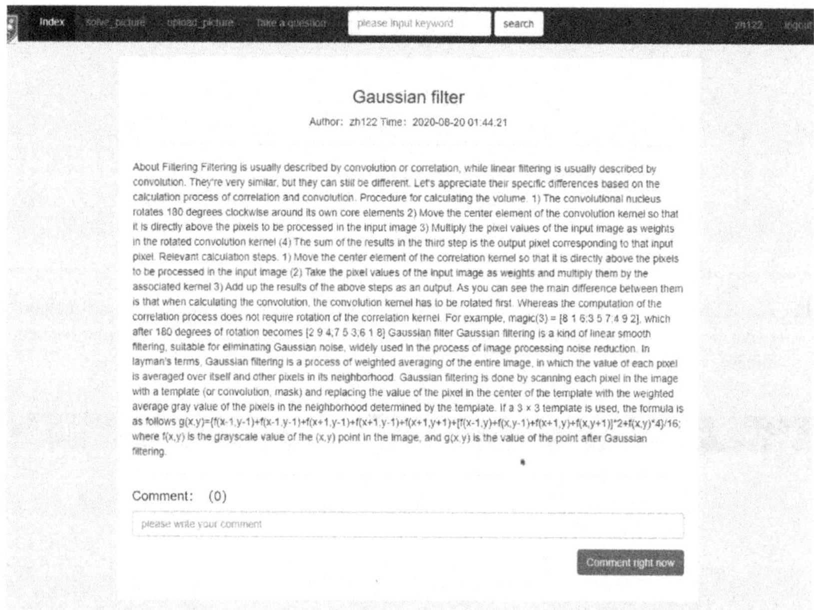


**FIG. 31** This interface is a supplemental page to Take a question in which other users can continue to add answers to the questions or answers raised. It enhances interaction between users in the form of comments, which has a positive effect on user stickiness.

## References

[1] J. Sang, et al., Improved crowd counting method based on scale-adaptive convolutional neural network, IEEE Access 7 (2019) 24411–24419.

[2] A. Krizhevsky, et al., ImageNet classification with deep convolutional neural networks, J. Commun. 60 (6) (2017) 84–90. ACM.

[3] Y. Zhang, et al., PSSPNN: PatchShuffle stochastic pooling neural network for an explainable diagnosis of COVID-19 with multiple-way data augmentation, Comput. Math. Methods Med. 2021 (2021). Article ID: 6633755.

[4] M.V.S. Santana, et al., De novo design and bioactivity prediction of SARS-CoV-2 main protease inhibitors using recurrent neural network-based transfer learning, BMC Chem. 15 (1) (2021) 20. Article ID: 8.

[5] Y. Zhang, et al., Single-image crowd counting via multi-column convolutional neural network, in: 2016 IEEE Conference on Computer Vision and Pattern Recognition (CVPR), 2016, pp. 589–597.

[6] S. Wang, et al., SCLNet: spatial context learning network for congested crowd counting, Neurocomputing 404 (2020) 227–239.

[7] M. Salehi, et al., A hybrid model based on general regression neural network and fruit fly optimization algorithm for forecasting and optimizing paclitaxel biosynthesis in *Corylus avellana* cell culture, Plant Methods 17 (1) (2021) 13. Article ID: 13.

[8] J. Qiu, et al., Crowd counting and density estimation via two-column convolutional neural network, in: 4th International Conference on Smart and Sustainable City (ICSSC 2017), 2017, pp. 1–5.

[9] J.C. Alcaraz, et al., Efficiency of deep neural networks for joint angle modeling in digital gait assessment, Eurasip J. Adv. Signal Process. 2021 (1) (2021) 20. Article ID: 10.

[10] Y. Chen, et al., Fast neighbor search by using revised k-d tree, Inf. Sci. 472 (2019) 145–162.

[11] J. Teunissen, et al., Controlling the weights of simulation particles: adaptive particle management using k-d trees, J. Comput. Phys. 259 (2014) 318–330.

[12] R. Ghosh, A recurrent neural network based deep learning model for offline signature verification and recognition system, Expert Syst. Appl. 168 (2021) 13. Article ID: 114249.

[13] S.-H. Wang, Covid-19 classification by FGCNet with deep feature fusion from graph convolutional network and convolutional neural network, Inform. Fusion 67 (2021) 208–229.

[14] S.C. Satapathy, A five-layer deep convolutional neural network with stochastic pooling for chest CT-based COVID-19 diagnosis, Mach. Vis. Appl. 32 (2021). Article ID: 14.

[15] B. McIlwaine, et al., JellyNet: the convolutional neural network jellyfish bloom detector, Int. J. Appl. Earth Obs. Geoinf. 97 (2021) 13. Article ID: 102279.

[16] S. Kim, et al., Efficient neural network compression via transfer learning for machine vision inspection, Neurocomputing 413 (2020) 294–304.

[17] S.-H. Wang, COVID-19 classification by CCSHNet with deep fusion using transfer learning and discriminant correlation analysis, Inform. Fusion 68 (2021) 131–148.

[18] S.-H. Wang, DenseNet-201-based deep neural network with composite learning factor and precomputation for multiple sclerosis classification, ACM Trans. Multimed. Comput. Commun. Appl. 16 (2s) (2020). Article ID: 60.

[19] S. Xie, Alcoholism identification based on an AlexNet transfer learning model, Front. Psych. 10 (2019). Article ID: 205.

[20] A.K. Sangaiah, Alcoholism identification via convolutional neural network based on parametric ReLU, dropout, and batch normalization, Neural Comput. & Applic. 32 (2020) 665–680.

[21] C. Pan, Multiple sclerosis identification by convolutional neural network with dropout and parametric ReLU, J. Comput. Sci. 28 (2018) 1–10.

[22] S. Wang, et al., Fruit category classification via an eight-layer convolutional neural network with parametric rectified linear unit and dropout technique, Multimed. Tools Appl. 79 (21–22) (2020) 15117–15133.

[23] Z. Chen, et al., Global-connected network with generalized ReLU activation, Pattern Recogn. 96 (2019) 106961.

[24] D.S. Guttery, Improved breast cancer classification through combining graph convolutional network and convolutional neural network, Inf. Process. Manag. 58 (2021). Article ID: 102439.

[25] C. Huang, Multiple sclerosis identification by 14-layer convolutional neural network with batch normalization, dropout, and stochastic pooling, Front. Neurosci. 12 (2018). Article ID: 818.

[26] Y.-D. Zhang, Advances in multimodal data fusion in neuroimaging: overview, challenges, and novel orientation, Inform. Fusion 64 (2020) 149–187.

[27] A. Apicella, et al., A simple and efficient architecture for trainable activation functions, Neurocomputing 370 (2019) 1–15.

[28] Y. Li, et al., CSRNet: dilated convolutional neural networks for understanding the highly congested scenes, in: 2018 IEEE/CVF Conference on Computer Vision and Pattern Recognition, 2018, pp. 1091–1100.

[29] D. McNeely-White, et al., Inception and ResNet features are (almost) equivalent, Cogn. Syst. Res. 59 (2020) 312–318.

[30] S. Peng, et al., More trainable inception-ResNet for face recognition, Neurocomputing 411 (2020) 9–19.

[31] Y.-D. Lv, Alcoholism detection by data augmentation and convolutional neural network with stochastic pooling, J. Med. Syst. 42 (1) (2018). Article ID: 2.

[32] K. Muhammad, Image based fruit category classification by 13-layer deep convolutional neural network and data augmentation, Multimed. Tools Appl. 78 (3) (2019) 3613–3632.

[33] A. Shakya, et al., Parametric study of convolutional neural network based remote sensing image classification, Int. J. Remote Sens. 42 (7) (2021) 2663–2685.

[34] C. Yu, et al., LLR: learning learning rates by LSTM for training neural networks, Neurocomputing 394 (2020) 41–50.

[35] J. Liang, et al., Barzilai–Borwein-based adaptive learning rate for deep learning, Pattern Recogn. Lett. 128 (2019) 197–203.

Chapter 4

# A cognitive system for lip identification using convolution neural networks

**Vishesh Agarwal[a] and Rahul Raman[b]**
*[a]SCOPE, VIT University, Vellore, India, [b]IIITDM, Kancheepuram, Chennai, India*

## 1 Introduction

Biometrics refers to the measurement and analysis of unique physical or behavioral characteristics, especially as a means of verifying personal identity. Biometric systems work by using sensors to detect and perceive a certain physical characteristic. The system then converts them into digital patterns and compares these patterns with patterns stored for personal identification.

A lip is a tactile sensory organ constituting the visible portion of the mouth. The external-most skin of the lip is the stratified squamous epithelium. The surface of the lips has visible wrinkles that can be considered identifiable. This forms the foundation of Cheiloscopy, a field of forensics that focuses on identification of people by the use of lip traces.

Each lip print has a different pattern or texture of grooves on its surface. A lip print may not consist of only one type of groove alone but may have a mixture of varying types of patterns. The uniqueness of a lip has been proven by the researchers by using color information and shape analysis. These measures of lips along with the movement patterns during speech are unique for every person.

Lip patterns may be altered by external factors, but lips reassume their original pattern on recovery. Lip patterns are unique for individuals and remain unchanged during their lifetime, making them a reliable basis for identification.

This chapter proposes the use of deep learning, specifically convolutional neural networks (CNNs), to perform feature extraction and identification of lip images. The proposed approached uses CNNs to extract high-level spatiotemporal features from images of lips. This is achieved by training the neural

Cognitive Systems and Signal Processing in Image Processing. https://doi.org/10.1016/B978-0-12-824410-4.00013-1

network on images created from the frames of videos of people speaking. The minor variation of the shape and size of lips in the frames allow the neural network to identify changes with respect to speech.

The approach has been designed to work for grayscale images of lips, and the model has been able to achieve a significant level of accuracy. The proposed CNN model has been tested out on the OuluVS database [1], and the results obtained are presented in this chapter.

The addition of a cognitive aspect adds more information to the features obtained from behavioral biometric measures; this allows for an increase in the accuracy and effectiveness of the approach, specifically in the case of authentication systems.

# 2 Survey of related work

## 2.1 Summary of existing approaches

The use of lips as a biometric measure is a relatively new area compared to other forms of identification, such as fingerprints, face detection, and so on. The consideration of lips as an important feature has seen a considerable increase in recent years due to the use of lip features in lip reading and multimodal biometry.

The work presented in one study [2] describes an identification approach based on static global characteristics of lips. The subject has to be stationary while having a neutral expression on his face to not change the shape of the lips. The chapter also compares different feature extraction techniques to determine which has the least processing time and is more accurate.

A different study [3] proposes the use of an ensemble of classifiers for the classification of lips. The paper compares the competencies of binary classifiers and uses the most competent classifiers to create an ensemble classifier. A new data structure for biometrics called the "Sim" is also proposed by the paper.

Another study [4] proposes the use of CNNs for the detection of lip region. The histogram of oriented gradients (HOOG) features of the lower half of the face are computed. The extracted features are passed to a support vector machine (SVM) for coarse detection and preliminary classification; based on the result of the SVM, the features are passed through the CNN for finer detection.

The work presented in one article [5] compares the physiological and behavioral information that can be obtained from the lip. The paper, based on a comparison of the existing approaches toward the information, concludes that behavioral information is more descriptive for speaker identification.

The work presented in a different article [6] proposes a lip feature-based identification using the Discrete Hidden Markov Model Kernel (DHMMK). Lip features were extracted and modeled by a DHMMK. The modeled features were learned by a SVM used for classification.

One study [7] presents a lip-reading model for audio-less video data of variable-length sequence frames. The lip region from each face image in the video sequence identified and concatenated into a single image. The created images are processed through a 12-layer CNN with 2 batch normalization layers for lip reading.

The work presented in another study [8] illustrates an approach toward lip reading using deep belief networks (DBNs). The features extraction is performed by applying principal component analysis (PCA) on the region of interest (ROI). A DBN with modification to its last restricted Boltzmann machine (RBM) is used in the classification the stage. The presented approach outperforms the conventional Hidden Markov Model (HMM) approach.

The work presented in a different study [9] uses dynamic features for lip reading. First-order regression coefficients are applied to the image along with its few neighboring frames for the extraction of dynamic features. The proposed approach is a better representation of the time derivatives compared to static images. The extracted dynamic features are processed through CNNs for lip reading.

One article [10] proposes the idea of ensemble features. The paper compared the individual accuracy achieved using features such as lip height, lip width, area of lip region, and angles at corners. These features are then combined for the creation of a new subset feature that improves the classification accuracy of certain weak features.

The work presented in one study [11] builds on the work presented in [8]. The DHMMK model was tested on multispeaker (MS) and speaker-independent) conditions using the proposed "hybrid" feature set and was evaluated at the phoneme level. The paper discussed some issues of the automatic lip-reading systems and how the proposed approach was able to rectify some of the issues.

One article [12] proposes a lightweight feature extraction approach based on psychological research into facial barcodes. The proposed idea used Gabor-based image patches to created three-dimensional features. This new approach can successfully extract lip features with a minimum of processing without the need for any trained models. Features generated in this manner are robust, allowing recovery from errors.

## 2.2 Shortcomings of previous work

Most of the present work in the domain of biometry using lips is based around the use of static features. These features do not take into account the change in shape, angle, lighting, or color. The shape of lips can vary due to movement, speech, or even facial expression while the change in appearance could be due to chaffing due to the weather or growth of facial hair.

In many of the present approaches, the results also vary with change in the visible region of lips due to the movement of the head. This makes them dependent on the subject remaining still throughout the entire process of collecting the sample.

Besides the limitations based on the nature of lips, there are limitations due to the approaches being used for processing the input. The present approaches either rely heavily on the use of filters for preprocessing the images or follow a lengthy process of classification, which makes them unsuitable for real-time applications.

A survey of papers [2–12] related to the field along with the key parameters related to the approach has been presented in Table 1.

Some of the conclusions related to the advantages and shortcomings of the approaches that can be drawn from the previously mentioned works [2–12] have been presented in Table 2.

### *2.2.1 Motivation*

The motivation behind this chapter was to create a biometric measure based on lips that would be suitable for use in real-time applications while sufficiently accurate.

This was achieved by using spatiotemporal features that can remain invariant to changes in shape while even accounting for idiosyncratic tendencies of people, such as the manner of speaking, pronunciation, and accent.

The use of CNNs makes this approach suitable for real-time applications, as once the model is trained, it can be deployed in multiple systems based on the saved weights. The model can also be retrained after intervals of time for keeping it updated and preventing any decline in its performance.

# 3 Feature extraction and classification using CNN

## 3.1 Cognitive computing

Cognitive computing at the most foundational level describes artificial intelligence systems that can simulate human thought and recreate human perceptions. Cognitive systems mimic human reasoning, which allows them to draw the best possible conclusion by weighing context and conflicting evidence.

These systems are capable of processing large quantities of data to make effective and efficient decisions, even as the amount of data scales up. The proposed idea is based on cognitive systems due to their probabilistic nature, which allows these systems to adapt to the complexity and unpredictability of unstructured or new information and behave accordingly.

The models built using cognitive systems are capable of generating context specific relationships between various entities present in a system. This enables them to develop hypotheses and arguments that can be used to reconcile ambiguous and even self-contradictory data, thus providing these systems with the

**TABLE 1** Survey of existing models and work.

| Serial number | Author | Acquisition | Source of image | Type of preprocessing | Local/global features | Static/dynamic |
|---|---|---|---|---|---|---|
| 1 | Rojas et al. [2] | Lip image | No movement, and neutral expressions | Color transformation using the equation $I = R + B - 6*G$ binarization | Global | Static |
| 2 | Porwik et al. [3] | Lip image | No information was provided about the database | The ROI for the face and mouth was designated after which features based on Sim coefficient were extracted and added to the feature vector | Global | Static |
| 3 | Lee et al. [4] | Lip image | LFW databases MUCT database | The database did not require the images to be preprocessed | Global/local | Static |
| 4 | Shi-Lin Wang and Alan Wee-Chung Liew [5] | Lip image | No information was provided about the database | Segmentation is performed through the MS-FCM algorithm. A 5–2–7 lip model (5 points representing the lower lip contour, 2 points for the lip corners, and 7 points for the upper lip contour) is employed to describe the outer lip contour | Global | Dynamic |
| 5 | Travieso et al. [6] | Lip image | GPDS-ULPGC Face Dataset, PIE Face Dataset, RaFD Face Dataset | RGB transformation is performed on the image to make the lip region brighter. Otsu binarization is used to segment the lip from the face | Global | Static |
| 6 | NadeemHashmi et al. [7] | Lip image | MIRACLE-VC1, audio-less video | Extraction of lips is done using the Haar Cascade Facial Landmark detector; $7 \times 7$ images of the lip are concatenated to form a single image | Global | Dynamic |

*Continued*

**TABLE 1** Survey of existing models and work—cont'd

| Serial number | Author | Acquisition | Source of image | Type of preprocessing | Local/global features | Static/dynamic |
|---|---|---|---|---|---|---|
| 7 | F. Vakhshiteh and F. Almasganj [8] | Lip image | CUAVE dataset | Scaling, reshaping, and PCA | Global | Dynamic |
| 8 | Li et al. [9] | Lip image | No information was provided about the database | PCA The Difference image is computed by merging the image with 3 images before and 3 images after it in the sequence | Global | Dynamic |
| 9 | K.M and S. Ayyappan [10] | Lip image | An author-defined dataset is used | Lips were colored pink for fast lip segmentation using color space transform. The face was detected through Viola-Jones detection The preprocessing of the image was done using histogram equalization and binary thresholding | Local | Dynamic |
| 10 | Vakshiteh et al. [11] | Lip image | CUAVE dataset | Scaling, Reshaping, and PCA | Global | Dynamic |
| 11 | Abel et al. [12] | Lip image | An author-defined dataset is used | Viola-Jones method used for face and lip detection | Global | Dynamic |

**TABLE 2** Features and gaps identified in the existing work.

| Serial number | Author | Method | Advantages | Disadvantages |
|---|---|---|---|---|
| 1 | Rojas et al. [2] | Feature extraction using lip contour MAs HMM, SVM, HMM + SVM | High accuracy and a robust system using polar coordinates | Images need to have a neutral expression with little or no variation |
| 2 | Porwik et al. [3] | Geometrical measurement of lip contours was taken as the features, Collection of ensemble classifiers were trained on the dataset | Ensemble classifiers provide better classification accuracy compared to any individual components used in classification | FAR mistakes occur as only mouth ROI is analyzed and no other biometric features are taken into consideration. FRR mistakes result from the inability to stabilize the lip muscles |
| 3 | Lee et al. [4] | Lip detection is done by using a combination of HOOG, SVM, and CNN. HOOG is used to fetch the input for the SVM, which classifies whether the detected region is a lip or not. The output from the SVM is passed through the CNN for fine-tuning. Canny edge detection is applied to get the final lip region | The proposed method minimizes the effects of light and background on lip detection | The method uses a complex architecture that is very slow and not suitable for any real-time analysis. The accuracy obtained is lesser compared to other present-day methods |
| 4 | Shi-Lin Wang and Alan Wee-Chung Liew [5] | Temporal shape descriptor and motion vector representation are dynamic features used. GMM-UBM and HMM are used for the classification | The proposed method accounts for *the deformation in the shape of lips* due to speech and uses it as the basis for speaker identification | Does not account for changes in *the local features of the lip or any* changes to the appearance of the global feature |
| 5 | Travieso et al. [6] | The extracted features are passed through an HMM kernel and then used as the input for the SVM for classification | DHMMK requires fewer image samples compared to other classifiers for training. The proposed approach is found less sensitive to scale and resolution changes | The approach is susceptible to errors caused due to changes in the skin tone and orientation of the subject |

*Continued*

**TABLE 2** Features and gaps identified in the existing work—cont'd

| Serial number | Author | Method | Advantages | Disadvantages |
|---|---|---|---|---|
| 6 | NadeemHashmi et al. [7] | A 13-layer CNN is used for the classification of words | The proposed model requires a lesser number of parameters compared to existing models | The validation accuracy of the neural network is low |
| 7 | F. Vakhshiteh and F. Almasganj [8] | A DBN with modification to its last RBM is used in the classification | The proposed DBN outperforms HMM | Works only for character recognition, does not support words |
| 8 | Li et al. [9] | A CNN model is used for the classification | The proposed model works better than static and discrete-cosine transform features | The training was done using only a single speaker. The proposed method is variant to changes in the angle |
| 9 | K. M and S. Ayyappan [10] | A multilayer perceptron network is used for the classification of commands | The use of ensemble features for classification creates a robust model that is resistant to noise present in the image | The testing was performed on a specifically constructed database that consisted of a limited number of words |
| 10 | Vakshiteh et al. [11] | A DBN with modification to its last RBM is used in the classification | The proposed DBN outperforms HMM | Works only for character recognition, does not support words |
| 11 | Abel et al. [12] | Horizontal Gabor features are calculated using a fast Fourier transform. Thresholding is applied to the resultant patches to reduce the noise | The proposed approach can extract lip features with minimum processing and parameters that can be quickly adapted and used for detailed analysis. The features can be generated online without the need for trained models and are also robust, allowing recovery from errors | The results vary with the presence of facial hair, turning of head, and direction of the subject |

ability to develop deep domain insights and provide expert assistance by leveraging the relationships between different entities and entities and their system.

Beyond mimicking human perception, cognitive systems are capable of decision-making. Their decision-making evolves with changes in or availability of new information, outcomes, and actions, which allows the system to be more robust.

The proposed idea can be easily modified and developed into a real-time application due to the adaptive nature of the cognitive systems, which allows it to handle any new data by relating it with the previously provided data. For example, in the case of an identification system, if the lips of an unknown person are provided, the system would be able to correlate it to the old data and suggest a person whose lips could be considered the most similar.

### *3.1.1 Convolution network*

As presented in one work [13], the shape of lips can be deliberately changed by a subject to a large extent with the change of expression, and the color of the lip is subject to acquisition conditions. Based on this, it can be concluded that the analysis and recognition of an individual by lip-shape and lip-color analysis can only work fine in a constrained scenario.

This chapter aims to present an appropriate architecture that would be capable of extraction and classification of lip features in real-life scenarios. The idea proposed is based on using deep learning, specifically CNNs. As presented in one study [9], CNNs can reduce the errors at the feature extraction level, which can be caused by wrong face alignment, blurring of the image, or shaking of the subject.

The design of the CNN is inspired by feature integration theory in psychology, which claims that all perceived features are registered in parallel first and the object identification and association takes place at a later stage. The cognitive model is designed to utilize human-interpretable feature like shape, texture, edges, movement, and human idiosyncrasies to reconstruct and classify the image.

**(1)** The hidden layers in CNNs are divided into two categories: (1) convolution layers, which extract features from the input; and
**(2)** dense layers, which uses data from the convolution layer to generate output.

A perceptron, which is a digitalized version of a formal neuron and can be created by reformulating a simplified biological neuron into a mathematical formula, is taken as the basis for the mathematical model of neural network. The digitalized neuron has N real inputs. These inputs are taken as the recreation of the signals incoming from dendrites connected to the synapses of the previous neuron. The inputs are labeled with weights corresponding to the synaptic weight that they represent. This presents a measure of their permeability in the network. According to neurophysiology, the synaptic weights may have a negative value to express their inhibitory character. The excitation level of the neuron is represented by the weighted sum of input values.

The input image is convolved with a multidimensional filter. This filter is known as kernel and is used to compare the pixel values. Convolution can be represented mathematically with an asterisk. If an input image represented as $X$ and a filter represented with f, then the expression would be given by,

$$Z = X * f$$

These features extracted by the CNN are converted from a two-dimensional matrix into a one-dimensional vector and sent to the fully connected layer for the generation of the final results. Each of the individual values in a vector is treated as a separate feature representing the image. The dense layer performs a linear transformation and a nonlinear transformation on the generated feature vector. The linear transformation is applied as follows:

$$Z = W^T \cdot X + b$$

The parameter values, such as the weights, biases, and filters, are randomly initialized during the creation of the network. The neural network tries to update the parameters such that the overall predictions are more accurate during its training phase. The weights in each epoch are updated as follows:

$$\text{Weight}_{\text{new}} = \text{Weight}_{\text{old}} - lr^*(\partial E/\partial W)$$

The rectified linear unit (ReLU) serves as the activation function for the model. It is used commonly in CNNs and mimics the behavior of linear functions but is a nonlinear function. Thus it allows the complex relationships present in the data to be learned.

$$\text{ReLU}(x) = \begin{cases} 0, & x \leq 0 \\ x, & x > 0 \end{cases}$$

The proposed idea aims to use a high-level feature of images of lips to validate the presence of a test subject in the database. These high-level features can be extracted using a CNN. This is achieved by using a dense layer of neurons as the final layer of the neural network instead of using an activation softmax layer for prediction, as shown in Fig. 1.

The images are converted into grayscale and are fed into the input layer in the form of matrices in which each element represents a pixel value. These numerical values denote the intensity of pixels in the image. To perform mathematical operations in the CNN, certain parameter values are present that are randomly initialized. Each hidden layer replicated the functioning of neurons using a mathematical computation post from which the output layer generates the final prediction.

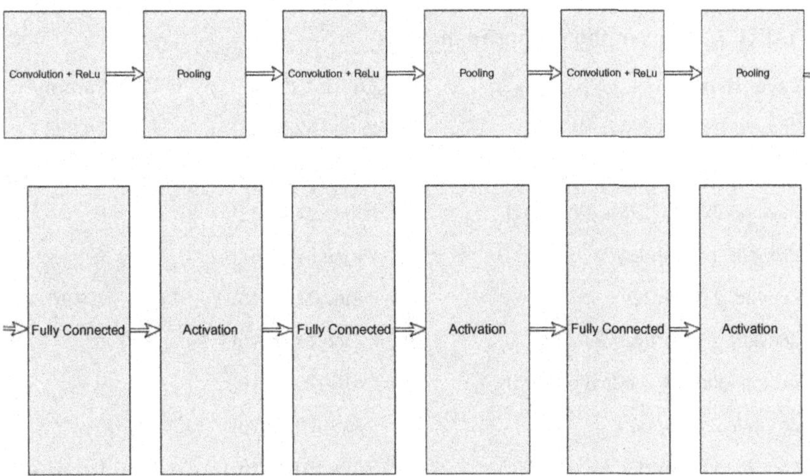


**FIG. 1** (A) Architecture of the CNN model (convolution layers). (B) Architecture of the CNN model (dense layers).

The database containing images of lips is used to train the CNN, which is then used to extract image features. The extracted feature vectors thus obtained are used to create a database of features. The user inputs an image of lips, the features of which are extracted. The extracted features are used as the query, and its similarity is computed with the feature vectors present in the feature database.

The proposed model is trained on images that represented the frames of the videos of the subject taken while the subject was speaking; as a result, the images have minor differences in the shape of the lips for each frame. The model is trained on these images, so it can also accommodate the changes in the shape of lips due to speech patterns. This allows for the model to be more robust and be less erroneous to variation in the shape and size of the lips.

The layers of the proposed CNN model based on the architecture presented in Fig. 1 are given in Table 3.

## 3.2 Database

The CNN model presented in this chapter was trained and tested on a component of the OuluVS dataset, which was originally presented in a different book [1]. The used component contains images of 20 subjects where the mouth region was determined by automatic face detection and eye detection for each frame, and Boosted Haar features were used for automatic coarse face detection along with two-dimensional Cascaded AdaBoost for localizing eyes in the detected faces.

**TABLE 3 Layers in the proposed model.**

| Layer (type) | Output shape | Param # |
|---|---|---|
| conv2d_1 (Conv2D) | (None,42,88,32) | 28,832 |
| activation_1 (Activation) | (None,42,88,32) | 0 |
| max_pooling2d_1 (MaxPooling2) | (None,21,44,32) | 0 |
| dropout_1 (Dropout) | (None,21,44,32) | 0 |
| conv2d_2 (Conv2D) | (None,21,44,16) | 204,816 |
| activation_2 (Activation) | (None,21,44,16) | 0 |
| max_pooling2d_2 (MaxPooling2) | (None,10,22,16) | 0 |
| dropout_2 (Dropout) | (None,10,22,16) | 0 |
| conv2d_3 (Conv2D) | (None,10,22,16) | 102,416 |
| activation_3 (Activation) | (None,10,22,16) | 0 |
| max_pooling2d_3 (MaxPooling2) | (None,5,11,16) | 0 |
| dropout_3 (Dropout) | (None,5,11,16) | 0 |
| flatten_1 (Flatten) | (None,880) | 0 |
| dense_1 (Dense) | (None,64) | 56,384 |
| activation_4 (Activation) | (None,64) | 0 |
| dropout_4 (Dropout) | (None,64) | 0 |
| dense_2 (Dense) | (None,32) | 2080 |
| activation_5 (Activation) | (None,32) | 0 |
| dropout_5 (Dropout) | (None,32) | 0 |
| dense_3 (Dense) | (None,10) | 330 |

The approach for processing the data in the previously mentioned study [1] was based on Haar-like features similar to Viola-Jones detection [14]. The approach used multiple rectangle features, which comprised shaded and unshaded regions. The value of a feature is calculated as the sum of pixels that are present in the unshaded parts of the rectangle subtracted from the shaded portion of the rectangle. An integral image representation is used to evaluate rectangular features in constant time. Viola Jones detection [14] creates a strong classifier by using AdaBoost to improve the learning process. This is done to maintain a cascaded architecture, which requires each layer to have a strong classifier and to be able to generate a fixed number of features.

The idea of using local spatiotemporal descriptors was presented by Zhao et al. [1] to represent and recognize spoken isolated phrases based solely on the use of visual inputs. Isolated phrase sequences were described by using spatiotemporal local binary patterns extracted from mouth regions.

The OuluVS dataset [1] includes images of 20 people uttering 10 short greetings five times each. It includes 17 males and 3 females, among whom 9 wear glasses. The chosen speakers belonged from four different countries to include different pronunciation habits, such as different speaking rates. The dataset [1] had a total of 817 spoken sequences from 20 speakers. Some sample images, which show the inclusiveness of the database, are presented in Table 4.

**TABLE 4** Sample images from OuluVS.

| Image | Description |
|---|---|
| 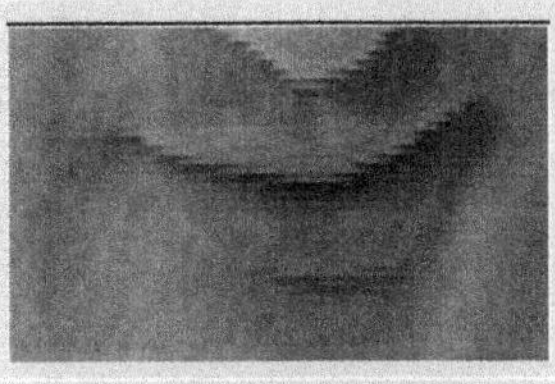 | Subject 1 saying "excuse" for the first time |
| 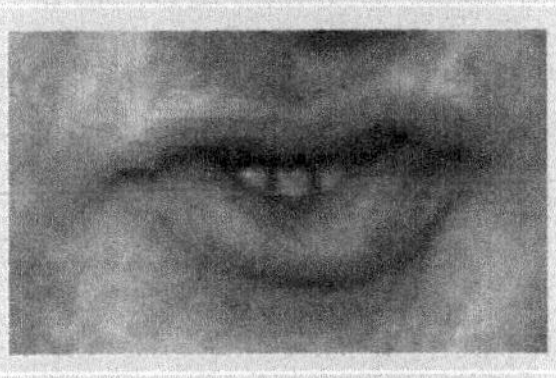 | Subject 1 saying "excuse" for the third time |
| 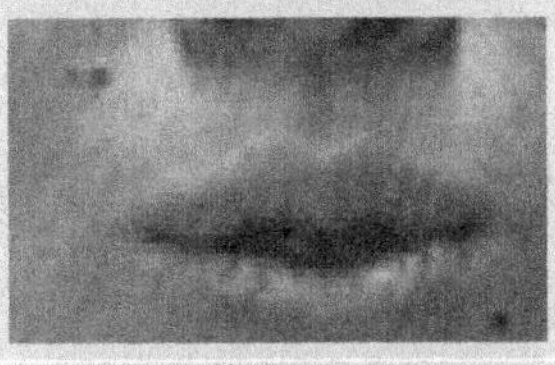 | Subject 2 saying "welcome" for the second time |
| 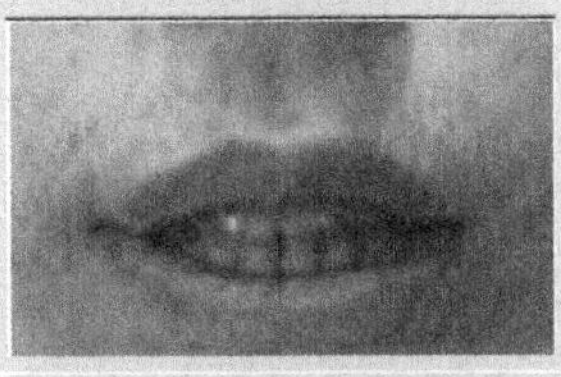 | Subject 7 saying "time" for the first time |
| 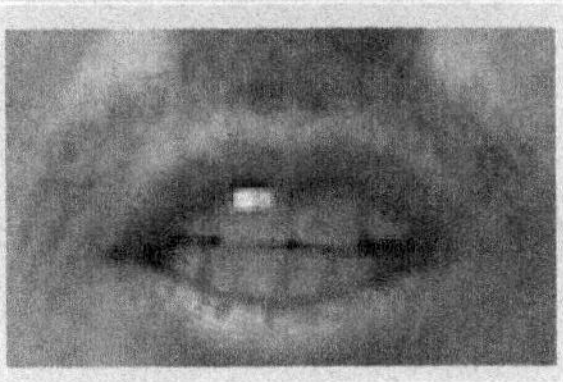 | Subject 9 saying "see you" for the first time |

This specific dataset was chosen due to the feature generation being similar to human perception, making it a suitable choice for training the CNN as a cognitive system. The face detection and its extension lip detection are based on cognitive features which are based on the common properties shared by the human face (such as "location and size: eyes, mouth, bridge of the nose", "eye region being darker compared to upper-cheeks", etc.).

## 4 Results

The evaluation results of the CNN model presented in this chapter are presented in Table 5. The training of the network was limited to three epochs to prevent overfitting caused by the high similarity of the images present in the dataset.

Binary accuracy has been used as the metric to calculate the training accuracy and validation accuracy for the model. The accuracy is measured based on the frequency with which the predicted labels match with the actual labels. This frequency is ultimately returned as binary accuracy: an idempotent operation that simply divides the total by count.

$$Accuracy = \frac{Count\left(y_{pred} = y_{actual}\right)}{Count\left(y_{pred}\right)}$$

The loss is calculated based on categorical cross-entropy. The categorical cross-entropy is used to generate a one-hot array that contains a probable match for each category being considered for classification.

$$Categorical\ Crossentropy = \prod_{c=1}^{C} y_c(x, w_c)^{t_c}$$

The following graphs contain the model loss plot against the number of training epochs and the model accuracy plot against the number of training epochs in the respected order (Figs. 2 and 3).

A subset of predictions performed by the model for the images presented in Table 4 is given in Fig. 4.

**TABLE 5** Metrics for the training of the CNN.

| Epoch | Training accuracy | Training loss | Validation accuracy | Validation loss |
|---|---|---|---|---|
| 1 | 0.7695 | 0.7389 | 0.7545 | 0.8121 |
| 2 | 0.9166 | 0.3028 | 0.8948 | 0.3379 |
| 3 | 0.9387 | 0.2277 | 0.9671 | 0.1124 |

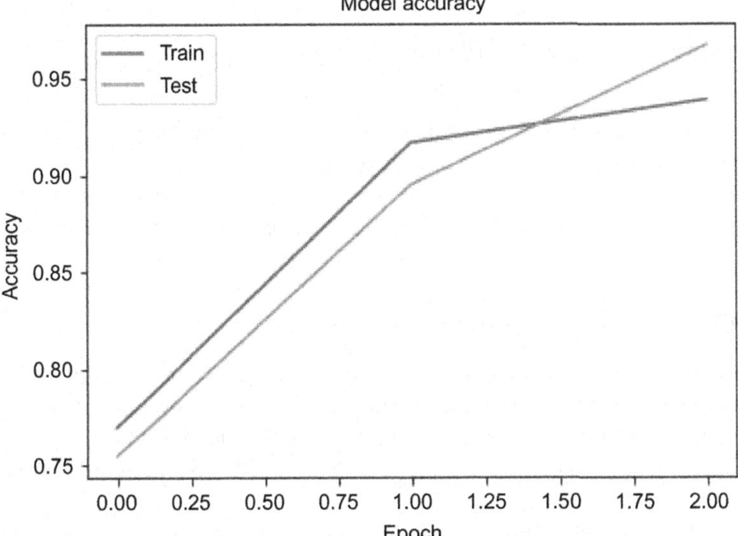


**FIG. 2** Graph of model accuracy plotted against the number of epochs.

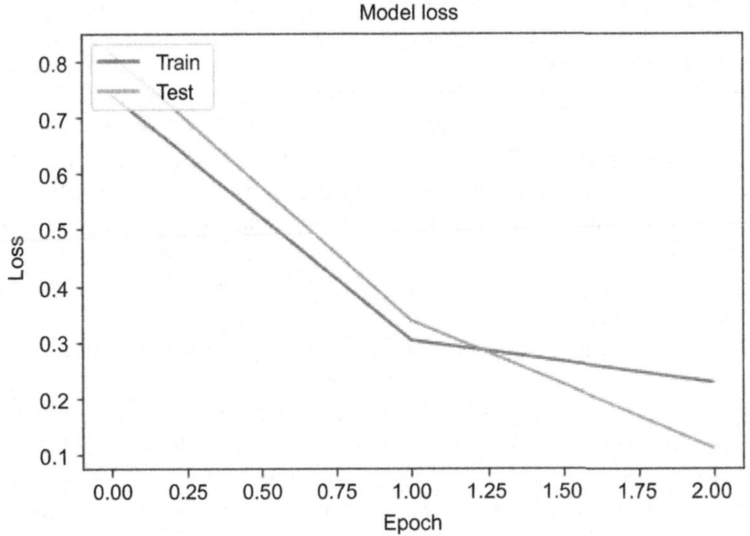


**FIG. 3** Graph of Model loss plotted against the number of epochs.

```
for i in range(0,len(mp)):
    print(x_img[i],"\n","Actual Category: ",Actual_category[i],"Predicted Category: ",mp[i])
```

```
<PIL.Image.Image image mode=L size=117x71 at 0x1789E5B70>
 Actual Category:  [1. 0. 0. 0. 0. 0. 0. 0. 0. 0.] Predicted Category:  [[1. 0. 0. 0. 0. 0. 0. 0. 0. 0.]]
<PIL.Image.Image image mode=L size=117x71 at 0x1789D6B00>
 Actual Category:  [1. 0. 0. 0. 0. 0. 0. 0. 0. 0.] Predicted Category:  [[1. 0. 0. 0. 0. 0. 0. 0. 0. 0.]]
<PIL.Image.Image image mode=L size=117x71 at 0x1789D6588>
 Actual Category:  [0. 1. 0. 0. 0. 0. 0. 0. 0. 0.] Predicted Category:  [[0. 1. 0. 0. 0. 0. 0. 0. 0. 0.]]
<PIL.Image.Image image mode=L size=117x71 at 0x1789D60F0>
 Actual Category:  [0. 0. 0. 0. 0. 0. 1. 0. 0. 0.] Predicted Category:  [[0. 0. 0. 0. 0. 0. 1. 0. 0. 0.]]
<PIL.Image.Image image mode=L size=117x71 at 0x1789D69B0>
 Actual Category:  [0. 0. 0. 0. 0. 0. 0. 0. 1. 0.] Predicted Category:  [[0. 0. 0. 0. 0. 0. 0. 0. 1. 0.]]
```

**FIG. 4** Predictions performed by the model.

The proposed model performed fairly well considering the limitations imposed due to the small size of the database and the number of training epochs being limited to just three. Despite the limitations, the model was able to reach a validation accuracy of 96.71% and perform the classification accurately.

## 5 Conclusion and future work

In this chapter, a CNN model for extraction of lip features and identification of people based on those features has been presented. The proposed model works well in the identification of people, images for whom are presented in the database, but being a neural network fails to classify any nonexisting image properly.

Lips have been attested to be a unique part of the human body, making them a suitable feature that can be used in biometric systems. Lips have been proven unique by researchers by the analysis of their shape along with their color information. The previously mentioned measures of human lips along with their movement patterns during speech are unique for every individual. The lip movement while speaking depends on the idiosyncrasies of a person such as the pronunciation and accent, which vary from person to person.

The chapter considers these unique properties and proposes the use of spatiotemporal features based on the movement of the lips while speaking. These features take into account the changes in the shape of the human lips with respect to time while speaking, making them a suitable choice for biometric detection based on lips.

Cognitive computing systems are most effective as intelligence augmentation systems, which allow them to act as great supplements to human thinking and analysis. Cognitive systems for specialized purposes (such as the proposed approach) are easier to adopt compared to broader scope systems due to their similarity to humans in performing the task. Cognitive systems can aggregate, integrate, and analyze unstructured data to provide deep domain insights.

Any nonexisting image is classified based on its similarity of features to the images, which are already present in the database. The future work for the proposed model includes the addition of a secondary classification mechanism that can filter out the images that are not part of the database while providing a similarity estimate for the person having the most similar lips. This chapter also serves as proof of concept that lips can be used as standalone biometric features and also as a part of the set of features that are being used in multimodal biometry.

## References

[1] G. Zhao, M. Barnard, M. Pietikainen, Lipreading with local spatiotemporal descriptors, IEEE Trans. Multimedia 11 (7) (2009) 1254–1265.

[2] A.M. Rojas, C.M. Travieso, J.B. Alonso, M.A. Ferrer, Automatic lip identification applied under soft facial emotion conditions, in: 2012 IEEE International Carnahan Conference on Security Technology (ICCST), Boston, MA, 2012, pp. 218–223.

[3] P. Porwik, R. Doroz, K. Wrobel, An ensemble learning approach to lip-based biometric verification, with a dynamic selection of classifiers, Expert Syst. Appl. 115 (2019) 673–683 (ISSN 0957-4174).

[4] W.-Y. Lee, K.-E. Ko, K.-B. Sim, Robust lip detection based on histogram of oriented gradient features and convolutional neural network under effects of light and background, Optik 136 (2017) 462–469 (ISSN 0030-4026).

[5] S.-L. Wang, A.W.-C. Liew, Physiological and behavioural lip biometrics: A comprehensive study of their discriminative power, Pattern Recogn. 45 (9) (2012) 3328–3335 (ISSN 0031-3203).

[6] C.M. Travieso, J. Zhang, P. Miller, J.B. Alonso, Using a discrete hidden Markov Model Kernel for lip-based biometric identification, Image Vis. Comput. 32 (12) (2014) 1080–1089 (ISSN 02628856).

[7] S.N. Hashmi, H. Gupta, D. Mittal, K. Kumar, A. Nanda, S. Gupta, A lip reading model using CNN with batch normalization, in: 2018 Eleventh International Conference on Contemporary Computing (IC3), Noida, 2018, pp. 1–6.

[8] F. Vakhshiteh, F. Almasganj, Lip-reading via deep neural network using appearance-based visual features, in: 2017 24th National and 2nd International Iranian Conference on Biomedical Engineering (ICBME), Tehran, 2017, pp. 1–6.

[9] Y. Li, Y. Takashima, T. Takiguchi, Y. Ariki, Lip reading using a dynamic feature of lip images and convolutional neural networks, in: 2016 IEEE/ACIS 15th International Conference on Computer and Information Science (ICIS), Okayama, 2016, pp. 1–6, https://doi.org/10.1109/ICIS.2016.7550888.

[10] K.M.S. Ayyappan, Investigation of effectiveness of ensemble features for visual lip reading, in: 2014 International Conference on Advances in Computing, Communications and Informatics (ICACCI), New Delhi, 2014, pp. 530–533.

[11] F. Vakhshiteh, F. Almasganj, A. Nickabadi, Lip-reading via deep neural networks using hybrid visual features, Image Anal. Stereol. 37 (2) (2018) 159–171 (ISSN 1854-5165).

[12] A. Abel, C. Gao, L. Smith, R. Watt, A. Hussain, Fast lip feature extraction using psychologically motivated gabor features, in: 2018 IEEE Symposium Series on Computational Intelligence (SSCI), Bangalore, India, 2018, pp. 1033–1040.

[13] S. Bakshi, R. Raman, P.K. Sa, Lip pattern recognition based on local feature extraction, in: 2011 Annual IEEE India Conference, Hyderabad, 2011, pp. 1–4.

[14] P. Viola, M. Jones, Rapid object detection using a boosted cascade of simple features, in: CVPR, 2001, pp. 511–518.

Chapter 5

# An overview of the impact of PACS as health informatics and technology e-health in healthcare management

Reinaldo Padilha França[a], Ana Carolina Borges Monteiro[a], Rangel Arthur[b], and Yuzo Iano[a]

*[a]School of Electrical and Computer Engineering (FEEC), State University of Campinas (UNICAMP), Campinas, São Paulo, Brazil, [b]Faculty of Technology (FT), State University of Campinas (UNICAMP), Limeira, São Paulo, Brazil*

## 1 Introduction

Picture archiving and communication systems (PACS) are widely used in imaging clinics and have had positive impacts on the work of the health industry, where this technology has been deployed in many health institutions for the purpose of organizing test results and are considered excellent support for biomedical engineering. However, its applications can be expanded to ensure greater productivity for healthcare companies, control of generated files, and safe medical information, with the main function of storing imaging exams to provide easier communication between clinics and hospitals. This system meets the entire flow of the healthcare facility, including imaging, diagnosis, reporting, and viewing of exam results by patients and doctors to process monitoring, which is of great value in healthcare management [1].

All patient clinical information can now be archived in computer programs, provided that laboratory test results, radiological reports, and therapeutic approaches are saved in electronic medical records (EMRs). However, the first point concerns the identification of the unit sectors that most need workflow improvements and can benefit from PACS. Setting goals is another very important aspect since there is a need to reduce waiting times and increase the number of calls. Moreover, with the PACS system, it is possible to have access to several types of radiological exams, such as mammography, tomography, and

Cognitive Systems and Signal Processing in Image Processing. https://doi.org/10.1016/B978-0-12-824410-4.00007-6

ultrasound, among others, and integrate them into the radiologist information system (RIS), which is integrated with the PACS system, enabling the promotion of links with medical images and tracking all information related to the paths taken by patients [1–3].

One of the great advantages of PACS is the elimination of the impression of radiological reports, which corroborates with paperless technology, mainly in the field of e-health. Then, one can notice the drastic reduction of physical space destined for the file of reports and exams. Moreover, this system has a kind of exam quality control, where after the insertion of the exams, there is a verification to identify failures in this process; if the exam is not pending, it is stored; otherwise, the trader will be advised to take appropriate action. With the PACS system, it is also possible to access clinical and radiological patient data remotely, thanks to the ability to securely and reliably connect data over the internet; it does all the work for radiologists as it enters data, checks for mismatch, and helps doctors read images retrieved from exams. The basic functions that a PACS must contain include allowing the storage of digital images output from medical equipment and providing remote access to stored images. This health informatics technology is highly promising, yet it is considered a powerful reading workflow platform that simplifies doctors' reading activities and centralizes management [4, 5].

This technology is an evolution compared to radiological films and printers, but not as efficient as cloud data storage. The PACS system is a platform that allows the insertion, evaluation, and storage of medical images in an organized and controlled manner, directly impacting e-health in which technology optimizes medical work, reducing operational activities and allowing concentration in the interpretation of exams [1, 6, 7].

Thus, this chapter offers a major scientific contribution concerning the discussion on the use of PACS with cognitive systems, assessing that machines with cognitive systems make use of huge volumes of data to generate predictive mathematical models that help clarify the various possibilities of this decision. In this sense, a PACS system is a platform that allows the insertion, evaluation, and storage of medical images in an organized and controlled manner, directly impacting e-health, optimizing medical work, reducing operational activities, and even allowing concentration (volumes of data) in the interpretation of exams. Cognitive systems also combine with documents from other sources, such as EMRs, radiology and pathology reports, laboratory results, and medical notes on the evolution of treatment, as they are directly aligned with the broad context of encompassing digital imaging. PACS technology archives many pictures, such as ultrasound, endoscopy, radiography, colonoscopy, mammography, dermoscopic, and electrocardiogram images. This provides proactive diagnosis through cognitive computing, making it possible to obtain a computerized approach to search and mine patient records in digital format, prescriptions, and disease statistics (i.e., through PACS data management). Thus, cognitive technology will play a role as a supplementary lens for the analysis of medical images, identifying more subtle changes in digitizations and reducing the time for planning treatment, analyzing large amounts of data.

The importance and novelty of this study derive from different factors since cognitive computing is a set of techniques and algorithms that help transform data into information through data extraction and interpretation, which incorporate cognitive systems that acquire properties to read new information, obtain learning, and recognize this information better with each interaction. This is dependent on technologies that provide this database for cognitive systems to operate. PACS enables the digitization of information in health organizations, especially in diagnostic medicine, which is a critical solution for medical image management as it manages the storage and sharing of images generated by various devices—usually computerized tomography (CT), ultrasound, nuclear medicine, positron emission tomography (PET), and even magnetic resonance imaging (MRI)—facilitating medical workflow.

It is worth noting that the contributions of this type of research point to the complement of two technologies, due to all the motivation previously highlighted, generating scientific knowledge, due to the wide discussion and overview carried out, adding academic value in this way.

Therefore, this chapter aims to provide an updated discussion (major scientific contribution) on health informatics and PACS in the context of health informatics, showing and approaching its success within technology in healthcare management, with a concise bibliographic background, categorizing and synthesizing the technological potential in e-health.

It is worth mentioning that this chapter differs from the existing literature because the existing literature is often used to describe and explain the theory, documenting how each discovery added to the store of knowledge, relating theoretical aspects, how the academics piece fits into a theoretical model, among others. While this presented overview is a scientific collection around the topics addressed, relating that this type of study is scarce in the literature, offering a new perspective on an element missing in the literature, dealing with an updated discussion of technological approaches.

## 2 Review literature on cognitive systems concepts

From the historical point of view, machines were used only to make complex calculations, and due to the advancement and popularization of computer technology, users started to develop their own programs (algorithms) and software. Society, especially companies that worked with digital data, realized the difficulty of managing the information obtained during the processes. In this sense, solutions such as cognitive computing (CC) have become a way to improve decision-making [8].

CC aims to automate and streamline processes, allowing these processes to reduce costs and offer a better experience over time. This is because the system with artificial cognition is capable of absorbing information, processing it, and proposing paths based on that data. ML algorithms make machines continue to learn throughout their cycles. As information is included in the system, it refines the way the system views problems and tends to be more accurate in offering viable alternatives [9].

The technological skills of this technological platform are inspired by the unique capabilities of the human brain related to analysis and problem-solving. Relating that just like in human beings, the process is given through the capture of the senses and then their perception. And then, this knowledge is processed and recorded in our memory and later used in decision making, that is, based on cognition [8, 9].

Considering that based on the use of sensors, artificial intelligence (AI) models, AI methodologies, algorithms, and data, systems are developed that are able to identify patterns, recognize objects, visualize countless possibilities among the data set, and validate hypotheses in order to generate responses and recommendations that can help make decisions and appropriate predictions [10].

Whether in medicine, by helping a doctor decide the ideal treatment for the patient, or in the legal field, by helping a judge decide whether or not to convict an offender, after comparing the process with the violated laws, through computing. Simulating human intelligence by computer systems efficiently replicates the way human beings think about problems and offers solutions to achieve interaction of this software within the reach of different types of professionals on a task that is no longer so complex due to its high processing power [11, 12].

Cognitive systems interact with humans naturally to interpret data, learning from virtually all interactions, and proposing new possibilities through probabilistic reasoning. This does not generate predetermined responses, rather it generate hypotheses, substantiated arguments, and recommendations. Using resources such as data mining, pattern recognition, natural language processing, and CC results in the creation of systems capable of solving complex situations without requiring human interaction [9, 12].

The main competencies of cognitive systems are digital reasoning obtained through methods and models to represent, store, research, evaluate, explore, and retrieve knowledge. This feature allows inferences, predictions, and abstractions, such as ontologies, semantic web, data mining, intelligent agents, and intelligent scheduling, among others. Additional characteristics of a cognitive system include those based on rules relating to probabilistic reasoning, approximate reasoning (fuzzy logic), deductive reasoning, and digital automated learning enabling classification and regression, prediction, and clustering through computational tools with similar ML capabilities to the human being [13].

Artificial neural networks are a set of methods and technologies for cognitive systems capable of interpreting images, similar to human vision, through metaheuristics (e.g., particle swarm, evolutionary computing), deep learning, and cognitive networks. They enable pattern recognition, information extraction, organization, and image processing, such as face biometrics, visual inspection, surveillance, process control, object recognition, and medical image analysis, among many others [14, 15].

Through speech recognition, speech synthesis, speech biometrics, speech analytics, speech filtering, and coding, cognitive systems are capable of interpreting and even producing speech analogous to human beings, generating dialogs that enable information extraction and organization, such as emotion analysis, automatic summarization, dynamic translation, language identification, and generation and understanding of natural language, among others. They even allow device control, dialog transcription, speaker recognition, dialysis, assistive speech, and emotion analysis, among others [14, 15].

The era of computing through cognitive systems is derived from computers capable of interpreting generic signals, not necessarily related to speech and vision, through image acquisition, performing filtering, segmentation, representation, and description, and through morphology, mathematics can obtain object recognition, such as applications involving signals obtained by sensors. Cognitive systems make sense of unstructured data and can scale it to keep up with the complexity and unpredictability of information in the modern world [8, 15].

In medicine, CC that solves questions about cancer treatment is complicated; however, from the analysis of a database by a digital image of a patient, it is possible to find the best treatment to care for skin cancer, lung cancer, anemia, leukemia, breast cancer, and other diseases that can be seen by digital imaging. What conventionally could take a long time, with cognitive technology its efficiency is very noticeable, in a more practical way, indicating which is the most appropriate treatment [16].

It is also worth highlighting the difference between CC, AI, and ML. AI aims to use computational devices to perform human activities autonomously; unlike CC, AI focuses on solving complex problems. ML consists of a technology whose principle is to check patterns within a process, being able to predict behaviors or insights through an analysis of the collected data, in order to solve a problem. CC is different from the aforementioned technologies, having the ability to process information similarly to the human brain, considering its differential in the most effective way of using the acquired knowledge, going beyond just reproducing information [13–16].

Finally, a cognitive system can understand, adapt, and make sense of all data, from a reading text, visualization of images, and digital perception of natural speech with context. Understanding the types of unstructured data, such as texts, images, voice, video, and music, that is, all forms of communication that human beings interact with. From a cognitive system, it is possible to interpret the information, organize it, and offer explanations about what it means, based on conclusions. This generates hypotheses (they are probabilistic and are created based on the domain of knowledge to which he was trained), creates ideas, predicts something to come. It is also possible to learn, accumulating data, and obtain information about each interaction, that is, the more information (data), the more tuned it gets, perpetually increasing the quality of your digital reasoning and decision-making process [17].

## 2.1 Cognitive systems in medical image processing

The emergence of the cognitive system marks a new era in computing through learning algorithms results in technology capable of interpreting data, generating logics, and insights from the structuring and crossing of information, just like humans [18].

With the advancement of imaging technologies, the challenge of analyzing results is increasing. However, cognitive technology can be used for a variety of purposes, such as categorizing tumor cells for a laboratory or cataloging photos of skin or breast cancer in patients (cognitive informatics in health). Given that this disruptive technology has the properties of performing a series of tasks, such as measuring the proportions of the image and identifying the colors of the pixels, to complete and generate insights from these results [16, 18].

In CC, equipped with learning algorithms, which are trained to perform a certain task, specifically for image recognition, the machine could be fed with exam pictures and, from them, establish its own rules and strategies to achieve the goal, that is, obtain a diagnosis [13, 16, 19].

These algorithms, which become increasingly complex and sophisticated, are one of the foundations of CC technology. Making the machine be able to "reason," generating new concepts, insights, and hypotheses. Since, based on examples, that is, a dataset with exam images, a neural network manages to generalize the results, still evaluating that the system can learn over time, gradually becoming more valuable and intelligent [20].

CC also improves predictions based on past trends, since one of the fundamentals of technology is the availability of data and, with the Big Data trend, relating the huge amount of information already available, which can be used in medicine. Test results and diagnostics help explain the behavior of a type of tumor, in addition to indicating the best form of treatment. Reflecting that traditionally doctors decides whether a patient is sick or not based on their experience, updating themselves through scientific congresses and additional studies but still having limited knowledge and making decisions based on that. With CC, it is proposed that doctors can be helped by a gigantic base of information, that is, cognitive informatics in health [18, 21].

Computers with cognitive systems make use of huge volumes of data to generate predictive mathematical models that help clarify the various possibilities of a decision. Making it possible to understand even those data that are not structured or translated into the digital language, such as natural human language, texts, and images. This information is then interpreted by mathematical cognitive algorithms capable of learning, considering that the more information these systems receive, the better they become for the performance of a given task, managing to absorb data stored over the years or even decades and make the necessary crossings [21, 22].

At the same time, there has been a major advance in medical technologies aimed at diagnostic imaging, such as: echocardiography; ultrasound, which replaces abdominal palpation and percussion; resonance imaging, which replaces contrasted radiology exams, and PET, allowing to check the areas involved in various brain activities; and mammography consisting of an imaging exam, belonging to the class of routine complementary exams in asymptomatic women, for early detection of possible causes of breast cancer. Nowadays, diagnosis is made by exams and not by reasoning and clinical judgment, evaluating chest expansion, auscultation, feeling the thoracic-vocal thrill, or even making a percussion to diagnose pneumonitis, through imaging tests such as a simple chest X-ray or CT scan [16, 22].

In this way, the medical community will be able to identify and reduce operational and financial inefficiencies once they have access to this data, cognitive systems will combine with documents from other sources, such as EMRs, radiology and pathology reports, laboratory results, medical notes on the evolution of treatment, medical journals, clinical treatment guidelines, and even studies with published results, that is, cognitive informatics in health. In addition to providing more personalized treatment, the combination of expertise aims to improve workflows and adopt a patient-centered approach to improve results and care [23].

In this sense, CC can transform the way the clinical staff performs diagnosis, treatment, and monitoring of patients. Cognitive technology creates opportunities for doctors and specialists to extract broad information through high-resolution images. Thus, cognitive technology in health has a generalized impact on the sector, assisting the physician in the diagnosis and choice of treatment, through CC and ML inserted in the daily lives of many hospitals, they can be fed with much more data and receive a layer of information. Intelligence that will optimize assistance [24].

The use of these disruptive tools, in addition to organizing and improving searches for patient information, suggesting the treatment of diseases based on clinical protocols and best practices that have recently proven to be effective, helping health professionals in diagnosing diseases and making decisions that should be taken about it. Rapid processing of this information gives the physician elements to make the decision on the best care to be taken with the patient [20, 24].

## 2.2 Cognitive systems in the context of predictive analytics

The concept of predictive analysis comes from a data mining tool used to improve results, identifying risks and opportunities, and guiding decision-making. In a simplified way, the predictive analysis uses Big Data, statistical algorithms, and ML techniques to predict the probability of future results and trends based on historical data. That is, predictive analysis helps discover patterns in the data that can help expose problems and identify opportunities [21, 24].

In health, due to a large amount of medical data and electronic health records, predictive analysis usually involves a greater amount of metrics, analyzing patient data, which can help doctors and specialists predict the possibility of diseases and help in early diagnosis. Carrying out predictive measures can reduce hospital readmissions, decrease surgery costs, identify high-risk patients, reduce hospital waiting times, and promote initiatives that improve patient satisfaction [22, 24].

This ability to use data, analysis, and systematic digital reasoning leads to more productive and effective planning with the term "analytics." There are several types of analyses, such as statistical modeling, forecasting, data mining, and design of experiments, among others. The most advanced analytics include sophisticated statistical models, such as ML, optimization, neural networks, and other sophisticated techniques of data mining through AI. Currently, one of the most used practices is Big Data, made through data mining techniques applied to a large volume of data, identifying patterns, and generating new information [14, 24].

Providing a more accurate assessment of what will happen enables the generation of new insights that lead to more effective decision making. Within the health area, predictive models allow the identification of existing patterns, and it is still possible to make predictions of hospitalization rates, probability of infections, and diseases, among others [20, 24].

In addition, these predictive analysis technologies increase the accuracy of diagnoses, mainly linked through imaging tests, assisting in preventive medicine and public health, since it is humanly impossible to analyze the millions of documents and digital images, and even existing medical studies. This results in a lot of time being saved by crossing this huge amount of data, even saving resources that could be spent on conventional medical care. As much as this technological revolution has changed the health paradigm, learning health systems requires the compilation and storage of data, feedback cycles of knowledge and practices of change, and the application of new forms of knowledge [21, 24].

Medical notes written by hand, identifying the symptoms of diseases, and lack of information remain as primary causes that hinder the efficiency of health professionals. Through proactive diagnosis using CC, it is possible to obtain a computerized approach to search and mine patient records in digital format, prescriptions, and disease statistics, making it possible to predict disease patterns or even help identify the chances of disease patterns in previously unknown diseases. Predictive analytics helps improve clinical workflows, thereby improving health services on a global scale [19, 24].

In this context, CC can eliminate all of these inefficiencies by providing insightful information through programmatic computing. With the same ease and efficiency, it also allows the translation of texts into different languages, with an understanding of the context and not just the translation of words but also image recognition [8, 22–24].

Since human tasks are no longer exclusive to human beings, machines are learning to learn. These techniques are not a substitute for human thinking, but definitely, they lead people to make better decisions by reducing the risk of duplicating or hiding relevant information and helping maintain a logical line of reasoning, clarifying possible doubts in any type of process [24].

In this broad context, it is undeniable that CC is giving rise to a new way of doing operations because technology improves the way institutions and their operations work. This includes health care, which requires delicate attention, to production and industry, which requires blunt processes. Consequently, it will also enhance the human life experience in the digital age. After all, computing is no longer about programming or building software solutions; instead, it is evolving into a way of life. Man and machine will merge to arrive at decisions for complex everyday problems, that is, eliminating the guesswork involved and presenting precision as a standard feature [8, 24].

## 3 Review literature on implementation of PACS systems

In this broad context encompassing CC and digital imaging, PACS archives various images, including ultrasound, endoscopy, radiography, colonoscopy, mammography, dermoscopic, and electrocardiogram images. Even a patient photo can be stored as long as the system accepts JPG and TIFF format files, thus demystifying the concept that it would be restricted to radiological content in the Digital Imaging and Communications in Medicine (DICOM) standard. In addition, as the reports can be issued electronically with digital signatures, without the need to be printed, it is also necessary to bear a timestamp, which is the stamp that attests to the date and time the report received a digital signature. Certification of the PACS solution is required to ensure the quality and security of confidential patient information. Recently, the trend of deconstructed PACS systems has emerged, which allows the use of multiple software that acts together and talks to each other, according to the needs of the diagnostic imaging center [25, 26].

Digital radiology has revolutionized diagnostic medicine by enabling more detailed imaging examinations and the elimination of costly and environmentally aggressive printing film. With it, the PACS system has become one of the main requirements for combining medical equipment with computers, enabling the combination of anatomical and metabolic mapping. Along with the technological revolution that has taken place over the last 20 years, the healthcare industry has been able to modernize and electronically handle sector-specific tasks, from scheduling and registering patients to performing examinations and issuing reports [27].

The implementation of the PACS system in a health institution arises, above all, from the need to have tools that help in managing the service and medical information of patients. In addition to removing the limitation offered by the activity and economic-financial reports, the PACS system integration enables the manager to reduce costs, increase operational efficiency, and decrease patient waiting time. This complexity called for flexibility, delivered with the concept of deconstructed PACS since in this mode, there is not only software to store and manage the images but also several programs that work together and talk to each other as needed. Deconstructed PACS was only made possible by the Vendor Neutral Archive (VNA), which is a technology for storing and managing images and data of various kinds, such as reports, in a standard format and a single interface. Put simply, VNA is a platform that enables healthcare professionals to centralize the most important patient information, from the baseline to the outcome of various scans, eliminating file and system incompatibility. The concept of deconstructing PACS is focused on eliminating the virtual walls that separate many different areas of imaging and patient care for imaging, meaning expanding the ability to access and view diagnostic images and results for all departments and specialties, beyond the traditional reports and information that is already stored in EMRs [1, 28–30].

VNA works in the cloud and therefore excludes the need for local servers to store images and reports, saving money and space. The VNA and deconstruction process offers a more efficient way to add new facilities to large hospital networks. The process would make access to complete imaging, tools, and diagnostic information, not just storage, vendor-independent, and accessible through a single access point, viewer, and system. By enabling data with different standards to talk to each other, technology promotes system integration and facilitates the use of business intelligence and analytics tools in conjunction with RIS, for example. The deconstructed PACS system also facilitates the routine of radiologists, as everything they need to work in different specialties can be concentrated on the same viewer, avoiding travel and delay. Having a common workflow engine that enables a consistent process, including ordering, imaging, information management, diagnostic review, reporting, storage, archiving, retrieval, and review (considering nondiagnostics and diagnostics), improves consistency and would set a broad standard of both quality and simplification of the process across the company's healthcare spectrum. Whereas hospitals add more facilities to their networks, integration is essential to getting the right information for the right doctor at the point of care or decision at a critical time [1, 31].

There are pros and cons to these alternatives, and it is important to focus on the main issue, which is tangible in terms of system redundancy. When image acquisition and workflow are dedicated to PACS, if it goes down, image accessibility will still be operational throughout the institution through VNA. By contrast, when it becomes the hub for this activity, as it falls, or even if it is disabled, all accessibility will be affected. In a single line-of-service application scenario, such as a small image center or hospital, such factors are not a problem as elements are not shared across the lines of service. The organization can choose different software that meets the needs of each of the five major processes involved in performing diagnostic imaging exams, ranging from image acquisition, worklist, and flow, diagnostic display, data (file) management, reaching even in clinical distribution and exhibition, everything is integrated and dialoguing with each other. Another factor to consider in a "deconstructed" environment, integration that falls more heavily on the installation as there may be multiple vendors involved. In contrast, a more classic PACS puts more burden on the vendor in terms of interoperability [32].

In terms of healthcare information technology (IT), this would simplify the process as long as resources are consolidated resulting in the cost savings and redundant storage space that currently exists in most healthcare configurations. It provides the ability to bring information to more centralized governance, which can bring improved consistency. It can also be instrumental in driving interoperability between different PACS, imaging, reporting, and EMR devices. It may be the beginning of the life cycle, but another notion of a deconstructed PACS is to avoid duplicate applications. It should also be considered that the number of vendors that have taken a deconstructed PACS approach is relatively small, and almost all are smaller independent vendors, although most major vendors connect to third-party software and solutions. Another point to consider is that not all solutions work well with others. Software upgrades of a solution can also have a negative impact on overall system operation. Evaluating the best solutions takes time, and most medical facilities do not have the time to do a detailed assessment and define what best suits certain needs. There are few facilities with built-in resources to deploy and support third-party solutions from multiple vendors. Even though VNAs remain the exception, they can support many different technologies [1, 31, 33].

Thus, it is currently possible to completely disassemble a PACS into separate, independent components just to aggregate them again to match the functionality of a built-in standards-based PACS, which consists of the known common structure, being a computational architecture designed to capture, store, distribute, and display medical images. With the features known for storing images on a server, it allows images to be analyzed on the screen. This makes it unnecessary to print exams, in addition to film disuse, PACS reduces the cost of chemistry, processing, storage, and manipulation, and allows immediate consultation of any patient information, as it is exclusively digital, ensuring the confidentiality of patient data. It is at the discretion of the medical imaging department to manage ordering, distribution, archiving, and retrieval of clinical examinations, since the ease of searching for information through PACS increases industry productivity and promotes improvement in the clinical workflow. Since the standardization that comes with PACS makes it easier to promote the integration of several heterogeneous systems, such as those in parallel operation for the most diverse specific tasks, ranging from scheduling and registration of the patient to the execution of exams and issuance of reports [1, 34].

Effective integration with PACS offers several benefits for healthcare professionals and technicians and for patients. Imaging technology offers cost-effective storage and access to images from various medical media where benefits do not limit one or two areas. The list of advantages is large and offers more efficiency for physicians with less screen switching, greater security, and consistency of information, reduced use and cost of printing exams and medical records, and reduced patient waiting time for diagnosis [1, 34].

## 4 PACS systems application

If in modern days people live in an era of health data sharing, this is due to tools such as PACS, a tool that enables communication and archiving of images in a safe and standardized way, arising from the need for integration between different technologies used in this task. Thanks to it, hospitals, medical clinics, and doctor's offices can send and receive medical files quickly and securely. PACS has also enabled the development and standardization of solutions that contribute to the democratization of exams and rapid outcomes, such as telemedicine. PACS consists of a filing and communication system focused on diagnostic imaging that allows ready access to medical images in digital format in any sector of a hospital and provides interaction between environments that have communication, visualization, manipulation, and storage of medical images in health services. Generally speaking, a PACS consists of equipment and systems for the acquisition, archiving, and presentation of medical data and images, where each component is properly integrated through computer networks and DICOM compliant computer applications [35].

Simply put, the system consists of performing five basic steps. First, the equipment used in diagnostic tests captures images of the body part studied. Second, the records are transmitted by the equipment to an image server via a transfer protocol that determines what format they will be in, whether DICOM, Health Level 7 (HL7), or others. Third, the transmitted data is stored in a server database itself and/or in an external data structure, which may be a cloud. Fourth, when stored, information is available for viewing on workstations (offline) or systems located on the web, such as platforms used by telemedicine companies. And fifth, data can be acquired by patients and healthcare professionals, provided they are accredited to download, print, or save this information [36].

RIS is one of the most complete management software systems for diagnostic imaging centers and has the main objective of automating the entire workflow of a radiology clinic. This automation ranges from scheduling the procedure to distributing the exam result, thus speeding up processes and reducing many errors. In addition, it has as the positive consequence of increasing team productivity, since from this system it is possible to track the status of each task and the search facilitated by information through personalized search with keywords and filters. RIS and PACS are two systems aimed at improving internal radiology management, and the integration of these systems is increasingly being used by managers. Because they are complete tools, when integrated, they generate many benefits for the medical institution. One of the greatest features this integration provides is the agility to work with more than one system. The integration between RIS and PACS is an important step toward a superior service in radiology, since, from this union, a solid foundation is formed that brings numerous and different benefits to the patients and professionals involved in the daily routine of a clinic [37].

This beneficial process begins at reception, where the patient's registered data is the basis for the other steps of the care process. At this stage, nurses, technologists, and doctors only need to validate the data registered with the patient. With this, doctors can work with a list of patients, thus signaling the priorities and pending reports. In addition, the patient can easily access the exams through an internet portal with a password and login that are offered at the time of registration at reception. This ease of data exchange ensures not only the smooth flow of patients within the institution but also the security of information without the risk of exchanging roles between different individuals. Among the many applications of PACS, it is worth mentioning the ability to store large amounts of medical data, the standardization of storage and transfer protocols, the ability to provide integration between different protocols and languages, the construction of autonomous and reliable databases, the feasibility of simple and quick access to information by different professionals, ensuring greater security in archiving patient data, which can only be accessed with authorization, and finally, searching and cross-checking information stored in databases [4].

Thus, the PACS adds to the health services quick access to patient images and reports, because at each service, new information about appointments, medication prescriptions, orders, and test reports are added to the medical record. Given that in the past, these documents were only available on paper, their sharing was quite restricted. Such restrictions were overcome to the digitization of files and adoption of PACS for data sharing, generating access to doctors and other health professionals, consulting the patient's entire medical history with just a few clicks, allowing health professionals to quickly find the information that interests them at that time. As a basic example, if diabetes is suspected, it is possible to refer to blood glucose test results [38].

A chronological view of patient exams provided that with the PACS system, it does not matter the order in which files are stored or consulted, as they can be organized by applying filters. What was previously done through paper medical records complicated the organization of the easily mingled procedures, making the doctor need to read each record if he wanted to have a chronological view of the patient's health events. As long as the security scanning and transmission of digital images (in pixels) is stored in databases, which decreases the risk of loss, even if the file is accidentally deleted it is likely that other digital copies are saved in the cloud, on servers, or shared via email. Alternatively, in the past, with the transportation of medical records and images by patients and health professionals, there was a risk of losing these documents, which generally required further examinations, as there was only one copy of the generated images [39, 40].

Developing radiological film through the use of chemicals is a costly process involving the purchase of equipment, film, and products and the separation of space for the development of radiological images. With the vast majority of files saved in the cloud, on servers, or on platforms that can be easily consulted after the exam, there is no need to purchase the printer, specific paper, and ink and there is no need for physical storage space. With greater standardization and quality of processes, with clear and simple steps, the system can be easily understood and used by different professionals, reducing bureaucracy and increasing its efficiency. This is because each user can contribute to the database in the right way and indirectly with diagnoses and assertive attitudes regarding patient treatment [2, 40].

Electronic Patient Record (PEP) refers to a health information management system, storage, and sharing of the digital exam, and when integrated with online reports, PEP helps organize and increase agility in meeting the demands. In the specific case of PACS, its use is indispensable for clinics that store and share images digitally, because it standardizes this type of communication. Its importance goes beyond being integrated with PEP and telemedicine, enabling clinics to be more accurate in medical examinations and reports and in managing clinical information. If the entire process is digitized from the beginning of care, failures to manually record information will be avoided, providing better support to the doctor during the consultation. In addition, PACS interoperability ensures that it communicates with other digital systems used by the clinic, such as PEP. While PACS manages the standard management of digital exam images, PEP goes beyond and organizes all clinic or patient information, each in a way and with a purpose. Telemedicine optimizes the performance of examinations and reports [41].

The PEP is the patient file, but fully digitized and online, which gathers all clinical and assistance information about care and stores the history. The idea of the EMR is to assist the care provided in any health institution. Therefore, PACS is important for the full use of PEPs, since the exam and the digital report need to be shared and stored by the medical records. Recalling that PEPs are also integrable to the management systems of public and private clinics, clinics, and hospitals. Just as when deploying the online report solution, the entire digital exam process is integrated with the PACS. For example, electrocardiogram (ECG), spirometry, electroencephalogram, mammography, and X-ray images are obtained directly from the devices and then sent via the internet to a team of medical specialists, enabled to remotely laud. Another good thing about telemedicine is that online reports can also be integrated with RIS and EMRs, keeping patient clinical information organized and accessible to different teams and professionals at any time [41, 42].

In short, is possible to consider that telemedicine, like PACS, is a facilitator for digital examination. The integration of the two technologies, also with RIS and PEP, allows clinics to have agility and efficiency in health service delivery. Collecting exam, registration, and clinical data will positively impact patient care, which gains quality with more accurate diagnoses, and facilitates workflow for staff. Advantages of PACS come from facilitating the routine of healthcare professionals, who save time in locating and sharing patient information. In this sense, doctors have an added advantage because they can access the entire patient history simply and quickly, making more assertive decisions. As mentioned earlier, there is no need to be in the health unit to consult them. Remote access also allows the formation of geographically distributed PACS, generating the integration of two or more systems that are physically distant, resulting in a wide sharing of information via the internet, while offering data selection for each terminal. While general information is available to everyone, specific data, such as images from an unaudited exam, can also select what information is restricted to some network terminals [40, 43, 44].

One disadvantage of PACS is that most users do not need to know the programming languages, yet the system requires periodic maintenance, which should be done by experts in the field. Failures in the operation of the PACS can result in difficulties in accessing databases, since another challenge is in the very choice of the company that will implement the system, which needs to be meticulous, checking the reputation and security protocols adopted by it, in order to preserve data protected by doctor-patient confidentiality [40, 43, 44].

## 5 PACS environments and systems management

Purchasing a PACS involves financial and time investments for any healthcare facility. It is very important for healthcare professionals to research and familiarize themselves with the PACS system before purchasing it, bearing in mind that one facility can consume hundreds of thousands of dollars in hardware, software, and training. Professionals, and training may take a few months. Installing a PACS system is a complex challenge that can consume hundreds of thousands of dollars, plus weeks or months of dedication, meaning a large portion of a budget will be used and a new recurring maintenance cost will be added. On the other hand, the system brings organization in the generation of reports and examinations, which stimulates the increase of productivity, a major breakthrough for radiologists who can laud a digital exam, especially when compared to places that still work with printers and film [45, 46].

The PACS system also allows a health facility to have its own server, replacing storage media with hard drives, CDs, and even USB flash drives, which is one of the main pillars for its sale and why so many hospitals and health centers have been opting for this solution. This decreases the chance of reports being lost, since, after the examination report process, the doctor needs to store the images and documents for the next patient consultation. When this is in physical form it is much easier for this material to be damaged over time. In PACS, everything is stored digitally in a highly secure system. Thus, in addition to preventing data from being lost, it makes the task of finding the necessary data by authorized persons much easier. It also increases security in relation to patient medical data, since PACS saves all exams and reports in encrypted form. Thus, only authorized people with login and password credentials can view the documents, bringing much more confidence to the patient and improving the work of the entire clinic staff [45, 46].

It enables data mobility, since, with PACS, imaging exams can be accessed not only by computers but also by mobile devices, such as tablets and smartphones, facilitating the routine of managers and health professionals. This mobility is possible from the moment data storage is made in the cloud, a scenario that breaks physical barriers and even allows the issuance of reports at a distance. Having a patient's history of exams readily available optimizes the monitoring of the patient's health condition and improves the patient's assessment of the clinic. Reduced costs means more money to invest in new equipment and improvement for employees. With PACS, the images can be analyzed on the screen; there is no need to print them. PACS contributes to a more sustainable planet, which goes far beyond reducing costs; failing to print images is a valuable attitude when it comes to sustainability, as the chemicals and materials used in this process generate waste and pollute the environment. Optimizing diagnosis due to the high resolution and quality of digital images generated by the PACS system implies the ease and speed with which a physician can interpret an examination result, issue diagnosis, and define the most appropriate treatment [44–46].

Exams are stored electronically and, due to this process simplification, the work of all professionals is streamlined, which increases productivity and appeals to the client who will have their results in hand much faster. PACS can be integrated with other systems, such as RIS, PEP, or EMR, which provides standardization and comprehensive business management. The routine is completely optimized because the systems store and make all information available on the same platform to which they are connected without having to switch screens and log in again each time it is necessary to access the data [41, 46].

The high cost of acquisition of servers and software for PACS is high, and some systems are more complex and it may take several months to complete installation and training. There are also additional costs associated with the need for IT teams; security of the information must be guaranteed due to the confidentiality of the data. There are also technological changes related to the periodic need to update equipment and software that over time become obsolete, resulting in more long-term associated costs. Many of the advantages of PACS systems have been taken advantage of by cloud computing technology applied to medical imaging management, and thus the main disadvantages have been virtually eliminated. Today's PACS systems are built on cloud computing technology and are based on delivering hardware and software services over the internet. This way, the storage system can be used on any mobile device with network access, and the images are shared online. The main advantages of PACS associated with cloud computing are: instant access to images from anywhere (even outside the health facility, such as at home); faster implementation; lower initial investment in equipment and maintenance; and reduction of infrastructure and maintenance costs [32].

The medical image management, storage, and transmission service is also being offered as software as a service and may be of interest to smaller institutions with low investment capacity in more robust solutions. Cloud computing, which is fast becoming an attractive alternative to traditional, centralized IT infrastructures, is a new paradigm that focuses on delivering hardware and software services over the internet. PACS, when available in cloud computing, can be accessed from anywhere, accelerating physician access to patient test results. Since adopting PACS in the cloud mode is much cheaper than the conventional format and radiology has an astronomical amount of data to store, specialized clinics can generate terabytes of data per day. Hiring a data center is much more expensive than cloud storage because you only pay for what be used in cloud storage [47].

Benefits include: easy access to data and the resources to manage it; lower initial investment in equipment, maintenance, and data center staff; scalable system; rapid implementation; and due to the Infrastructure as a Service cloud model, cloud scalability is complete and there are no idle services, allowing the company to pay only for what it consumes; reduced cost of ownership, infrastructure, and storage; flexibility and adaptability to different technology levels and business models; instant access to high-resolution, high-quality images from anywhere; resilience against system failures; and operational efficiency. It is also advisable for fast-growing companies with no capital to invest in infrastructure, maintenance, or skilled labor [47, 48].

Opting for private clouds is the best choice for PACS environments. Certifications must be ensured that the environment is highly secure and relies on encryption to protect communication between servers and target identification so that data is not brought to a criminal server. The cloud should be chosen for quality and security, not investment value, where the price must be combined with quality and cannot be a purely financial decision. Challenges that are faced by PACS in the cloud can sometimes include: a conservative view of doctors and radiologists about cloud computing; the financial impact if the decision is for a private cloud; difficulties transferring large amounts of on-site stored data to the cloud; and even cloud interoperability and security concerns. Obstacles exist, but they need to be overcome, since running PACS in the cloud is a logical step for imaging IT, and its benefits are material, not only in terms of cost, time savings, and reduced risk but primarily in how hospitals can better support all their clinical functions. The cloud solution is not only capital equipment-intensive, but it is on the rise in the market, improving systems every day, with better usability and a much more affordable cost [32, 48].

## 5.1 PACS extension in the healthcare management

PACS VNAs are critical tools for storing imaging, where healthcare organizations struggle to store and migrate medical image data using such tools, making them viewable to providers at the point of care. VNA is a medical archive system that allows planning and managing the life cycle of the medical files stored on it. It is a technology of storage and management of images and data of the most diverse nature, such as reports, images, and videos, and accessible in a single interface, allowing to differentially compress them and export to cheaper storage systems, and to index and save all the medical files, such as DICOM and non-DICOM images, DICOM information objects, PDFs, video files, proprietary, and standard machine output files. Put simply, VNA is understood as a platform that enables healthcare professionals to centralize the most important patient information, from the patient's baseline to the outcome of multiple scans, with no problems with file and system compatibility. Being such a tool it must become the final archive of the PACS, RIS, and other medical systems, allowing to save final studies and reports either by DICOM connection, HL7 delivery, direct upload, FTP, or any other valid method [1, 2, 49].

Today's move toward collaborative care means more physicians need to have access to image, data just like radiology reports, to be able to make care management decisions that provide a 360-degree view of the patient, as long as this view makes it easy to identify, The best and most effective treatments for individual patients, or even specific populations, derived from combining and analyzing structured and unstructured information. PACS has some limitations, in general, its use is restricted to the workplace and may take up space with hardware for proper, secure storage of images, and as technology becomes obsolete over the years, requiring new investments or even an integral substitute in all cases, cloud VNA is an indispensable complement to enable working with the capabilities of PACS optimally and efficiently. PACS and VNAs provide the means for organizations to store and manage their image data [50]

Similar to PACS, VNAs are archives for DICOM-based images and content, integrating the viewing and storage of different health IT systems independently of vendor restrictions. VNAs dissociate PACS and workstations at the archiving layer, developing an application engine that receives, integrates, and transmits data, yet provides a viewing experience regardless of the source of images. For large healthcare organizations with thousands of physicians, a single interface can save time and money by reducing the need to train end-users on each individual PACS. Since VNA supports all types of data formats so that any system can interpret them, having stored not only standardized files like DICOM (non-proprietary) but also format files like jpg, tiff, pdf, mp4, and txt. VNA is capable of handling content in other formats, such as HL7, RIS, and Hospital Information System context-wide archives. Radiology image management is no longer just PACS since VNA has solidified its market share, changing the way and practices for storing and manipulating patient data [51].

One of the reasons why neutrality is already highlighted in the VNA name is the ease with which it is possible to store and make available, for consultation and sharing, patient information in different formats. It also adapts to PACS and other systems from any manufacturer. When one of these systems needs to be replaced with a newer or even branded version, for example, VNA remains functional. While high-quality customer service is not a tangible feature of any PACS or VNA system, it is essential to the selection process. Choosing which infrastructure components to deploy, how to upgrade, how to migrate data between different systems, and how to enable enterprise-wide collaboration can be a challenge for executive leaders [51].

In a scenario of a clinic with three PACS systems, a physician who wants to look at a patient's images across all systems will need to open three different viewers, log in three different times, and search for the patient in three different ways, while keeping in mind that the physician would need to manually look at, process, and remember the images. This process can be problematic for doctors since multiple logins are time-consuming, and it is difficult to use fragmented data for patient care. While PACS can reliably store large amounts of image data, it can quickly become inefficient in complex organizations. Or even consider an acute scenario of a doctor dealing with a stroke, in which case time is of the essence. When doctors are given access to PACS or VNA images faster, they can make a faster diagnosis and initiate the appropriate treatment process faster [51].

VNAs address two important interoperability issues brought about by PACS, related to the ability to share data between multiple PACSs within the same organization, and the ability to read files when organizations switch PACS providers. Since PACS providers commonly use their own proprietary software, this causes problems when doctors need to view a file. And if an organization changes its PACS provider, the new system will have difficulty reading data because the format used could only be read by the original provider system. All VNA vendors are in agreement with the storage and network interface for DICOM images and administrative updates. DICOM enables compatibility between systems and software from different vendors, so entities can access files without any interoperability issues. Like PACS, VNAs is a difficult technology to deploy, but they improve image workflows and ensure proper storage and access [51].

So, selecting the right solution whether PACS or VNA is a complex decision, but the most important step is to identify a true VNA product or a rebranded PACS solution. VNA has neither a clinical viewer nor a display tool that doctors can use effectively; the system is not a professional medical visualization system. It is in fact and, by definition, a medical file system, while

PACS is an image display and manipulation system that includes functions for measurements, windowing, reporting, along with a storage system. In short, VNA is a backend system, and PACS is a frontend system [51].

VNA is a multi-PACS system, intending to connect to different products from different suppliers, that is, it is possible to consolidate in a single store all the medical image files of a company and has the ability to cross-reference studies with different access numbers and patients with different IDs as a single patient. It is also multienterprise given the amount of medical information that has to be dealt with which tends to get bigger every day. Noncloud-based clinics and hospitals need a complex and often extensive hardware structure [52].

All information can be stored in the cloud, but it is also possible to limit local hardware to store only some volume of information and can transfer old history to the cloud storage platform. Online information needs to have the integrity of this information, given that a serious problem in local hardware could irreversibly compromise the data. That is why backup is so important, since the best medical imaging services are more than just a backup, where they duplicate information entirely, and they rely on specialized IT teams [51, 52].

Thus, before choosing the VNA provider, it is important to verify that it works according to the requirements of internationally recognized certifications, such as the Health Insurance Portability and Accountability Act (HIPAA), a US law that standardizes electronic healthcare transactions in the US market. Organizations can still successfully use PACS to deal with medical imaging quickly and effectively, nevertheless, VNAs should be considered a promising option to reduce long-term costs and enable greater interoperability around critical image data [53].

## 6 Discussion

Another advantage is that radiologists who wish to give a second opinion according to patient results are allowed access and can even transfer this clinical data to the DICOM system and save the images in JPG format or CD media. While deploying the PACS system requires considerable financial investment and personnel training, the long-term consequences justify its practice, because this software reduces long-term operating costs.

RIS is a system used by the radiology department for: patient registration and scheduling; interfacing with equipment (worklist); image and patient tracking; digitization of documents; typing and issuance of reports; and materials management. Conceptually RIS and PACS are separate modules but can be organized in other ways, working together.

PACS can be viewed as a computer network that stores, retrieves, distributes, and displays medical images and data, and has the ability to handle different types of medical device images, such as mammography, ultrasound, and X-ray, among other machines. The workflow that ranges from capturing image data to archiving it on PACS, CT, and X-ray devices follows its basic applicability by performing the preprocessing, compression, and security of PACS image metadata in the acquisition of these different types of equipment and converts them into standard DICOM formats, being sent to a PACS controller or a workstation display.

Some standards allow integration between different systems. The best known are HL7and DICOM, which are ANSI standards established in 1987 that allow data to be exchanged between different health information systems. Among the various types of messages present in healthcare systems are: patient admission; laboratory test result; and patient account billing.

Problems encountered in HL7 are derived from the fact that it does not determine which parts of the protocol to implement, so vendor compatibility testing is not possible, which leads to interoperability issues. As far as is known, the new version 3.0 promises to solve these HL7 problems. One standard found for documents that are structured is according to the Clinical Document Architecture, which proposes a framework for exchanging clinical documents; using Extensible Markup Language, Reference Information Model, HL7 Data Types, and controlled vocabularies (such as SNOMED, LOINC, and others) to ensure interoperability. The DICOM standard was published in 1993 by the American College of Radiology and the National Electrical Manufacturers Association, where it was adopted by the manufacturers of imaging equipment (resonance, tomographs, ultrasound, among others), defining primarily how a medical image should be stored on permanent media and how it is transmitted over a network.

Cloud computing is a topic that has been widely discussed in many areas, especially in healthcare because of the benefits that technological developments bring to the sector, which can reduce costs, increase efficiency, give more flexibility, scale resources, and reduce software deployment time. Also, it is seen as the promise for PACS to generate more agility and security. This method helps store, manage, and process data from different locations by providing hosted services over the internet. Cost savings are still the biggest appeal to the service industries. In this digital caravan, there is no shortage of other advantages for the healthcare market, such as the ability to share patient information among healthcare professionals, the increased speed and flexibility of services, or the real-time management of medical images, which will each have PACS cloud availability. Similarly, mobile devices will become increasingly popular in the medical field, with thousands of mobile health (mHealth) applications supporting healthcare professionals and patients. This integration tends to be done in cloud environments where operating costs are lower and constraints are more contained in the connectivity vector.

In the local PACS model, the company needs to configure a server and network to do this management, requiring a hiring investment that serves to install the equipment in the unit. As a result, the imaging center needs to provide a room that has ideal conditions for this, remembering that this equipment is where all exams and patient information are stored and, like any device, is at risk of malfunction. Besides, it is also necessary to provide qualified personnel to manage the new software purchased. Still, in this same PACS model, there are systems sold as cloud services, but they work the same way as local ones. The difference is that the equipment is located in the headquarters of the service provider itself but is subject to the same risks. In the PACS cloud model, all these processes occur differently, since the contracted service does not require investment for installation and since the information is all stored in the cloud, it is not necessary to install any kind of equipment. Therefore, the clinic does not need to have physical space or hire responsible staff. The cloud PACS service also offers qualified support to meet all demands on the tool. In addition, this model offers much greater security, since it is not dependent on a physical server, is not at risk of being damaged, and has many backup options. Investing is also customized, where each unit has a monthly subscription according to its exam volume. And yet, this format further facilitates communication with patients and medical staff, with login and password, and it is possible to access the system from anywhere.

In short, there are two main cloud applications in diagnostic medicine, and storing images in PACS will make images produced in resonances, CT scans, and other types of exams stored in the cloud easier to use tools that allow image reconstruction on other planes, such as multiplanar reconstruction, projection of maximum, minimum, and average intensity, and even the use of three-dimensional (3D) views. Cloud storage facilitates deployment of a report center and increases productivity in diagnostic medicine and patient safety and reduces healthcare costs, allowing for excellent services to be brought to locations farther away from large urban centers, locations that often lack trained professionals and adequate equipment. The mobility of cloud computing makes exams and reports stored through the integration between PACS and RIS available anywhere, such as in the operating room, in the office of a professional who assesses the evolution of a cancerous tumor, or even when doctor and patient are in different locations.

Although data handling by PACS systems brings a lot of benefits, as detailed and previously mentioned, it can also offer challenges in data storage, indexing, and sharing. Data security may be one of the biggest challenges of this technology. When dealing with this type of digital integration, above all, it is necessary to preserve internal and patient information, that is, sensitive data, in order to prevent possible leaks (in line with the General Data Protection Law in force in several countries).

New technology trends associated with the handling of digital images via PACS for cloud computing technology brings many benefits associated with easy access to data and the resources to manage it, including: access to high-resolution, high-quality images from anywhere; a scalable system generating flexibility, making it adaptable to different levels of technology and business models; resilience against system failures and operational efficiency; less of an initial investment in equipment and maintenance; "pay when and how much to use" data centers, which reduces the cost of ownership, infrastructure, and storage, resulting in rapid implementation. There are also challenges for storing, indexing, and sharing data, such as: difficulty transferring a large volume of data stored on-site to the cloud; a conservative view of doctors and radiologists about cloud computing; doubts about interoperability and security in the cloud; difficulty obtaining the necessary commitment from the supplier regarding data confidentiality.

In this sense, the obstacles exist, but they need to be overcome, since running PACS in the cloud is a logical step for IT aimed at medical images, considering that the benefits are material, not only in terms of cost, time, and risk savings reduced but primarily on how hospitals can better support all of their clinical functions.

## 7 Future trends

Three-dimensional printing can make use of images stored by PACS for numerous healthcare applications, since it is a technology known for its ability to create low-cost prostheses, the technique has been refined and already allows other types of uses, such as the construction of team training prototypes before high-risk surgical procedures. From the tomography-generated 3D model, doctors can produce a life-size copy, and with it, rehearse, combine, and propose solutions to everything that could go wrong, and as soon as it is actually applied, surgery is a success. Since it is necessary to manipulate the sectional images of computed tomography to select the region or organ to be represented in 3D. This step depends on both anatomical knowledge and familiarity with graphical features. There is specific software that allows this segmentation and exports the selected area in a graphic file format that can be printed in 3D, but increasingly, this functionality has been incorporated by PACS [54, 55].

From the evolution of the equipment of CT scanners and magnetic resonance scanners to produce sharper 3D images with extremely high resolution and less noise, it will be possible to view 3D image exams and create photorealistic images of the anatomy, helping in planning and interpretation of surgery to determine whether a tumor is cancerous. In addition, breast tomosynthesis (3D mammography) is now the standard of care for screening mammography, while 3D ultrasound ensures that the ultrasound has captured the entire anatomy with scanning. Many of these advances are possible due to the computational power that is currently available at a relatively low cost, and the increase in network speed allows the transmission of large data sets in 3D images [56].

In this regard, cognitive technology will play a role as a supplementary lens for the analysis of medical images, identifying more subtle changes in digitizations and reducing the time for planning treatment and analyzing large amounts of data. The use of this technology and the evolution of the 3D image are complementary, as there is an enormous amount of information in the images that can be analyzed by a computer and presented to the specialist or responsible physician. Through cognitive technology, it will be possible to achieve an advanced tomography, whose algorithms promise to identify the most delicate changes in organ tissues, which can lead to the earlier identification of diseases [56].

Also through cognitive technology, it will be possible to achieve advanced MRI, accelerating the adoption of diagnostic medicine, exemplifying the case of brain MRI, and through the deep learning algorithm, accessing a vast database of clinical images to identify anatomical structures of the brain. It is trained to automatically select the brain slices to be scanned, which should help reduce manual effort and eliminate redundancies [57].

With the cognitive technology in mammography exams, it will be possible to obtain precision helping in the breast cancer detection process (especially in the initial stage) through the deep learning algorithm, allowing more accurate diagnoses by automatically identifying tissue lesions and calcifications, and even combining the findings of all available visualizations in a single breast cancer suspicion index [58, 59].

Related outcome indicators in the pursuit of an increasingly intelligent information network lead to a demand for systems that allow the mining of raw data, turning it into contextualized information that supports management and clinical decisions. Investing in improving RIS and PACS systems promises greater clarity and correlation of information. Increasing system integration across systems, grouping, and correlating PEP data with PACS and RIS ensures greater efficiency. The integration of the systems allows greater security in the diagnosis since control protocols are created and used at the time of issuing the reports. These protocols have the role of avoiding risks such as name changes at the time of issue. Cloud-based report collaboration enables a joint analysis of an image or even submission to experts in other regions of the country, increasing diagnostic accuracy [60].

## 8 Conclusions

In summary, CC is a set of techniques and algorithms that help transform data into information through data extraction and interpretation, given that technology allows knowledge to be shared intelligently. CC allows computers and applications to digitally understand problems with capabilities similar to those of the human brain, querying the vast libraries of knowledge (dataset), which a person would never be able to process on time, to offer a better solution found for each data medical issue.

Making a comparison, just like a human being, cognitive systems have properties to read new information, learning and recognizing this information better with each interaction. Cognitive systems also learn in a supervised manner, that is, they need a data curator, who has deep knowledge about the domain of knowledge, and through this system is trained and taught so that it learns correctly. While the system evolves over time, it is possible to have unsupervised learning or even reinforced learning.

And so, it is a fact that by integrating and analyzing large data sets, systems based on CC learn to interpret technical and specific medical jargon, apply high-level intelligent digital reasoning, and in some cases, predictive modeling, to develop solutions and comprehensive results that result in a higher quality of data analysis, as is done in diagnostic imaging exams.

At the same step that the advancement of technology enables several changes in health organizations, especially in diagnostic medicine, the digitization of information through the use of PACS and the storage of data in the cloud change the work routine of the radiologist, allowing mobility. This scenario breaks physical barriers and allows the elaboration of reports at a distance. It is possible to access image exams not only from computers but also from mobile devices, such as mobile phones and tablets, which facilitates access to information and changes the routines of professionals and managers. The PACS solution is critical for medical image management as it manages the storage and sharing of images generated by various devices, facilitating workflow and increasing productivity.

A PACS consists of a multiplicity of devices, the first step in typical PACS systems is the modality. The modalities are usually CT, ultrasound, nuclear medicine, PET, and MRI. Depending on the installation workflow, most modalities send to a workstation, which is a checkpoint for certifying that the exam is correct, and other important attributes are present for analyzing this image.

Despite the early stages of the cloud-based PACS concept, it makes many advances for healthcare providers and patients possible in the end. Mobility can increase medical productivity and support diagnosis, as having a patient's history of exams at hand, at all times and places, allows better monitoring of their health. With proper care in the protection of information, mobility can help to speed up work routines and even influence the profitability of the diagnostic center, as it allows more reports to be prepared in less time.

## References


[1] A. Peck, Clark's Essential PACS, RIS and Imaging Informatics, CRC Press, 2017.

[2] M. Abdekhoda, K.M. Salih, Determinant factors in applying picture archiving and communication systems (PACS) in healthcare, Perspect. Health Inf. Manag. 14 (Summer) (2017).

[3] S. Bryan, G. Weatherburn, J. Watkins, M. Roddie, J. Keen, N. Muris, M.J. Buxton, Radiology report times: impact of picture archiving and communication systems, AJR Am. J. Roentgenol. 170 (5) (1998) 1153–1159.

[4] M.D. Kovacs, M.Y. Cho, P.F. Burchett, M. Trambert, Benefits of integrated RIS/PACS/reporting due to automatic population of templated reports, Curr. Probl. Diagn. Radiol. 48 (1) (2019) 37–39.

[5] S. Bryan, G.C. Weatherburn, J.R. Watkins, M.J. Buxton, The benefits of hospital-wide picture archiving and communication systems: a survey of clinical users of radiology services, Br. J. Radiol. 72 (857) (1999) 469–478.

[6] M.S. Tabatabaei, M. Langarizadeh, K. Tavakol, An evaluation protocol for picture archiving and communication system: a systematic review, Acta Inform. Med. 25 (4) (2017) 250.

[7] M. Santos, L. Bastiao, C. Costa, A. Silva, N. Rocha, Clinical data mining in small hospital PACS: contributions for radiology department improvement, in: Healthcare Administration: Concepts, Methodologies, Tools, and Applications, IGI Global, 2015, pp. 47–65.

[8] Y. Wang, B. Widrow, L.A. Zadeh, N. Howard, S. Wood, V.C. Bhavsar, D.F. Shell, Cognitive intelligence: deep learning, thinking, and reasoning by brain-inspired systems, Int J. Cogn. Inform Nat. Intell. (IJCINI) 10 (4) (2016) 1–20.

[9] J. Xu, W. Lu, F. Xue, K. Chen, Cognitive facility management: definition, system architecture, and example scenario, Autom. Constr. 107 (2019) 102922.

[10] R.P. França, Y. Iano, A.C.B. Monteiro, R. Arthur, Intelligent applications of WSN in the world: a technological and literary background, in: Handbook of Wireless Sensor Networks: Issues and Challenges in Current Scenario's, Springer, Cham, 2020, pp. 13–34.

[11] A.C.B. Monteiro, et al., Development of a laboratory medical algorithm for simultaneous detection and counting of erythrocytes and leukocytes in digital images of a blood smear, in: Deep Learning Techniques for Biomedical and Health Informatics, Academic Press, 2020, pp. 165–186.

[12] R.P. França, et al., Potential proposal to improve data transmission in healthcare systems, in: Deep Learning Techniques for Biomedical and Health Informatics, Academic Press, 2020, pp. 267–283.

[13] J. Hurwitz, et al., Cognitive Computing and Big Data Analytics, Wiley, Indianapolis, IN, 2015.

[14] R.P. França, et al., An overview of Web 2.0 and its technologies and their impact in the modern era, in: Handbook of Research on User Experience in Web 2.0 Technologies and Its Impact on Universities and Businesses, 2020, pp. 73–93.

[15] R.P. França, A.C.B. Monteiro, R. Arthur, Y. Iano, An overview of internet of things technology applied on precision agriculture concept, in: Precision Agriculture Technologies for Food Security and Sustainability, 2021, pp. 47–70.

[16] A.C.B. Monteiro, Proposta de uma metodologia de segmentação de imagens para detecção e contagem de hemácias e leucócitos através do algoritmo WT-MO, 2019.

[17] S. Gupta, A.K. Kar, A. Baabdullah, W.A. Al-Khowaiter, Big data with cognitive computing: a review for the future, Int. J. Inf. Manag. 42 (2018) 78–89.

[18] S.A. Shah, X. Yang, Q.H. Abbasi, Cognitive health care system and its application in pill-rolling assessment, Int. J. Numer. Modell. Electron. Netw. Dev. Fields 32 (6) (2019), e2632.

[19] A.C.B. Monteiro, et al., Health 4.0 as an application of industry 4.0 in healthcare services and management, Med. Technol. J. 2 (4) (2018) 262–276.

[20] A.C.B. Monteiro, et al., Health 4.0: applications, management, technologies and review, Pers. Med. 5 (2019) 6.

[21] R.P. França, et al., Big data and cloud computing: a technological and literary background, in: Advanced Deep Learning Applications in Big Data Analytics, IGI Global, 2021, pp. 29–50.

[22] R.P. França, et al., A proposal based on discrete events for improvement of the transmission channels in cloud environments and big data, in: Big Data, IoT, and Machine Learning: Tools and Applications, CRC Press, 2020, pp. 185–204.

[23] M. Chen, et al., Edge cognitive computing-based smart healthcare system, Futur. Gener. Comput. Syst. 86 (2018) 403–411.

[24] M. Chen, et al., A 5G cognitive system for healthcare, Big Data Cogn. Comput. 1 (1) (2017) 2.

[25] S.A. Clark, Secure Integration of Information Systems in Radiology, Murray State University, 2018.

[26] J. Papp, Quality Management in the Imaging Sciences E-Book, Elsevier Health Sciences, 2018.

[27] D. Kessel, I. Robertson, Interventional Radiology: A Survival Guide E-Book, Elsevier Health Sciences, 2016.

[28] B.P. Chang, A.F. Arriaga, S.M. Hassan, P. Kidik, D.L. Hepner, S.R. Lipsitz, D.J. Correll, Improving efficiency in preoperative assessment: a pilot study on visit times for preoperative evaluation, Perioper. Care Operat. Room Manag. 11 (2018) 1–9.

[29] V. Desai, A. Flanders, A.C. Zoga, Leveraging technology to improve radiology workflow, Semin. Musculoskelet. Radiol. 22 (05) (2018, November) 528–539. Thieme Medical Publishers.

[30] R. Álvarez, J.H. Legarreta, L. Kabongo, G. Epelde, I. Macía, Towards a deconstructed PACS-as-a-service system, in: International Conference on Innovation in Medicine and Healthcare, Springer, Cham, 2017, June, pp. 234–243.

[31] M. Karthiyayini, V. Thavavel, N.S. Selvam, Cloud-based vendor neutral archive: reduces imaging rates and enhances patient care, in: 2015 International Conference on Advanced Computing and Communication Systems, IEEE, 2015, January, pp. 1–4.

[32] S.J. Berkowitz, J.L. Wei, S. Halabi, Migrating to the modern PACS: challenges and opportunities, Radiographics 38 (6) (2018) 1761–1772.

[33] J.W. Gardner, K.K. Boyer, J.V. Gray, Operational and strategic information processing: complementing healthcare IT infrastructure, J. Oper. Manag. 33 (2015) 123–139.

[34] J.M. Ehrenfeld, J.D. Gonzalo, Health Systems Science Review E-Book, Elsevier Health Sciences, 2019.

[35] T. Benson, G. Grieve, Standards development organizations, in: Principles of Health Interoperability, Springer, Cham, 2016, pp. 103–118.

[36] M. Diehl, T. Klein, V. Powell, American National Standards for health data integration, in: Integration of Medical and Dental Care and Patient Data, Springer, Cham, 2019, pp. 253–266.

[37] L. Mineiro, P. Tomé, The integration of radiology information systems, in: 2015 10th Iberian Conference on Information Systems and Technologies (CISTI), IEEE, 2015, June, pp. 1–6.

[38] S.E. Vaala, J.M. Lee, K.K. Hood, S.A. Mulvaney, Sharing and helping: predictors of adolescents' willingness to share diabetes personal health information with peers, J. Am. Med. Inform. Assoc. 25 (2) (2017) 135–141.

[39] J.A. Awokola, J.O. Emuoyibofarhe, C. Meinel, F.A. Ajala, Performance evaluation of A cloud-based picture archiving and communication system (PACS), Ann. Comput. Sci. Ser 17 (1) (2019).

[40] M.S. Marcolino, J.A.Q. Oliveira, M. D'Agostino, A.L. Ribeiro, M.B.M. Alkmim, D. Novillo-Ortiz, The impact of mHealth interventions: systematic review of systematic reviews, JMIR Mhealth Uhealth 6 (1) (2018), e23.

[41] W.A. Ribeiro, M. Andrade, D.M. Frash, P.P.C. Santana, D.M. Souza, V.L. Almeida, Implementação do prontuário eletrônico do paciente: um estudo bibliográfico das vantagens e desvantagens para o serviço de saúde, Revista Pró-UniverSUS 9 (1) (2018) 07–11.

[42] Z.S.N. Reis, R.J.C. Correia, A.D.C. Pereira, Sistemas eletrônicos de informação na assistência e pesquisa em saúde da mulher: para quando um maior envolvimento dos profissionais de saúde, Rev. Bras. Ginecol. Obstet. 33 (3) (2011) 107–110.

[43] T.F. Heston, Introductory chapter: telemedicine, in: Telemedicine, IntechOpen, 2018.

[44] R. Marcu, D. Popescu, I. Danila, Healthcare integration based on cloud computing, UPB Sci. Bull 77 (2) (2015) 31–42.

[45] J.W. Song, M.C. Mango, L.M. Museru, A. Kesselman, K. Foryoung, O. Kiloloma, F.J. Minja, Successful implementation of a PACS in Tanzania, J. Am. Coll. Radiol. 14 (5) (2017) 710–713.

[46] W. Budianto, D. Napitupulu, K. Adiyarta, A.P. Windarto, Requirement analysis of PACS and RIS hospital management information system on radiology installation based on Kano method, J. Phys. Conf. Ser. 1255 (1) (2019, August), 012053. IOP Publishing.

[47] L. Liu, W. Chen, M. Nie, F. Zhang, Y. Wang, A. He, G. Yan, iMAGE cloud: medical image processing as a service for regional healthcare in a hybrid cloud environment, Environ. Health Prev. Med. 21 (6) (2016) 563–571.

[48] C.T. Yang, W.C. Shih, L.T. Chen, C.T. Kuo, F.C. Jiang, F.Y. Leu, Accessing medical image file with co-allocation HDFS in cloud, Futur. Gener. Comput. Syst. 43 (2015) 61–73.

[49] E. Seeram, Medical imaging informatics: an overview, in: Digital Radiography, Springer, Singapore, 2019, pp. 165–183.

[50] A. Parikh, N. Mehta, PACS: next generation, in: Medical Imaging 2015: PACS and Imaging Informatics: Next Generation and Innovations, vol. 9418, International Society for Optics and Photonics, 2015, March, p. 94180G.

[51] D. Haak, C.E. Page, S. Reinartz, T. Krüger, T.M. Deserno, DICOM for clinical research: PACS-integrated electronic data capture in multi-center trials, J. Digit. Imaging 28 (5) (2015) 558–566.

[52] L.J.R. Pereira, Serão todos os exames radiológicos pedidos posteriormente acedidos pelos médicos? Análise de registos de um Sistema de Informação Radiológico, 2012.

[53] P.F. Edemekong, M.J. Haydel, Health insurance portability and accountability act (HIPAA), in: StatPearls [Internet], StatPearls Publishing, 2019.

[54] G. Kuhn, T. Zhao, D.J. Guigonis, J.L. Sorenson, D.W. MacCutcheon, U.S. Patent No. 10,275,927, U.S. Patent and Trademark Office, Washington, DC, 2019.

[55] H. Feldman, P. Kamali, S.J. Lin, J.D. Halamka, Clinical 3D printing: a protected health information (PHI) and compliance perspective, Int. J. Med. Inform. 115 (2018) 18–23.

[56] K. Doi, Diagnostic imaging over the last 50 years: research and development in medical imaging science and technology, Phys. Med. Biol. 51 (13) (2006) R5.

[57] C.D. Papadaniil, et al., Cognitive MMN and P300 in mild cognitive impairment and Alzheimer's disease: a high-density EEG-3D vector field tomography approach, Brain Res. 1648 (2016) 425–433.

[58] S. Wang, et al., Accelerating magnetic resonance imaging via deep learning, in: 2016 IEEE 13th International Symposium on Biomedical Imaging (ISBI), IEEE, 2016.

[59] Y. Zheng, et al., Early breast cancer detection with digital mammograms using Haar-like features and AdaBoost algorithm, in: Sensing and Analysis Technologies for Biomedical and Cognitive Applications 2016, vol. 9871, International Society for Optics and Photonics, 2016.

[60] J. Muschelli, Recommendations for processing head CT data, Front. Neuroinform. 13 (2019) 61.

Chapter 6

# Change detection techniques for a remote sensing application: An overview

**Rohini Selvaraj and Sureshkumar Nagarajan**
*School of Computer Science and Engineering, Vellore Institute of Technology, Vellore, Tamil Nadu, India*

## 1 Introduction

Change detection is a way to identify changes in the condition of land features by sensing them at different times. Pinpointing the geographical location, measuring the form of change, and testing the precision of the changes are all common goals for the detection of a change in remote sensing (RS). Auspicious and accurate change detection of the Earth's surface feature helps identify the relationship and interaction between the human and nature to use and better manage the resource. Change detection is suitable for numerous applications like coastal change, rate of land degradation, urban sprawl, and land-use change. Land use/ land cover (LULC) change detection is among the most relevant applications of change detection in this chapter. Land cover [1] states that the physical attributes of the Earth's surface, encapsulated in the exchange of vegetation, sea, topsoil, and some additional environmental aspects of the Earth, including all those created purely by human activities. Land use indicates how land is being used by individuals and their surroundings, usually with an emphasis on the systematic role of land for commercial development. In broad, change detection includes the utilization of a multitemporal dataset to systematically assess the quantitative influences of the occurrence.

Change detection usability for real-world applications is complicated and requires various processing steps, like the detection of correct periods of an image, the preprocessing of images, and the specification of an application-specific algorithm. This method begins with the finding of an image, which is a series of RS images of the same location founded at various times. Such images are influenced by geospatial and atmospheric interference and should be corrected to remove the interference. This method is achieved by

**Cognitive Systems and Signal Processing in Image Processing. https://doi.org/10.1016/B978-0-12-824410-4.00015-5**

preprocessing. After that, the change identification algorithm is used to identify changes to distinguish them into change and no change areas.

In the earlier stage, change detection is done by the visual interpretation method. Martin and Howrath [2] proposed a method for rural to urban change detection by visual analysis of spot multispectral image. Singh [3] reviewed some traditional change detection methods like thresholding and digital change detection method. Stow et al. [4] compared the rationing multisensor, multidate satellite imagery with the principal component (PC) method for change detection. They used the Landsat/Multispectral Scanner (MSS) with SPOT/High Resolution Visible (HRV) multispectral (XS) data or Landsat/Thematic Mapper (TM). Manavalan et al. [5] proposed a change detection method with IRS-LISS 2 data. Metternicht [6] practiced fuzzy set pixel-based change detection for land cover detection. The switch over from pixel-based to object-based [7] practices were experimented with by Willhauck [8]. Zhanguo and Dent [9] applied a vegetation index differencing technique intended for land cover change detection and decreased the impact of topographic effects and illumination. Listner and Niemeyer [10] explained different object-based image analyses (OBIA) with IR-MAD for change detection. Combinations of pixel-based and object-based change detection are called hybrid change detection. Xu et al. [11] had given details about these techniques. Fig. 1 shows the evolution of the change detection technique from 1985 to 2019.

This article highlights approaches for detecting changes, reviews their implementations, and gives the basics for selecting appropriate methods for detecting changes. This article is organized into five sections as follows. The first section elaborates the introduction about the change detection method and related work. The second section discusses the RS data and its type. The third section discusses data preprocessing. The fourth section provides a review of comparative change detection techniques. The final section discusses the conclusion of this article.

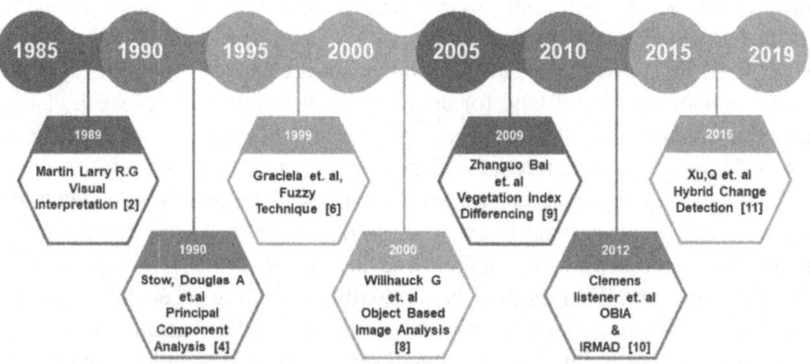


**FIG. 1** Timeline chart for the evolution of change detection technique.

## 2 Remote sensing data

RS images are widely used to detect changes in LULC identification. The images acquired from the satellite vary as far as brightness, color, and wavelength. The resolution of an image determines the quality of the detail in the image pixel. The kind of sensor utilized and the highness of the satellite's path mostly decide the resolution of the image. The following elements pretend the change detection using satellite data, such as atmospheric condition, spatial, temporal, spectral, and thematic constraints, soil moisture condition, and radiometric resolution. Selection of appropriate data and change detection may reduce the effect of satellite data. The data from the same satellite eliminate radiometric and spatial constrain and relatively close data eliminate the effect of seasons. An image preprocessing technique is used to compensate for the other effect. Most of the researchers practice with spatial resolution data, such as Landsat, MODIS, SPOT, and radar. Very-high resolution optical satellites, such as Quick Bird, IKONOS, Rapid Eye, and Geo Eye, are used only for qualitative analysis and object-based image analysis. Md. Inzamul Haque [12], Islam et al. [13], Zhanguo and Dent [9], and Mashame and Akinyemi [14] used Landsat (3,4,5,7,8) images for their research. Spot (1–7) images were used for change detection by Martin and Howarth [2], Zhanguo and Dent [9], and Akay and Sertel [15]. Johansen et al. [16] uses Quick Bird images for change detection analysis.

## 3 Data preprocessing

Data preprocessing is known to be the most critical stage of image processing to achieve greater accuracy. Satellite data is influenced by multiple factors, including geographical, spectral, temporal, and atmospheric conditions. Image preprocessing eliminates this effect by some correction processes such as geometric correction and radiometric correction. Geometric [17] is an inevitable process in change detection, geometric correction involves image registration and rectification. Geometric disasters are carried out because of the changes in sensor, sensor positioning, Earth axis, and terrain effect. Radiometric correction [12, 18] resolves the error produced by the variant in atmospheric circumstance, solar angle, sensor characteristic, and view angle. Radiometric correction [19] is carried out in different ways such as absolute radiometric correction (ARC) and relative radiometric correction (RRC).

## 4 Change detection technique

Change detection techniques are classified into various categories: (1) algebra, (2) transformation, (3) classification, (4) geographic information system (GIS) approaches, (5) visual inspection, and (6) other approaches. The sixth category contains some change detection algorithms that are not appropriate for

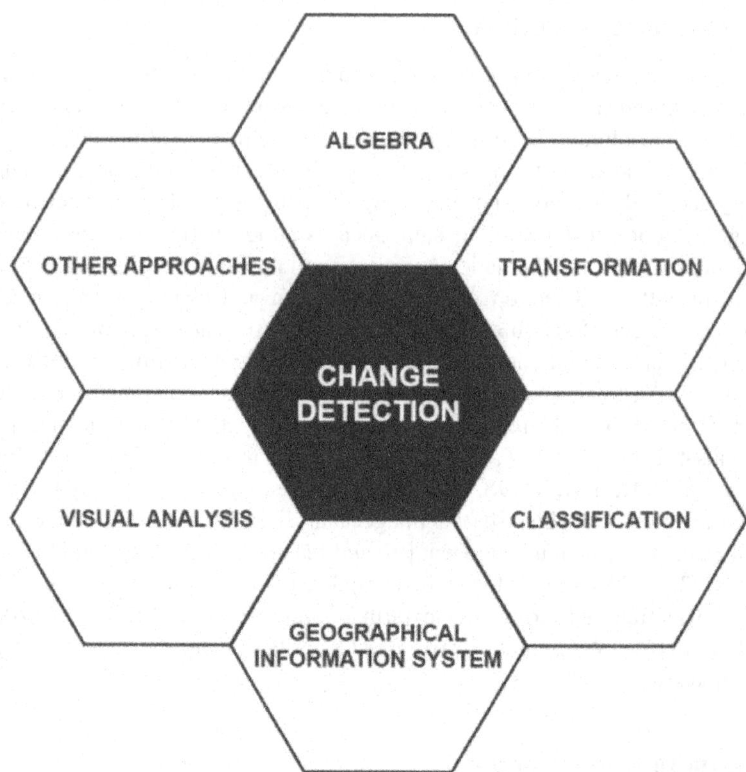


**FIG. 2** Categories of change detection technique.

classification into any of the five groups and are not yet commonly used in nature. Fig. 2 demonstrates the groups of the methodology for detecting change.

## 4.1 Algebra approach

The algebra category comprises image regression, image differentiation, vegetation index differentiation, image rationing, and change vector analysis (CVA). These algebraic groups have a mutual feature, such as the distribution of thresholds to identify modified areas. Besides the CVA, these approaches are relatively straightforward, easy to execute, and easy to follow, but they cannot provide full change matrix knowledge. The major disadvantage of the algebra type is the complexity of choosing appropriate thresholds to identify changed regions. In this type, two attributes are very difficult to detect, one selecting acceptable image bands or vegetation indices and the other selecting appropriate thresholds to recognize the modified areas. The list of methods used in the algebra approach is shown in Fig. 3.

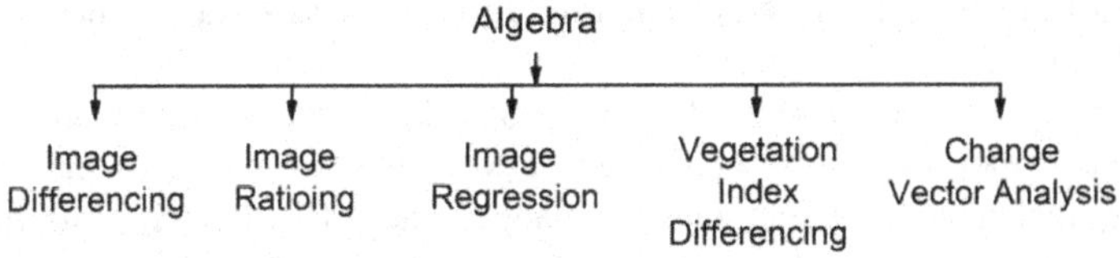

**FIG. 3** List of methods in algebra approach.

### *4.1.1 Image differencing*

Subtracting the imagery of one date from that of another is called image differencing. In this process, the representation of a related spatial space, obtained from times $t1$ and $t2$, is subtracted by pixel insight. Quantitatively, the difference in the image is:

$$Id(x,y) = I_1(x,y) - I_2(x,y) \tag{1}$$

Here $I_1$ and $I_2$ are the images taken from $t1$ and $t2$ $(x, y)$ and are also the positions of the pixels. The resultant image is $Id$, representing the difference in intensity between $I_1$ and $I_2$. This approach only works if the images are registered. Manavalan et al. [5], Karthik and Shivakumar [20], and Karnieli et al. [21] use the image differencing technique for their research. This technique mostly suits urban land cover changes at the urban fringe from SPOT HRV imagery and change detection in forest ecosystems. With this technique, the difficult thing is to find the threshold values for change and no change in the resulting images. For the selection of the threshold value, the standard deviation is used as a means. The fundamental principle on the use of RS data for the detection of changes is that changes in the land cover must result in changes in radiance values that must be significant concerning radiance changes caused by other factors due to land cover changes. Based on this guidance, people could expect that dissimilarity in intensity due to land cover change resides at the tails of the image's difference distribution. Considering that land distribution changes are not as much as changes by various factors, we assume that a big part of the thing that matters is spread across the average.

### *4.1.2 Image ratioing*

Like image differencing, pictures are viewed pixel-wise in this technique. Images must always be registered in advance. The image ratio, an employed strategy used here, is determined by:

$$I_r(x,y) = \frac{I_1(x,\ y)}{I_2(x,\ y)} \tag{2}$$

In Eq. (2), the $I_r$ image takes values in the range $[0,\infty)$. The order of the images in the division is not significant, unlike in image differencing, as the effects of the change are represented in ratios, and areas that are not changed should generally have a value of 1.

In the area of conversion, the ratio would be greater or less than 1 and is contingent upon the nature of change between the two dates. If the value of $I_r$ is equivalent to 1, it specifies no change. The difficulty with this method is that the choice of threshold value between change and no change is an interesting task. This technique is analyzed because of the semidistribution of the resultant image histogram. Liu et al. [22], Lu et al. [23], and Tomowski et al. [24] compare the image rationing technique with other techniques for land cover change detection. This approach reduces the effects of the shadow, angle, and topography of the sun. The nonnormal distribution of the outcome is frequently used.

### 4.1.3 Image regression

The image regression method establishes the correlation among bitemporal images, then uses a regression function to evaluate the pixel values of the second-date image and subtract the regressed image from the first-date image. It is assumed that the $I_2$ image obtained from $t2$ is a linear function of the $I_1$ image. Hereunder the assumption, by using least-squares regression as a minimum-squares regression, we can find an estimate of $I_2$.

$$I_2(x,y) = aI_1(x,y) + b \tag{3}$$

To calculate parameters $a$ and $b$, we define the squared error between the measured data. Luppino et al. [25] and Chen et al. [26] uses the image regression technique. This technique reduces the effects of the atmospheric, sensor, and environmental transformations between two-date images. The problem with methods is that accurate regression functions are required for the selected bands before implementing change detection.

### 4.1.4 Vegetation index differencing

The vegetation index is a statistical transition and is calculated to determine the impact of vegetation on multispectral mode interpretations. Based on high plant absorbance in the red and strong reflectance in the near-infrared band, these indices enrich the spectral variances. The vegetation indexes are normally developed separately for two images for change detection, and then standard pixel-based change detection (e.g., separation or rationing) is applied. Various vegetation indexes include: (1) the normalized difference vegetation index (NDVI); (2) the ratio-based ratio vegetation index (RVI); (3) orthogonal indexes, including the difference vegetation index (DVI) and the perpendicular vegetation index (PVI); and (4) the soil adjusted vegetation index (SAVI) and the modified SAVI (MSAVI).

$$RVI = \frac{n}{r} \tag{4}$$

$$NDVI = \frac{n - r}{n_r} \tag{5}$$

$$DVI = \sqrt{\frac{n - r}{n + r} + 0.5} \tag{6}$$

$$SAVI = \frac{n - r}{n - r + 1}(1 + L) \tag{7}$$

$$MSAVI = \frac{2n + 1 - \sqrt{(2n+1)^2 - 8(n - r)}}{2} \tag{8}$$

Where $n$ is the near-infrared band, and the red band is $r$. The same bond between NDVI and SAVI reinforces the $L$ in SAVI. By calculating the angle vegetation index, RVI and NDVI were updated and bitemporal vegetation time-dependent vegetation indices (TDVI) were created. It highlights variations in the spectral response of various characteristics and eliminates the impact of topographic and illumination effects. Julien et al. [27], Gillespie et al. [28] and Higginbottom and Symeonakis [29] apply this technique for land cover change detection. It decreases the impact of topographic effects and illumination, but it fails to attempt the random and coherence noise.

### 4.1.5 Change vector analysis

CVA is a technique where it is possible to analyze multiple image bands at the same time. As its name suggests, CVA not only serves as a means of identifying changes but also helps analyze and identify changes. In CVA, pixel values are spectral band vectors. Change vectors (CVs) are calculated by pixel-wise subtraction of vectors as in image differentiation. For change analysis, the magnitude and orientation of the CVs are used. As follows, this approach produces two outputs. Initial is spectral CV, which describes the direction and magnitude of change for a different date, and the next one is the cumulative magnitude of change per pixel, which is measured by calculating the Euclidean distance between endpoints across the $n$-dimensional space of change.

This method delivers detailed data about the change that occurred. The problems related to this method are that it is hard to describe the threshold of magnitude with the help of which perception between change and no change is interpreted and inferring the direction of the vector with the nature of change. CVA can also be conducted on training datasets (e.g., Kauth-ThomasTransformation, KTT). CVA based on LULC change detection is used in Chen et al. [30] and Salih et al. [31]. This method is used for application, which needs a full-dimensional data processing and analysis technique. The limitation of this method is only applied to the same phonological period data.

## 4.2 Transformation approach

The transformation groups include Gramm-Schmidt (GS), KTT, PC analysis (PCA), and Chi-square transformations. The benefit of these approaches is to minimize data redundancy between bands and to highlight various details in the resulting components On either hand, they never deliver comprehensive change matrixes and need to pick thresholds as an algebra category to define modified areas. A further drawback to these approaches is the complexity in understanding and marking improvements in the material on transformed images. A list of methods in the transformation approach is shown in Fig. 4.

### 4.2.1 *Principal component analysis*

This method depends on the covariance matrix or the eigenvector of the variance of the mixed data collection. This method is a multivariate analysis procedure that is utilized to lessen the spectral components to the lesser number of PCs, which are the purpose for the event of the majority of the difference in the primary multispectral images. For the decrease of spectral components, a regularly linear transformation is utilized. The linear transformation is performed on the multidate images and is consolidated to get a private dataset.

The idea in PCA is that the regions of no change are strongly correlated when areas of change are not. PC1 and PC2 are likely to represent the unchanged areas of multitemporal image processing, while PC3 and later PCs provide details about the transition. Two CD methodologies focused on PCA are used. The main distinct rotation is to separately obtain PCs from images and then use other CD techniques, such as differentiating images. The second is a consolidated approach in which bitemporal images are compiled into one collection and PCs are added. Compared to changes, PCs have a negative correlation to bitemporal data. Fung and Ledrew [32], Dharani and Sreenivasulu [33], and Listner and Niemeyer [10] use PCA for both pixel-based and object-based change detection.

### 4.2.2 *Kauth-Thomas transformation/tasseled cap transformation*

The KTT is a multiband and multidate dataset in linear transformation and differs from PCA in terms of being fixed. The greenness, brightness, and wetness reflect these performance characteristics. This method was presented by Kauth and Thomas in their 1976 spectral data pattern analysis. The definition of this approach is like a PCA. The only distinction is that PCA relies on the scene of

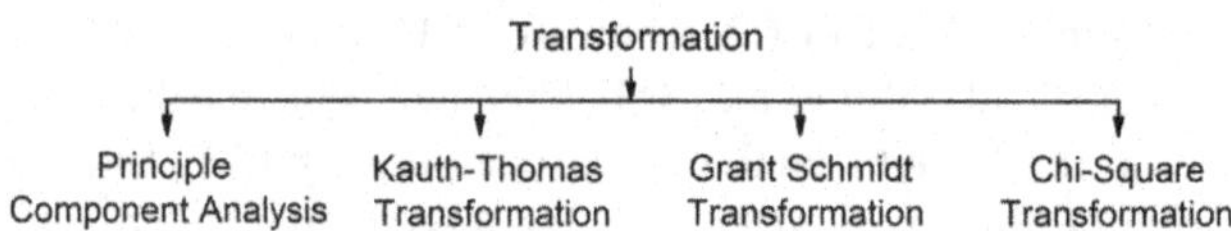


**FIG. 4** List of methods in the transformation approach.

the image, and the transformation of KTT is irrespective of the scene. This approach decreases redundant information between bands and focuses on various data in the derived components. Jin and Sader [34] worked on KTT transformation for indexing the disturbance. The KTT transition is independent of the scene, but it struggles to define and identify information about changes, it does not include a full change matrix, and to classify the modified places, it needs to decide the threshold value. Accurate calibration of the atmosphere for each image data is necessary.

By changing KTT, GS is designed to manage multitemporal data that generates constant components equivalent to multitemporal analogs of KTT illumination, greenness, and wetness, and a component of the transition.

### *4.2.3 Chi-square transform*

$$Y = (X - M)^T \sum\nolimits^{-1} \times (X - M) \tag{9}$$

Where $Y$: change the image with digital values, $M$: vector of the mean residuals of each band, $X$: vector of the variance of the six digital values among the two dates, $T$: transverse of the matrix, and $\sum^{-1}$: inverse covariance matrix of the six bands. The benefit of this approach is that several bands are concurrently measured to generate a single image shift. The concept that the value of $Y = 0$ reflects a pixel of no change is not valid when a significant part of the image is shifted. Also, the change related to the particular spectral orientation is not easily detected.

## 4.3 Classification approaches

Classification type involves expectation-maximixation (EM) algorithm change detection, postclassification comparison, artificial neural network (ANN), hybrid change detection, unsupervised change detection, and spectral-temporal blended analysis. The consistency of the identification shall be determined by the quality and quantity of the training results. The key benefit of this approach is that it can provide reliable adjustment information that is not much influenced by external influences, such as atmospheric change interferences, and these approaches are capable of producing information on the matrix of transition. It is always difficult to select high-quality and sufficiently various training sample sets for image classification, particularly for the classification of past image data. These approaches are time-consuming methods, and the demanding challenge of generating highly precise classifications frequently leads to errors in the outcomes of change identification, particularly when high-quality sample data for training is not available. The list of classification strategies in the technique of shift detection is presented in Fig. 5.

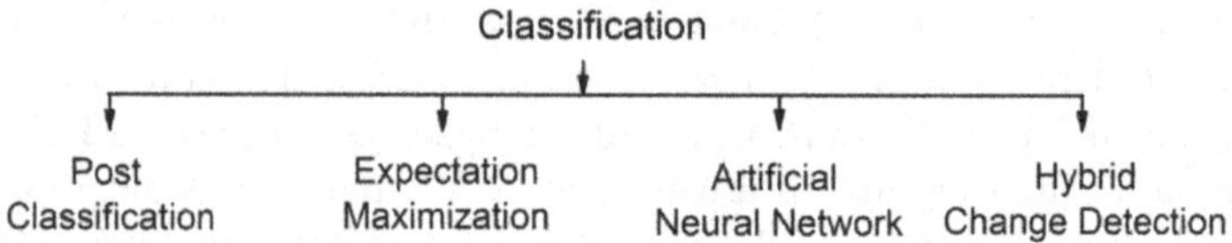


**FIG. 5** List of classification techniques in change detection.

### 4.3.1 Postclassification comparison

Postclassification comparison is probably the most quantitative change detection technique. The methodology of this system is based independently on the rectification of the classified images, and then the thematic maps are created, followed by the comparison of the corresponding labels to classify the places where the change occurred. Unless the classification accuracy is correctly coded for T1 and T2, it is simple to obtain change maps that display a total change matrix. There are many benefits associated with this process, such as reducing sensor, atmospheric, and environmental variations, since data from two dates are individually classified, thus minimizing the issue of normalizing atmospheric and sensor differences between two dates. Mamdouh El-Hattab [35] and Kantakumar and Neelamsetti [36] use postclassification algorithms for correction and hybrid classification, respectively. This approach takes a great deal of time and experience to produce items for labeling. The final precision is affected by the accuracy of each date's classified image.

### 4.3.2 Expectation-maximization algorithm

If the data is incomplete, has missing data points, or has unnoticed (hidden) latent variables, the EM algorithm is a way to find maximum likelihood estimates for model parameters. It is an iterative method of approximating the equation of maximum probability. EM detection is a classification-based approach that uses an algorithm of EM to approximately two times the probabilities of the previous joint class. These probabilities are directly estimated from the images under study. The advantage of this approach was stated to have better accuracy of change detection than other methods of change detection. Hao et al. [37] practices the EM algorithm for the unsupervised change detection method. The problem with this method requires estimating the a priori joint class probability.

### 4.3.3 Hybrid change detection

Hybrid change detection combines two or more techniques (pixel and object-based) for change detection, and it is categorized as procedure-based and result-based detections. To separate modified pixels, this approach utilizes an overlay enhancement from a chosen image and then uses supervised classification. From the classification outcomes, a binary shift mask is created.

This change mask filters out the modified themes created for each date from the LULC maps. Procedure-based means combining two methods in a different phase of change detection. Result-based means analysis of the result of different methods for change detection. Xu et al. [11] combined the pixel-based IR-MAD method and GEOBIA for hybrid change detection. Xu et al. [38] proposed a new fusion in feature level and produced a novel iterative slow feature analysis by combining pixel and object spectral feature. This methodology involves the setting of thresholds for classification implementation; it is quite difficult to define trajectories of change.

### *4.3.4 Artificial neural network*

ANNs are not involving any assumptions as to the form n and independence. Without specifying mathematically how outcomes reflect on inputs, they dynamically evaluate continuous functions from results. The spectral data of the time of transition is the feedback used to train the neural network. A back-propagation algorithm is also used to practice the multilayer vision neural network model. The ANN algorithm learns the relationships (networks) between input (image) and output nodes (changes) from the training dataset and type. The trained network then is applied to the main dataset to create a change map. An ANN algorithm was used for change detection by Kolios and Stylios [39]. When land-cover groups are not usually allocated, the ANN approach can produce better shift detection outcomes.

## 4.4 Geographical information system approach

In order to discern shift, GIS participates in the various source material. The key benefit of using GIS for change detection is its ability to give a broader perspective on the area under study and the frequent coverage of the area. Be that as it may, the presence of various source data accuracies affects the change detection outcome. This method combines earlier and recent land-use maps with topographic and geological details. Image overlapping and binary masking strategies are helpful for quantitatively exposing the patterns of transition in each category. This approach allows the integration of aerial photography data from present and past land-use data with other map details. Hegazy and Kaloop [40] uses GIS data for mapping urban growth. With this approach, the consistency of the results depends on the various GIS data with different geometric precision and classification systems.

## 4.5 Visual analysis

Visual analysis visually interprets the color formula in order to distinguish the modified regions. The alternative is to introduce on-screen digitization of the modified region using visual representation based on overlaid photographs of different dates. Human experience and knowledge are useful for visual interpretation. Two or three picture dates may be examined at one time. The analyst can integrate texture, form, size, and patterns into the visual interpretation to decide on the LULC update. Martin and Howarth [2] uses the visualization analysis method for change detection on multidated spot images. This method cannot deliver complete change data. The results are determined by the expert's expertise in image analysis. The disadvantage with this method is difficulty in bring up to date the results and time-consuming process.

### 4.6 Other approaches

Besides the popular categories of change detection, there are several other approaches that are often used to respond to changes in multitemporal RS images. Ayele et al. [18] uses the Bayesian ML classification method for change detection. The evaluation of long-lasting spatial-temporal land cover patterns of change and the basic aims of the study were to measure the pace, trend, and magnitude of change with topography for the collection, preparation, and execution of growth strategies. To achieve these objectives, use the rich archive and spectral resolution Landsat data sets, the Bayesian ML-supervised classifier to map the land-use class, and shift detection comparison techniques to recognize the intra-image land cover change. Gholoobi et al. [41] utilized a fuzzy c-means algorithm to define cluster centers of vegetation and nonvegetation class. For object-based classification, they used fuzzy c-means algorithm classification Ganasri and Dwarakish [42]. Maximum likelihood algorithm, the minimal distance to mean algorithm, and the parallelepiped algorithm use three different approaches. Among them, the parallelepiped algorithm assigns a pixel to one of the predefined classes of information in terms of its value concerning the DN spectrum of each class in the same band.

## 5 Conclusion

Analysis of change detection remains an active research area that seeks to develop innovative approaches. It is imperative to provide the option to implement it successfully and to have accurate change detection outcomes aligned with change trajectories with a new change detection technique. Despite the fact that a number of strategies for detecting change have been developed, it is still difficult to select a reasonable strategy to conduct precise detection of change for a specific research purpose or field of study. Choosing a suitable strategy for identifying improvements requires close analysis of important effect factors. In exercise, so many techniques of change detection are repeatedly used to implement change detection, the results of which are then compared by visual assessment or quantitative precise evaluation to identify the best product. There is now no general method for identifying improvements that can be thoroughly extended to various types of satellite images. In recent years, deep neural networks in many image recognition systems have gained a great deal of success.

Smearing deep neural networks for the detection of change will improve the accuracy of detection of change. The benefits of individual methods of change detection can also be used to combine different change detection approaches to form a composite detection system and thereby increase the precision of change detection.

## References


[1] T. Ramachandra, U. Kumar, Geographic resources decision support system for land use, land cover dynamics analysis, in: *Proceedings of the FOSS/GRASS Users Conference*, no. September, 2004, pp. 12–14.

[2] L.R.G. Martin, P.J. Howarth, Change-detection accuracy assessment using SPOT multispectral imagery of the rural-urban fringe, Remote Sens. Environ. 30 (1) (1989) 55–66.

[3] A. Singh, Review article: digital change detection techniques using remotely-sensed data, Int. J. Remote Sens. 10 (6) (1989) 989–1003.

[4] D.A. Stow, D. Collins, D. Mc Kinsey, Land use change detection based on multi-date imagery from different satellite sensor systems, Geocarto Int. 5 (3) (1990) 3–12.

[5] P. Manavalan, K. Kesavasamy, S. Adiga, Irrigated crops monitoring through seasons using digital change detection analysis of IRS-LISS 2 data, Int. J. Remote Sens. 16 (4) (1995) 633–640.

[6] G. Metternicht, Change detection assessment using fuzzy sets and remotely sensed data: an application of topographic map revision, ISPRS J. Photogramm. Remote Sens. 54 (4) (1999) 221–233.

[7] T. Blaschke, Object based image analysis for remote sensing, ISPRS J. Photogramm. Remote Sens. 65 (1) (2010) 2–16.

[8] G. Willhauck, Comparison of object oriented classification techniques and standard image analysis for the use of change detection between SPOT multispectral satellite images and aerial photos, Int. Arch. Photogramm. Remote Sens. XXXIII (2000) 214–221.

[9] Z. Bai, D. Dent, Recent land degradation and improvement in China, Ambio: J. Human Environ. 38 (3) (2009) 150–156.

[10] J.C. Listner, I. Niemeyer, Object-based change detection, Int. J. Remote Sens. 33 (14) (2012) 4434–4457.

[11] Q.Q. Xu, Z.J. Liu, M.Z. Yang, H.C. Ren, C. Song, F.F. Li, A hybrid change detection analysis using high-resolution remote sensing image, IOP Conf. Ser. Earth Environ. Sci. 46 (1) (2016).

[12] M.I. Haque, R. Basak, Land cover change detection using GIS and remote sensing techniques: a spatio-temporal study on Tanguar Haor, Sunamganj, Bangladesh, Egypt. J. Remote Sens. Space Sci. 3 (2017) 417–451.

[13] K. Islam, M. Jashimuddin, B. Nath, T.K. Nath, Land use classification and change detection by using multi-temporal remotely sensed imagery: the case of Chunati wildlife sanctuary, Bangladesh, Egypt. J. Remote Sens. Space Sci. 21 (1) (2018) 37–47.

[14] G. Mashame, F. Akinyemi, Towards a remote sensing based assessment of land susceptibility to degradation: examining seasonal variation in land use-land cover for modelling land degradation in a semi-arid context, ISPRS Ann. Photogramm. Remote Sens. Spatial Inf. Sci. 3 (July) (2016) 137–144.

[15] S.S. Akay, E. Sertel, Urban land cover/use change detection using high resolution SPOT 5 and SPOT 6 images and urban atlas nomenclature, Int. Arch. Photogramm. Remote Sens. Spatial Inf. Sci.—ISPRS Arc. 41 (July) (2016) 789–796.

[16] K. Johansen, L.A. Arroyo, S. Phinn, C. Witte, Comparison of geo-object based and pixel-based change detection of riparian environments using high spatial resolution multi-spectral imagery, Photogramm. Eng. Remote Sens. 76 (2) (2013) 123–136.

[17] D. Lu, M. Batistella, P. Mausel, E. Moran, Mapping and monitoring land degradation risks in the Western Brazilian Amazon using multitemporal Landsat TM/ETM+ images, Land Degrad. Dev. 18 (1) (2007) 41–54.

[18] G.T. Ayele, A.K. Tebeje, S. Demissie, M.A. Belete, M.A. Jemberrie, W.M. Teshome, D.T. Mengistu, E.Z. Teshale, Time series land cover mapping and change detection analysis using geographic information system and remote sensing, Northern Ethiopia, Air Soil Water Res. 11 (2018).

[19] O. Dubovyk, G. Menz, C. Conrad, F. Thonfeld, A. Khamzina, Object-based identification of vegetation cover decline in irrigated agro-ecosystems in Uzbekistan, Quat. Int. 311 (2013) 163–174.

[20] Karthik, B.R. Shivakumar, Change detection using image differencing: a study over area surrounding Kumta, India, in: *Proceedings of the 2017 2nd IEEE International Conference on Electrical, Computer and Communication Technologies, ICECCT 2017*, no. February, 2017.

[21] A. Karnieli, U. Gilad, M. Ponzet, T. Svoray, R. Mirzadinov, O. Fedorina, Assessing land-cover change and degradation in the Central Asian deserts using satellite image processing and geostatistical methods, J. Arid Environ. 72 (11) (2008) 2093–2105.

[22] Y. Liu, S. Nishiyama, T. Yano, Analysis of four change detection algorithms in bi-temporal space with a case study, Int. J. Remote Sens. 25 (11) (2004) 2121–2139.

[23] D. Lu, P. Mausel, M. Batistella, E. Moran, Land-cover binary change detection methods for use in the moist tropical region of the Amazon: a comparative study, Int. J. Remote Sens. 26 (1) (2005) 101–114.

[24] R. Tomowski, S. Klonus, M. Ehlers, U. Michel, P. Reinartz, Change visualization through a texture-based analysis approach for disaster applications, ISPRS—Int. Arch. Photogramm. Remote Sens. Spatial Inf. Sci. XXXVIII (2010) 263–268.

[25] L.T. Luppino, F.M. Bianchi, G. Moser, S.N. Anfinsen, Remote sensing image regression for heterogeneous change detection, IEEE Int. Workshop Mach. Learn. Signal Process. MLSP vol. 2018 (Sep, 2018).

[26] X. Chen, L. Vierling, D. Deering, A simple and effective radiometric correction method to improve landscape change detection across sensors and across time, Remote Sens. Environ. 98 (1) (2005) 63–79.

[27] Y. Julien, J.A. Sobrino, J.-C. Jiménez-Muñoz, Land use classification from multitemporal landsat imagery using the yearly land cover dynamics (YLCD) method, Int. J. Appl. Earth Obs. Geoinf. 13 (5) (2011) 711–720.

[28] T.W. Gillespie, S. Ostermann-Kelm, C. Dong, K.S. Willis, G.S. Okin, G.M. MacDonald, Monitoring changes of NDVI in protected areas of southern California, Ecol. Indic. 88 (2018) 485–494. June 2017.

[29] T.P. Higginbottom, E. Symeonakis, Assessing land degradation and desertification using vegetation index data: current frameworks and future directions, Remote Sens. 6 (10) (2014) 9552–9575.

[30] J. Chen, P. Gong, C. He, R. Pu, P. Shi, Land-use/land-cover change detection using improved change-vector analysis, Photogramm. Eng. Remote Sens. 69 (4) (2013) 369–379.

[31] A.A.M. Salih, E.T. Ganawa, A.A. Elmahl, Spectral mixture analysis (SMA) and change vector analysis (CVA) methods for monitoring and mapping land degradation/desertification in arid and semiarid areas (Sudan), using Landsat imagery, Egypt. J. Remote Sens. Space Sci. 20 (2017) S21–S29.

[32] T. Fung, E. Ledrew, Application of principal components analysis to change detection, Photogramm. Eng. Remote. Sens. 53 (12) (1987) 1649–1658.
[33] M. Dharani, G. Sreenivasulu, Land use and land cover change detection by using principal component analysis and morphological operations in remote sensing applications, Int. J. Comput. Appl. (2019) 1–10.
[34] S. Jin, S.A. Sader, Comparison of time series tasseled cap wetness and the normalized difference moisture index in detecting forest disturbances, Remote Sens. Environ. 94 (3) (2005) 364–372.
[35] M. El-Hattab, Applying post classification change detection technique to monitor an Egyptian coastal zone (Abu Qir Bay), Egypt. J. Remote Sens. Space Sci. 19 (1) (2016) 23–36.
[36] L.N. Kantakumar, P. Neelamsetti, Multi-temporal land use classification using hybrid approach, Egypt. J. Remote Sens. Space Sci. 18 (2) (2015) 289–295.
[37] M. Hao, W. Shi, H. Zhang, C. Li, Unsupervised change detection with expectation-maximization-based level set, IEEE Geosci. Remote Sens. Lett. 11 (1) (2014) 210–214.
[38] J. Xu, C. Zhao, B. Zhang, Y. Lin, D. Yu, Hybrid change detection based on ISFA for high-resolution imagery, in: 2018 IEEE 3rd International Conference on Image, Vision and Computing (ICIVC), 2018, pp. 76–80.
[39] S. Kolios, C.D. Stylios, Identification of land cover/land use changes in the greater area of the Preveza peninsula in Greece using Landsat satellite data, Appl. Geogr. 40 (2013) 150–160.
[40] I.R. Hegazy, M.R. Kaloop, Monitoring urban growth and land use change detection with GIS and remote sensing techniques in Daqahlia governorate Egypt, Int. J. Sustain. Built Environ. 4 (1) (2015) 117–124.
[41] M. Gholoobi, A. Tayyebib, M. Taleyi, A.H. Tayyebib, Comparing pixel based and object based approaches in land use classification in mountainous areas, Int. Arch. Photogramm. Remote Sens. Spatial Inf. Sci.—ISPRS Arch. XXXVIII (2) (2010) 573–581.
[42] B.P. Ganasri, G.S. Dwarakish, Study of land use/land cover dynamics through classification algorithms for Harangi catchment area, Karnataka State, India, Aquat. Procedia 4 (2015) 1413–1420. no. Icwrcoe.

Chapter 7

# Facial emotion recognition via stationary wavelet entropy and particle swarm optimization

**Xiang Li and Junding Sun**
*College of Computer Science and Technology, Henan Polytechnic University, Jiaozuo, People's Republic of China*

## 1 Introduction

Facial emotion is a kind of psychological and physiological response used to convey emotions. As an important nonverbal information in daily communication, it can help us better understand each other's real emotions. Referring to the definition of facial emotion by US psychologists Ekman and Friesen [1], we classified facial emotion as neutral, happy, sadness, surprise, angry, fear, and disgust. Facial emotion recognition uses computers to recognize and classify the emotions of people. The main problem of current facial emotion recognition is how to effectively extract the features of the input image. Many scholars use support vector machine or wavelet transform (WT) for feature extraction, and we input different facial emotion images into the computer, and it can identify emotions of people by analyzing image features. Which is of great significance to the development of psychological testing, human-computer interaction, advanced driver assistance systems, and other work. Therefore, facial emotion recognition is one of the important research directions in the field of computer vision.

### 1.1 Related work of facial emotion recognition

In recent years, many scholars have worked on facial emotion recognition. Ali et al. [2] proposed to use the support vector machine (SVM) method. Evans [3] used the Haar WT (HWT) method. Yang [4] introduced cat swarm optimization (CSO) and achieved good results in facial emotion recognition. Lu [5] used fuzzy SVM (FSVM) to detect facial emotion. Phillips [6] applied the Jaya algorithm to recognizing facial emotion. These methods have the shortcomings of low detection accuracy, weak robustness, and poor parameters optimization ability.

Cognitive Systems and Signal Processing in Image Processing. https://doi.org/10.1016/B978-0-12-824410-4.00005-2

To solve these problems, this chapter proposed a facial emotion recognition model with stationary wavelet entropy (SWE) as the feature extraction method, single-hidden-layer feedforward neural network (SHLFNN) as the classifier and particle swarm optimization (PSO) as the optimization method. Among them, the PSO algorithm has the characteristics of easy implementation, fast convergence speed, few algorithm parameters, and stronger global search ability. Therefore, the high efficiency and convergence of SHLFNN training can be guaranteed. Experimental simulation results prove that the proposed method is superior to the state-of-the-art approaches in detection performance.

### 1.2 Structure of this chapter

The rest of this chapter is structured as follows. In the following section, we introduced the research object and data set. In the third section, we introduced the concepts and basic principles of research methods. In the fourth section, we analyzed and discussed the results of the experiment. In the final section, we summarized and anticipated this chapter.

## 2 Dataset

To facilitate the experiment and increase the comparability of experimental results, the data set used in this chapter is the data in Zhang et al. [7]. The data is collected from 20 subjects of different ages (23–37 years old), different occupations, and different skin colors. An experienced photographer used a digital camera (Canon EOS 70D) to collect seven kinds of facial emotion images of each subject (neutral, happy, sadness, surprise, angry, fear and disgust). There are 700 images in total. All images are approved by three experienced psychologists. At the same time, the collected images are slightly modified according to the face model proposed by Shih et al. [8] to obtain better experimental results. Fig. 1 shows samples of our data set. The first row in Fig. 1 is the seven facial emotions images of a male. And the second row in Fig. 1 is the seven facial emotions images of a female.

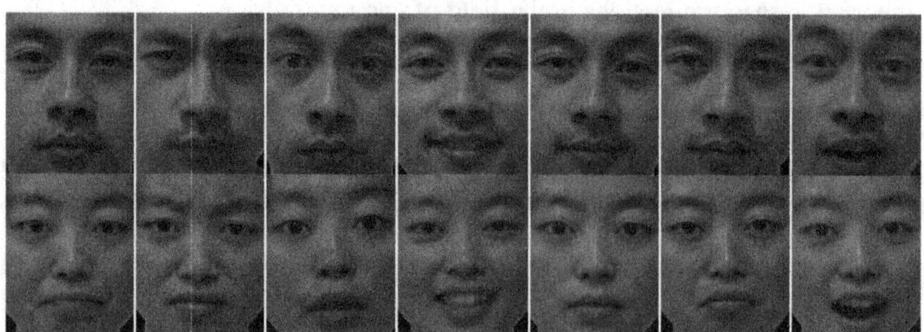

**FIG. 1** Samples of dataset.

# 3 Methodology

## 3.1 Stationary wavelet entropy

Wavelet refers to the wave generated by a function over a distance. The wavelet basis function is obtained by adjusting the size and position of the mother wavelet and the scale function, which can conduct multiresolution analysis of the signal. Entropy is a physical quantity used to describe the complexity or confusion of a system. The traditional wavelet entropy (WE) is based on WT. Since WT can be used to localize the signal in terms of time and frequency, it is highly sensitive to the signal details and can be used to extract the transient local details of nonstatic signals. Therefore, WE is often used for physiological signal analysis [9, 10].

According to information entropy theory [11], $T$ represents all possibilities of the state characteristics of a partially uncertain system. Then the probability $p_v$ of the state value $t_v$ of the system is:

$$p_v = \Pr(T = t_v),\ v = 1,2,3\ldots,Z \tag{1}$$

$$\sum_{v}^{Z} p_v = 1 \tag{2}$$

where, $Z$ is the number of state characteristics. $v$ represents the index of state characteristics. The information entropy of the system in a state of $t_v$ can be expressed as:

$$I_v = \log\left(\frac{1}{p_v}\right),\ v = 1,2,3,\ldots,Z \tag{3}$$

The information entropy of a system in all possible states of $T$ can be defined as:

$$L(T) = -\sum_{v=1}^{Z} p_v \cdot \log(p_v) \tag{4}$$

Therefore, $W_E$ can be expressed as:

$$Q_l = \sum_{v=1}^{Z} |y_l(v)|^2 \tag{5}$$

$$U_l = \frac{Q_l}{\sum_{l=1}^{J} Q_l} \tag{6}$$

$$W_E = -\sum_{l=1}^{J} U_l \cdot \log(U_l) \tag{7}$$

where, $Q_l$ represents the relative energy of the wavelet coefficient at the $v$ scale. $U_l$ represents the distribution of different wavelet scales after the normalization of the original signal energy. $J$ represents the number of levels of wavelet decomposition. And $l$ represents the index of levels of wavelet decomposition.

When WE is used to extract features from the image, it is necessary to normalize the image first. Otherwise, slight changes in the image will directly affect the result of image recognition. In recent years, some scholars have proposed the stationary wavelet entropy theory to solve this problem of WE, that is, to use the SWT to replace the WT [12–15].

When SWE performs one-level feature extraction on the original image, a low-pass filter and a high-pass filter are used to decompose the original image into four subbands [16–18], which are respectively marked as: $B_1$, $C_1$, $D_1$, and $E_1$. Here, subband $B_1$ represents the horizontal quadrant, subband $C_1$ represents the vertical quadrant, subband $D_1$ represents the diagonal quadrant, and subband $E_1$ represents the approximate component of the original image. Subband $E_1$ can be decomposed into four new subbands at a higher level. For a two-level stationary wavelet entropy, the subband $E_1$ is sent to perform another one-level stationary wavelet entropy decomposition, the corresponding four subbands ($B_2$, $C_2$, $D_2$, and $E_2$) will be produced. The decomposition process of SWE is shown in Fig. 2.

From Table 1, we can know that after $(g-1)$-level image decomposition of the original image, the subbands results are as follows:

$$Decompose(E_{g-1}) = (B_g, C_g, D_g, E_g) \tag{8}$$

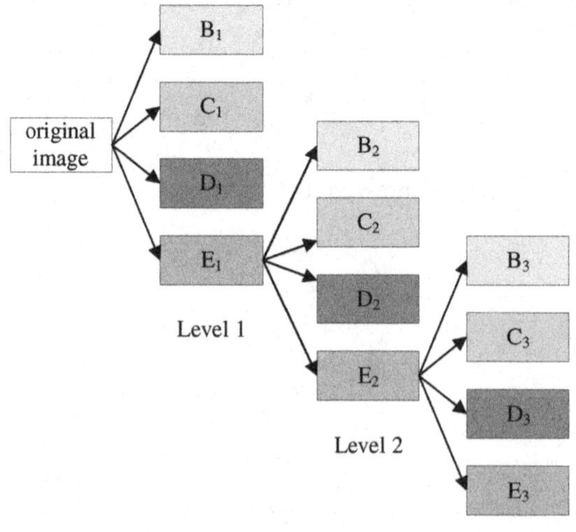


**FIG. 2** Diagram of a three-level image decomposition.

**TABLE 1** Relationship between decomposition level and number of subbands.

| Level | Subbands | Number of subbands |
|---|---|---|
| 1 | $B_1$, $C_1$, $D_1$, $E_1$ | 4 |
| 2 | $B_1$, $C_1$, $D_1$, $B_2$, $C_2$, $D_2$, $E_2$ | 7 |
| 3 | $B_1$, $C_1$, $D_1$, $B_2$, $C_2$, $D_2$, $B_3$, $C_3$, $D_3$, $E_3$ | 10 |
| ... | ... | ... |
| $g$ | $B_1$, $C_1$, $D_1$, $B_2$, $C_2$, $D_2$, $B_3$, $C_3$, $D_3$, $E_3$, …, $B_g$, $C_g$, $D_g$, $E_g$ | $3g+1$ |

where, $E_{g-1}$ represents the approximate component of the original image from the $(g-1)$-level image decomposition. Subband $B_g$ represents the horizontal quadrant. Subband $C_g$ represents the vertical quadrant. Subband $D_g$ represents the diagonal quadrant. And subband $E_g$ represents the approximate component of the original image from the $g$-level image decomposition.

## 3.2 Single-hidden-layer feedforward neural network

Single-hidden-layer feedforward neural network belongs to the research content of feedforward neural network. The feedforward neural network is composed of many neurons, which also is the basic unit of information processing. Each neuron in the feedforward neural network is highly interconnected, and its processing mode of all information borrows from the working mode of the human central nervous system, which has high relativity with cognitive signal processing. Therefore, it belongs to a relatively intelligent system. In practical application, feedforward neural network shows many satisfactory characteristics: strong self-learning ability, strong robustness, and high fault tolerance. Without doubt, feedforward neural network is widely used in computer image processing and pattern recognition and other fields [19–21].

The single-hidden-layer feedforward neural network is developed from feedforward neural network, the structure of which is as follows: input layer, hidden layer, and output layer. The connection mode between the neurons of each layer is the full connection. The structure of neurons is shown in Fig. 3. Because it can complete difficult nonlinear mapping without other operations, it has a strong approximation ability [22–25]. Meanwhile, the structure of SHLFNN is simple and practical, which can be applied to many complex classification problems. In our experiments, we put the extracted feature into the SHLFNN. After the calculation of SHLFNN, the classification result is output. Therefore, SHLFNN has a wide range of applications and strong practicability.

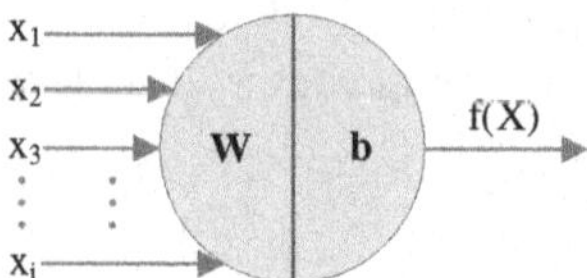


**FIG. 3** Diagram of a neuron.

Here, $f(X)$ represents the output of the neuron. $X=(x_1,x_2,x_3,\ldots,x_i)^T$ represents the input vector of $i$ dimensions. $W$ represents the weight of the neuron. $b$ represents the bias of the neuron. $f(X)$ can be expressed as:

$$f(X)=\gamma\left(\sum_{n=1}^{i} w_n x_n + b\right) \tag{9}$$

For the output of the SHLFNN can be expressed as:

$$F(X)=\sum_{m=1}^{S} h_m\gamma\left(\sum_{n=1}^{i} w_{mn}x_n + b_m\right) \tag{10}$$

$$=\sum_{m=1}^{S} h_m\gamma\left(W_m^T X + b_m\right) \tag{11}$$

where, $F(X)$ represents the output of SHLFNN [26–28]. $X=(x_1,x_2,x_3,\ldots,x_i)^T$ represents the input vector of $i$ dimensions. $h_m$ represents the output weight of the $m$ th neuron in the hidden layer. $S$ represents the number of neurons in the hidden layer. $m$ represents the index of neurons in the hidden layer. $\gamma$ represents the activation function of each neuron in the hidden layer. $i$ represents the dimension of the input vector. $n$ represents the index of dimension of the input vector. $W_m=(w_{m1},w_{m2},w_{m3},\ldots,w_{mi})^T$ represents the input weight of the $m$ th neuron in the hidden layer. $b_m$ represents the bias of the $m$ th neuron in the hidden layer. The structure of SHLFNN is shown in Fig. 4.

After obtaining the output of the classifier, the difference between the output value and the real value can be calculated, which is called the loss value of SHLFNN. It can be described as:

$$|F(X)-Y(X)|<\tau \tag{12}$$

where, $Y(X)$ represents the real value of data. $\tau$ represents a real number, which is used to measure the loss value of SHLFNN. The following will show how to use PSO to minimize $\tau$.

### 3.3 Particle swarm optimization

PSO [29] is a swarm intelligence algorithm proposed by Kennedy and Eberhart in 1995. The algorithm is derived from a complex adaptive system (CAS)—that is, a bird flock social system. The optimization process of PSO can be regarded as the foraging process of birds, and its basic idea is to find the optimal solution

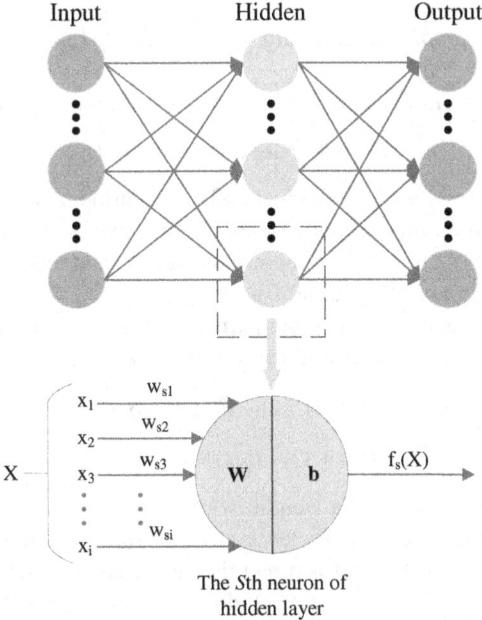


FIG. 4 Diagram of a SHLFNN.

through the coordination and information sharing among individuals in the swarm. When PSO is used to optimize the problem, the independent variables in the problem to be optimized are regarded as different dimensions of each particle, and each particle is regarded as a solution of the problem to be optimized.

By comparing particle swarm to bird swarm, in the process of bird swarm foraging (PSO), each bird (particle) constantly changes its position and direction through the surrounding environment information and sharing information with other birds to achieve fast and accurate food search. Through continual learning and information sharing, the scattered birds will continue to gather together in the process of seeking food. Eventually, they will stop and gather at the location of the food. From this, it can be seen that the PSO algorithm has a fast convergence speed, is not easy to fall into a local optimal solution, and is good at handling multi-objective and high-dimensional optimization problems.

In the optimization process of PSO, each particle has two properties: position and velocity. All particles adjust their structure and behavior by tracking the individual optimal solution and the global optimal solution [30–33]. The individual optimal solution is the optimal value that a particle can find. The global optimal solution is the optimal value that the whole particle swarm can find. Suppose $N$ represents the number of particles in the particle swarm. $V$ represents the velocity of the particle. $P$ represents the position of the particle. $H$ represents the objective function of the PSO, and the value of $H$ is the fitness value of each particle. In each iteration, the individual optimal solution of each particle and the global optimal solution of particle swarm are updated. The solution formula of the individual optimal solution can be defined as:

$$pBest(j,t) = \arg \min_{k=1,2,\ldots,t} \left[H\left(P_j(k)\right)\right] \tag{13}$$

The solution formula of the global optimal solution is defined as:

$$gBest(t) = \arg \min \left[pBest(j,t)\right] \tag{14}$$

where, *pBest* represents the individual optimal solution of a particle. *gBest* represents the global optimal solution of the particle swarm. *j* represents the index of particle, $j \in (1,2,3,\ldots,N)$. *t* represents the current number of iterations. *k* represents the index of iteration, $k \in (1,2,3,\ldots,t)$.

According to Eqs. (13), (14), the particle velocity and position update formula of the whole particle swarm can be expressed as:

$$v_j(t+1) = uV_j(t) + c_1 \times r_1\left(pBest(j,t) - P_j(t)\right) + c_2 \times r_2\left(gBest(t) - P_j(t)\right) \tag{15}$$

$$P_j(t+1) = P_j(t) + V_j(t+1) \tag{16}$$

where, $u$ represents the inertia weight, which is used to balance the local and global search capabilities of particles. $c_1$, $c_2$ represent the learning factor, which is the acceleration coefficient to correct the distance between the particle to the two optimal positions. $r_1$, $r_2$ are two random numbers, $r_1, r_2 \in [0,1]$. The speed limit method is used to prevent particles from flying out of the search space, which is defined in Eq. (17).

$$V_j(t+1) \leftarrow \min\left(V_{max}, V_j(t+1)\right) \tag{17}$$

where, $V_{max}$ represents the upper limit of particle velocity.

The PSO algorithm provides shared information through the individual optimal solution of each particle and the global optimal solution of particle swarm [34]. The whole optimization process always follows the current optimal position, and most particles in the particle swarm can converge to the optimal solution quickly. The concrete implementation of the PSO algorithm is shown in Table 2.

## 3.4 Implementation

First, we collected facial information from subjects to build a database of facial models. Second, SWE is used to extract the facial emotion features and input to SHLFNN. Third, the SHLFNN is trained with PSO. Finally, output the identification performance. The flowchart of our method is shown in Fig. 5.

When SHLFNN is trained by particle swarm algorithm, the unoptimized weights and biases of SHLFNN need to correspond to the dimension of each particle in the particle swarm respectively. The fitness value of each particle is calculated by the objective function, and the individual optimal solution of each particle (*pBest*) and the global optimal solution of particle swarm (*gBest*) are recorded in each iteration. Each particle continuously improves its structure and behavior by tracking the two optimal solutions to obtain the final optimization result (optimized weights and biases of SHLFNN). The flowchart of PSO optimizes the SHLFNN, as shown in Fig. 6.

**TABLE 2 Algorithm process.**

Initial parameters: number of particles, dimension of particles, maximum velocity and position of particle motion, position and velocity of particles, individual optimal solution, global optimal solution.

```
do
  for each particle
      calculate the fitness value
      if fitness value < the individual optimal solution for the current particle
         set the fitness value to the current individual optimal solution
      if fitness value < the global optimal solution for the current particle swarm
         sets the fitness value to the current global optimal solution
      end
    end
  end
for each particle
      calculate the velocity of the particle to determine if the velocity constraint is met
      updates the position of the particle to determine if the position constraint is met
end
while   the maximum number of iterations or the minimum error criterion is not met
        perform the iteration
else    satisfy the stop condition
        stop the iteration, output the result
```

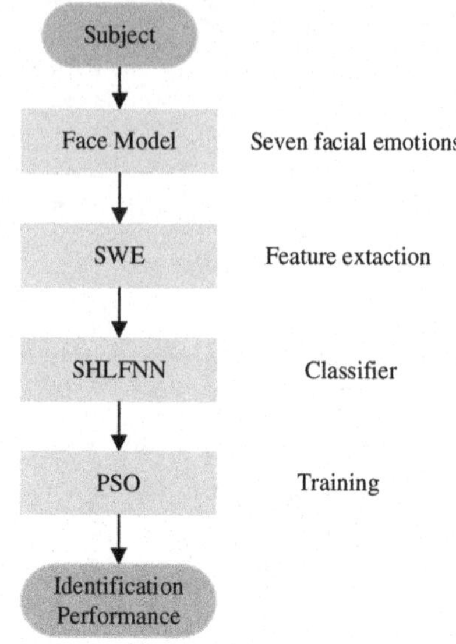


**FIG. 5** Block diagram of our developed system.

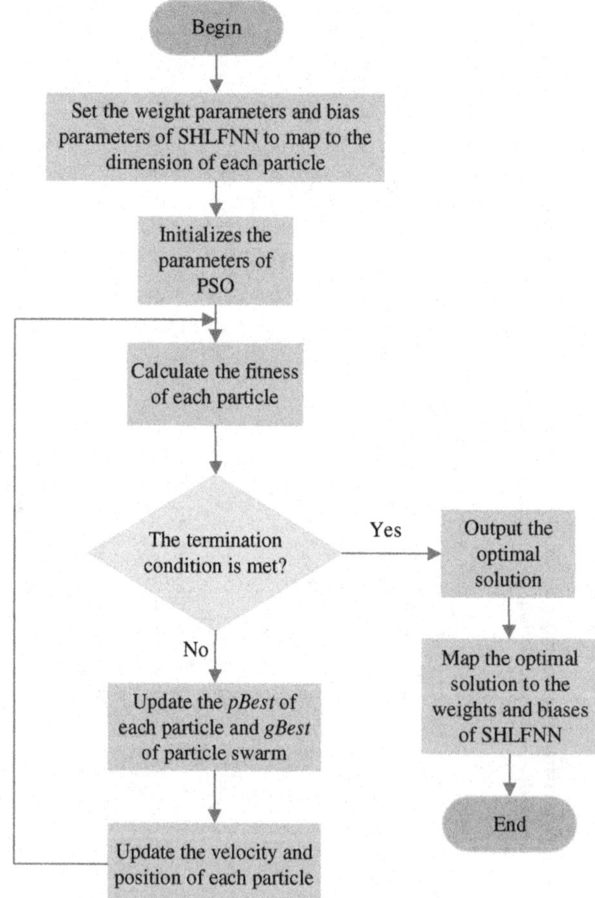


**FIG. 6** Diagram of PSO algorithm.

During the perform of PSO, it generates the particle optimal solution *pBest* of each particle and the global optimal solution *gBest* of the current particle swarm through the objective function. We sorted the *pBest* of each particle from small to large and recorded the smallest *pBest* value as *gBest* value, as shown in Eqs. (13), (14). During each iteration, if the newly generated fitness value $<pBest$, then assign fitness value to *pBest*. Similarly, if $pBest < gBest$, assigns *pBest* to *gBest*, then perform speed calculation and position update for each particle to make all particles move forward toward the optimal solution, as shown in Eqs. (15), (16). By repeating the previous operations, the PSO algorithm can gradually optimize the weights and biases of SHLFNN and improve the performance of the network.

## 3.5 Measure

In this chapter, the 10-fold cross validation [35–37] is introduced to prevent overfitting. The specific implementation process is as follows. The data set is divided into 10 equal subsets and numbered from 1 to 10. Each subset contained seven emotions: neutral, happy, sadness, fear, anger, surprise, and disgust. At the same time, there were 70 images in each subset, with 10 images for each emotion. First, set the subset No. 1 as the test set and the remaining subsets as the training set. This newly generated dataset is set to number I. Then, set the subset No. 2 as the test set and the remaining subsets as the training set. This newly generated dataset is set to number II. Take turns to set the subset No. 3 to No. 10 as test set and set the corresponding remaining subsets as the training set. The seven data sets generated by this way are numbered III to X. Finally, the results of the X (X = 10) data sets can be obtained through experiments to evaluate the accuracy of the algorithm. To evaluate the accuracy of the algorithm more accurately, we will perform 10 runs of 10-fold cross validation. To represent the experimental results more concisely, the confusion matrix is introduced in Table 3.

Where, TP represents both the predicted class and the actual class are positive. FP represents that the predicted class is positive and the actual class is negative. FN represents that the predicted class is negative and the actual class is positive. And TN represents that both the predicted class and the actual class are negative. Therefore, the ideal confusion matrix $K(e = 1, q = 1)$ can be shown as follows.

**TABLE 3 Confusion matrix.**

| Confusion matrix | | Actual class | |
|---|---|---|---|
| | | Positive | Negative |
| Predicted class | Positive | TP | FP |
| | Negative | FN | TN |

$$K(e=1,q=1)=\begin{bmatrix}10&0&0&0&0&0&0\\0&10&0&0&0&0&0\\0&0&10&0&0&0&0\\0&0&0&10&0&0&0\\0&0&0&0&10&0&0\\0&0&0&0&0&10&0\\0&0&0&0&0&0&10\end{bmatrix}\tag{18}$$

where, $K$ represents the confusion matrix, $e$ represents the run number, and $q$ represents the fold number. The ideal confusion matrix of 10-fold cross validation is as follows.

$$K(e=1,q=10)=\begin{bmatrix}100&0&0&0&0&0&0\\0&100&0&0&0&0&0\\0&0&100&0&0&0&0\\0&0&0&100&0&0&0\\0&0&0&0&100&0&0\\0&0&0&0&0&100&0\\0&0&0&0&0&0&100\end{bmatrix}\tag{19}$$

The ideal confusion matrix of 10 runs 10-fold cross validation is as follows.

$$K(e=10,q=10)=\begin{bmatrix}1000&0&0&0&0&0&0\\0&1000&0&0&0&0&0\\0&0&1000&0&0&0&0\\0&0&0&1000&0&0&0\\0&0&0&0&1000&0&0\\0&0&0&0&0&1000&0\\0&0&0&0&0&0&1000\end{bmatrix}\tag{20}$$

We can define overall accuracy (OA) and the sensitivity $I$ of $d$th class after performing 10 runs of 10-fold cross validation as follows:

$$OA=\frac{\sum_{s=1}^{7}K_{ss}(e=10,q=10)}{\sum_{s=1}^{7}\sum_{a=1}^{7}K_{sa}(e=10,q=10)}\tag{21}$$

$$I(d)=\frac{K_{dd}(e=10,q=10)}{\sum_{s=1}^{7}K_{ds}(e=10,q=10)}\tag{22}$$

where, $I(d)$ is the sensitivity of class $d(d\in[1,7],d\in N^{+})$, which means the $d$th element in the diagonal of $K(e=10,q=10)$ divided by the sum of the $d$th row. $K_{ds}$ represents the $d$th class recognized as $s$th class in the confusion matrix.

# 4 Experiment results and discussions

## 4.1 Confusion matrix of proposed method

Through the analysis of the experiment results, we can obtain the confusion matrix that runs $10 \times 10$-fold cross validation, as shown in Table 4. Among them, the value on the diagonal is the number of times that the facial emotion identified by our model is consistent with the actual facial emotion results (the predicted results are correct). The number of other positions is the number of times that the facial emotion identified by our model is inconsistent with the actual facial emotion results (the predicted results are wrong).

According to Eqs. (21), (22), it can be known that the *OA* of SWE + PSO (ours) is 93.89%, *I* (*neutral*) is 94.88%, *I* (*happy*) is 94.60%, *I* (*sadness*) is 94.55%, *I* (*fear*) is 93.29%, *I* (*angry*) is 94.11%, *I* (*surprise*) is 92.61%, and *I* (*disgusted*) is 93.19%. The accuracy of these calculated percentages is retained to two decimal places.

## 4.2 Statistical results

Table 5 shows the data of our method after 10 runs, including the accuracy of weachfacialemotionineachrun,theoverallaccuracyofeachrun,andthemean + standarddeviationofeachfacialemotionclassafter10runs.Here,C1representstheneutral emotion,C2representsthehappyemotion,C3representsthesademotion,C4represents thefearemotion,C5representstheangryemotion,C6representsthesurpriseemotion, andC7representsthedisgustemotion.ByanalyzingthedataintheTable5,wecanclearly seethatourmodelhasthebestrecognitioneffectforC2(happy),withmean + standard deviationof94.60 ± 2.12%.C1(neutral)isfollowedbymean + standarddeviationof 94.50 ± 1.84%, ranking third is C7 (disgust) and mean + standard deviation of 94.40 ± 2.59%.

**TABLE 4** Confusion matrix of SWE + PSO (proposed method).

| Confusion matrix | | Actual class | | | | | | |
|---|---|---|---|---|---|---|---|---|
| | | Neutral | Happy | Sadness | Fear | Angry | Surprise | Disgusted |
| Predicted class | Neural | 945 | 11 | 12 | 8 | 5 | 9 | 10 |
| | Happy | 13 | 946 | 8 | 11 | 2 | 4 | 16 |
| | Sadness | 11 | 12 | 936 | 9 | 13 | 12 | 7 |
| | Fear | 8 | 12 | 8 | 931 | 12 | 16 | 13 |
| | Angry | 3 | 0 | 15 | 12 | 942 | 17 | 11 |
| | Surprise | 6 | 14 | 11 | 15 | 14 | 928 | 12 |
| | Disgusted | 10 | 5 | 0 | 12 | 13 | 16 | 944 |

**TABLE 5** Statistical analysis of 10 runs of data (unit: %).

| Run | C1 | C2 | C3 | C4 | C5 | C6 | C7 | OA |
|---|---|---|---|---|---|---|---|---|
| 1 | 96.00 | 97.00 | 98.00 | 98.00 | 98.00 | 97.00 | 97.00 | 97.29 |
| 2 | 92.00 | 93.00 | 90.00 | 87.00 | 95.00 | 93.00 | 91.00 | 91.57 |
| 3 | 94.00 | 94.00 | 87.00 | 93.00 | 95.00 | 93.00 | 94.00 | 92.86 |
| 4 | 92.00 | 95.00 | 85.00 | 89.00 | 94.00 | 81.00 | 94.00 | 90.00 |
| 5 | 95.00 | 93.00 | 95.00 | 93.00 | 91.00 | 94.00 | 95.00 | 93.71 |
| 6 | 94.00 | 96.00 | 98.00 | 93.00 | 91.00 | 94.00 | 96.00 | 94.57 |
| 7 | 97.00 | 90.00 | 93.00 | 95.00 | 95.00 | 89.00 | 89.00 | 92.57 |
| 8 | 95.00 | 96.00 | 96.00 | 93.00 | 92.00 | 94.00 | 96.00 | 94.57 |
| 9 | 93.00 | 96.00 | 97.00 | 93.00 | 95.00 | 96.00 | 95.00 | 95.00 |
| 10 | 97.00 | 96.00 | 97.00 | 97.00 | 96.00 | 97.00 | 97.00 | 96.71 |
| Mean + SD | 94.50 ± 1.84 | 94.60 ± 2.12 | 93.60 ± 4.72 | 93.10 ± 3.28 | 94.20 ± 2.25 | 92.80 ± 4.76 | 94.40 ± 2.59 | 93.89 ± 2.24 |

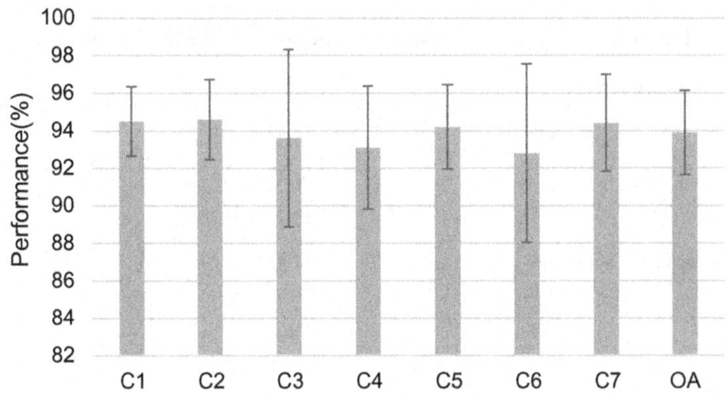


**FIG. 7** Diagram of average and standard deviation of each class after 10 runs.

It can be seen from Fig. 7 that the standard deviation of C6 (surprise) is the largest, which is 4.76%. The second is that the standard deviation of C3 (sadness) is 4.72%. This is also consistent with the result shown in Fig. 8. The curve fluctuation of C6 (surprise) is the largest, and that of C3 (sadness) is second. The other types of curves fluctuate relatively smoothly, which shows that the model has good robustness.

## 4.3 Comparison to state-of-the-art approaches

In order to prove that our method has a better effect on facial emotion detection, we compared three state-of-the-art approaches: SVM [2], HWT [3], and CSO [4]; the results are shown in Table 6. The overall accuracy of SVM is

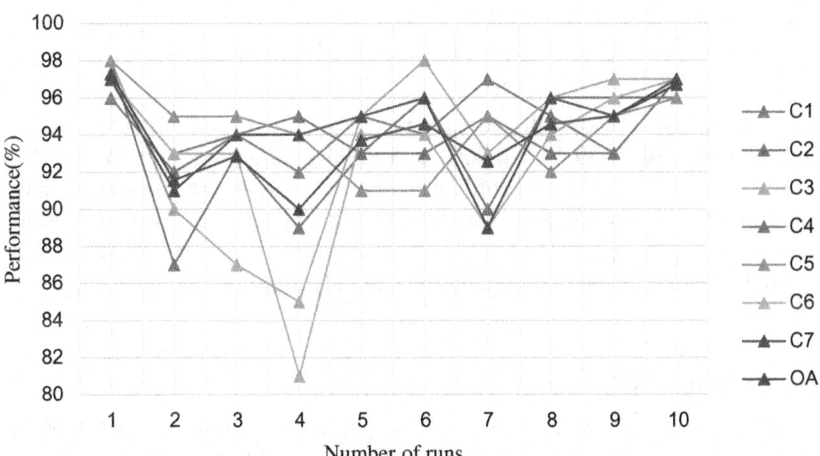


**FIG. 8** Diagram of accuracy for each run of each class.

**TABLE 6 Comparison to state-of-the-art approaches (unit: %).**

| Approach | OA |
|---|---|
| SVM | 83.43 ± 2.15 |
| HWT | 78.37 ± 1.50 |
| CSO | 89.49 ± 0.76 |
| SWE + PSO (Ours) | 93.89 ± 2.24 |

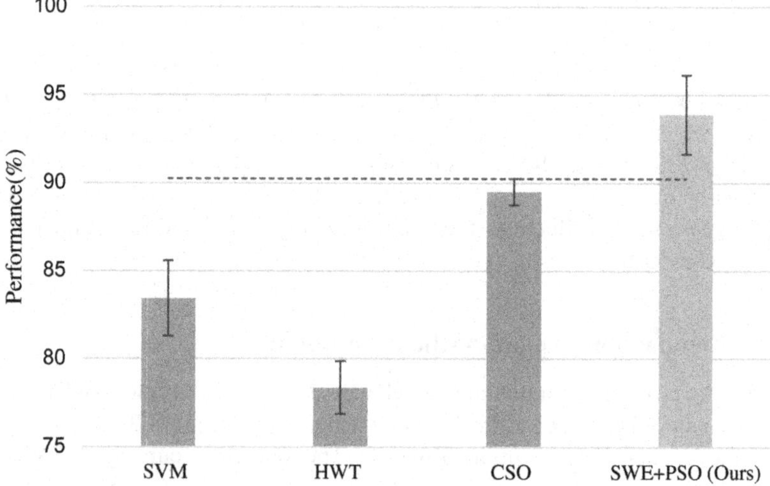


**FIG. 9** Diagram of comparison to state-of-the-art approaches.

83.43 ± 2.15%. The overall accuracy of HWT is 78.37 ± 1.50%. The overall accuracy of CSO is 89.49 ± 0.76%, and the overall accuracy of SWE + PSO (ours) is 93.89 ± 2.24%. According to the calculation, the overall accuracy of our method is 4.4% higher than that of CSO. Fig. 9 shows this more clearly. Among them, the red dotted line (black in print version) represents the highest overall accuracy value obtained by the CSO algorithm in the experiment.

## 5 Conclusions

In this chapter, we proposed a facial emotion recognition model with SWE as feature extraction method, SHLFNN as classifier, and PSO as training method. Through experiments, it can be proved that the overall accuracy of facial emotion detection of our model is significantly better than the state-of-the-art approaches. Finally, the overall accuracy of our method is $93.89 \pm 2.24\%$.

In future studies, we will continue to focus on the study of facial emotion recognition and try to test the newly proposed optimization algorithm, such as the grey wolf optimization algorithm. In addition, we will try to apply deep learning technology to facial emotion recognition.

## References

[1] P. Ekman, W.V. Friesen, Facial action coding system (FACS): a technique for the measurement of facial action, Riv. Psichiatr. 47 (2) (1978) 126–138.

[2] H. Ali, M. Hariharan, S. Yaacob, A.H. Adom, Facial emotion recognition based on higher-order spectra using support vector machines, J. Med. Imaging Health Infor. 5 (6) (Oct 2015) 1272–1277. (in English), Article; Proceedings Paper.

[3] F. Evans, Haar wavelet transform based facial emotion recognition, Adv. Comput. Sci. Res. 61 (2017) 342–346. 2017/03.

[4] W. Yang, Facial emotion recognition via discrete wavelet transform, principal component analysis, and cat swarm optimization, Lect. Notes Comput. Sci. 10559 (2017) 203–214.

[5] H.M. Lu, Facial emotion recognition based on biorthogonal wavelet entropy, fuzzy support vector machine, and stratified cross validation, IEEE Access 4 (2016) 8375–8385.

[6] P. Phillips, Intelligent facial emotion recognition based on stationary wavelet entropy and Jaya algorithm, Neurocomputing 272 (2018) 668–676.

[7] Y.D. Zhang, Z.J. Yang, H.M. Lu, X.X. Zhou, S.H. Wang, Facial emotion recognition based on biorthogonal wavelet entropy, fuzzy support vector machine, and stratified cross validation, IEEE Access 4 (99) (2016) 8375–8385.

[8] F.Y. Shih, C.-F.C.J.O. Research, Automatic Extraction of Head and Face Boundaries and Facial Features, vol. 45, 2005, pp. 83–84. no. 1.

[9] L. Han, Identification of Alcoholism based on wavelet Renyi entropy and three-segment encoded Jaya algorithm, Complexity 2018 (2018). Art. no. 3198184.

[10] D.S. Guttery, Abnormal breast detection by an improved AlexNet model, Ann. Oncol. 31 (S4) (2020) S277. 2020/09/01.

[11] C.E. Shannon, A mathematical theory of communication, Reprinted with corrections from, Bell Syst. Tech. J. 27 (1948) 379–423. 623-656, July, October.

[12] X.-X. Zhou, Comparison of machine learning methods for stationary wavelet entropy-based multiple sclerosis detection: decision tree, k-nearest neighbors, and support vector machine, Simulation 92 (9) (2016) 861–871.

[13] D.R. Nayak, Detection of unilateral hearing loss by stationary wavelet entropy, CNS Neurol. Disord. Drug Targets 16 (2) (2017) 15–24.

[14] J.M. Gorriz, Multivariate approach for Alzheimer's disease detection using stationary wavelet entropy and predator-prey particle swarm optimization, J. Alzheimer's Dis. 65 (3) (2018) 855–869.

[15] A. Atangana, Application of stationary wavelet entropy in pathological brain detection, Multimed. Tools Appl. 77 (3) (2018) 3701–3714.

[16] Y. Huo, Feature extraction of brain MRI by stationary wavelet transform and its applications, J. Biol. Syst. 18 (S) (2010) 115–132.

[17] X.-X. Zhou, H. Sheng, Combination of stationary wavelet transform and kernel support vector machines for pathological brain detection, Simulation 92 (9) (2016) 827–837. March 2.

[18] A. Liu, Magnetic resonance brain image classification via stationary wavelet transform and generalized eigenvalue proximal support vector machine, *J. Med. Imag.Health Infor*. Research Article 5 (7) (2015) 1395–1403.

[19] R. Bastami, A.A. Bazzazi, H.H. Shoormasti, K. Ahangari, Prediction of blasting cost in limestone mines using gene expression programming model and artificial neural networks, J. Min. Environ. 11 (1) (2020) 281–300. (in English), Win.

[20] L. Wu, Magnetic resonance brain image classification by an improved artificial bee colony algorithm, Prog. Electromagn. Res. 116 (2011) 65–79.

[21] L. Wu, Crop classification by forward neural network with adaptive chaotic particle swarm optimization, Sensors 11 (5) (2011) 4721–4743.

[22] M. Chen, Y. Li, L. Han, Detection of dendritic spines using wavelet-based conditional symmetric analysis and regularized morphological shared-weight neural networks, Comput. Math. Methods Med. (2015). Art. no. 454076.

[23] R.V. Rao, A. Liu, L. Wei, Abnormal breast detection in mammogram images by feed-forward neural network trained by Jaya algorithm, Fundam. Inform. 151 (1–4) (2017) 191–211.

[24] Y.-D. Lv, Alcoholism detection by data augmentation and convolutional neural network with stochastic pooling, J. Med. Syst. 42 (1) (2018). Art. no. 2.

[25] X. Wu, Diagnosis of COVID-19 by wavelet renyi entropy and three-segment biogeography-based optimization, Int. J. Comput. Intell. Syst. 13 (1) (2020) 1332–1344. 2020-09-17T09:29:20.000Z.

[26] S.-H. Wang, Covid-19 classification by FGCNet with deep feature fusion from graph convolutional network and convolutional neural network, Inf. Fusion 67 (2021) 208–229. 2020/10/09.

[27] S.C. Satapathy, A five-layer deep convolutional neural network with stochastic pooling for chest CT-based COVID-19 diagnosis, Mach. Vis. Appl. 32 (2021). Art. no. 14.

[28] S.-H. Wang, COVID-19 classification by CCSHNet with deep fusion using transfer learning and discriminant correlation analysis, Inf. Fusion 68 (2021) 131–148.

[29] J. Kennedy, R. Eberhart, Particle swarm optimization, in: *Icnn95-international Conference on Neural Networks*, 2002.

[30] M. Hoseiniasl, J.J. Fesharaki, 3D optimization of gear train layout using particle swarm optimization algorithm, J. Appl. Comput. Mech. 6 (4) (2020) 823–840. (in English), Fal.

[31] X.-X. Hou, Alcoholism detection by medical robots based on Hu moment invariants and predator-prey adaptive-inertia chaotic particle swarm optimization, Comput. Electr. Eng. 63 (2017) 126–138.

[32] J.F. Yang, P. Sun, Magnetic resonance brain classification by a novel binary particle swarm optimization with mutation and time-varying acceleration coefficients (in English), Biomed. Eng.-Biomed. Tech. 61 (4) (Aug 2016) 431–441.

[33] L. Wu, UCAV path planning by fitness-scaling adaptive chaotic particle swarm optimization, Math. Probl. Eng. (2013). Art. no. 705238.

[34] H. Behbahani, S.M. Hosseini, S.A. Samerei, A. Taherkhani, H. Asadi, Driving time prediction at freeway interchanges using artificial neural network and particle swarm optimization (in English), Iran. J. Sci. Technol.-Trans. Civil Eng. 44 (3) (Sep 2020) 975–989.

[35] Y. Chen, Cerebral micro-bleeding identification based on a nine-layer convolutional neural network with stochastic pooling, Concurr. Comp. Pract. Exp. 31 (1) (2020) e5130.

[36] A.K. Sangaiah, Alcoholism identification via convolutional neural network based on parametric ReLU, dropout, and batch normalization, Neural Comput. Appl. 32 (2020) 665–680.

[37] A. Buccini, L. Reichel, An l(P)-l(q) minimization method with cross-validation for the restoration of impulse noise contaminated images, J. Comput. Appl. Math. 375 (Sep 2020) 16. (in English), Art. no. 112824.

Chapter 8

# A research insight toward the significance in extraction of retinal blood vessels from fundus images and its various implementations

**Nimisha Anns Oommen and P. Darsana**
*Department of Electronics and Communication Engineering, Amal Jyothi College of Engineering, Kottayam, Kerala*

## 1 Introduction

The eye is the most tenuous and highly developed sensory organ in our body. A great deal of attention has to be provided to pamper our visual health. The fundus is the inside portion of an eye, which includes retina, fovea, optic disc, and blood vessels. A specialized optical apparatus called fundus cameras are used for retinal imaging. This provides a digital image of the fundus that can help an ophthalmologist make an early diagnosis of ocular and other diseases relative to the changes with the vascular structure of the eyes. The structural changes happening within the retinal blood vessels can be scrutinized as the direct indication of retinal disorders, such as diabetic retinopathy (DR), hypertension, and age-related macular degeneration (AMD). Recent studies show that blood vessels in the retina share some similarity in size, structure, and function with blood vessels in the brain [1], which helps detect cerebrovascular diseases, such as stroke and Alzheimer's [2]. Many systemic cardiovascular diseases like arterial hypertension and coronary heart disease are also related to structural vascular changes in the retina [3]. Thus, a retinal blood vessel is proved to be a transparent window to the eye, heart, and brain. These are the only vessels that can be photographed directly, and it does not create any panic, stress, or discomfort in patients. Changes exhibited in the structure of the retinal blood vessels are a reliable biomarker of various retinal, cardiovascular, and cerebrovascular

**Cognitive Systems and Signal Processing in Image Processing. https://doi.org/10.1016/B978-0-12-824410-4.00011-8**

diseases. The main motivation behind this research work is the higher possibility in the early detection of several maladies before its fatal stage by using retinal blood vessels.

Hence, accurate extraction of retinal blood vessels from the fundus image is the pivotal and primary step before disease identification and detection. Retinal blood vessel segmentation is one of the hot topics in the biomedical field from early 1990s and is still trending. Many researchers have introduced several novel techniques for the same but encountered with several difficulties. In general, retinal blood vessel segmentation can be performed by using two techniques: supervised and unsupervised. Both of the methods have their own advantages and disadvantages. Supervised methods are complex but more accurate than unsupervised methods.

Keeping in mind about the average complexity involved in both of the techniques, we have found that some methods [4–9] possess higher execution time and complexity just to process one image in the database. In variable cases, some of the images in the databases are distorted due to technical faults, noises, and lighting variations, which leads to the degradation of performance of the algorithms like in Refs. [8, 10]. And most of the algorithms find it difficult to handle pathological images [8, 11, 12] and high-resolution images [4, 13]. These are the main challenges that arise in the entire process of extraction of retinal blood vessels from fundus images. Many researchers have tried to increase the performance by eliminating the existing flaws. But it tends in a way that every algorithm has to compromise in terms of either complexity or accuracy. It means that there always exist a trade-off between accuracy and complexity while performing the retinal blood vessel extraction.

So our prime challenge is to break the trade-off between accuracy and complexity by eliminating the flaws in the previous literature so as to improve the overall performance. The contributions of our chapter are as follows:

- Technical faults, lighting variations, noises, and abnormalities due to diseases can be eliminated by incorporating a strong preprocessing phase. Here, we have implemented a double enhancement technique to avoid these flaws.
- Since most of the algorithms fail to work with high-resolution images, we have utilized lossless compression by discrete wavelet transform (DWT) to analyze both low- and high-resolution images in our unsupervised algorithm.
- The trade-off between accuracy and execution time has managed to a better extent in our unsupervised approach.

## 1.1 Organization of the chapter

The organization of our chapter is as follows:

The initial phase of our research was mainly engrossed to know about the importance of retinal blood vessel segmentation, its research scope in the future, relation of retinal blood vessels to disease detection, and various methods adopted for retinal blood vessel extraction. So a detailed study was conducted based on this aspect. Many of the existing methods are referred using the previous literature. The explanations of the literature are briefed in Section 2. As a result of this analysis, inferences are made by considering the strength and drawback of each method. Section 3 deals with the extraction of retinal blood vessels by a simple supervised method using the naive Bayes classifier. The proposed methodology, results, and performance evaluation are explained in this chapter. Section 4 deals with the extraction of retinal blood vessels using a simple unsupervised method, and this section explains the methodology, results, and performance assessment of the proposed algorithm. Section 5 deals with the conclusion, and Section 6 details about the future scopes.

## 2 Literature review

The foundation to any research is a strong background study about the topic and the techniques implemented so far and hence extracting its strengths and flaws by analyzing these methods. Mainly literature survey was conducted:

- to understand the importance of retinal vessel segmentation by considering its involvement in detecting various retinal pathologies, cerebrovascular diseases, and cardiovascular diseases; and
- to know about various existing methods in retinal blood vessel extraction and their flaws and strengths.

### 2.1 Role of retinal blood vessels in disease detection

Examination of the retinal blood vessel structure opens up a window to the eye, heart, and brain. Apart from retinal pathologies, diseases related to heart and brain can also be detected by observing the changes in retinal vessels.

#### *2.1.1 Retinal pathologies*

Retinal pathologies like DR, AMD, retinopathy of prematurity (ROP), hypertensive retinopathy, and so on can be detected by considering various changes happening to the retinal vessel structure. DR is caused as a result of diabetes and leads to permanent vision loss in its advanced stage. It is a leading cause of blindness in people [14]. In [15], Yun et al. proposed a method to identify four different stages of DR: normal retina, moderate nonproliferative DR, severe nonproliferative DR, and proliferative DR. In this method, classification of the four stages are done by using a feedforward neural network. Hypertensive retinopathy is caused due to retinal microvascular signs that are developed as a result of raising blood pressure [16]. AMD is a major cause of central blindness among older people [17]. Wet AMD is caused by abnormal growth of blood vessels. ROP is a vasoproliferative disorder of the retina that occurs in newborn preterm infants [18]. Glaucoma is a progressive neurodegeneration of the optic nerve resulting in vision loss [19]. In [20], Thomas and Titus proposed a multiclass convolutional neural network (CNN)-based system that is capable of classifying a fundus image either as normal or to different stages of DR or AMD.

#### 2.1.2 Cardiovascular diseases

The eye can be considered as a window to the heart. Many systemic cardiovascular diseases like arterial hypertension, coronary heart disease, diabetes mellitus, and obesity are associated with structural vascular changes in the retina [3].

#### 2.1.3 Cerebrovascular diseases

In [1], Shalev et al. observed that the retinal blood vessels share some similarity in size, structure, and function with blood vessels in the brain. Their study concluded that venular caliber in the eye is related to mental test scores of individuals in their 30s and even to IQ scores in childhood.

In [21], Jeena and Sukesh Kumar proposed a machine learning approach, which is based on an artificial neural network (ANN) to predict the possibility of stroke by analyzing the retinal parameters.

In [22], Baker et al. conducted a study to present an evidence on the association between retinal signs and stroke. They concluded that many retinal conditions are associated with stroke that reflects possible concomitant pathophysiological processes, which affect both the eye and the brain.

In [2], Valenti performed a study on Alzheimer's and visual system impact. The results showed that during the generative process of Alzheimer's, the visual system shows an early deficit that helps detect it before there are classic cognitive and memory losses.

#### 2.1.4 Cancers

In [23], Madanagopalan et al. reported a case study that demonstrates the rare association of breast carcinoma and central retinal vein occlusion. In [24], Ravi Babu et al. conducted a study to observe the incidence of retinopathy in various blood dyscrasias, such as leukemia, lymphoma, and polycythemia.

### 2.2 Different methods for segmentation

Retinal blood vessel extraction can be performed mainly by using two techniques: supervised and unsupervised. Supervised technique involves training of the system with input and labeled outputs. The outcome is more accurate and shows robust performance. But the limitation of this approach is its increased computational complexity and higher execution time. Unsupervised technique does not involve a training phase, but it learns and adapts through structural characteristics of the input patterns. It is less complex, and the outcome is not as accurate as a supervised technique but is comparable.

### 2.2.1 Supervised techniques

In [25], Marin et al. proposed a supervised approach where a neural network is used for pixel classification and a 7D feature vector is extracted for pixel characterization. This 7D feature vector is composed of gray-level and moment invariant features.

In [26], Zhua et al. proposed a supervised technique based on an extreme learning machine (ELM) as the classifier. ELM is a simple feedforward neural network with a single layer of hidden nodes. A set of 39D features is extracted for pixel representation.

In [27], Oliveira et al. proposed a supervised technique that fuses multiscale analysis provided by stationary wavelet transform (SWT) with a multiscale CNN. It uses rotation operations as the basis for data augmentation and prediction.

In [28], Jebaseeli et al. proposed a method to extract retinal blood vessels from a DR fundus image. The authors suggested a tandem pulse coupled neural network (TPCNN) for automatic feature generation, and classification is done by using deep learning-based support vector machine (DLBSVM).

In [29], Aslani and Sarnel suggested a method that combines a set of robust features from different algorithms into a hybrid feature vector. It builds a 17D feature vector, which is trained with a random forest (RF) classifier.

In [30], Aslani and Sarnel proposed an adaptive local thresholding method to extract large vessels and an SVM-based classifier to extract the residual fragments obtained as the result of thresholding. Multiscale transforms such as wavelet and curvelet transform at different scales are used. They are now recognized as useful feature extraction methods to represent image features at different scales.

Fraz et al. [10] implemented a supervised method that exploits an ensemble classifier of bagged and boosted decision trees to classify vessels and nonvessels. It extracts a 9D feature vector that analyzes both healthy and pathological images.

Fu et al. [31] proposed a novel approach that combines CNN and conditional random field (CRF) to form an integrated deep network termed as deep vessel. It incorporates a multiscale and multilevel CNN with a side output layer and utilizes CRF to model the interactivity between the pixels.

Memari et al. [32] proposed an automatic retinal blood vessel extraction by using a matched filter and AdaBoost classifier. Enhancement of the image is done by utilizing B-COSFIRE and Frangi-matched filters, and a blood vessel network is extracted by AdaBoost classifier.

Jin et al. [6] proposed an extension of the U-Net known as Deformable U-Net (DUNet) by replacing various convolutional layers by convolutional blocks that are deformable. It exploits local features of retinal blood vessels with U-shape architecture. High execution time is the main drawback of this method.

In [33], Yan et al. introduced a deep learning method that proposes a new segment-level loss that jointly adopts both the segment-level and the pixel-wise losses to extract thick and thin vessels efficiently. In the joint-loss framework, the basic deep learning model with reference to the U-Net model is designed by adding two separate branches to train the model with the segment-level loss and the pixel-wise loss simultaneously.

In [34], Leopold et al. proposed a fully residual autoencoder batch normalization network ("PixelBNN") to automate the segmentation of fundus morphologies. PixelBNN makes use of gated residual convolutional and deconvolutional layers activated by concatenated rectifying linear units (CReLU).

### 2.2.2 Unsupervised technique

In [11], Shah et al. introduced a simple, unsupervised method based on Gabor wavelet transform and multiscale line detector for the extraction of retinal vessels. Here, the blood vessels are enhanced by the linear superposition of complemented green channel and first scale Gabor wavelet image. Then, the multiscale line detector is used to extract the blood vessels.

In [35], Zhang et al. proposed a system composed of a matched filter followed by the first-order derivative of Gaussian exploiting the fact that the cross-section of a vessel is symmetric Gaussian function. Here, the first-order derivative filter is used to determine the threshold that separates vessels and nonvessels.

In [36], Mapayi et al. proposed a method for retinal blood vessel segmentation based on gray-level cooccurrence matrix (GLCM) energy information, which is followed by local adaptive thresholding. Here, the information based on energy feature is applied to the thresholding technique.

In [4], Odstrcilik et al. developed a novel method to extract the blood vessel at varying widths. This method enables the segmentation of a wide range of blood vessel sizes. This method is based on utilizing a matched filter with different shapes followed by Kittler minimum error thresholding technique.

In [37], Al-Rawi and Karajeh improved the sensitivity of a matched filter by using genetic algorithms. Here, genetic algorithms are used to generate high-quality solutions to optimize the matched filter parameters, thus enhancing its performance. The area under ROC is used as the fitness function for genetic algorithms, which selects the fittest individual by comparing each edge-detected image to a manually labeled image.

In [38], Aqeel and Ganesan proposed an unsupervised technique based on texture features followed by global thresholding and a set of morphological operations, such as dilation, thinning, and filling. Here, entropy is considered as the texture feature. Entropy is the measure of inconsistency of intensity values in an image.

In [39], Cinsdikici and Aydn introduced a hybrid model comprising of ant-based clustering and matched filtering algorithm. It is shown that an ant-based approach increases the accuracy of a matched filter.

In [40], Dash and Bhoi introduced a simple, unsupervised method based on local adaptive thresholding. Here, the algorithm is performed by means of mean-C thresholding. The method is found to be simple and less complex.

In [41], Jiang et al. proposed a novel approach to extract retinal blood vessels. In this method, major blood vessel structure and the capillaries are extracted separately by using two different techniques. The major blood vessel is extracted by means of morphology-based global intensity thresholding, while the capillaries are detected by matched filtering. Then the output of both techniques is overlapped to get the final segmented output.

In [12], Dash and Bhoi used a local adaptive thresholding method relied on an energy function that incorporates a data term and a regularization term. The threshold surface and weighting parameters are obtained by using a variational minimax optimization algorithm. Here, the authors have utilized a double enhancement technique.

In [42], Gao et al. has proposed an automatic, unsupervised method by using random walk algorithms based on the centerlines to extract retinal blood vessels. Here, Hessian-based multiscale vascular enhancement filtering is used to extract centerlines of vessels, which in turn is used to locate the labeled seeds in the random walks for segmentation.

A quick glimpse of remarks obtained from some of the significant literature is given in Table 1.

**TABLE 1** A glimpse of remarks obtained from the literature.

| Literature | Year | Method | Remarks |
|---|---|---|---|
| ***Supervised techniques*** | | | |
| Soares et al. [8] | 2006 | Bayesian classifier | Problem with pathological images |
| | | | Do not perform well for very large variations in lighting throughout the image |
| | | | Lack of strong preprocessing phase |
| Fraz et al. [10] | 2012 | Ensemble classifier | Less performance |
| | | | Do not include preprocessing phase |
| Li et al. [13] | 2015 | Deep neural network | Good accuracy |
| | | | Longer training time for low-resolution images |
| | | | Cannot handle high-resolution images |

*Continued*

**TABLE 1 A glimpse of remarks obtained from the literature—cont'd**

| Literature | Year | Method | Remarks |
|---|---|---|---|
| Yan et al. [33] | 2018 | Deep learning method | Better accuracy and sensitivity |
| | | | Training procedure complicated |
| Jin et al. [6] | 2019 | Deformable U-Net | Good accuracy |
| | | | High execution time |
| Leopold et al. [34] | 2019 | PixelBNN | Problem in detecting fine vessels |
| | | | Difficulty in handling pathological images |
| Tian et al. [43] | 2020 | Multipath CNN | Better accuracy |
| | | | Good connectivity of vessels |
| ***Unsupervised techniques*** | | | |
| Odstrcilik et al. [4] | 2013 | Matched filter | Lower ability to extract thin capillaries |
| | | | Large computational complexity for high-resolution images |
| Dash and Bhoi [40] | 2017 | Mean-C thresholding | Simple |
| | | | Comparable accuracy |
| Jiang et al. [41] | 2017 | Thresholding and matched filtering | Good performance |
| Dash and Bhoi [12] | 2018 | Local adaptive-thresholding | Good accuracy |
| | | | Problem in dealing with pathological images |
| Shah et al. [11] | 2019 | Gabor wavelet and multiscale line detector | Comparable accuracy |
| | | | Less performance with pathological images |
| | | | Problem in detecting fine vessels |
| Gao et al. [42] | 2020 | Random walk algorithm | The real-time performance of the algorithm has to be improved |

Based on the inferences made from the study, the common challenges encountered are the ambiguity of fundus images due to technical hitches, lighting conditions, and abnormalities due to maladies. The implementation of most of the algorithms is focused mainly for low-resolution images and are found to be complex while dealing with high-resolution images, and there always exists a trade-off between accuracy and execution time. Our research primarily focuses on implementing a strong algorithm that can manage these flaws to a better extent. Some authors have also tried the combination of unsupervised and supervised techniques [44–46], but in our perspective, it tends to make the algorithm more complex.

## 3 Extraction of retinal blood vessels using supervised technique

Extraction of retinal blood vessels by using efficient machine learning methods are generally proved to be more accurate and efficient than unsupervised methods. But the major disadvantage is its increased computational complexity and higher execution time. Highly efficient machine learning algorithms, like deep learning methods, neural network classifiers, and so on, are available. Their performance only improves with an increase in complexity. Most of the previous literature uses high-end networks, but their average execution time can be long hours, which are not reliable while dealing with real-time cases. Efficient machine learning algorithms require advanced hardware, which may not be always possible with students. Keeping all of this in mind, here we have tried to implement a different approach by applying a simple supervised technique that can manage the flaws to a certain extent.

In our research, a simple, supervised method is utilized by using a simple classifier known as naive Bayes classifier. The methodology consists of a sequential application of the preprocessing phase, feature extraction phase, supervised technique, and postprocessing phase. Preprocessing phase involves a double enhancement method using an adaptive gamma correction (AGC) and contrasts limited histogram equalization (CLAHE) with color space transformation and extraction of channels. The green channel and multiscale Gabor feature from the input image are utilized in the feature extraction phase. Ten dimensional features are extracted and provided to the succeeding stage. The algorithm is trained and tested by naive Bayes classifier followed by postprocessing phase.

The method is assessed by using two publicly available databases: DRIVE and STARE. It has achieved an average accuracy, sensitivity, and specificity of 0.9085, 0.2252, and 0.9132 for DRIVE database and 0.9182, 0.2293, and 0.9253 in STARE database. The algorithm has attained an average execution time of 31.23 s for DRIVE and 34.14 s for STARE databases.

## 3.1 Materials

The performance of the algorithm is appraised on two publicly available databases: DRIVE and STARE.

Digital Retinal Image for Vessel Extraction (DRIVE) [47] database consists of two sets of fundus images: train and test images. Each set has a total of 20 images. The images were acquired using a Canon CR5 nonmydriatic 3CCD camera with a 45-degree field of view (FOV). Each image was captured using 8 bits per color plane (i.e., 24 bits RGB color) with a resolution of 768 by 584 pixels. Manual segmentation of the retinal images by the human experts are also provided along with the database. A single ground truth is available for the training set and two sets of ground truths are available in the testing set. Here, the first manual segmentation by the human observer is considered for performance evaluation. FOV masks are also provided along with the database.

Structured Analysis of the Retina (STARE) [48] consists of a total of 20 images. This database does not include separate sets for training and testing. Here, the first 10 images in the database are used for training, and the whole 20 images are used for testing. Each image is captured using a TopCon TRV-50 retinal camera with a resolution of 700 by 605 pixels. The images are acquired at 35-degree FOV and 50% of the images contain pathologies. Manual segmentation results by the two experts A. Hoover and V. Kouznetsova are available for the images. Here, we have considered the result by A. Hoover as the ground truth. FOV masks are not available in the database. Thus, masks are created for the STARE database.

## 3.2 Methodology

The proposed methodology consists of mainly three phases, such as the preprocessing phase, feature extraction phase, supervised phase, and postprocessing phase. Fig. 1 shows the proposed methodology of the work.

### *3.2.1 Preprocessing*

Image preprocessing is the pivotal step for improving segmentation performance due to the nonuniform illumination of fundus images. It enhances the image features by suppressing unwanted noise and thereby improves the quality of the image. Different databases offer different images. Some images can be degraded due to any technical faults or noise, which affects the visibility of vessels. This problem is crucial while dealing with medical diagnosis. Here, a double enhancement method [12] is adopted to avoid such predicaments and promotes robust performance. It helps in better perceivability of the images. Double enhancement technique involves AGC and contrasts limited adaptive histogram equalization (CLAHE) to enhance the contrast and image quality. Fig. 2 shows the output after preprocessing.

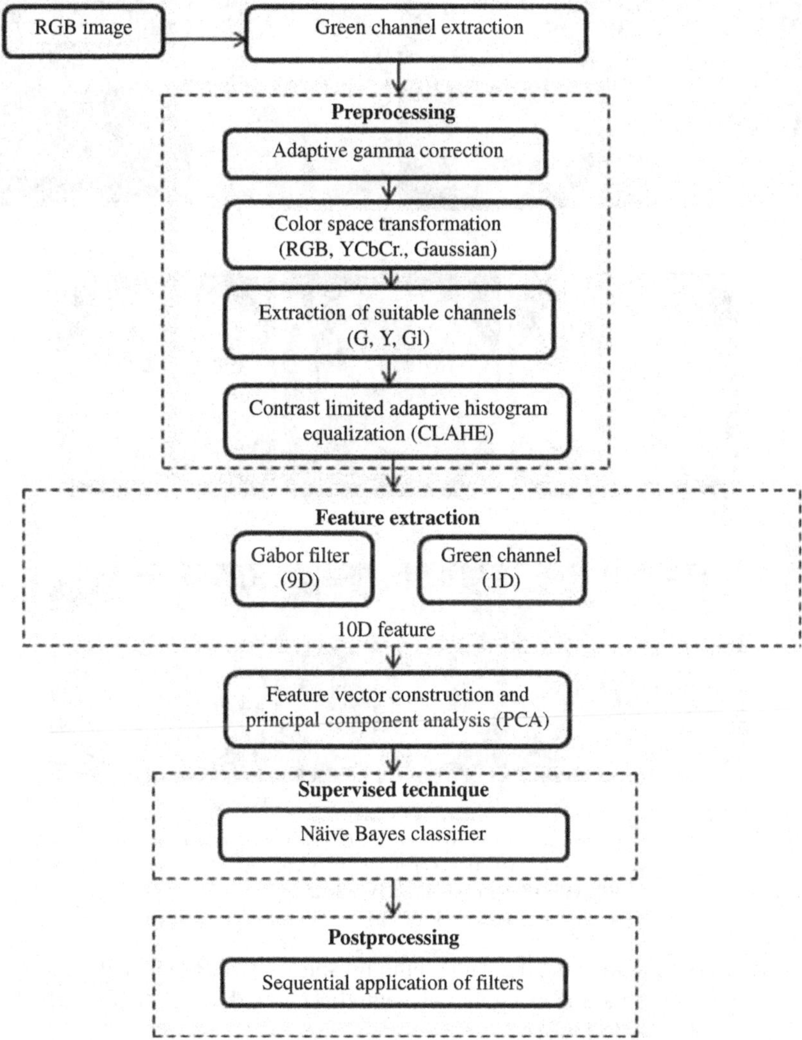


**FIG. 1** Methodology.

**(a)** Adaptive gamma correction.

AGC is performed to enhance the contrast of the image by setting the parameters of AGC dynamically based on the characteristics of input image. This is effective while dealing with real-life medical situations where we have to confront with different types of images. Several methods were analyzed and evaluated. Among those, Rahman et al. [49] is found to be the best method for retinal images. It helps to control the brightness of

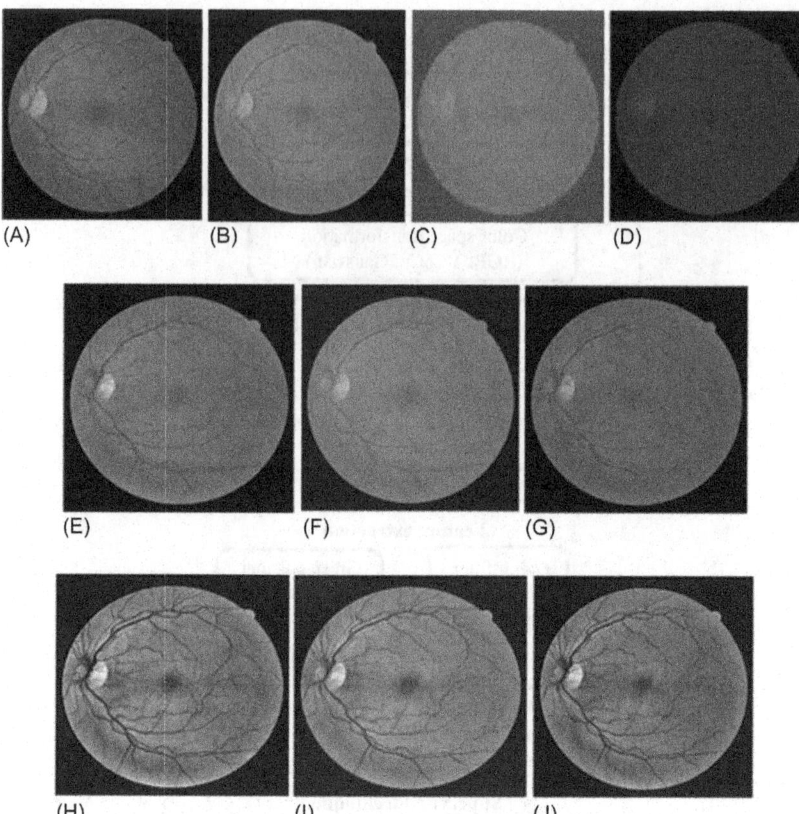


**FIG. 2** Preprocessing phase: (A) Input RGB image; (B) adaptive gamma correction; (C) YCbCr color space; (D) Gaussian color space; (E) G channel; (F) Y channel; (G) G1 channel; (H–J) G, Y, and G1 channels after CLAHE (first image in DRIVE database).

the image automatically. The method inspired from Rahman et al. [49] is implemented at the same in our method. The working of AGC method is described as follows:

- Read the input image.
- Check whether it is a color image or not, if yes, convert RGB to HSV and extract the V channel. HSV color model exhibits good representation of color for human perception.
- Check whether the image is low contrast (c1) or high contrast (c2). This is done by using the condition:

$$h(i) = \begin{cases} \text{c1}, & \text{if } d \leq \frac{1}{\tau} \\ \text{c2}, & \text{otherwise} \end{cases} \tag{1}$$

- If the image is high contrast, $\gamma$ is obtained by using exponential function as follows:

$$\gamma = \exp\left[\frac{(1-(\mu+\sigma))}{2}\right] \tag{2}$$

where $\mu$ is the mean and $\sigma$ is the standard deviation of the image intensity and $\tau$ is a factor that defines the contrast of an image.
If the image is low contrast, $\gamma$ is obtained by using logarithmic function as follows:

$$\gamma = -\log_2(\sigma) \tag{3}$$

- The high-contrast or low-contrast images are then categorized for dark or bright subclasses based on the mean value. The image is classified as bright if the mean is greater than or equal to 0.5 and dark if the mean is less than 0.5.
- If the image is bright, adaptive gamma corrected image is given as:

$$V = U^{\gamma} \tag{4}$$

If the image is dark, adaptive gamma corrected image is given as:

$$V = \frac{(U^{\gamma})}{U^{\gamma} + (1-U^{\gamma})\mu^{\gamma}} \tag{5}$$

**(b)** Color space transformation.

The adaptive gamma corrected image is then converted into YCbCr and Gaussian color models other than an RGB model. These color models expose the vessels clearly, which is essential for efficient segmentation. YCbCr and Gaussian color models are uniform and also are helpful in texture analysis. RGB image is converted into Gaussian color model by using the transformation equation:

$$\begin{bmatrix} G1 \\ G2 \\ G3 \end{bmatrix} = \begin{bmatrix} 0.06 & 0.63 & 0.27 \\ 0.3 & 0.04 & -0.35 \\ 0.34 & -0.6 & 0.17 \end{bmatrix} \begin{bmatrix} R \\ G \\ B \end{bmatrix} \tag{6}$$

**(c)** Extraction of color channels.

Suitable color channels have to be extracted from the color spaces. The RGB color model consists of red channel (R), green channel (G), and blue channel (B) from which green channel is extracted because red and blue channels have poor illuminance and also green channel has good visibility of vessels. The YCbCr color model consists of the Luma component (Y), the chroma of the blue difference (Cb), and the chroma of the red difference (Cr) from which Y channel is extracted. The Gaussian model consists of G1, G2, and G3 channels from which G1 channel is extracted.

**(d)** Contrast limited adaptive histogram equalization.

CLAHE is a variant of adaptive histogram equalization (AHE), which limits the overamplification of noise in uniform areas of an image and thereby enhances the contrast in images. CLAHE operates on tiny tiles in an image rather than the complete image. Contrast of each region is enhanced, and the output histogram nearly matches the histogram defined by the "Distribution" parameter. Then they are merged by bilinear interpolation.

### *3.2.2 Feature extraction*

Ten features are extracted from the input image where 9 features are obtained by applying Gabor filters on histogram-equalized color channels, and the 10th feature is the extracted green channel of the RGB color model after histogram equalization.

#### Gabor filtering

Multiscale Gabor filtering inspired from the research [44] is used in the proposed work. To extract the maximum possible vessels in the image, the image is scanned in different orientations in multiple scales. The parameters that influence the construction of the Gabor filter kernel are wavelength, aspect ratio, and bandwidth. The best performance of Gabor filtering is obtained at wavelengths 9, 10, 11, aspect ratio of 0.5, and orientation starting from zero with an increment of 15 degrees until 360 degrees. The resultant images are converted to binary by using half wave rectification used in Ref. [44]. Thus, the Gabor filtering applied on three color channels at three different wavelengths result in nine Gabor images and is shown in Fig. 3.

### *3.2.3 Feature vector construction and principal component analysis*

The 10 images resulted from the feature extraction phase is converted into 10-dimensional feature vector where each pixel in the image is represented by these 10 values. Prior to the supervised technique, principal component analysis is applied to the 10-dimensional feature vector to reduce the feature redundancy. It projects the feature space (*n* d-dimensional) onto a smaller subspace that represents our data well, with minimal loss of information. Before the output is given to the next stage, the retinal image is converted into binary.

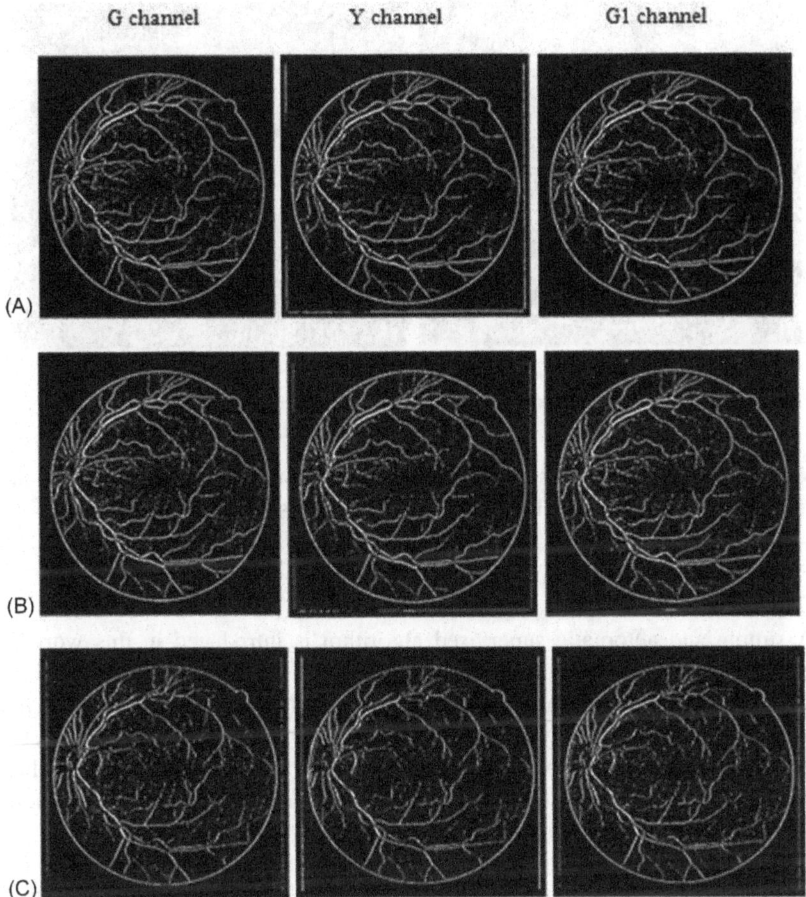


**FIG. 3** Output after Gabor filtering: (A) wavelength = 9, (B) wavelength = 10, and (C) wavelength = 11 (first image in DRIVE database).

### 3.2.4 *Supervised technique*

The result from the previous stage consisting of both vessels and nonvessels are given for classification purpose. The classification is done by using a simple classifier known as naive Bayes classifier. It is a family of probabilistic classifiers. It is a supervised machine learning algorithm that exploits Bayes theorem assuming that the features are statistically independent. It is fast, scalable, and requires only less data.

### 3.2.5 *Postprocessing*

Postprocessing phase is performed to remove the isolated nonvessels and noise. It is done by the sequential application of median filter and wiener filter to

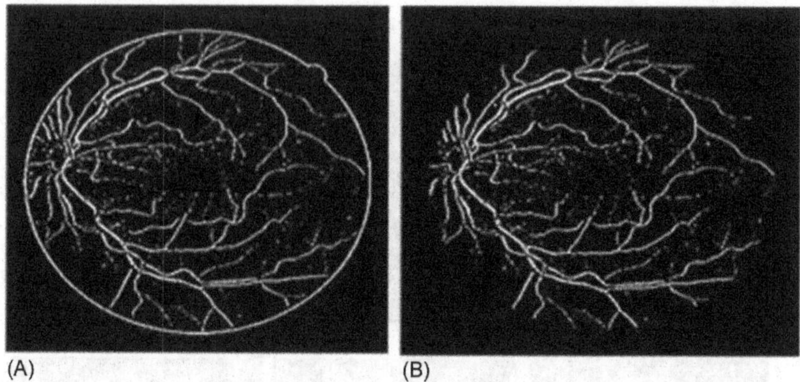

FIG. 4 (A) Supervised phase and (B) postprocessing phase (first image in DRIVE database).

remove unwanted nonvessels and noise, and FOV mask is used to remove the regions outside the FOV. Fig. 4B shows the final segmented output.

## 3.3 Result

A simple and automatic supervised algorithm is introduced in this work to extract the retinal blood vessels automatically from fundus images. In this work, Gabor features at different wavelengths and orientation are extracted from the input data. Gabor filtering shows its excellence in enhancing the blood vessels due to the fact that the blood vessels are Gaussian shaped. Then, a simple classifier called naive Bayes classifier is used for distinguishing vessels and nonvessels. The work focuses on better accuracy and low execution time.

The performance of the algorithm is assessed by using two publicly available databases: DRIVE and STARE. STARE has a total of 20 images. Fig. 5 shows the output of 12th image in STARE database.

### *3.3.1 Qualitative analysis*

From Figs. 3 and 4, it can be seen that the retinal blood vessels are accurately segmented from the fundus image. In case of both the DRIVE an STARE database, the algorithm maintains the connectivity of blood vessels to a good extent. Our algorithm handles pathological images with less complexity and execution time. It holds a good generalized effect on both normal and pathological images. No major vascular breaks can be observed after the postprocessing phase, but some of the fine vessels are suppressed.

### *3.3.2 Quantitative analysis*

The performance of the algorithm is appraised by using the metrics, such as accuracy, sensitivity, and specificity. Sensitivity estimates the ratio of real positives

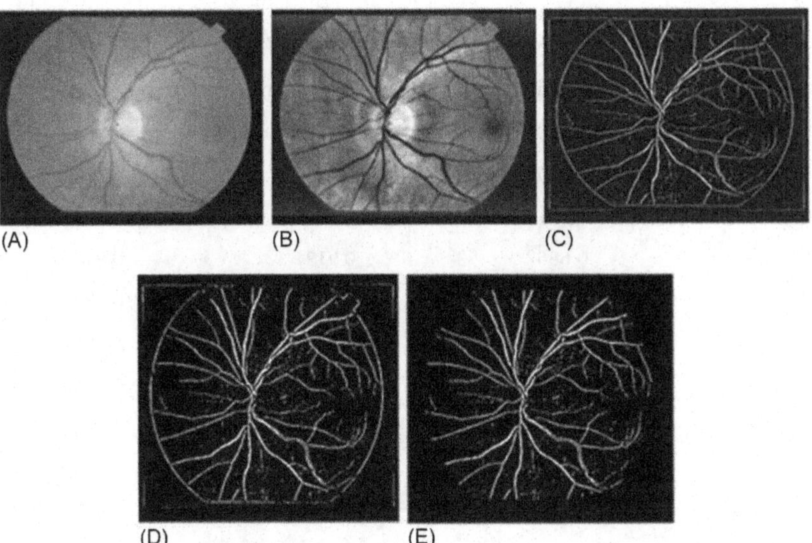

FIG. 5 Output of STARE database: (A) input image; (B) preprocessing phase (green channel); (C) feature extraction phase (after PCA); (D) supervised technique; and (E) postprocessing phase (12th image in STARE database).

that are precisely identified, and it shows the ability of the algorithm to detect true vessels. Specificity is the ratio of actual negatives that are truly identified, and it is the ability to detect nonvessels. Accuracy (ACC) is the degree to which the resultant output gets close to manually segmented output by the experts.

$$Sensitivity = \frac{TP}{TP + FN} \tag{7}$$

$$Specificity = \frac{TN}{TN + FP} \tag{8}$$

$$Accuracy = \frac{TP + TN}{TP + FN + TN + FP} \tag{9}$$

where TP is true positives, TN is true negatives, FP is false positives, and FN is false negatives.

In the DRIVE database, the classifier is trained by 20 train images and is completed at the time span of 190 s. Testing is performed on the 20 test images and attained an average execution time of 31.23 s. Table 2 shows the metrics computed for the images in DRIVE database.

In STARE database, the first 10 images are used for training and testing is performed on the whole 20 images. Training is done at a duration of 99.45 s, and testing has achieved an average execution time of 34.14 s. Table 3 shows the accuracy, sensitivity, and specificity computed for the images in STARE database.

**TABLE 2** Performance evaluation on DRIVE database.

| Images | Sensitivity | Specificity | Accuracy |
|---|---|---|---|
| (1) | 0.2380 | 0.9121 | 0.9063 |
| (2) | 0.1755 | 0.8983 | 0.8911 |
| (3) | 0.1911 | 0.9010 | 0.8955 |
| (4) | 0.6862 | 0.9121 | 0.9106 |
| (5) | 0.2283 | 0.9074 | 0.9021 |
| (6) | 0.1677 | 0.9031 | 0.8984 |
| (7) | 0.1743 | 0.9093 | 0.9035 |
| (8) | 0.2160 | 0.9148 | 0.9104 |
| (9) | 0.1683 | 0.9195 | 0.9149 |
| (10) | 0.1608 | 0.9183 | 0.9123 |
| (11) | 0.1667 | 0.9110 | 0.9057 |
| (12) | 0.2113 | 0.9144 | 0.9104 |
| (13) | 0.1644 | 0.9028 | 0.8967 |
| (14) | 0.1733 | 0.9198 | 0.9143 |
| (15) | 0.4451 | 0.9301 | 0.9279 |
| (16) | 0.1838 | 0.9105 | 0.9044 |
| (17) | 0.1705 | 0.9162 | 0.9110 |
| (18) | 0.2183 | 0.9218 | 0.9166 |
| (19) | 0.2088 | 0.9181 | 0.9123 |
| (20) | 0.1561 | 0.9238 | 0.9268 |
| Average | 0.2252 | 0.9132 | 0.9085 |

**TABLE 3** Performance evaluation on STARE database.

| Images | Sensitivity | Specificity | Accuracy |
|---|---|---|---|
| (1) | 0.1064 | 0.9205 | 0.9115 |
| (2) | 0.1012 | 0.9336 | 0.9283 |
| (3) | 0.1217 | 0.9406 | 0.9350 |
| (4) | 0.2384 | 0.9264 | 0.9243 |
| (5) | 0.2852 | 0.9114 | 0.9060 |

**TABLE 3** Performance evaluation on STARE database—cont'd

| Images | Sensitivity | Specificity | Accuracy |
|---|---|---|---|
| (6) | 0.1904 | 0.9318 | 0.9231 |
| (7) | 0.1199 | 0.9203 | 0.9123 |
| (8) | 0.2019 | 0.9265 | 0.9202 |
| (9) | 0.2241 | 0.9228 | 0.9158 |
| (10) | 0.1594 | 0.9207 | 0.9101 |
| (11) | 0.1479 | 0.9292 | 0.9245 |
| (12) | 0.4835 | 0.9289 | 0.9222 |
| (13) | 0.2151 | 0.9128 | 0.9030 |
| (14) | 0.2598 | 0.9116 | 0.9034 |
| (15) | 0.1964 | 0.9144 | 0.9097 |
| (16) | 0.1940 | 0.8989 | 0.8910 |
| (17) | 0.2008 | 0.9115 | 0.9051 |
| (18) | 0.4131 | 0.9505 | 0.9489 |
| (19) | 0.0763 | 0.9578 | 0.9356 |
| (20) | 0.6507 | 0.9360 | 0.9347 |
| Average | 0.2293 | 0.9253 | 0.9182 |

From the tabular computations, it is observed that the algorithm is simple and less complex. Training and testing of the classifier can be accomplished at lower execution time. But sensitivity is much lower when compared to other methods. Accuracy and specificity are satisfying but need to be improved as a future scope.

### *3.3.3 Performance comparison of our method with the state-of-the-art methods in terms of execution time*

The performance comparison of the proposed method with the state-of-the-art methods shows that our method outperforms all other methods in terms of execution time (Tables 4 and 5). But the drawback is that our method could not break the trade-off between accuracy and execution time. Here, we have selected a very simple classifier by considering many factors. Most of the recent methods use highly complicated and efficient learning networks, which of course results in better accuracy. But most of them are very complex, and

**TABLE 4** Comparison of average training time with other methods for DRIVE or STARE database.

| Dataset | Methods | Average processing time |
|---|---|---|
| DRIVE or STARE | Soares et al. [8] | 8 h |
| | Fraz et al. [10] | 100 s |
| | Li et al. [13] | 7 h |
| | Proposed | 190 s |
| | | 99.45 s |

**TABLE 5** Comparison of average processing time with other methods for DRIVE or STARE database.

| Dataset | Methods | Average processing time |
|---|---|---|
| DRIVE or STARE | Mendonca and Campilho [7] | 2.5 min |
| | Soares et al. [8] | 3 min |
| | Al-Diri et al. [9] | 11 min |
| | Cinsdikici and Aydn [39] | 35 s |
| | Marin et al. [25] | 1.5 min |
| | Fraz et al. [10] | 100 s |
| | Zhao et al. [50] | 2 min |
| | Li et al. [13] | 1.2 min |
| | Proposed | 31.23 s |
| | | 34.14 s |

the authors do not dare to mention the execution time. We can also incorporate a high-end network, which might result in very good theoretical values. But here, we have worked with many networks and selected a simple classifier that can track the vessels and true vessels accurately with low complexity and execution time. As an important note, here we have extracted only simple features like intensity and Gaussian. Our main focus is to build a system that can be incorporated for real-life medical situations. This is the primary phase of our research where we build a system with low complexity and comparable metrics. As a future work, we tend to improve the metrics by customizing the feature vector, which is more reliable with the classifier.

## 4 Extraction of retinal blood vessels using unsupervised technique

A simple unsupervised method is proposed to mitigate the shortcomings encountered in extracting retinal blood vessels from fundus images in the previous works. Most of the existing methods mainly focus on the segmenting blood vessels from low-resolution fundus images, which have become outdated with the advancement in imaging science.

The proposed method presents a simple but efficient algorithm to extract retinal blood vessels using DWT followed by multilevel Otsu thresholding. The methodology involves preprocessing, segmentation, and postprocessing stages. A double enhancement method is adopted during the preprocessing stage for better segmentation accuracy. The segmentation phase applies DWT followed by multilevel Otsu thresholding. The multiresolution analysis using wavelet transform perfectly blends with Otsu thresholding to extract the blood vessels accurately. Finally, the postprocessing stage embraces a series of morphological operations to remove the isolated nonvessels and noise. The technique is experimentally tested, and performance is evaluated on a child heart and health study in England (CHASE_DB1) database and high-resolution fundus (HRF) database, which are explained in the following section.

The proposed method offers good performance for both of the databases, with less computational complexity and execution time. The algorithm has achieved an accuracy of 0.9523 with an execution time of 6.76 s for CHASE_DB1 database and an accuracy of 0.9468, 0.9508, and 0.9380 with an average execution time of 16.01 s for normal, glaucomatous, and DR images with HRF database, respectively.

### 4.1 Materials

CHASE_DB1 is a retinal image database of multiethnic school children, obtained from a child heart and health study in England [10]. The images are captured using a Nidek NM-200-D fundus camera with a high-resolution of 1280 by 960 pixels and 30-degree FOV. It consists of 28 paired images from the left and right eye of 14 children, and its manual segmentation results are also provided by two observers. Here, we have considered only the images of the right eye in the database for performance evaluation. The manual segmentation suggested by the first human observer is considered as ground truth in this work.

HRF database consists of retinal images of healthy, glaucomatous and DR people. Each set consists of 15 images along with its ground-truth images obtained from experts [4]. The images are captured by using a Canon CR-1 fundus camera. They have a higher resolution of 3504 by 2336 and FOV of 60 degrees.

CHASE_DB1 database comprises of low-resolution images while the HRF database comprises of high-resolution images. These databases are chosen to test whether the proposed algorithm works for different resolutions without any complication.

## 4.2 Proposed method

The proposed methodology for the segmentation of retinal blood vessels mainly consists of three phases: preprocessing, segmentation, and postprocessing, as shown in Fig. 6. Here also, we have extracted the green channel of the input image and given as input to the preprocessing phase.

### 4.2.1 Preprocessing

Preprocessing is an important step in improving the performance of segmentation due to nonuniform illumination of the input retinal images. Hence as in Section 3.2.1, we are adopting a double enhancement method for the better perceivability and visibility of blood vessels. The preprocessing phase incorporates: Gamma correction and CLAHE followed by median filtering.

**(a)** Gamma correction.

Power-law transform is given by:

$$q = ca^{\gamma} \tag{10}$$

where $q$ is the output image, $c$ and $\gamma$ are constants greater than zero, and $a$ is the input.

Gamma correction can be used to control the overall brightness of an image. It can be used with images that are found to be either bleached out or too dark [12]. Expansion and compression of pixel intensity values are desired for darker and faded images [51]. Here, to save time we have used the algorithm used in Rahman et al. [49] to obtain the values of $g$ and $\gamma$. The average values obtained are 1 and 1.5 for $g$ and $\gamma$. These values are obtained by analyzing the statistical characteristics, such as the mean and standard deviation of the image. It handles both darker and brighter images on the databases in an appropriate and acceptable manner. The equation utilized to find $\gamma$ is shown in Eq. (11). The next phase is contrast limited histogram equalization.

$$\gamma = \exp\left[\frac{1-(M+S)}{2}\right] \tag{11}$$

where $M$ is the mean and $S$ is the standard deviation of the image.

**(b)** Contrast Limited Adaptive Histogram Equalization.

CLAHE is better explained in Section 3.2.1, the outcome of which is given for median filtering.

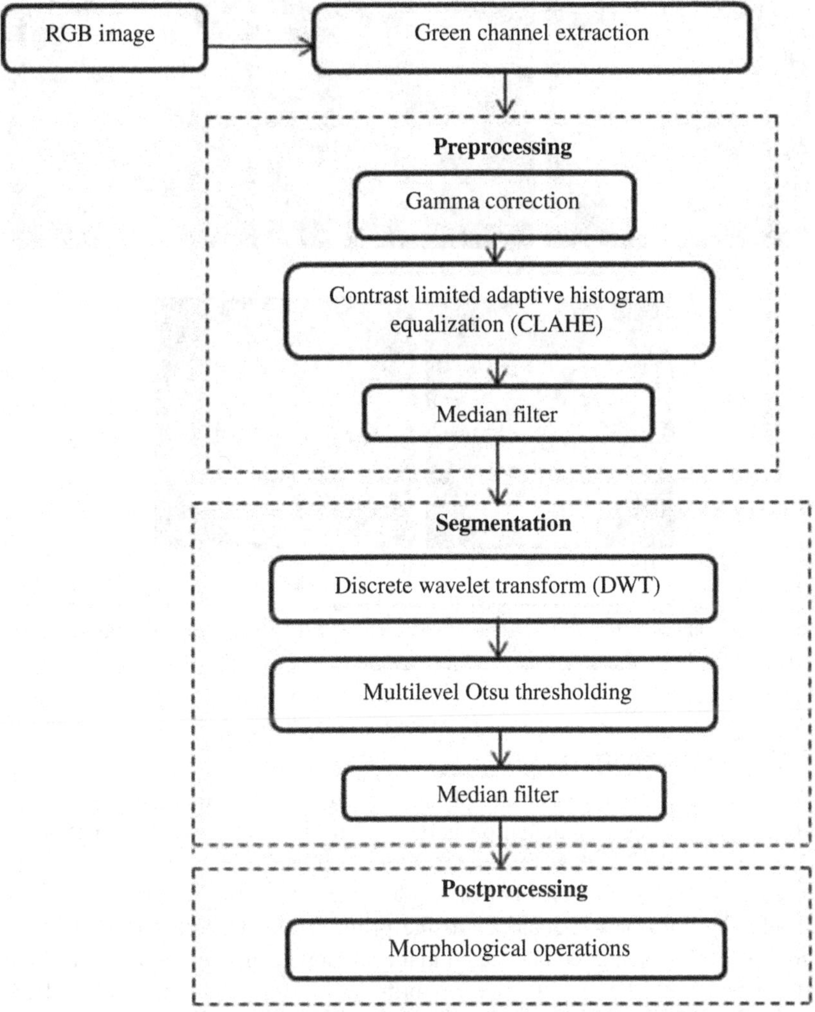


**FIG. 6** Methodology.

**(c)** Median filtering.

The output after double enhancement undergoes median filtering to prepare the image for the next stage. It is a nonlinear digital filtering method and is employed to eliminate salt-and-pepper noise in an image [52]. It reduces noise from an image without diminishing the sharpness of the image. Each image pixel is displaced with the median value of the surrounding m-by-m neighborhood by the median filter. Fig. 7 shows the result of preprocessing phase of fifth image in CHASE_DB1 database.

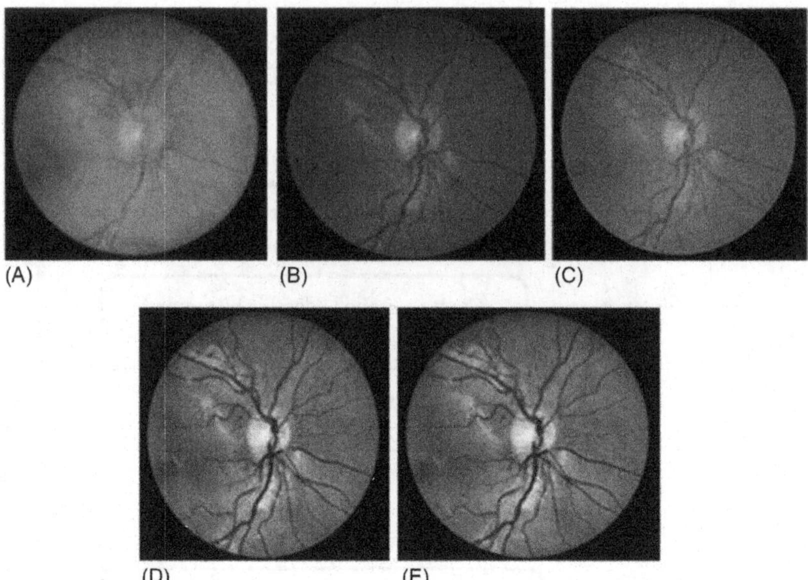


**FIG. 7** Preprocessing phase: (A) original RGB image; (B) green channel; (C) Gamma correction; (D) contrast limited adaptive histogram equalization; and (E) median filtering (fifth image in CHASE DB_1).

### *4.2.2 Segmentation*

The output of the preprocessing phase is given to the segmentation phase for further processing. Segmentation is done using DWT followed by multilevel Otsu thresholding. In this process, the intensified image from the previous stage is convolved with a mean filter of window size 19 × 19. The window size is decided by considering accuracy as the prime factor. Different window sizes from 3 × 3 is considered and found that accuracy keeps on incrementing from 3 × 3 to 19 × 19 and starts decrementing after 19 × 19. Hence, 19 × 19 is selected. Then, DWT is applied to the residue image, which is procured by subtracting the enhanced image from the convoluted image. The residue or difference image contains of a handful of spatial information, which is preserved by both convoluted and enhanced image. Numerous types of wavelets, such as Haar, Daubechies, Morlet, Symlet, and more, are available in the wavelet family. Here, db 1 wavelet of Daubechies family is used because it provides better output than other wavelets in this context.

DWT produces the approximation and detail coefficients. The approximation coefficients are extracted and advanced to the next step due to the fact that they contain more information about the original images. In other words, they are the compressed version of the original images. DWT provides lossless

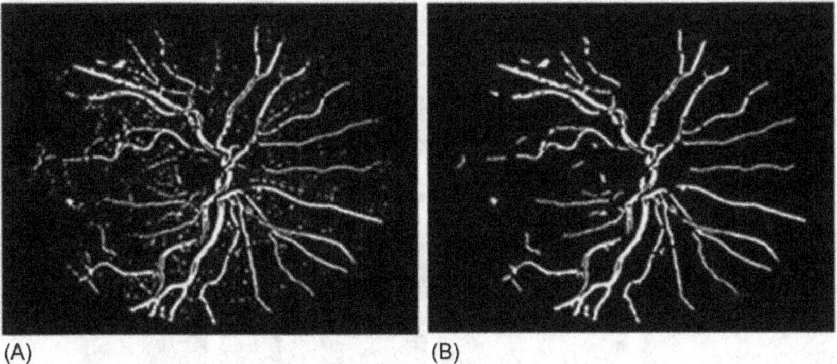


**FIG. 8** (A) Segmentation phase and (B) postprocessing phase (fifth image in CHASE_DB1).

compression. Approximation coefficients contain the spatial characteristics of the image and to which multilevel Otsu thresholding is applied. It can be defined as follows:

$$c(x,y) = \begin{cases} 1, & \text{if } d(x,y) > T \\ 0, & \text{otherwise} \end{cases} \tag{12}$$

where $c(x, y)$ is the threshold output, $d(x, y)$ is the output of DWT, and $T$ is the threshold obtained as a result of Otsu thresholding. The median filtering is reapplied to suppress noise. Fig. 8A shows the output of fifth image in CHASE_DB1 database after segmentation.

### 4.2.3 Postprocessing

The result of the foregoing stage shows the presence of noise and some nonvessels, which can be eliminated with the aid of a set of morphological operations. A top hat transform is applied to the image to enhance the vessels and smoothen the background. This is significant for pathological images. Top hat transform can be defined as follows:

$$g(h) = h - h \circ s \tag{13}$$

where $g(h)$ is the top-hat transformed image, $h$ is the input image, $\circ$ is the opening operation, and $s$ is the structuring element. Fig. 8B shows the final segmented output after postprocessing.

## 5 Result

The performance appraisal of the method is validated by computing various performance metrics like sensitivity, specificity, and accuracy. Fig. 9 shows the results in the HRF database.

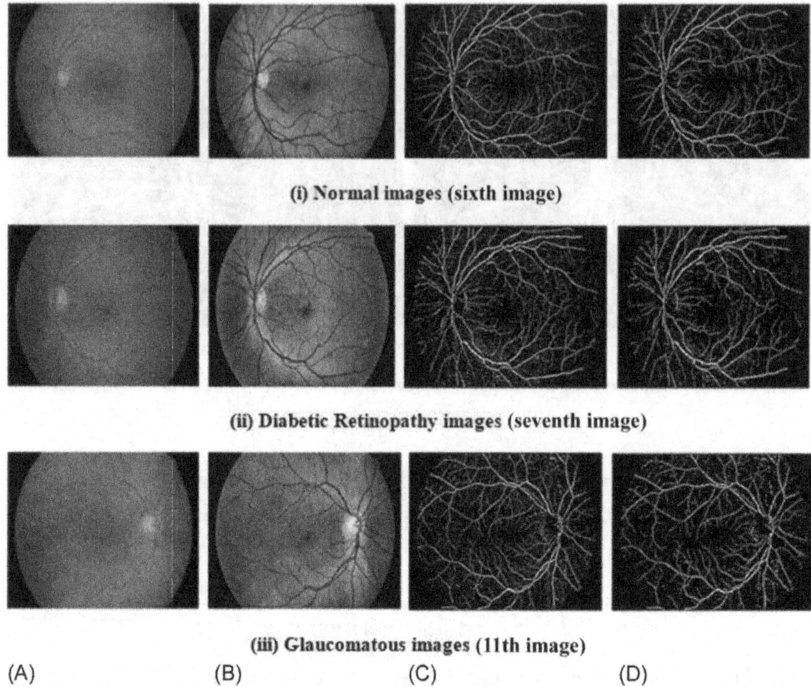


**FIG. 9** (A) Original RGB images; (B) preprocessed images; (C) images after segmentation phase; and (D) images after postprocessing phase (HRF database).

## 5.1 Qualitative analysis

CHASE_DB1 does not generalize the background contrast of fundus images more uniformly than the HRF. This is managed by utilizing a double enhancement technique adopted in preprocessing stage. From Figs. 8 and 9, it is visually evident that the retinal blood vessels are more accurately segmented from the fundus image. In case of HRF database, the thin blood vessels are efficiently extracted than CHASE_DB1 database. The algorithm also handles pathological images with less complexity and execution time. Here, it is not found to be essential to consider the extraction of thick and thin vessels separately as in Ref. [41], since our algorithm does that effectively. The algorithm maintains the connectivity of blood vessels to a good extent, which makes it better for the extraction of thin blood vessels. It holds a good generalization effect on both normal and pathological images. There exist no major vascular breaks and effectively suppresses the noise after postprocessing phase. From Fig. 9, the algorithm extracts the vessels with more details in junction areas and also successfully segments the tied vessels. It is more evident from the HRF database than the CHASE_DB1 database. Our algorithm succeeds in extracting most of the vessels and can be made better in future research.

## 5.2 Quantitative analysis

The performance appraisal of this method is validated by computing various performance metrics, like true positive predictive value (PPV), negative predictive value (NPV), false discovery rate (FDR), Matthews's correlation coefficient (MCC) other than accuracy (ACC), sensitivity, and specificity. This is done to emphasize the significance and caliber of our algorithm.

Sensitivity is also termed as true positive rate (TPR), and specificity is also known as true negative rate (TNR). Positive and negative predictive values can be defined as the amount of positives and negatives detected during the procedure, which are actual positives and actual negatives, respectively. The false discovery rate (FDR) measures the ratio of false prediction to the set of predictions. MCC assesses the caliber of binary classifications and varies between − 1 and + 1. MCC equals − 1 shows that there is no match between resultant output and the ground truth output and 1 is a perfect match between resultant and the ground-truth output.

$$TPR = \frac{TP}{TP + FN} \tag{14}$$

$$TNR = \frac{TN}{TN + FP} \tag{15}$$

$$PPV = \frac{TP}{TP + FP} \tag{16}$$

$$NPV = \frac{TN}{TN + FN} \tag{17}$$

$$FDR = \frac{FP}{FP + TN} \tag{18}$$

$$MCC = \frac{TP*TN - FP*FN}{\sqrt{(TP + FP)(TP + FN)(TN + FP)(TN + FN)}} \tag{19}$$

$$ACC = \frac{TP + TN}{TP + FN + TN + FP} \tag{20}$$

where TP is true positives, TN is true negatives, FP is false positives, and FN is false negatives.

Table 6 shows the performance metrics for CHASE_DB1 database. From a total of 28 images of left and right eye, the algorithm efficiently works for both of the sets in the database. But here, we consider only the right eye images for the evaluation purpose. The algorithm is performed with an average execution time of 6.76 s.

Table 7 represents the performance evaluation of normal retinal images in the HRF database.

Table 8 represents the performance evaluation of DR retinal images in the HRF database.

**TABLE 6** Performance validation on CHASE_DB1 database.

| Images | Accuracy | Sensitivity | Specificity | PPV | NPV | FDR | MCC |
|---|---|---|---|---|---|---|---|
| (1) | 0.9533 | 0.7256 | 0.9683 | 0.6005 | 0.9817 | 0.0317 | 0.6356 |
| (2) | 0.9421 | 0.6213 | 0.9691 | 0.6291 | 0.9810 | 0.0309 | 0.5938 |
| (3) | 0.9562 | 0.7449 | 0.9706 | 0.6335 | 0.9824 | 0.0294 | 0.6638 |
| (4) | 0.9517 | 0.6923 | 0.9720 | 0.6578 | 0.9759 | 0.0280 | 0.6488 |
| (5) | 0.9560 | 0.8131 | 0.9657 | 0.6174 | 0.9870 | 0.0343 | 0.6861 |
| (6) | 0.9515 | 0.7038 | 0.9682 | 0.5990 | 0.9798 | 0.0318 | 0.6237 |
| (7) | 0.9407 | 0.5770 | 0.9790 | 0.7430 | 0.9565 | 0.0210 | 0.6236 |
| (8) | 0.9560 | 0.6401 | 0.9786 | 0.6821 | 0.9743 | 0.0214 | 0.6373 |
| (9) | 0.9529 | 0.5236 | 0.9812 | 0.6482 | 0.9689 | 0.0188 | 0.5581 |
| (10) | 0.9483 | 0.5776 | 0.9739 | 0.6036 | 0.9710 | 0.0261 | 0.5629 |
| (11) | 0.9623 | 0.6268 | 0.9834 | 0.7046 | 0.9766 | 0.0166 | 0.6448 |
| (12) | 0.9475 | 0.6214 | 0.9781 | 0.7277 | 0.9649 | 0.0219 | 0.6444 |
| (13) | 0.9523 | 0.6568 | 0.9676 | 0.5115 | 0.9820 | 0.0324 | 0.5551 |
| (14) | 0.9612 | 0.6964 | 0.9750 | 0.5935 | 0.9840 | 0.0250 | 0.6227 |
| | 0.9523 | 0.6581 | 0.9736 | 0.6394 | 0.9761 | 0.0264 | 0.623 |

**TABLE 7** Performance evaluation on HRF-normal retinal images.

| Images | Accuracy | TPR | TNR | PPV | NPV | FDR | MCC |
|---|---|---|---|---|---|---|---|
| (1) | 0.9442 | 0.8104 | 0.9543 | 0.5739 | 0.9852 | 0.0457 | 0.6539 |
| (2) | 0.9486 | 0.8561 | 0.9549 | 0.5617 | 0.9899 | 0.0451 | 0.6688 |
| (3) | 0.9367 | 0.7711 | 0.9499 | 0.5507 | 0.9812 | 0.0501 | 0.6194 |
| (4) | 0.9453 | 0.7487 | 0.9613 | 0.6117 | 0.9792 | 0.0387 | 0.6477 |
| (5) | 0.9531 | 0.8428 | 0.9601 | 0.5747 | 0.9896 | 0.0399 | 0.6732 |
| (6) | 0.9504 | 0.7866 | 0.9659 | 0.6847 | 0.9796 | 0.0341 | 0.7070 |
| (7) | 0.9459 | 0.8932 | 0.9482 | 0.4281 | 0.9951 | 0.0518 | 0.5968 |
| (8) | 0.9482 | 0.8501 | 0.9551 | 0.5735 | 0.9890 | 0.0449 | 0.6730 |
| (9) | 0.9535 | 0.7760 | 0.9635 | 0.5441 | 0.9871 | 0.0365 | 0.6267 |
| (10) | 0.9513 | 0.8406 | 0.9573 | 0.5183 | 0.9910 | 0.0427 | 0.6375 |
| (11) | 0.9481 | 0.7509 | 0.9652 | 0.6519 | 0.9781 | 0.0348 | 0.6717 |
| (12) | 0.9405 | 0.7175 | 0.9653 | 0.6977 | 0.9684 | 0.0347 | 0.6744 |
| (13) | 0.9428 | 0.7992 | 0.9449 | 0.4408 | 0.9897 | 0.0501 | 0.5679 |
| (14) | 0.9452 | 0.7208 | 0.9623 | 0.5926 | 0.9784 | 0.0377 | 0.6245 |
| (15) | 0.9476 | 0.8180 | 0.9529 | 0.4136 | 0.9923 | 0.0471 | 0.5594 |
|  | 0.9468 | 0.7988 | 0.9571 | 0.5612 | 0.9849 | 0.0423 | 0.6401 |

Table 9 shows the performance evaluation of glaucomatous retinal images in the HRF database.

The algorithm is executed with mean execution time of 16.01 s for the images in the HRF database. From the tabular computation, it is witnessed that the algorithm possess robust performance for both of the databases. The higher value of PPV and lower value of FDR evinces that the vessels and nonvessel objects are marked with more exactness and efficiency. The higher the value of MCC, the more robust is the performance. The algorithm handles low- and high-resolution images effectively. From the visually and mathematically evidential results, it is deduced that our algorithm implies good performance both qualitatively and quantitatively.

Table 10 shows the comparison of our algorithm with the state-of-the-art methods for the CHASE_DB1 database. It can be seen that the proposed method has a much more preferable accuracy than all other methods in the literature. Sensitivity is lower when likened to other methods but is much more satisfying and comparable with the literature.

Table 11 shows the comparison of the proposed algorithm with different methods for normal, DR, and glaucomatous retinal images in the HRF database.

**TABLE 8** Performance evaluation on HRF-DR retinal images.

| Images | Accuracy | TPR | TNR | PPV | NPV | FDR | MCC |
|---|---|---|---|---|---|---|---|
| (1) | 0.9582 | 0.6060 | 0.9717 | 0.4500 | 0.9847 | 0.0283 | 0.5011 |
| (2) | 0.9491 | 0.6295 | 0.9648 | 0.4683 | 0.9814 | 0.0352 | 0.5170 |
| (3) | 0.9217 | 0.3923 | 0.9719 | 0.5693 | 0.9440 | 0.0281 | 0.4324 |
| (4) | 0.9272 | 0.3887 | 0.9722 | 0.5384 | 0.9501 | 0.0278 | 0.4198 |
| (5) | 0.9567 | 0.6894 | 0.9700 | 0.5352 | 0.9842 | 0.0300 | 0.5853 |
| (6) | 0.9345 | 0.5672 | 0.9620 | 0.5271 | 0.9675 | 0.0380 | 0.5116 |
| (7) | 0.9372 | 0.5840 | 0.9696 | 0.6386 | 0.9621 | 0.0304 | 0.5766 |
| (8) | 0.9282 | 0.5143 | 0.9657 | 0.5759 | 0.9564 | 0.0343 | 0.5055 |
| (9) | 0.9382 | 0.5426 | 0.9630 | 0.4794 | 0.9710 | 0.0370 | 0.4772 |
| (10) | 0.9407 | 0.6937 | 0.9589 | 0.5535 | 0.9771 | 0.0411 | 0.5884 |
| (11) | 0.9420 | 0.6584 | 0.9668 | 0.6337 | 0.9701 | 0.0332 | 0.6144 |
| (12) | 0.9419 | 0.5755 | 0.9659 | 0.5245 | 0.9721 | 0.0341 | 0.5185 |
| (13) | 0.9387 | 0.5425 | 0.9706 | 0.5972 | 0.9635 | 0.0294 | 0.5363 |
| (14) | 0.9225 | 0.4893 | 0.9623 | 0.5441 | 0.9535 | 0.0377 | 0.4740 |
| (15) | 0.9343 | 0.4914 | 0.9650 | 0.4930 | 0.9648 | 0.0350 | 0.4571 |
| | 0.9380 | 0.5577 | 0.9667 | 0.5418 | 0.9668 | 0.0333 | 0.5143 |

**TABLE 9** Performance evaluation on HRF-glaucomatous retinal images.

| Images | Accuracy | TPR | TNR | PPV | NPV | FDR | MCC |
|---|---|---|---|---|---|---|---|
| (1) | 0.9450 | 0.5758 | 0.9737 | 0.6308 | 0.9672 | 0.0263 | 0.5681 |
| (2) | 0.9435 | 0.6297 | 0.9659 | 0.5685 | 0.9734 | 0.0341 | 0.5170 |
| (3) | 0.9553 | 0.7746 | 0.9593 | 0.3009 | 0.9947 | 0.0407 | 0.4658 |
| (4) | 0.9576 | 0.7056 | 0.9714 | 0.5749 | 0.9837 | 0.0286 | 0.6150 |
| (5) | 0.9542 | 0.7346 | 0.9633 | 0.4534 | 0.9887 | 0.0367 | 0.5554 |
| (6) | 0.9514 | 0.7252 | 0.9613 | 0.4514 | 0.9876 | 0.0387 | 0.5489 |
| (7) | 0.9578 | 0.7548 | 0.9670 | 0.5098 | 0.9886 | 0.0330 | 0.5998 |
| (8) | 0.9489 | 0.6181 | 0.9730 | 0.6244 | 0.9723 | 0.0270 | 0.5939 |
| (9) | 0.9574 | 0.7265 | 0.9696 | 0.5588 | 0.9853 | 0.0304 | 0.6154 |

**TABLE 9** Performance evaluation on HRF-glaucomatous retinal images—cont'd

| Images | Accuracy | TPR | TNR | PPV | NPV | FDR | MCC |
|---|---|---|---|---|---|---|---|
| (10) | 0.9590 | 0.7493 | 0.9695 | 0.5508 | 0.9872 | 0.0305 | 0.6219 |
| (11) | 0.9401 | 0.5847 | 0.9762 | 0.7146 | 0.9585 | 0.0238 | 0.6144 |
| (12) | 0.9403 | 0.6225 | 0.9716 | 0.6839 | 0.9631 | 0.0284 | 0.6200 |
| (13) | 0.9546 | 0.7006 | 0.9690 | 0.5627 | 0.9827 | 0.0310 | 0.6043 |
| (14) | 0.9477 | 0.6377 | 0.9682 | 0.5706 | 0.9758 | 0.0318 | 0.5754 |
| (15) | 0.9485 | 0.6993 | 0.9623 | 0.5056 | 0.9830 | 0.0377 | 0.5686 |
| | 0.9508 | 0.6826 | 0.9680 | 0.5507 | 0.9795 | 0.0319 | 0.5827 |

**TABLE 10** Performance comparison with other methods in the CHASE_DB1 database.

| Dataset | Methods | Year | TNR | TPR | Accuracy |
|---|---|---|---|---|---|
| CHASE_DB1 | Fraz et al. [10] | 2012 | 0.9711 | 0.7224 | 0.9469 |
| | Fraz et al. [53] | 2014 | 0.9770 | 0.7250 | 0.9520 |
| | Azzopardi et al. [5] | 2015 | 0.9587 | 0.7585 | 0.9387 |
| | Roychowdhury et al. [54] | 2015 | 0.9824 | 0.7201 | 0.9530 |
| | Roychowdhury et al. [55] | 2015 | 0.9575 | 0.7615 | 0.9467 |
| | Fu et al. [31] | 2016 | – | 0.7130 | 0.9489 |
| | Zhang et al. [56] | 2016 | 0.9661 | 0.7626 | 0.9452 |
| | Dash et al. [40] | 2017 | 0.9760 | 0.7040 | 0.9540 |
| | Memari et al. [32] | 2017 | 0.9591 | 0.8192 | 0.9482 |
| | Orlando et al. [57] | 2017 | 0.9712 | 0.7277 | – |
| | Zhang et al. [58] | 2017 | 0.9716 | 0.7644 | 0.9502 |
| | Dash et al. [12] | 2018 | 0.9807 | 0.7555 | 0.9521 |
| | Jin et al. [6] | 2019 | 0.9752 | 0.8155 | 0.9610 |
| | Sundaram et al. [59] | 2019 | 0.9600 | 0.7100 | 0.9500 |
| | Khawaja et al. [60] | 2019 | 0.9697 | 0.7974 | 0.9528 |
| | Tian et al. [43] | 2020 | 0.9680 | 0.8778 | 0.9601 |
| | Proposed | 2020 | 0.9736 | 0.6581 | 0.9523 |

It can be seen that our algorithm offers good comparable results with other methods.

Table 12 shows the comparison of average execution time of the proposed algorithm with the state-of-the-art methods for both CHASE_DB1 and HRF databases. From Table 12, it can be concluded that our algorithm outperforms all other methods in respect of execution time. For both of the databases, our method achieves the lowest running time, which implies that the proposed algorithm is computationally less complex. It can handle both low- and high-resolution images efficiently.

**TABLE 11** Performance comparison with other methods in HRF database.

| Dataset | Methods | Year | | TNR | TPR | Accuracy |
|---|---|---|---|---|---|---|
| HRF | Budai et al. [61] | 2013 | Normal | 0.9920 | 0.6620 | 0.9610 |
| | | | DR | 0.9770 | 0.6580 | 0.9550 |
| | | | Glaucomatous | 0.9860 | 0.6870 | 0.9650 |
| | Odstrcilik et al. [4] | 2013 | Normal | 0.9750 | 0.7861 | 0.9539 |
| | | | DR | 0.9619 | 0.7463 | 0.9445 |
| | | | Glaucomatous | 0.9638 | 0.7900 | 0.9497 |
| | Dash and Bhoi [62] | 2017 | Normal | 0.9807 | 0.7260 | 0.9568 |
| | | | DR | 0.9604 | 0.7755 | 0.9478 |
| | | | Glaucomatous | 0.9610 | 0.7330 | 0.9770 |
| | Yan et al. [33] | 2018 | – | 0.9592 | 0.7881 | 0.9437 |
| | Lu et al. [63] | 2018 | – | 0.9760 | 0.7762 | 0.9608 |
| | Jin et al. [6] | 2019 | – | 0.9874 | 0.7464 | 0.9651 |
| | Proposed | 2020 | Normal | 0.9571 | 0.7988 | 0.9468 |
| | | | DR | 0.9667 | 0.5577 | 0.9380 |
| | | | Glaucomatous | 0.9680 | 0.6826 | 0.9508 |

**TABLE 12** Comparison of average execution time with other methods.

| Dataset | Methods | Average execution time (s) |
|---|---|---|
| CHASE_DB1 | Azzopardi et al. [5] | 25 |
| | Roychowdhury et al. [55] | 7.9138 |
| | Roychowdhury et al. [54] | 11.711 |
| | Jin et al. [6] | 47.7 |
| | Proposed | 6.76 |
| HRF | Attila et al. [61] | $26.693 \pm 0.92$ |
| | Odstrcilik et al. [4] | 92 |
| | Proposed | 16.01 |

## 5.3 Comparison of our method against existing methods

Since our algorithm is unsupervised, it is more suitable to compare it with other unsupervised algorithms. But the performance of our technique is comparable to several supervised techniques, such as Refs. [10, 31–33, 53, 54, 57, 58], or slightly lower to others, such as Refs. [6, 43, 63]. The advantage of our method is the lower execution time when compared with Refs. [4–6, 54, 55, 61] for both of the databases, and the main highlight is the lower executional complexity of high-resolution images, with better performance metrics.

Jin et al. [6] are capable of detecting complicated vessel structures with better accuracy than our method but possess higher computational time. Tian et al. [43] effectively suppressed noise and ensured good connectivity of vessels with better accuracy than our method. Yan et al. [33] showed desirable performance, but the training procedure is complicated and its accuracy and sensitivity is comparable to our method. Odstrcilik et al. [4] had lower ability to extract thin capillaries and had a longer execution time for the computation of high-resolution images, that is, 92 s. Sundaram et al. [59] propounded a hybrid segmentation method, but they encounter difficulty with pathological images. Azzopardi et al. [5] proposed a trainable filter in an unsupervised way but had lower accuracy and higher execution time than our technique. Zhang et al. [56] and Dash and Bhoi [12] show difficulty with pathological images, but their results are comparable with our method. Fraz et al. [10] does not involve any preprocessing for retinal images before the feature extraction to avoid computational complexity, but the accuracy is lower than our method. Lower accuracy for Memari et al. [32] is also due to the same reason. Strong preprocessing is required due to the erratic illumination merged with central reflexes on the images and low contrast between the vessels. This is more significant with CHASE_DB1 database. It can be avoided by proper preprocessing phase. Our method adopts double enhancement technique for better segmentation accuracy. Roychowdhury et al. [54, 55] show robust performance while dealing with pathological images. Their accuracy is comparable with our method but have large execution time. From the previously mentioned works, it is concluded that there always exists a trade-off between accuracy and execution time, but our method achieves better accuracy with low execution time.

Here, we can observe that the performance of our unsupervised method is very much reliable and efficient. It could tackle the following flaws to a very good extent:

- Technical hitches, lighting conditions, noises, and abnormalities due to diseases are resolved by adopting a double enhancement method in the preprocessing phase. Moreover, we have incorporated an AGC algorithm for retinal images, which brings novelty to our technique.
- The trade-off that exists between efficiency and computational complexity was broken by our unsupervised technique. Though the supervised technique possesses lower complexity, its accuracy is only satisfying.
- Some algorithms may not be able or find it more complex to work with high-resolution images. But here, we have tackled the problem wisely by incorporating lossless compression technique in the segmentation phase, which resulted in an efficient and less complex algorithm with high-resolution images, which can also be marked as a novelty in our method.
- The pathological areas in the fundus image make the work of blood vessel extraction more difficult. But our algorithm works with pathological images without any difficulty.

## 6 Conclusion

Retinal blood vessel extraction is a crucial step for the early detection and diagnosis of many retinal, cardiovascular, and cerebrovascular diseases. During the initial phase of our research, literature study was conducted to know the relation between retinal blood vessels with several complicated diseases and the existing methods adopted for the extraction of retinal blood vessel. In real-time medical applications, it is essential to deal with multiresolution, vague, and abnormal images, which calls for a strong algorithm that can deal with such shortcomings in an efficient way with good accuracy, low complexity, and low execution time.

In this work, we have proposed a supervised and an unsupervised method for the segmentation of retinal blood vessels from fundus images in an aim to tackle the flaws in the existing literature.

Supervised technique employs a naive Bayes classifier, and the algorithm is evaluated on DRIVE and STARE databases. It has achieved an average accuracy, sensitivity, and specificity of 0.909, 0.225, and 0.913 with a mean execution time of 31.23 s for DRIVE and 0.918, 0.229, and 0.925 with a mean execution time of 34.14 s for STARE databases.

Unsupervised method exploits the effective blend of DWT and multilevel Otsu thresholding. The lossless compression provided by DWT is utilized as a boon in our method for multiresolution analysis that helps analyze both low- and high-resolution images with less complexity and execution time. It also aids in extracting the fine details of the image, which can be made useful for medical diagnosis procedure. The algorithm is assessed by CHASE_DB1 and HRF databases. These two databases are specifically chosen to examine and evaluate the performance of our algorithm in dealing with low- and high-resolution images. It has achieved an average accuracy, sensitivity, and specificity of 0.9523, 0.658, and 0.974 with an average execution time of 6.76 s for CHASE_DB1 and 0.9468, 0.7988, and 0.9571 for normal, 0.9380, 0.5577, and 0.9667 for DR, and 0.9508, 0.6826, and 0.9680 for glaucomatous retinal images in the HRF database with a mean execution time of 16.01 s.

The algorithm adopted for the supervised technique possesses comparable performance and less complexity. The method provides good results in terms of complexity when compared with other literature but could not tackle the flaws that we sought to meet. But the difficulties and failures faced in this technique paved us a scope for the future research. We have used a new insight for our unsupervised method that helped us in tackling the drawbacks efficiently. The algorithm for unsupervised method has met our requirements, and it effectively managed the flaws to a very good extent. The failures and challenges faced in our research paved us a path for future works.

## 7 Future scope

The ultimate aim of our research is to identify the abnormalities and symptoms of any diseases of the retina, at an early stage, such that a fast diagnosis could be possible in hospitals for the patients. Thus, a strong and real-time efficient algorithm is necessary for the segmentation as an initial phase, for the keen observation of retinal vessels. As a future scope, the proposed algorithm can be improved and analyzed to detect diseases from the segmented output. Also, we could build a hardware system that can be incorporated with medical equipment to obtain the segmented result, as soon as the retinal photograph of the patient is taken.

## References

[1] I. Shalev, T.E. Moffitt, T.Y. Wong, M.H. Meier, R.M. Houts, J. Ding, C.Y. Cheung, M.K. Ikram, A. Caspi, R. Poulton, Retinal vessel caliber and lifelong neuropsychological functioning: retinal imaging as an investigative tool for cognitive epidemiology, Psychol. Sci. 24 (7) (2013) 1198–1207, https://doi.org/10.1177/0956797612470959.

[2] D.A. Valenti, Alzheimer's disease: visual system review, Optometry 81 (1) (2010) 12–21.

[3] J. Flammer, K. Konieczka, R.M. Bruno, A. Virdis, A.J. Flammer, S. Taddei, The eye and the heart, Eur. Heart J. 34 (17) (2013) 1270–1278, https://doi.org/10.1093/eurheartj/eht023.

[4] J. Odstrcilik, R. Kolar, A. Budai, J. Hornegger, J. Jan, J. Gazarek, Retinal vessel segmentation by improved matched filtering: evaluation on a new high-resolution fundus image database, IET Image Process. 7 (2013) 373–383.

[5] G. Azzopardi, N. Strisciuglio, M. Vento, N. Petkov, Trainable COSFIRE filters for vessel delineation with application to retinal images, Med. Image Anal. 19 (1) (2015) 46–57.

[6] Q. Jin, Z. Meng, T.D. Pham, Q. Chen, L. Wei, R. Su, DUNet: a deformable network for retinal vessel segmentation, Knowl. Based Syst. 178 (2019) 149–162.

[7] A.M. Mendonca, A. Campilho, Segmentation of retinal blood vessels by combining the detection of centerlines and morphological reconstruction, IEEE Trans. Med. Imaging 25 (9) (2006) 1200–1213.

[8] J.V.B. Soares, J.J.G. Leandro, R.M. Cesar, H.F. Jelinek, M.J. Cree, Retinal vessel segmentation using the 2-D Gabor wavelet and supervised classification, IEEE Trans. Med. Imaging 25 (9) (2006) 1214–1222.

[9] B. Al-Diri, A. Hunter, D. Steel, An active contour model for segmenting and measuring retinal vessels, IEEE Trans. Med. Imaging 28 (9) (2009) 1488–1497.

[10] M.M. Fraz, P. Remagnino, A. Hoppe, B. Uyyanonvara, A.R. Rudnicka, C.G. Owen, S.A. Barman, An ensemble classification-based approach applied to retinal blood vessel segmentation, IEEE Trans. Biomed. Imaging 59 (9) (2012) 2538–2548.

[11] S.A.A. Shah, A. Shahzad, M.A. Khan, C. Lu, T.B. Tang, Unsupervised method for retinal vessel segmentation based on Gabor wavelet and multiscale line detector, IEEE Access 7 (2019) 167221–167228.

[12] J. Dash, N. Bhoi, An unsupervised approach for extraction of blood vessels from fundus images, J. Digit. Imaging 31 (2018) 857–868, https://doi.org/10.1007/s10278-018-0059-x.

[13] Q. Li, B. Feng, L. Xie, P. Liang, H. Zhang, T. Wang, A cross-modality learning approach for vessel segmentation in retinal images, IEEE Trans. Med. Imaging (2015), https://doi.org/10.1109/TMI.2015.2457891.

[14] B.E. Klein, Overview of epidemiologic studies of diabetic retinopathy, Ophthalmic Epidemiol. 14 (4) (2007) 179–183, https://doi.org/10.1080/09286580701396720.

[15] W.L. Yun, U.R. Acharya, Y.V. Venkatesh, C. Chee, L.C. Min, E.Y.K. Ng, Identification of different stages of diabetic retinopathy using retinal optical images, Inf. Sci. 178 (1) (2008) 106–121, https://doi.org/10.1016/j.ins.2007.07.020.

[16] T. Wong, P. Mitchell, The eye in hypertension, Lancet 369 (9559) (2007) 425–435.

[17] S. Ramin, M. Soheilian, G. Habibi, R. Ghazavi, R. Gharebaghi, F. Heidary, Age-related macular degeneration: a scientometric analysis, Med. Hypothesis Discov. Innov. Ophthalmol. J. 4 (2) (2015) 39–49.

[18] P.K. Shah, V. Prabhu, S.S. Karandikar, R. Ranjan, V. Narendran, N. Kalpana, Retinopathy of prematurity: past, present and future, World J. Clin. Pediatr. 5 (1) (2016) 35–46, https://doi.org/10.5409/wjcp.v5.i1.35.

[19] M. Mishra, M.K. Nath, S. Dandapat, Glaucoma detection from color fundus images, Int. J. Comput. Commun. Technol. (2011) 7–10.

[20] S.A. Thomas, G. Titus, Design of a portable retinal imaging module with automatic abnormality detection, Biomed. Signal Process. Control 60 (2020), https://doi.org/10.1016/j.bspc.2020.101962.

[21] R.S. Jeena, A. Sukesh Kumar, Artificial neural network based classification of healthy retina and retina of stroke patients, in: AMSE Conference Calcutta, 2017.

[22] M.L. Baker, P.J. Hand, J.J. Wang, T.Y. Wong, Artificial neural network based classification of healthy retina and retina of stroke patients, Retinal Signs Stroke 39 (2008) 1371–1379, https://doi.org/10.1161/STROKEAHA.107.496091.

[23] V.G. Madanagopalan, V.P. Selvam, N.V.S. Sivan, N.V. Govindaraju, Central retinal vein occlusion in a patient with breast carcinoma, GMS Ophthalmol. Cases 9 (2019) 1–4,-https://doi.org/10.3205/oc000093.

[24] G. Ravi Babu, L.J. Sandhyavali, K.S. Divya, Retinopathy in blood dyscrasias: case-series and review of literature, IOSR J. Dental Med. Sci. 15 (5) (2016) 44–48, https://doi.org/10.9790/0853-1505104448.

[25] D. Marin, A. Aquino, M.E. Gegundez-Arias, J.M. Bravo, A new supervised method for blood vessel segmentation in retinal images by using gray-level and moment invariants-based features, IEEE Trans. Med. Imaging 30 (1) (2011) 146–158, https://doi.org/10.1109/TMI.2010.2064333.

[26] C. Zhu, B. Zou, R. Zhao, J. Cui, X. Duan, Z. Chen, Y. Liang, Retinal vessel segmentation in colour fundus images using extreme learning machine, Comput. Med. Imaging Graph. 55 (2017) 68–77, https://doi.org/10.1016/j.compmedimag.2016.05.004.

[27] A. Oliveira, S. Pereira, C.A. Silva, Retinal vessel segmentation based on fully convolutional neural networks, Expert Syst. Appl. 112 (2018) 229–242, https://doi.org/10.1016/j.eswa.2018.06.034.

[28] J. Jebaseeli, C.A.D. Durai, J.D. Peter, Segmentation of retinal blood vessels from ophthalmologic diabetic retinopathy images, Comput. Electr. Eng. 73 (1) (2019) 245–258, https://doi.org/10.1016/j.compeleceng.2018.11.024.

[29] S. Aslani, H. Sarnel, A new supervised retinal vessel segmentation method based on robust hybrid features, Biomed. Signal Process. Control 30 (2016) 1–12, https://doi.org/10.1016/j.bspc.2016.05.006.

[30] L. Xu, S. Luo, A novel method for blood vessel detection from retinal images, BioMed. Eng. OnLine 9 (14) (2010) 1–10, https://doi.org/10.1186/1475-925X-9-14.

[31] H. Fu, Y. Xu, S. Lin, D.W. Kee Wong, J. Liu, DeepVessel: retinal vessel segmentation via deep learning and conditional random field, in: S. Ourselin, L. Joskowicz, M. Sabuncu, G. Unal, W. Wells (Eds.), Medical Image Computing and Computer-Assisted Intervention, MICCAI 2016, MICCAI Lecture Notes in Computer Science, vol. 9901, Springer, Cham, 2016.

[32] N. Memari, A.R. Ramli, M.I. Bin Saripan, S. Mashohor, M. Moghbel, Supervised retinal vessel segmentation from color fundus images based on matched filtering and AdaBoost classifier, PLoS One 12 (12) (2017) e0188939, https://doi.org/10.1371/journal.pone.0188939.

[33] Z. Yan, X. Yang, K. Cheng, Joint segment-level and pixel-wise losses for deep learning based retinal vessel segmentation, IEEE Trans. Biomed. Eng. 65 (9) (2018) 1912–1923.

[34] H.A. Leopold, J. Orchard, J.S. Zelek, V. Lakshminarayanan, PixelBNN: augmenting the PixelCNN with batch normalization and the presentation of a fast architecture for retinal vessel segmentation, J. Imaging 5 (2) (2019) 26, https://doi.org/10.3390/jimaging5020026.

[35] B. Zhang, L. Zhang, L. Zhang, F. Karray, Retinal vessel extraction by matched filter with first-order derivative of Gaussian, Comput. Biol. Med. 40 (4) (2010) 438–445, https://doi.org/10.1016/j.compbiomed.2010.02.008.

[36] T. Mapayi, S. Viriri, J.R. Tapamo, Adaptive thresholding technique for retinal vessel segmentation based on GLCM-energy information, Comput. Math. Methods Med. 2015 (2015) 1–11, https://doi.org/10.1155/2015/597475. 597475.

[37] M. Al-Rawi, H. Karajeh, Genetic algorithm matched filter optimization for automated detection of blood vessels from digital retinal images, Comput. Methods Programs Biomed. 87 (3) (2007) 248–253, https://doi.org/10.1016/j.cmpb.2007.05.012.

[38] A.F. Aqeel, S. Ganesan, Retinal image segmentation using texture, thresholding and morphological operations, in: IEEE International Conference on Electro/Information Technology, 2011.

[39] M.G. Cinsdikici, D. Aydn, Detection of blood vessels in ophthalmoscope images using MF/ant (matched filter/ant colony) algorithm, Comput. Methods Programs Biomed. 96 (2) (2009) 85–95, https://doi.org/10.1016/j.cmpb.2009.04.005.

[40] J. Dash, N. Bhoi, A thresholding based technique to extract retinal blood vessels from fundus images, Fut. Comput. Inform. J. 2 (2) (2017) 103–109, https://doi.org/10.1016/j.fcij.2017.10.001.

[41] Z. Jiang, J. Yepez, S. An, S. Ko, Fast, accurate and robust retinal vessel segmentation system, Biocybern. Biomed. Eng. 37 (2017) 412–421.

[42] J. Gao, G. Chen, W. Lin, An effective retinal blood vessel segmentation by using automatic random walks based on centerline extraction, BioMed. Res. Int. (2020), https://doi.org/10.1155/2020/7352129. Article ID 7352129.

[43] C. Tian, Multi-path convolutional neural network in fundus segmentation of blood vessels, Biocybern. Biomed. Eng. 40 (2020) 583–595.

[44] R. GeethaRamani, L. Balasubramanian, Retinal blood vessel segmentation employing image processing and data mining techniques for computerized retinal image analysis, Biocybern. Biomed. Eng. 36 (1) (2016) 102–118, https://doi.org/10.1016/j.bbe.2015.06.004.

[45] M. Hashemzadeh, B.A. Azar, Retinal blood vessel extraction employing effective image features and combination of supervised and unsupervised machine learning methods, Artif. Intell. Med. 95 (2019) 1–15, https://doi.org/10.1016/j.artmed.2019.03.001.

[46] L. Xu, S. Luo, A novel method for blood vessel detection from retinal image, BioMed. Eng. OnLine 14 (2010) 1–10, https://doi.org/10.1186/1475-925X-9-14.

[47] M. Niemeijer, J. Staal, V. Ginnekan, B. Loog, M.D. Abramoff, Comparative study of retinal vessel segmentation methods on a new publicly available database, Med. Imaging 5370 (2004) 648–656. https://ui.adsabs.harvard.edu/link_gateway/2004SPIE.5370..648N/doi:10.1117/12.535349.

[48] STARE, STructured Analysis of the Retina, 2000. https://cecas.clemson.edu/ahoover/stare/.

[49] S. Rahman, M.M Rahman, M. Abdullah-Al-Wadud, et al., An adaptive gamma correction for image enhancement, EURASIP J. Image Video Process. 35 (2016) 1–13, https://doi.org/10.1186/s13640-016-0138-1.

[50] Y.Q. Zhao, X.H. Wang, X.F. Wang, F.Y. Shih, Retinal vessels segmentation based on level set and region growing, Pattern Recogn. 47 (7) (2014) 2437–2446.

[51] Trifas, A. Monica, Medical Image Enhancement (Ph.D. thesis), LSU Doctoral Dissertations, 2005.

[52] R.C. Gonzalez, R.E. Woods, S.L. Eddins, Medical Image Enhancement (Ph.D. thesis), LSU Doctoral Dissertations 2005.

[53] M.M. Fraz, A.R. Rudnicka, C.G. Owen, S.A. Barman, Delineation of blood vessels in pediatric retinal images using decision trees-based ensemble classification, Int. J. CARS 9 (5) (2014) 795–811.

[54] S. Roychowdhury, D.D. Koozekanani, K.K. Parhi, Blood vessel segmentation of fundus images by major vessel extraction and sub-image classification, IEEE J. Biomed. Health Inform. 19 (3) (2015) 1118–1128.

[55] S. Roychowdhury, D.D. Koozekanani, K.K. Parhi, S. Roychowdhury, D.D. Koozekanani, K.K. Parhi, Iterative vessel segmentation of fundus images, IEEE Trans. Biomed. Eng. 62 (7) (2015) 1738–1749.

[56] J. Zhang, B. Dashtbozorg, E. Bekkers, J.P.W. Pluim, R. Duits, B.M. ter Haar Romeny, Robust retinal vessel segmentation via locally adaptive derivative frames in orientation scores, IEEE Trans. Med. Imaging 35 (12) (2016) 2631–2644.

[57] J.I. Orlando, E. Prokofyeva, M.B. Blaschko, Discriminatively trained fully connected conditional random field model for blood vessel segmentation in fundus images, IEEE Trans. Biomed. Eng. 64 (1) (2017) 16–27.

[58] J. Zhang, Y. Cheng, E. Bekkers, M. Wang, B. Dashtbozorg, B.M. ter Haar Romeny, Retinal vessel delineation using a brain-inspired wavelet transform and random forest, Pattern Recogn. 69 (2017) 107–123.

[59] R. Sundaram, K.S. Ravichandran, P. Jayaraman, B. Venkatraman, Extraction of blood vessels in fundus images of retina through hybrid segmentation approach, Mathematics 7(2) (169) (2019) 3–17.

[60] A. Khawaja, T.M. Khan, M.A.U. Khan, S.J. Nawaz, A multi-scale directional line detector for retinal vessel segmentation, Sensors (Basel) 19 (22) (2019) 4949.

[61] A. Budai, R. Bock, A. Maier, J. Hornegger, G. Michelson, Robust vessel segmentation in fundus images, Int. J. Biomed. Imaging 2013 (2013) 154860.

[62] J. Dash, N. Bhoi, Detection of retinal blood vessels from ophthalmoscope images using morphological approach, Electron. Lett. Comput. Vis. Image Anal. 16 (1) (2017) 1–14.

[63] J. Lu, Y. Xu, M. Chen, Y. Luo, A coarse-to-fine fully convolutional neural network for fundus vessel segmentation, Symmetry 10 (607) (2018) 1–16.

Chapter 9

# Hearing loss classification via stationary wavelet entropy and cat swarm optimization

**Chong Yao**
*School of Computer Science and Technology, Henan Polytechnic University, Jiaozuo, Henan, People's Republic of China*

## 1 Introduction

Sensorineural hearing loss (SNHL), also known as "sensorineural deafness," is caused by damage of cochlear receptor cells and auditory nerve fibers. This is often accompanied by fatal behaviors such as dementia, falls, and mental retardation. Aging, drug side effects, disease, and genetics can all cause SNHL. Currently there is no complete cure for SNHL, so timely diagnosis is very necessary.

In recent years, neural networks have developed rapidly and become a common method in the field of computer vision. Neural networks have developed hundreds of models and have achieved very successful applications in technical fields such as handwriting recognition, image annotation, semantic segmentation, and speech recognition. Different optimization algorithms are gradually discovered and applied. They all show good performance in the detection of medical images. Profant et al. [1] mainly studied the physiological changes of hearing loss patients, which made a great contribution to the image analysis research of later scholars. Bao and Nakamura [2] extracted features using wavelet entropy (WE) and optimized the classification of support vector machine using particle swarm optimization (PSO). Ranjan et al. [3] used stationary wavelet entropy (SWE) and single-hidden-layer neural network. PSO algorithm and hybrid technology of artificial bee swarm are used to train the network. Pereira [4] employed Hu moment invariant (HMI) to detect hearing loss. Nayeem [5] combined WE and genetic algorithm (GA). Tang and Lee [6] proposed a hybrid algorithm that mixes Tabu search (TS) and PSO. Gao and Liu [7] combined WE and cat swarm optimization (CSO).

**Cognitive Systems and Signal Processing in Image Processing. https://doi.org/10.1016/B978-0-12-824410-4.00014-3**

Based on the previous studies, we carefully analyzed the merits and demerits of each experiment and made our experimental choice. First, we chose to use magnetic resonance imaging (MRI) images as our primary form of data. Although computed tomography and MRI can show the occurrence of disease, MRI is more advantageous and more authoritative for the diagnosis of disease. Secondly, compared with some common feature extraction methods, we found that the stable WE has a higher accuracy under the same conditions, so we finally chose SWE and determined the two levels after comparing the results of various levels. Finally, we choose the single-hidden-layer neural network as the classifier, and after comparing different evolutionary algorithms, we choose the CSO, which has a good performance in finding the optimal solution.

The remaining parts of this chapter are organized as follows: Section 2 provides the dataset. Section 3 introduces the selection of each part of our experiment and the principle one by one. Section 4 introduces the experimental results and data analysis. Section 5 gives the conclusion.

## 2 Dataset

For a fairer comparison, we selected the same number of datasets as other experiments. 180 subjects have been selected: 60 HC, 60 patients with RHL, and 60 patients with LHL. After collecting the data, we analyzed from age, sex, duration of illness, pure tone average (PTA), and education level. The analysis results of epidemiological investigation of all subjects are shown in Table 1. In the selection process, we excluded patients with brain injuries (such as tumors or strokes), mental illnesses, neurological diseases, and contraindications to MRI.

From Table 1 we can see that the value of PTA of HC is kept within the range of 19–25 (dB). Patients with hearing loss have PTA values significantly higher than this normal range. Furthermore, we can see that the value of PTA on the right is lower than that on the left, possibly because the sensitivity of the human left ear is higher than that of the right ear. This is due to greater amplitude in the right hemisphere, and the neural pathways from the left ear to the cerebral cortex are crossed.

## 3 Methodology

### 3.1 Stationary wavelet entropy

In the past, there are many complex feature extraction methods, such as the stationary wavelet transform (SWT), discrete wavelet transform, and WE [8]. They all showed good performance in their respective experiments. Finally, by comparing with other wavelets, we chose stationary WE (SWE), which combined SWT and Shannon entropy. Many experiments have proved the stability and effectiveness of this method.

**TABLE 1** The data analysis of all subjects.

| | Age (year) | Gender (m/f) | Disease duration (year) | Education level (year) | PTA of left ear (dB) | PTA of right ear (dB) |
|---|---|---|---|---|---|---|
| Control | 53.2 ± 5.9 | 27/33 | 0 | 11.7 ± 3.2 | 23.1 ± 2.1 | 20.3 ± 2.2 |
| RHL | 51.3 ± 8.3 | 29/31 | 13.8 ± 14.5 | 12.3 ± 2.5 | 22.0 ± 3.5 | 80.4 ± 18.8 |
| LHL | 51.4 ± 9.0 | 32/28 | 17.1 ± 18.2 | 12.8 ± 1.5 | 77.3 ± 17.2 | 20.1 ± 4.5 |

In feature extraction, the original image is firstly decomposed into four subbands with the filter, which are marked as $LL_1, LH_1, HL_1$, and $HH_1$. Then we use Shannon entropy, which has been verified and widely used, to calculate the entropy of the four subbands. Shannon entropy is defined as follows:

$$\text{Entropy} = -\sum_j X_j^2 \log X_j^2 \tag{1}$$

Here $X_j$ represents the $j$th element of a given subband.

In each subsequent level SWE, the $LL_k$ subband of the previous level is decomposed ($k$ stands for level). The decomposition is expressed as follows:

$$LL_{k+1} = (LL_k) *_r (h_k) *_c (h_k) \tag{2}$$

$$LH_{k+1} = (LL_k) *_r (h_k) *_c (g_k) \tag{3}$$

$$HL_{k+1} = (LL_k) *_r (g_k) *_c (h_k) \tag{4}$$

$$HH_{k+1} = (LL_k) *_r (g_k) *_c (g_k) \tag{5}$$

where $*_r$ represents row-wise filter, $*_c$ represents column-wise filter, and $l$ and $h$ represent the low-pass and the high-pass filters, respectively.

According to the previous, Table 2 lists the subbands contained in different image decomposition levels and the number of subbands. Finally, we can get the relationship between the decomposition level and the total number is: $number = 3n + 1$. The diagram of N-level decomposition is shown in Fig. 1. Start with the original image and decompose it one by one until the $n$th layer.

To sum up, we can summarize the extraction process using SWE features as follows:

1. Get the preprocessed dataset.
2. Decompose the images in the dataset. (We can conduct experiments with different levels of decomposition and make a choice after comparison.)

**TABLE 2** Number of subbands at different decomposition levels.

| Level | Subbands | Total number of subbands |
|---|---|---|
| 1 | $LL_1$, $LH_1$, $HL_1$, $HH_1$ | 4 |
| 2 | $LH_1$, $HL_1$, $HH_1$, $LL_2$, $LH_2$, $HL_2$, $HH_2$ | 7 |
| 3 | $LH_1$, $HL_1$, $HH_1$, $LH_2$, $HL_2$, $HH_2$, $LL_3$, $HL_3$, $LH_3$, $HH_3$ | 10 |
| … | … | … |
| $n$ | $LH_1$, $HL_1$, $HH_1$, $LH_2$, $HL_2$, $HH_2$, $LL_3$, $HL_3$, $LH_3$, $HH_3$…$LL_n$, $HL_n$, $LH_n$, $HH_n$ | $3n+1$ |

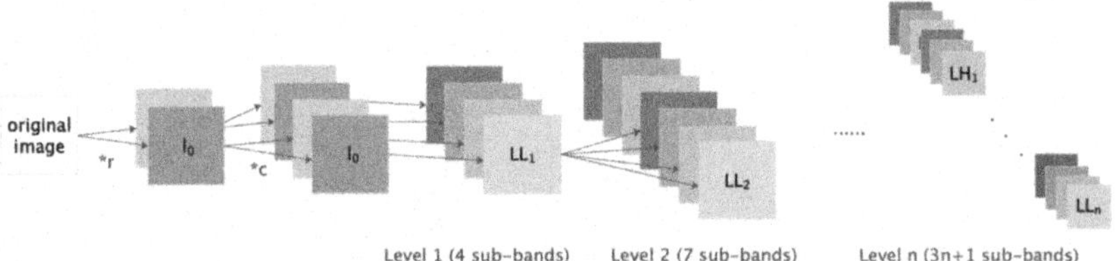


**FIG. 1** Diagram of image decomposition.

3. Calculate entropy over each subband.
4. Quantize all entropy results so that they can be provided to the next operation.

## 3.2 Single-hidden-layer feedforward neural network

As a model inspired by the human nervous system, neural networks have shown good performance in the field of deep learning [9–12], in which the single-hidden-layer feedforward neural network (SLFN) is used as a classifier. There are also many other efficient classifiers such as support vector machines, multilayer neural networks, and naive Bayesian classifier. But support vector machines are sensitive to parameter and kernel function selection. Naive Bayesian classifiers require that the attributes of the dataset are independent of each other. This is difficult for our experimental dataset. Multilayer neural network is time-consuming. After comprehensive consideration, we chose a single-hidden-layer neural network, which only has three layers due to its simplicity compared to deep learning approaches [13–20].

SLFH has a good ability of nonlinear fitting. Therefore, the input can be classified by proper activation function selecting and multiple hidden layer nodes setting. The structure of the SLFH and the mathematical model of neurons can be seen in Fig. 2. The number of nodes in the input layer and the output layer are set according to our image features and classification results, respectively.

From the mathematical model in Fig. 2, we can know that the calculation formula of each node in the hidden layer is as follows:

$$\psi(x) = \sum_{i=1}^{n} w_i x + b \tag{6}$$

where $i$ is the $i$th input node, $w_i$ is the weight received by the current node from the previous layer nodes, and $b$ is the bias value of the current node. Then an activation function is used to make the neural network have nonlinear fitting ability. The learning function of neural network can be described as follows:

$$\xi(x) = \sum_{j=1}^{m} \beta_j G(\psi(x)) \tag{7}$$

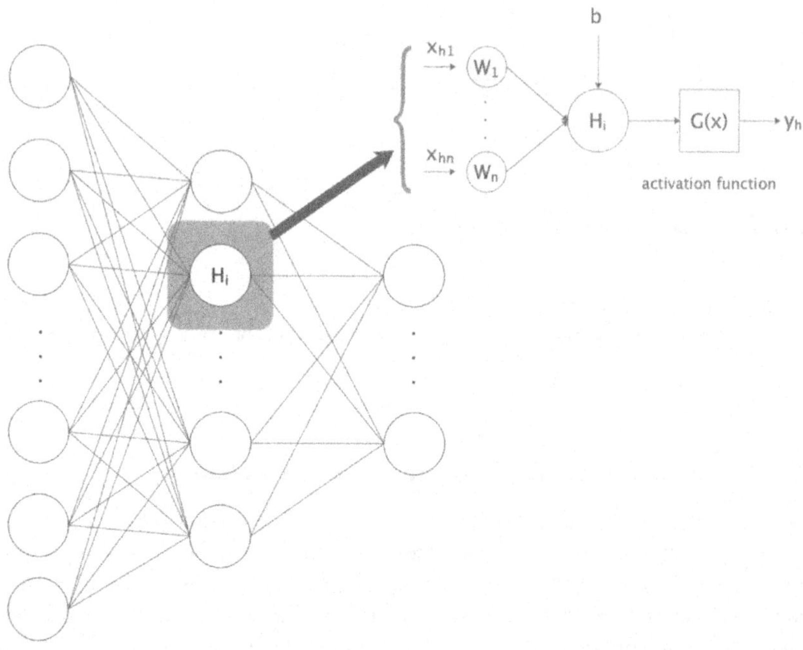


**FIG. 2** Diagram of SLFN structure and neuron mathematical model. (The node at the top right is randomly selected from the hidden layer and marked as $H_i$. As the input and output of the mathematical model, $X_{h1}$, $X_{hn}$, and $Y_h$ represent the values connected to the current node in the input layer and output layer, respectively. $W$ is the weight, $b$ is the bias value, and $G(x)$ is the activation function.)

where $j$ is an integer. $\beta_j$ is weight connecting the hidden layer with the output layer. After the whole classifier output is obtained, the difference between the output and the reality can be calculated, which is called loss. This is also the focus of our subsequent optimization. It can be defined as follows:

$$|\xi(x) - y(x)| < \varepsilon \tag{8}$$

where $y(x)$ represents real data. In subsequent chapters we will focus on how to minimize $\varepsilon$.

## 3.3 Cat swarm optimization

There are optimization methods been used to train SLFN [21–30]. This study will use a relatively new method—CSO. In biology, although there are many kinds of cats, they have similar living habits. In summary, there are two characteristics: cats have high alertness and are curious about their targets. Therefore, the cat is always searching around and tracking the target as soon as it finds it. CSO is an algorithm based on these two characteristics. It is a global optimization algorithm of swarm intelligence, first proposed by Chu et al. [31] in 2006 and proved to have better performance than PSO.

Two submodels are defined in the CSO: some cats perform tracing mode and others perform seeking mode [32]. The two modes interact through the mixture ratio (MR), which represents the proportion of the population of cats in the run tracking mode, and it should be a small value in the program.

**a. Seeking mode**

There are four basic elements in the seeking mode: counts of dimension to change (CDC), seeking range of selected dimension (SRD), seeking memory pool (SMP), and self-position consideration (SPC). The meaning of these parameters is shown in Table 3.

The search process can be described in Algorithm 1. The position change of copies can be described as follows:

$$X_{mn} = (1 + SRD \times R) \times X_m \tag{9}$$

Here $X_m$ is current position, and $X_{mn}$ is new position. $R \in [0,1]$. If all fitness function (FS) is not exactly the same during the search, we will calculate the probability of each candidate point, otherwise set all the selecting probability of each candidate point be 1. The probability of each candidate can be written as follows:

$$P_m = \frac{|FS_m - FS_{min}|}{FS_{max} - FS_{min}} \tag{10}$$

where $0 < m < j$.

**TABLE 3** The meaning of the parameters in the seeking model.

| Parameter | Type | Role |
|---|---|---|
| CDC | Integer | Number of dimensions of variation |
| SRD | Integer | Mutative ratio for the selected dimensions |
| SMP | Integer | Number of copies of cat |
| SPC | Boolean | Whether to use a passed position as one of the candidates to move to |

**Algorithm 1. Pseudocode of seeking mode**

```
If SPC is true
    j=SMP-1
Else
    j=SMP
End
```

```
Make j copies of the selected cat position
For m = 1 to SMP
    Randomly compute present value X_mn using SRD and CDC by
    equation (9)
    Replace the old one
       Calculate selection probability P_m by equation (10)
    End
```

**b. Tracking mode**

In the algorithm, it is assumed that each cat has its own position made up of $M$ dimensions, the velocities of movement of each dimension, a fitness value (representing the cat's adaptability to the fitness function), and a flag to identify whether the cat is in seeking mode or tracking mode. For cats entering tracking mode, the procedure can be described in Algorithm 2.

**Algorithm 2. Pseudocode of tracking mode**

1. Update the velocities of each cat by Eq. (11).
2. Check that whether the update speed is within the specified range and if it is exceeded, set it to the specified maximum speed.
3. Update the position of each cat by Eq. (12).

The update of the tracking phase velocities can be defined as follows:

$$v_{l,i} = v_{l,i} + r \times q \times (X_{best,i} - X_{l,i}) \tag{11}$$

where $i = 1, 2, \ldots, M$; $l$ represents cat number; $r$ is a random value in the range of [0,1]; $q$ is a constant; $X_{best,\ i}$ is the position of the cat with the optimal FS; $X_{l,\ i}$ is the position of $cat_l$.

The update of position can be defined as:

$$X_{l,i} = X_{l,i} + v_{l,i} \tag{12}$$

**c. Cat swarm optimization**

Cats spend most of their time seeking in the real world, so we use a small MR value to connect the two patterns to form the cat swarm algorithm. A small number of cats are tracking, and most of them are searching. Based on the previous two modes, the cat swarm algorithm realizes the interaction with MR and connects them to find the optimal solution. The whole process is described by Fig. 3. First we initialize some of the necessary parameters: the number of cats and the value of MR. Then, according to the value of MR, we randomly set the number of cat groups of the two modules, and set the flag as the corresponding value. According to the value of the flag, the corresponding operations previously mentioned are performed. Finally,

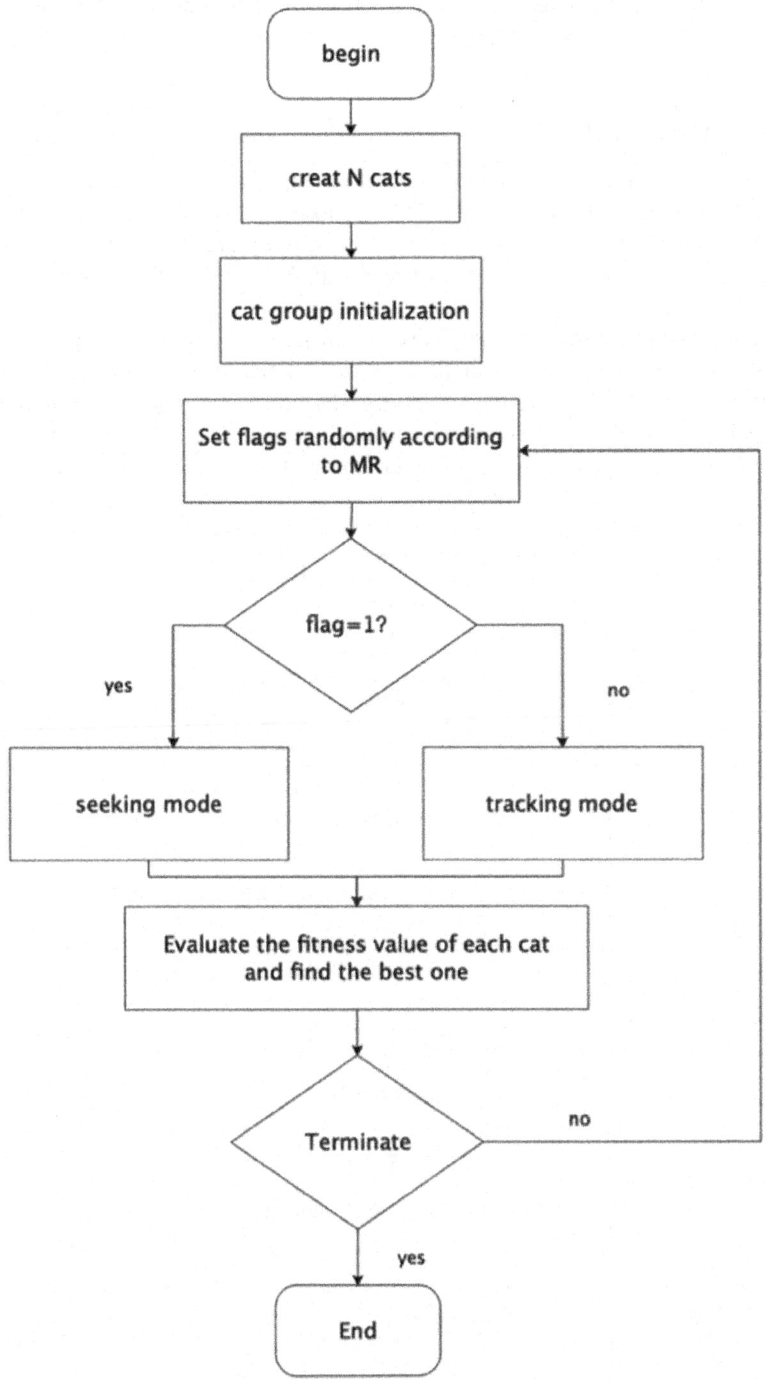


**FIG. 3** Pipeline of CSO algorithm. (Flag is a constant that stands for cat mode [seeking or tracking mode].)

according to the fitness function to calculate the value and judge whether the program terminates or continues.

### 3.4 Implementation

In our experiment, SWE was used to extract image features, SLFN was used to classify images, and CSO was used for optimization. We treat each solution of the neural network as a cat, so that the cat in the optimal position is the optimal solution after iterative optimization. The overall flow chart of this experiment is shown in Fig. 4.

This diagram shows us a complete experimental process. In this experiment, the methods of different fields in the previous sections were combined to form a method for medical image classification. The most important part is how to apply CSO to optimize the classifier and set iteration conditions appropriately. The CSO judges the number of iterations and finds the optimal solution

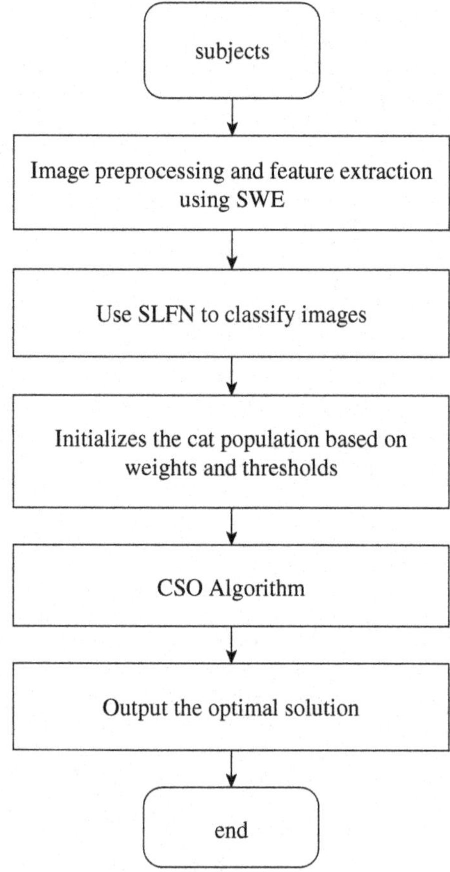


**FIG. 4** Block diagram of the whole system.

according to the fitness function [33]. The process of SLFN training by CSO is shown in Algorithm 3.

**Algorithm 3. Pseudocode of CSO**

1. Create *n* cats. Set the parameters of cat swarm and randomly initialize the population. It consists of connection weights and thresholds between the layers.
2. Input training sample set and expected output.
3. Determine the fitness function.
4. Randomly divide the cat population into seeking mode and tracking mode according to the MR.
5. Update position separately.
6. Calculate fitness and keep the optimal cat.
7. Judge whether the conditions are met. If so, output the optimal solution and end the process. Otherwise go on to step 4.

## 3.5 Measure

Cross-validation is to divide the original data into two parts: train set and validation set. Firstly, the classifier is trained with the training set, and then the model is tested with the validation set to evaluate the performance of the classifier [34–36]. The goal of cross-validation is to get a reliable and stable model.

In order to make the experiment more accurate, we adopt the method of 10 runs of 10-fold cross-validation. Eight folds are used for training, the final two folds are used for validation and test, respectively, in each trial. Overall accuracy (OA) and sensitivity of *t*th class $s(t)$ are used as our evaluation indexes during the experiment. The OA is defined as follows:

$$OA = \frac{\sum_{i=1}^{3} E_{ii}(r=10, f=10)}{\sum_{i=1}^{3}\sum_{j=1}^{3} E_{ij}(r=10, f=10)} \tag{13}$$

The sensitivity of *t*th class $s(t)$ is defined as follows:

$$s(t) = \frac{E_{tt}(r=10, f=10)}{\sum_{i=1}^{3} E_{ti}(r=10, f=10)} \tag{14}$$

Here $r$ represents run number, and $f$ represents the fold number. $E(r,f)$ represents the confusion matrix, which can be shown in Fig. 5.

In this chapter, the dataset has 60 objects under each category. We used 10-fold cross-validation and ran it 10 times. Ideally, the confusion matrix for this experiment should be as follows:

$$E(r=10, f=10) = \begin{bmatrix} 600 & 0 & 0 \\ 0 & 600 & 0 \\ 0 & 0 & 600 \end{bmatrix} \tag{15}$$

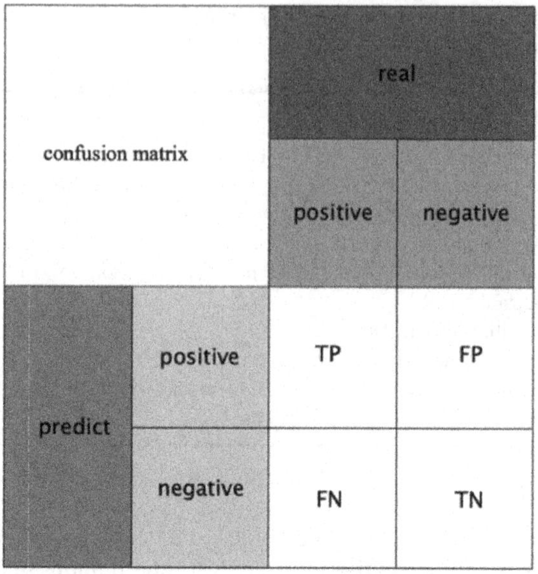

| confusion matrix | | real | |
|---|---|---|---|
| | | positive | negative |
| predict | positive | TP | FP |
| | negative | FN | TN |

**FIG. 5** Diagram of confusion matrix. (This is a confusion matrix for binary classification. The four indicators in the lower right corner represent the number of samples in different situations. Their meanings are shown in Table 4.)

**TABLE 4** The meanings of TP, FP, FN, and TN.

| Indicator | Meaning |
|---|---|
| TP | Both the predicted value and the real value are positive |
| FP | The real value is negative, and the model thinks it is positive; this is the type I error in statistics |
| FN | The real value is positive, and the model thinks it is negative; this is the type II error in statistics |
| TN | Both the predicted value and the real value are negative |

where $r$ represents the run number and f represents the fold number. They are all integers from 1 to 10.

# 4 Experiment results and discussions

## 4.1 Confusion matrix of proposed method

As defined in the previous sections, we perform a visual analysis of the experiment.

Table 5 lists the confusion matrix of our proposed method over $10 \times 10$-fold cross-validation. The values on the diagonal of the table are the correct values

**TABLE 5** Confusion matrix of SWE-CSO.

| Confusion matrix | HC | LHL | RHL |
|---|---|---|---|
| HC | 546 | 21 | 33 |
| LHL | 38 | 534 | 28 |
| RHL | 25 | 31 | 544 |

that our method identifies. They belong to the TP type in Fig. 5. The rest are respectively the numbers of errors identified.

As can be seen from Table 5: 21 HCs are misclassified as LHLs, 33 HCs are~misclassified as RHLs, 38 LHLs are misclassified as HCs, 28 LHLs are misclassified as RHLs, 25 RHLs are misclassified as HCs, and 31 RHLs are misclassified as LHLs. They belong to the FN type in Fig. 5.

Fig. 6 shows the different values of the matrix in different colors, which makes the distribution of observed values more obvious. Each value in the row is standardized. We list the values in each square and match the colors. It is not difficult to see that there is a significant difference between the colors

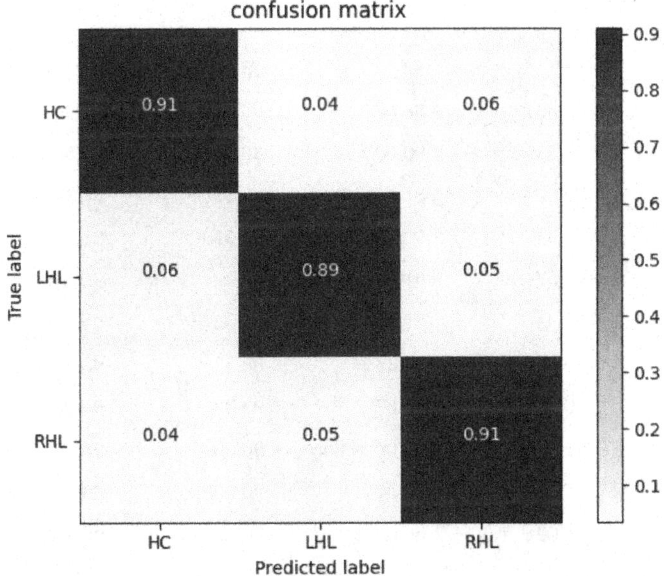


**FIG. 6** Diagram of confusion matrix of SWE-CSO. (The darker the color in the diagonal, the better the performance of the classifier.)

of the diagonal and those of other positions, which exactly indicates that our model has good performance. The values of the light color position in the figure do not exceed 0.07. Image classification can be completed with a low error rate. In the following sections, we will introduce our experimental results in more detail and make comparisons.

## 4.2 Statistical results

Following the results shown in the previous section, we present the OA and sensitivity analysis, which was defined in Section 3.5, of the experiment in this section. Table 6 lists the OA and sensitivity data of the 10 trials and the final mean results. We can see from Table 6 that the final OA is 90.22 ± 0.95%. The sensitivities over the three subject classes are 91.00 ± 1.96%, 89.00 ± 3.87%, and 90.67 ± 2.38%, respectively.

Also, to make us more sensitive to perceptual data, Figs. 5, 7 and 8 visualize the data. We can clearly perceive that the data fluctuates around 90% in Fig. 7. Except for the polyline S2, the other two polylines do not fluctuate much. This can be intuitively felt in Fig. 8, and the error bar of S2 has the maximum error bar length. These are sufficient to demonstrate the robustness of our model.

**TABLE 6** Performance analysis of SWE-CSO.

| | Sensitivity | | | Overall |
|---|---|---|---|---|
| Fold | *S1* | *S2* | *S3* | accuracy |
| 1 | 88.33 | 86.67 | 93.33 | 89.44 |
| 2 | 93.33 | 90.00 | 88.33 | 90.56 |
| 3 | 90.00 | 81.67 | 93.33 | 88.33 |
| 4 | 88.33 | 93.33 | 93.33 | 91.67 |
| 5 | 91.67 | 91.67 | 88.33 | 90.56 |
| 6 | 93.33 | 91.67 | 88.33 | 91.11 |
| 7 | 90.00 | 93.33 | 88.33 | 90.56 |
| 8 | 90.00 | 86.67 | 93.33 | 90.00 |
| 9 | 91.67 | 90.00 | 90.00 | 90.56 |
| 10 | 93.33 | 85.00 | 90.00 | 89.44 |
| Mean + SD | 91.00 ± 1.96 | 89.00 ± 3.87 | 90.67 ± 2.38 | 90.22 ± 0.95 |

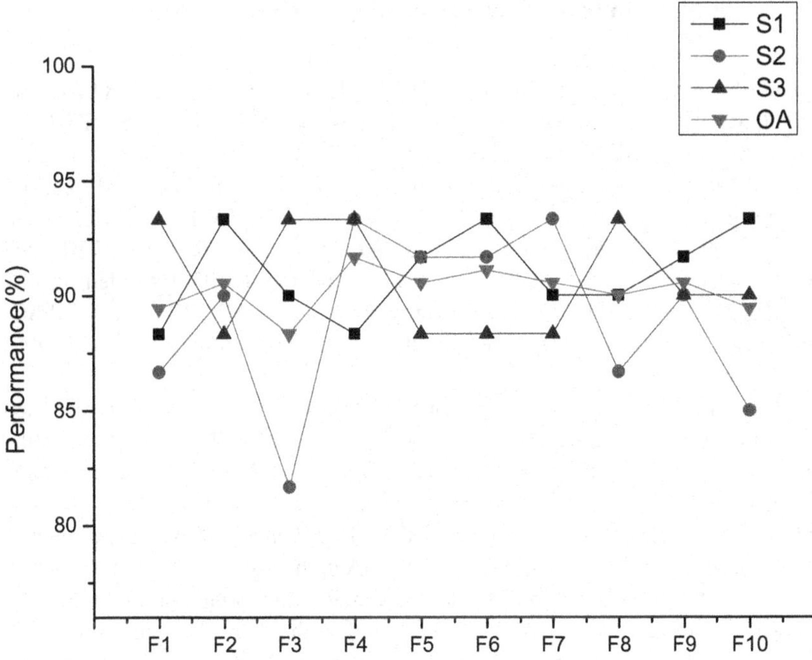


**FIG. 7** Line chart of performance of SWE-CSO.

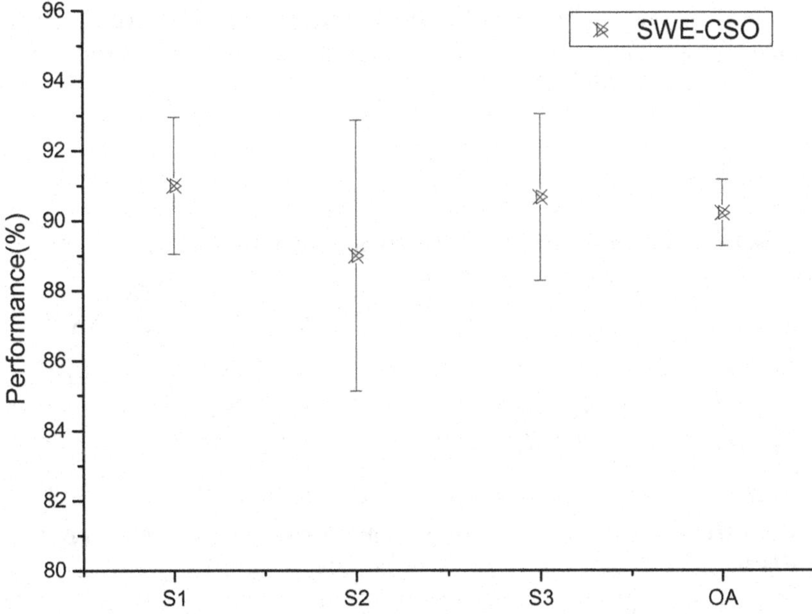


**FIG. 8** Error bar of SWE-CSO.

## 4.3 Comparison to state-of-the-art approaches

At the end of the experiment we compared our proposed "SWE + CSO" with some of the most advanced methods: HMI [4], WE-GA [5], TS-PSO [6], and WE-CSO [7]. The three sensitivity values of HMI, WE-GA, TS-PSO, WE-CSO, and SWE-CSO are about 77%, 81%, 86%, 84%, and 90%, respectively. Table 7 reports the OA and sensitivity of these methods and lists our results in the last row of the table. The results show SWE-CSO yielded an OA of 90.22 ± 0.95%, the HMI yielded an OA of 77.47 ± 1.17%, the WE-GA yielded an OA of 81.11 ± 1.34%, and the TS-PSO yielded an OA of 86.17 ± 0.41%. The three sensitivity values of HMI, WE-GA, TS-PSO, WE-CSO, and SWE-CSO are about 77%, 81%, 86%, 84%, and 90% respectively.

From Fig. 9, we can observe that the OA and sensitivity of our proposed method are the highest. They all stayed around 90%. To make the results clearer, we draw a dotted line between the values of "SWE-CSO" and the values of other methods, which makes the boundary between them more obvious. These are sufficient to demonstrate the effectiveness of our experimental method. By comparing WE-CSO and WE-GA in the figure, we found that under the same feature extraction method, replacing the optimization algorithm improved the OA by nearly 3%. Compared with SWE-CSO and WE-CSO, under the same classification optimization method, replacing the feature extraction method improved the OA by nearly 6%. This indicates that selecting more effective feature extraction methods and matching appropriate optimization algorithms can greatly improve classification efficiency. In future work, we will continue to explore more effective classification strategies and apply them to help doctors make better diagnoses.

**TABLE 7** Comparison of state-of-the-art approaches.

| Approach | S1 | S2 | S3 | Overall accuracy |
|---|---|---|---|---|
| HMI [4] | 77.60 ± 5.72 | 77.60 ± 4.30 | 77.20 ± 5.98 | 77.47 ± 1.17 |
| WE-GA [5] | 81.25 ± 4.91 | 80.42 ± 5.57 | 81.67 ± 6.86 | 81.11 ± 1.34 |
| TS-PSO [6] | 86.50 ± 3.09 | 86.50 ± 2.77 | 85.50 ± 2.23 | 86.17 ± 0.41 |
| WE-CSO [7] | 85.50 ± 6.85 | 84.50 ± 4.97 | 83.50 ± 5.80 | 84.50 ± 0.81 |
| **SWE-CSO (Ours)** | **91.00 ± 1.96** | **89.00 ± 3.87** | **90.67 ± 2.38** | **90.22 ± 0.95** |

The bold one is the best one.

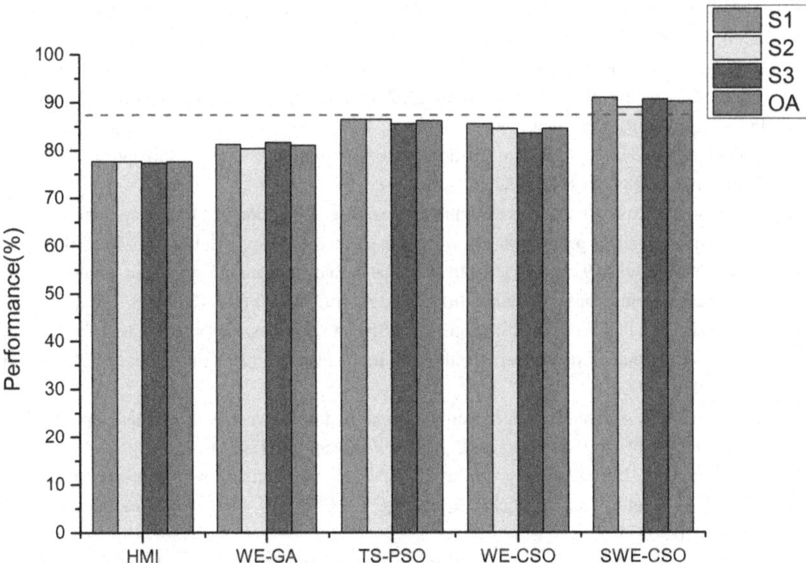


**FIG. 9** Histogram of five state-of-the-art approaches.

## 5 Conclusions

In this experiment, we compared a number of other experimental research methods, selected more effective stable WE to extract image features, single-hidden-layer neural network as the classifier, and used the cat swarm algorithm to optimize the classifier. The comparison results are given in this last section of this chapter. The final results show that our OA and sensitivity are superior to other methods, and the final OA reaches $90.22 \pm 0.95\%$. Overall, our results are excellent, but not 100% accurate, so there is room for improvement. There are many excellent classifiers and optimization algorithms that we will actively explore in order to achieve higher accuracy in medical diagnoses.

## References

[1] O. Profant, A. Škoch, Z. Balogová, J. Tintěra, J. Hlinka, J. Syka, Diffusion tensor imaging and MR morphometry of the central auditory pathway and auditory cortex in aging, Neuroscience 260 (2014).

[2] F. Bao, K. Nakamura, Hearing loss via wavelet entropy and particle swarm optimized trained support vector machine, in: DEStech Transactions on Engineering and Technology Research, 2019.

[3] N.D. Ranjan, Z. Yudong, Y. Ming, Y. Ti-Fei, L. Bin, L. Huimin, et al., Detection of unilateral hearing loss by stationary wavelet entropy, CNS Neurol. Disord. Drug Targets 16 (2017).

[4] A. Pereira, Hu moment invariant: a new method for hearing loss detection, Adv. Eng. Res. 153 (2017) 412–416.

[5] A. Nayeem, Hearing loss detection based on wavelet entropy and genetic algorithm, Adv. Intell. Syst. Res. 153 (2017) 49–53.

[6] C. Tang, E. Lee, Hearing loss identification via wavelet entropy and combination of Tabu search and particle swarm optimization, in: 23rd International Conference on Digital Signal Processing (DSP), Shanghai, China, 2018, pp. 1–5.

[7] R. Gao, J. Liu, Hearing loss identification by wavelet entropy and cat swarm optimization, AIP Conf. Proc. 2073 (2019) 020082.

[8] M. Bakhoday-Paskyabi, A wavelet-entropy based segmentation of turbulence measurements from a moored shear probe near the wavy sea surface, SN Appl. Sci. 2 (2020) 22102.

[9] S.-H. Wang, Covid-19 classification by FGCNet with deep feature fusion from graph convolutional network and convolutional neural network, Inf. Fusion 67 (2021) 208–229.

[10] S.-H. Wang, COVID-19 classification by CCSHNet with deep fusion using transfer learning and discriminant correlation analysis. Inf. Fusion (2021)https://doi.org/10.1016/j.inffus.2020.11.005.

[11] S.C. Satapathy, A five-layer deep convolutional neural network with stochastic pooling for chest CT-based COVID-19 diagnosis, Mach. Vis. Appl. 32 (2021) 14.

[12] S.C. Satapathy, L.Y. Zhu, A seven-layer convolutional neural network for chest CT based COVID-19 diagnosis using stochastic pooling. IEEE Sens. J. (2020)https://doi.org/10.1109/JSEN.2020.30258551-1.

[13] A.K. Sangaiah, Alcoholism identification via convolutional neural network based on parametric ReLU, dropout, and batch normalization, Neural Comput. Appl. 32 (2020) 665–680.

[14] Y. Chen, Cerebral micro-bleeding identification based on a nine-layer convolutional neural network with stochastic pooling, Concurr. Comput. Pract. Exp. 31 (2020) e5130.

[15] V.V. Govindaraj, High performance multiple sclerosis classification by data augmentation and AlexNet transfer learning model, J. Med. Imaging Health Inform. 9 (2019) 2012–2021.

[16] J. Ramirez, Unilateral sensorineural hearing loss identification based on double-density dual-tree complex wavelet transform and multinomial logistic regression. Integr. Comput. Aided Eng. (2019)https://doi.org/10.3233/ICA-190605.

[17] C. Tang, Cerebral micro-bleeding detection based on densely connected neural network, Front. Neurosci. 13 (2019) 422.

[18] S. Xie, Alcoholism identification based on an alexnet transfer learning model, Front. Psychiatry 10 (2019) 205.

[19] K. Muhammad, Image based fruit category classification by 13-layer deep convolutional neural network and data augmentation, Multimed. Tools Appl. 78 (2019) 3613–3632.

[20] G. Zhao, Polarimetric synthetic aperture radar image segmentation by convolutional neural network using graphical processing units, J. Real-Time Image Proc. 15 (2018) 631–642.

[21] L. Wu, Weights optimization of neural network via improved BCO approach, Prog. Electromagn. Res. 83 (2008) 185–198.

[22] L. Wu, Crop classification by forward neural network with adaptive chaotic particle swarm optimization, Sensors 11 (2011) 4721–4743.

[23] L. Wu, UCAV path planning by fitness-scaling adaptive chaotic particle swarm optimization, Math. Probl. Eng. (2013) 705238

[24] J.F. Yang, P. Sun, Magnetic resonance brain classification by a novel binary particle swarm optimization with mutation and time-varying acceleration coefficients, Biomed. Eng. Biomed. Tech. 61 (2016) 431–441.

[25] X. Wu, Smart detection on abnormal breasts in digital mammography based on contrast-limited adaptive histogram equalization and chaotic adaptive real-coded biogeography-based optimization, Simulation 92 (2016) 873–885.

[26] P. Li, G. Liu, Pathological brain detection via wavelet packet Tsallis entropy and real-coded biogeography-based optimization, Fundam. Inform. 151 (2017) 275–291.

[27] X.-X. Hou, Alcoholism detection by medical robots based on Hu moment invariants and predator-prey adaptive-inertia chaotic particle swarm optimization, Comput. Electr. Eng. 63 (2017) 126–138.

[28] Y.-J. Li, Single slice based detection for Alzheimer's disease via wavelet entropy and multi-layer perceptron trained by biogeography-based optimization, Multimed. Tools Appl. 77 (2018) 10393–10417.

[29] J.M. Gorriz, Multivariate approach for Alzheimer's disease detection using stationary wavelet entropy and predator-prey particle swarm optimization, J. Alzheimers Dis. 65 (2018) 855–869.

[30] P. Doke, D. Shrivastava, Using CNN with Bayesian optimization to identify cerebral micro-bleeds, Mach. Vis. Appl. 31 (2020) 36.

[31] S.-C. Chu, P.-w. Tsai, J.-S. Pan, Cat swarm optimization, in: PRICAI 2006: Trends in Artificial Intelligence, 2006, pp. 854–858.

[32] P. Qian, Cat swarm optimization applied to alcohol use disorder identification, Multimed. Tools Appl. 77 (2018) 22875–22896.

[33] P. Bansal, S. Kumar, S. Pasrija, S. Singh, A hybrid grasshopper and new cat swarm optimization algorithm for feature selection and optimization of multi-layer perceptron, Soft Comput. (2020) 27.

[34] S.-H. Wang, DenseNet-201-based deep neural network with composite learning factor and pre-computation for multiple sclerosis classification, ACM Trans. Multimedia Comput. Commun. Appl. 16 (2020) 60.

[35] X. Jiang, Fingerspelling identification for Chinese sign language via AlexNet-based transfer learning and Adam optimizer, Sci. Program. 2020 (2020) 3291426.

[36] X. Jiang, L. Chang, Classification of Alzheimer's disease via eight-layer convolutional neural network with batch normalization and dropout techniques, J. Med. Imaging Health Inform. 10 (2020) 1040–1048.

Chapter 10

# Early detection of breast cancer using efficient image processing algorithms and prediagnostic techniques: A detailed approach

G. Boopathi Raja
*Department of ECE, Velalar College of Engineering and Technology, Erode, Tamil Nadu, India*

## 1 Introduction

Cancer cells are malignant cells that grow uncontrollably in any part of the human body. These irregular cells are called cancer (or) tumor (or) malignant cells. Such types of cells can enter easily through typical tissue. Numerous malignancies and abnormal cells from the affected tissue region are named after the abnormal tissue cells, for instance, breast cancer, lung cancer, and aggressive cancer [1]. There are more than 250 types of cancer.

Anything that can make normal immune cells develop unusually can cause cancer. The most well-known classifications of disease-related or causative agents are as per the following: synthetic or toxic (chemical) exposure, ionizing radiation, different infections, and human genes.

The cell also dies at the point where natural cell division occurs, and the cell is destroyed or altered without its structure being restored. When such types of cells remains alive, it leads to cancer cells. It shows uncontrolled detachment and growth. Therefore, the frequency of malignancy is developing. Cancer cells often originate in this host cell and migrate across the circulatory system, tissues, and organs, where they may replicate the unregulated growth cycle. Metastatic proliferation or metastasis is a continuous chain of cancer cells, leaving an area and trying to emerge in another organ of the body. Table 1 indicates the estimated number of new cases and death rates for each cancer type, as given by the National Cancer Institute in 2016 and 2021 (Source: https://www.cancer.gov/types/common-cancers).

Signs and symptoms of cancer are based on the category and extent of cancer, although the usual signs and symptoms may not be clear. Even though there

**Cognitive Systems and Signal Processing in Image Processing. https://doi.org/10.1016/B978-0-12-824410-4.00009-X**

**TABLE 1** Cancer type vs estimated cases in the year 2016 and 2021.

| Cancer type | Estimated new cases | | Estimated deaths | |
|---|---|---|---|---|
| | 2016 | 2021 | 2016 | 2021 |
| Bladder | 76,960 | 83,730 | 16,390 | 17,200 |
| Colorectal cancer | 134,490 | 1,49,500 | 49,190 | 52,980 |
| Breast cancer | 2,46,660 | Female: 2,81,550, Male: 2650 | 40,450 | Female: 43,600, Male: 530 |
| Kidney cancer | 62,700 | 76,080 | 14,240 | 13,780 |
| Leukemia | 60,140 | 61,090 | 24,400 | 23,660 |
| Lung cancer | 2,24,390 | 2,35,760 | 1,58,080 | 1,31,880 |
| Melanoma cancer | 76,380 | 1,06,110 | 10,130 | 7180 |
| Pancreatic cancer | 53,070 | 60,430 | 41,780 | 48,220 |
| Thyroid cancer | 64,300 | 44,280 | 1980 | 2200 |

are several prognostic tests for cancer, specific diagnoses are made by analyzing a biopsy sample of suspected cancer tissue.

The finding of the disease is typically determined by the results of the biopsy and decides the kind of malignant growth and the degree of the disease. The stage additionally helps caregivers decide on treatment goals. In general, in many stages, when the set number rises, it usually varies from 0 to 4 when the kind of malignant growth is more aggressive or more prevalent in the body. Stage-based strategies shift from disease to malignant growth.

Therapy contracts vary due to the type and level of cancer. Many drugs are formulated to match the illness of each patient. Many treatments contain one or more of the following, and in some cases, all of them: surgery, chemotherapy, and radiation. Many home remedies and other malignancy therapies are listed, yet patients are firmly urged to consult their disease specialists before utilizing them.

Malignant development can vary from mild to extreme growth. Depending on the type of cancer, the visualization varies, but mostly equals aggressive cancers, those ranked high, or 3 or 4.

Cancer cases and types of diseases are impacted by numerous elements, for example, age, sex, race, natural components, diet, and hereditary qualities.

Therefore, disease cases and sorts of malignant growth shift as indicated by these changes. For instance, the World Health Organization (WHO) gives the following general data on disease around the world:

- Cancer is the main factor for human death. The most recent information from the WHO estimates that each year 8.2 million deaths (roughly 22% of all deaths) are due to cancer.
- The mortality rate from lung, stomach, liver, colon, and breast cancers increases each year.
- Cancer deaths are expected to keep ascending, with an expected 13.1 million deaths by 2030 (about 70% increments).

Cancer can be identified in different parts of the world, and cancer in other parts of the world may be more widespread than cancer in the United States. For example, stomach cancer is more common in Japan than in the United States. This also applies to a combination of distinctive and genetic features.

The outline of this chapter is structured as described in this paragraph. Section 2 describes the various literature reviews related to breast cancer. The various types of breast cancer and their symptoms are explained under Section 3. The necessity of cognitive techniques is introduced in Section 4. In Section 5, the better methodology for early diagnosis of breast cancer is introduced. Finally, the experimental results are analyzed and examined in Section 6.

## 2 Literature review

A considerable number of female deaths is due to breast cancer [2]. It is estimated that one of every six women will be affected by breast cancer [3, 4]. Furthermore, the detailed results show that more than four million women worldwide are diagnosed with breast cancer each year [5]. Early detection and treatment is needed to decrease the death rate from breast cancer [6]. X-ray and magnetic resonance imaging (MRI) are entrenched imaging procedures to recognize and alleviate cancer. This is done by creating a progression of three-dimensional (3D) pictures. For this, a radiologist works to physically distinguish the infected part and distinguish issues [7, 8]. This process is tedious due to the high number of pictures [9, 10]. Subsequently, for the early detection of breast cancer, programmed PC-based image investigation has become important today. For the prediagnosis of breast cancer, several studies were undergone. It was expected to provide brief yield and help the radiologist precisely find the ailing region.

The fundamental goal of the investigation includes the detection of BD (breast density) and breast region of interest (BROI) by using suitable segmentation algorithms for the obtained breast MRI images. To begin with, the BROI division must fill in as the key advance to maintain a strategic distance from superfluous structures, for example, an undesirable foundation and organs like the lung, heart, and liver, developing effectiveness and precision during additional examination like tumor segmentation [11]. The segmentation of the tumor-affected region in obtaining MRIs has been viewed as a difficult and blunder-inclined methodology. Likewise, tumors regularly dwell inside the BROI. In this manner, before the segmentation of the tumor, it is necessary to distinguish the BROI. This is the basic and most essential step in BROI [12].

The segmentation of BROI is also valuable for a few specific applications. The BD estimation [13] and execution improvement of DCE-MRI as far as pharmacokinetics-model alignment (PMC) [14] is the best example of this type of segmentation. The features of the inside chest chamber ought to be resolved during PMC. The pectoral muscle segmentation was required [15]. Then, the proportion of BD must be included as a solid marker for the assessment of risk factors involved in breast cancer. Additionally, breast tissue design imbalance in the left and right bosom is viewed as an irregular organic cycle that prompts disease [16]. There is no specific particular shape for BD, and the design might be found any place in the image. Besides, a typical issue faced by breast MRIs is intensity inhomogeneity. Since the inclination field includes more difficulties by delivering comparative intensity around the BROI.

The various procedures have been accounted for BROI segmentation. Ertas et al. [17] analyzed the morphological activity and threshold based on intensity for the segmentation. Nonetheless, the outcomes are better when there is high contrast in the chest chamber. A few different techniques, for example, intensity histogram [18], wavelet investigation and active contour [19], fuzzy C-means algorithm [20], region-based segmentation [21], are introduced.

The difference in the uniform density distribution of intensity among the border region and failure is considered to be an important strategy. The complete mechanized strategy was revealed by Wang et al. [22]. The breast region is extracted completely from nonfat stifled MRI pictures. In this work, he clarified that the characteristics of breast air limits and pectoral muscle are comparative in 3D. It shows smooth sheet surfaces. Also, it is necessary to minimize the effects such as lower contrast and vague structures; hence it utilizes the Hessian-based filter. Notwithstanding, this technique may exclude BD-based segmentation. Also, the exact mask cannot create in this. The multiatlas segmentation algorithm was proposed by Khalvati et al. [23]. Thus, the breast atlas were formed by the assistance of stage congruency.

The probabilistic atlas-based methodology was introduced for effective breast segmentation by Gubern-Merida et al. [24]. Nonetheless, accuracy is considered a major factor in analyzing performance. It relies on the amount and the inconstancy of the database. This may require an atlas that is illustrative of the population. The computation cost is the maximum on comparisons with other techniques. Milenkovic et al. have discussed edge-based methodology [25]. They are autonomous from the obvious difference among the breast region of interest (ROI) and the chest wall. The edge information taken from the tunable Gabor filter and utilized by the cost function is discussed in this strategy. The exactness of this strategy relies on the data from the nearby slices and precise starting outskirt assurance. Despite the developments in BROI segmentation, the completely programmed, exact, and quick division of BROI requires a lot of consideration. This is due to the following:

1. Usually breast structures are in various shapes and are shown in MR breast images. There is no clear boundary between breast landmarks. It is difficult to find the boundary that requires manual revision [26].
2. The two-sided unevenness may be present among the left and right side of breast areas. It requires a different examination [27].
3. The pectoral muscle is firmly connected. On comparing with BROI, it has more power. It requires manual adjustments and also provides bogus positives [28].
4. Based on the past research work, it was clear that few existing techniques are supervised and need earlier data before the segmentation process. It provides detailed results about the computational multifaceted nature [29].

Several noteworthy scopes of research studies were carried out in BD segmentation. An intuitive threshold-based strategy [30] and user-assisted clustering techniques [31] were utilized in semiautomated segmentation techniques. Most of the noncomputerized techniques are subjective. It makes interreader and intrareader inconstancy [32]. It may be very tedious and, accordingly, unacceptable for handling a huge database. A few endeavors on automated techniques have been concentrated to adapt to previously mentioned troubles, for example, adaptive thresholding [33], Chartbook-based strategy [34], Gaussian appropriation curve fitting [35], progressive support vector machine (SVMs) [36], and Otsu thresholding calculation [37].

Several supervised techniques were observed, and it gives efficient and precise outcomes. However, it requires complicated and expensive labeling. The analysis was done by master radiologists before segmentation. Consequently, unsupervised techniques produce proficient outcomes for the automatic segmentation of BD. Likewise, the computation time of segmentation was effectively minimized by the reduction of the number of pixels processed. The novel structure was proposed to overcome these issues. It is completely unsupervised, automatic, quick, and proficient. The proposed model is classified into two categories: (1) BROI segmentation; and (2) BD segmentation.

Initially denoising the MR picture was done in the BROI segmentation process. It was defined to eliminate air-background utilizing pixel-wise wiener filtering (PAWF) method and k-means grouping. The edges of an image may persevere in the PAWF strategy. The k-means grouping and normal filtering technique will consequently group the entire image into various groups. It is based on the correlation between pixel intensities. After this, in the heart region, an image with high intensity is segmented by utilizing the active contour-based level-set technique.

The computation of the initial contour was done by utilizing convolution and the greatest entropy threshold method [38]. This is the novelty of this segmentation approach. It gives exact segmentation and a decrease in calculation speed. Then the pectoral muscle was segmented based on a threshold value. Both the location of the pectoral muscle and the BD are different. As a result, the morphological technique was used oppositely to expand the distance between the pectoral muscle and breast width. The picture is digitized using an active threshold approach to prevent the pectoral muscle.

At last, for smoothening the obtained BROI segmented image, the polynomial curve fitting was preferred. During BD segmentation, at first, denoising is applied to the resultant image obtained after BROI segmentation. Based on the observation received from the analysis, the amount and gray values of the BD image on the right and left breast may vary. Subsequently, the single threshold value could not give precise segmentation. The BROI segmented image was partitioned as indicated by its mathematical data. The corresponding threshold value for the left and right breast was determined by utilizing four different levels of fuzzy cognitive maps (FCMs). The investigation may compute FCM for the BROI instead of on a whole image.

Several existing models were developed based on efficient image processing algorithms based on machine learning and deep learning approaches. Each model provides accuracy in the classification of breast cancer up to a certain extent. In critical cases, these models failed to classify or deviate from its accuracy. Hence, it is necessary to propose a new model to classify the breast cancer image irrespective of age, gender, affected region, stage, and more. Cognitive-based approaches fulfill all these objectives.

## 3 Breast cancer: A brief introduction

### 3.1 Overview of breast cancer

Cancer occurs when mutations known as genetic transformations happen in the genes that control cell development. Transformations permit cells to split and duplicate in an unpredictable and nonstoppable manner.

The most common disease that occurs in the breast is known as breast cancer. Usually, it is formed either in the ducts or lobules of the breast. The milk-producing glands are called lobules, and ducts are channels that convey milk from parts to the nipple. The fatty tissue of the breast is connective tissue [39].

### 3.2 Symptoms of breast cancer

Typically, breast cancer cannot create any manifestations at the beginning phase. As a rule, the tumor might be too little to be felt, but abnormalities present can be found on the mammogram. At the point when a tumor is felt, the primary sign is normally another irregularity in the breast that was not there previously.

Each sort of breast cancer may provide an assortment of symptoms. A considerable number of such manifestations are comparable; however, few might be unique. Side effects of the most widely recognized breast cancer include:

- lump or muscle stiffness that may differ from the surrounding tissues;
- severe pain in the breast region;
- peeling, estimating, or glowing skin on nipple or breast;
- red, irritated skin all over the breast;
- swelling in breast and underarm;
- curved nipple;
- discharge from nipple continuously;
- blood bleeding from the nipple;
- depending on the type of cancer, the visualization varies but mostly equals aggressive cancers, those ranked high or 3 or 4; and
- sudden modification in the skin on the breast.

## 3.3 Categories of breast cancer

Women can experience severe breast cancer, yet all are sorted into just two groups [39]:

**a.** Invasive category—This cancer spreads from the breast or glands to other parts of the breast.
**b.** Noninvasive category—This type of cancer does not spread beyond the breast tissue.

These two categories are used to represent the most well-known types of breast cancer, which include the following:

- Ductal carcinoma in situ (DCIS): DCIS is a noninvasive technique. In this, the malignant growth cells are observed from the ducts or channels of the breast. This problem does not show my effects on surrounding breast tissues.
- Lobular carcinoma in situ (LCIS): LCIS is the malignant growth that spreads in the milk-delivering portions of the breast. The malignant cells did not attack encompassing tissues like DCIS.
- Infectious ductal carcinoma (IDC): IDC is the most well-known form of breast cancer. This classification is found in the lining of breast milk. It affects the tissues in the breast. When breast cancer continues to spread to the tissues beyond the breast, it may continue to spread to other surrounding organs and tissues.
- Invasive Lobular carcinoma (ILC): ILC starts to show up on breast lobes and attacks close-by tissues.

Some other common types of breast cancer are: Paget's nipple disease; phyllode tumors; and angiosarcoma.

### 3.3.1 *Inflammatory breast cancer*

The uncommon however aggressive type of breast cancer is inflammatory breast cancer (IBC). IBC only builds up to 5% reliable sources for all types of breast cancer. In such a case, the lymph nodes can be hindered by cancer cells close to the breast. Consequently, the lymph vessels in the breast cannot discharge appropriately. Rather than spreading cancer, IBC prompts swelling of the breast and reddish color and feels extremely warm. Breast cancer can look like a rash and can look thick, like an orange peel.

This is severe and can develop rapidly. Therefore, it is necessary to consult a doctor immediately if any symptoms occur.

### 3.3.2 *Triple-negative breast cancer*

IDC is the most well-known form of breast cancer. The lining of breast milk comes into this definition. Breast tissues are affected. It will continue to spread to other organs and tissues nearby as breast cancer begins spreading to the tissues beyond the breast.

- It does not have estrogen receptors. Estrogen can invigorate malignant growth to develop when a tumor contains estrogen receptors.
- It does not have progesterone receptors. These cellular receptors bind to the hormone progesterone. Progesterone may trigger the growth of cancer if the tumor contains progesterone receptors.
- It does not have any other HER2 protein on its surface. HER2 is a protein that improves breast cancer growth.

When a tumor meets these three mechanisms, it is called breast cancer with triple-negative.

### 3.3.3 *Metastatic breast cancer*

Metastatic breast cancer is otherwise considered the fourth level of breast cancer. It is a malignant growth that extends from the breast to other areas of the body, such as the bones, lungs, and liver. This is a ridiculous final breast cancer process. The oncologist (cancer specialist) will formulate a therapeutic plan to prevent the tumor or tissue from developing and spreading.

## 3.4 Male breast cancer

Breast cancer will affect men at any stage. According to the American Cancer Society (ACS), breast cancer affects white women at a far higher rate than white men. It is, however, 70 times more prevalent in black women than it is in black men [39].

Similar to women having breast cancer, men also suffered from the same symptoms and health problems. A few manifestations may happen, and these indications may change starting with one individual then onto the next.

## 3.5 Breast cancer stages

Breast cancer can be partitioned into stages depending on the size of the tumor or the size of the tissue. Significant tumors and/or attacks of close-by tissues or organs are at a more elevated level than other diseases and/or still in the bosom. To create breast cancer growth, specialists need to:

- know if the disease has spread or not;
- know the size of tumor spread;
- identify the association of lymph hub; and
- know if the malignancy has spread to the entire body.

Breast cancer has five primary stages: stage 0 to stage 5.

(i) Stage 0 breast cancer: DCIS disease cells stay caught in the channels and do not spread to close-by tissues.
(ii) Stage 1 breast cancer:
  - Stage 1A: Initially tumor influenced roughly equivalent to or under 2 cm wide. In this stage, the lymph hubs are not influenced.
  - Stage 1B: This sort of malignant growth is regularly found nearer to lymph hubs. In this stage, tumor side effects are not found even in the chest or a tumor more modest than 2 cm.
(iii) Stage 2 breast cancer:
  - Stage 2A: It can spread up to 1–3 lymph hubs, or anywhere between the 2 and 5 cm range. This form of cancer should not spread to lymph nodes afterward.
  - Stage 2B: The affected region is someplace in the scope of 2 and 5 cm. It can spread up to 1–3 lymph hubs, or anywhere between the 2 and 5 cm range. This form of cancer should not spread to lymph nodes afterward.
(iv) Stage 3 breast cancer:
  - *Stage 3A:* The internal lymph nodes are extended, and the tumor can be of any dimension. Tumors are more than 5 cm in diameter at this point, and the damage has spread to the lymph center or auxiliary 1–3.
  - Stage 3B: The tumor has attacked the mass of the chest or skin. It may or may have tainted up to nine lymph hubs.
  - Stage 3C: Cancer is found in at least 10 lymph hubs, lymph hubs close to the collarbone, or inside lymph hubs.
(v) Stage 4 breast cancer:

In this stage, cancer might be any size. Cancer cells have spread to close-by and far-off lymph hubs and organs.

## 3.6 Diagnosis of breast cancer

It is important to decide the side effects brought about by bosom malignant growth. The malignant growth master will play out an intensive actual assessment alongside the bosom test. They may likewise request to go through at least one analytic test for affirmation on the off chance that someone is having manifestations.

Sometimes tests are generally recommended to analyze the bosom malignancy [39]. Some of them are the following:

- Mammogram: The most widely recognized approach to see underneath the bosom surface by an imaging test called a mammogram. Numerous women in their 40s and older get mammograms consistently to get tested for cancer disease. On the off chance that the specialist finds that the patient may have a tumor or a dubious zone, they will suggest going through a mammogram test. On the off chance that an anomalous territory shows up on a mammogram, a specialist may demand further tests.
- Ultrasound: This technique utilizes sound waves to make a picture of profound tissue in the chest. An ultrasound can assist the pro with recognizing a strong mass, for example, a tumor, and a dangerous sore.
- Breast biopsy: If the specialist discovers bosom disease, they can arrange a mammogram and ultrasound. On the off chance that the two tests do not affirm the malignant growth, at that point the specialist may have a test known as a breast biopsy. In this test, the specialist must take a sample of tissue from the influenced region for testing. There are numerous kinds of breast biopsies. For a portion of these tests, a specialist utilizes a needle to take a tissue test. With others, they make an opening in the bosom and eliminate the example.

## 3.7 Breast cancer treatment

Cancer treatment depends on the stage, influenced area, age, and so on. To start with, the specialist must dissect the malignancy size, stage, and grade. From that point forward, proper treatment must be looked over, and the alternatives depends on those boundaries. The most widely recognized therapy for breast cancer is surgery. A large number of women have alternative treatments, for example, radiation, chemotherapy, targeted therapy, or hormone treatment.

### *3.7.1 Surgery*

Numerous medical procedures can be utilized to eliminate the growth of breast cancer, including the following:

- Lumpectomy: In this strategy, the tumor-influenced part will be removed alongside other encompassing tissues, leaving different segments of the breast unblemished.
- Mastectomy: In this, the whole breast is removed. Both breasts are removed if there should be an occurrence of a twofold mastectomy.

- Sentinel hub biopsy: This medical procedure removes a few lymph hubs that get liquid from the tumor. These lymph hubs will be tried. On the off chance that they do not have malignant growth, a further medical procedure is not required to eliminate a large portion of the lymph hubs.
- Axillary hub analysis: During a sentinel node biopsy, if harmful development cells are located in the lymph nodes, the specialists can remove additional lymph nodes.
- Contralateral prophylactic mastectomy: Even though breast cancer can only affect one breast, this form of operation to remove the healthy breast will lower the chance of getting breast cancer again.

#### *3.7.2 Radiation therapy*

In a radiation treatment, high-dose radiation is utilized to distinguish and destroy the malignant growth of cancer cells. A significant number of therapies utilize external radiation. This technique utilizes large equipment set up outside of the human body.

The recent advancement in cancer treatment has allowed specialists to remove cancer or malignant cells from the body. This radiation-based therapy is known as brachytherapy. The specialist inserts a radio containing seeds, or pills, in the body near the site of the tumor to perform brachytherapy. The seeds remain there for a short time and work to demolish malignant growth cells.

#### *3.7.3 Chemotherapy*

Chemotherapy is a treatment that is used to kill cancer cells. A few people may get this treatment all alone, yet this sort of treatment is regularly utilized related to different treatments, particularly surgery.

Sometimes specialists need to give patients chemotherapy before a medical procedure. It is believed that this treatment will diminish the tumor, and a medical procedure will not be required at this point. Chemotherapy has numerous unfortunate results; the correct meeting is needed to discuss concerns before beginning treatment.

#### *3.7.4 Hormone therapy*

Sometimes, estrogen and progesterone may increase suddenly and stimulate the growth of breast cancer cells in women. Hormone treatment blocks the excess production of these hormones or impedes hormone receptors in disease cells. This activity reduces and reasonably avoids the spread of cancer.

### 3.8 Medications

Several therapies are intended for abnormal attacks or mutations inside the malignant growth of cancer cells. For example, Herceptin (trastuzumab) may inhibit the activity of the HER2 protein in the human body. Since HER2 stimulates the development of breast cancer cells, taking a drug that prevents its synthesis may help delay the spread of cancer cells.

As per the Center for Disease Control and Prevention (CDC) Trusted Source, today, approximately 1 in every 25 women is suffering from breast cancer. As per ACS figures, 268,600 new cases of breast cancer are expected to hit the United States by 2019. Breast cancer can also spread to other areas of the body, according to the report. Furthermore, nearly 41,000 women are predicted to die from cancer.

## 3.9 Risk factors for breast cancer

Several risk factors play a part in the growth of breast cancer. A few of these causes, such as family history and smoking, can be avoided. Some of the risk factors for breast cancer include the following:

- Age: As age increases, the risk of forming breast cancer also increases. The majority of invasive breast cancer is diagnosed in women over the age of 55.
- Drinking alcohol: Excessive alcohol consumption increases risk.
- Dense breast tissue: Thick breast tissue can make mammograms impossible to read. It also raises the risk of breast cancer.
- Gender: Breast cancer is more prevalent in white women than in white men, and breast cancer is more common in black women than in black men.
- Genetics: Breast cancer is more likely to develop in women who have BRCA1 and BRCA2 mutations than in women who do not. A few changes can also have an impact on the risk factor.
- Early menstruation: Breast cancer is more likely to occur in women whose first period was before they were 12 years old.
- Giving birth at old age: Breast cancer risk is raised in women who do not have their first child until after the age of 35.
- Hormone treatment: Women who have taken or are taking postmenopausal estrogen and progesterone drugs to alleviate menopausal symptoms are more likely to develop breast cancer.
- Inherited risk: When a woman's closest relative has breast cancer, she is more likely to have it herself.
- The beginning of menopause: Women who do not begin menopause until after the age of 55 are more likely to get breast cancer.
- Never get pregnant: Breast cancer is more common in women who have never been pregnant.
- Previous breast cancer: Women who had breast cancer in one breast are more likely to get cancer in their other breast or in another part of the recently affected breast.

## 3.10 Breast cancer survival rate

The survival rate of breast cancer varies greatly depending on many factors. The two significant factors are the sort of cancer and the phase of the disease when diagnosed [39]. Different factors may incorporate age, sex, and race, among others.

## 3.11 Breast cancer prevention

Even though there are uncontrollable risk factors, following a healthy lifestyle, getting regular checkups, and taking any of the preventive measures suggested by a specialist can help lessen the danger of developing breast cancer.

### *3.11.1 Lifestyle factors*

Lifestyle factors may influence the danger of breast cancer. For instance, overweight women are at high danger of affecting breast cancer. Maintaining a healthy diet and getting plenty of exercise can help lose weight and reduce risk.

Excessive drinking also increases risk. This is valid for having at least two beverages every day and for heavy drinking. Nonetheless, one examination found that even one beverage daily expanded the danger of bosom malignancy.

## 3.12 Breast cancer screening

Regular mammograms cannot avoid breast cancer completely, but they may reduce the risk of undiagnosed complications. The American College of Physicians (ACP) offers the following general recommendations for women at higher risk of breast cancer:

- Women 40–49 years: No annual mammogram is recommended, but women must consult with their doctors.
- Women 50–74 years: A mammogram test is recommended every year.
- Women 75 years and older: Mammograms are no longer recommended.
- The ACP has not recommended mammograms for females age 10 years or less.

According to the ACS, each woman should start testing every year at age 45, and then go for a test every other year beginning at the age of 55.

## 3.13 Preemptive treatment

Few women are at severe risk for breast cancer because of genetic reasons. For example, if the parent has a genetic mutation in BRCA1 or BRCA2, then the child has a greater risk of having it. This greatly increases the risk of breast cancer.

If anyone has this type of mutation, they must consult a doctor about their diagnostic and prophylactic treatment options. This may reduce the risk of developing breast cancer. Such measures may incorporate prophylactic mastectomy (surgical removal of the chest).

### 3.14 Breast test

Breast tests are an alternate approach to search for symptoms of breast cancer along with mammogram test.

#### *3.14.1 Self-test*

Many women examine their breasts. It is better to do this test once every month. This examination can help them get acquainted with any changes that are taking place.

#### *3.14.2 Breast test by a doctor*

A doctor or other health care provider performs the test following the same self-examination guidelines. This does not hurt the patient, and the doctor is required to do a breast test.

During the test, the doctor will examine abnormal areas of the breast for signs of breast cancer. The doctor may also examine other parts of the body to identify symptoms that are related.

### 3.15 Breast cancer awareness

In recent days, people know more about the problems associated with cancer. The awareness campaigns for breast cancer may be arranged, and it has helped individuals realize what the dangers are, how to lessen their danger, what side effects to search for, and what tests to take.

Every year, several awareness programs are conducted in October, since it is Breast Cancer Awareness Month. But many organizations, nongovernmental organizations, and social workers are working continuously to spread awareness in the word throughout the year.

## 4 Cognitive approaches in breast cancer techniques

### 4.1 Cognitive image processing

The primary reason for computer vision is to give visual data to the desired application. To perform this, viewing programs must be integrated into a variety of subactivities grouped under three categories:

1. Lower Vision (or) Low-level Perspective:

   Low-level viewing tasks include image capture, sampling, and preprocessing.

**2.** Intermediate Vision (or) Middle-level Perspective:

Medium-level activities are concerned with enhancement, symbolic representation, segmentation, and recognition.

**3.** High-level Perspective:

High-level viewing activities are concerned with accomplishing intellectual comprehension of data from low-level vision modules.

The integration of these three levels results in the formation of a complete visual perception system. It includes all the functions required to identify the objects of the image and to build relationships between them or between objects and the viewer. A conceptual framework or cognitive vision system may be classified based on this; it depends on a bunch of smaller activities that a framework needs to play out certain exercises.

Researchers have used this approach to overcome certain problems, such as the optimistic concept of "shall not be neutral in any basic model," which supports a common definition of subjective perception of the system. Computer vision is currently a well-established research area with a heavy emphasis on media frameworks, for example, the automation of operations in production lines in industrial areas. The solutions can be found for many of these vision problems in terms of mathematical interpretations that omit the need for prior knowledge.

The disadvantages of this technique are that the parameters cannot match with the real-time factors and cannot measure the unknown. The present challenge is to create robust frameworks that wipe out interference and deviations from data-driven models. It must be more successful regarding computer specifications and memory aspects. Reducing dependency on broad training datasets, inefficiency, and handling data training exploitation are all problems that need to be tackled.

## 4.2 Knowledge-based vision systems

The main aim of computer-aided vision frameworks is the capacity to decipher conventional picture and semantic meaning. Geometric presentations have a flaw in that they could not handle a large number of possible variations for an object. Models with additional details on the object's functionality were suggested to help people understand things in practical terms [40].

Along with better object recognition comes the ability to provide knowledge about the context of a scene. The structure in a picture (which is a collection of objects) will enhance the visual performance in terms of location. In this context, it can provide insight into the functioning of an object in the event. Also, it minimizes the effects of sensory noise or occlusions [41].

Studies from other fields of cognition-based approaches have shown that visual perception of the world around us transcends perception. Also, the combination of cognitive knowledge cannot be ignored. Conceptual knowledge includes the knowledge about the surroundings, such as learning from past and present experiences [42]. The system could incorporate information and how people remember data needed to understand new situations based on past experiences. The information can be updated and modified to suit reality with systematic and concise methods of organizing information [40].

## 4.3 Integration of knowledge bases in vision systems

Along with empowering computers to translate images, integration, information has been suggested for individual visual modules. The visual modules were significantly affected by low- and mid-range visual activities such as segmentation. Also, contextual information has been raised to minimize computer resources as it places less load on the system compared to maintaining the geometric representation of all types of one object [40]. Finally, using explicit image recognition in vision implementations has a range of advantages over traditional knowledge-based applications, including the ability to add rules without changing existing code, data extraction, and data recovery.

A cognitive vision accomplishes the following four levels of computer viewing activities:

- Acquisition or detection of something in visual support
  - The localization of an object found
  - Recognition of type of the object
  - Understanding the part of an object in a scene

This usefulness can be acquired by:

- the ability of faculty to read semantic information;
- the importance of preserving contextual data and how it contributes to the system; and
- discussing environmental concerns, things, and events.

The use of knowledge bases in vision systems is explored in this session. Cognitive-based visual systems are classified as programs that conduct "subactivities" of cognitive theories.

## 4.4 Image processing, annotation, and retrieval

The automatic annotation of the image datasets obtained interest given the enormous measure of preparing subtleties needed for artificial intelligence (AI) classifiers. For example, automatic image annotation is obtained by automatically obtaining information from data [43] using a complex representation system based on the official representation of the Fuzzy Petri Net. The proposed framework utilizes a strategy to view scenes and ideas that cannot be connected to pictures without utilizing background information. This data structure information has been applied using labeled and unencrypted images with a moderated reading model, enhancing image annotation performance [44].

Transfer learning has enhanced the functional classification of texture representations by using input rather than raw data in image processing. Nontarget knowledge between the raw source database and targets is often revealed in this way. The utilization of past data removed from other surface pictures has been discovered to be keener and more averse to be sounder than different techniques. This has been accomplished by setting up a combined relationship of assembled models among sources and focused on areas [45].

## 4.5 Human activity recognition

Knowledge-based activity recognition systems handle the prior data, for example, what assignments are relied upon to be performed and human life systems, and relevant data, that is, where pictures are gathered and occupation acknowledgment. These applications can be separated into three classifications: (1) mathematical methods (or) statistical approach; (2) synthetic methods (or) syntactic approach; and (3) description-based method [46].

Research has shown that the exploitation of information has been used to select appropriate strategies for segregation and to improve overall performance. Practices define a set of baseline-based foundations, with well-structured businesses, jobs, and relationships. Different researchers have used this way to represent knowledge as logical rules (logic-order logic), hypothetical thinking (for example, knowledge of a professional human resource), the basis for belief in modeling processes), and ontologies (an official description of information within the domain).

Finally, definition-based methods are dependent on human activity spatial frameworks. These measures help people remember what transitory structures mean in terms of progression and current paths [46].

Human activity has been recognized using a visual semantic preparation, which predicts the sequence of events that will accomplish the desired goal. The proposed architecture demonstrated promising abilities for knowledge transmission through activities, enabling the system to reach common solutions [47]. Task visibility has also been enhanced by using common sense knowledge. Given the user's GPS position, adjacent commercial operations were detected using the encoding tool to undo the satellite imagery of the area [48].

## 4.6 Medical images analysis

Present manual annotation techniques for semantic recognition of histopathology photographs [49] have improved with medical expertise in the diagnosis of breast cancer [50]. Comprehensive computer technology has been used to perform background correction and removal of archeological material (such as nonruptured blood vessels or two arteries connected when not present) in MRIs

[51]. Classic techniques such as Markov Random Field can jeopardize tissue details that are important in classifying malignant lesions in low-computed tomography (LdCT) that produces noise. To achieve the texture that allowed LdCT reconstruction to last, researchers used data from a full-scale computed tomography (CT) [52].

Some treatment programs present difficulties because of the handling of images. For example, spontaneous prostate separation in MRI images is challenging, as bladder formation can produce wide variations between different individuals. Also, the boundaries of the most interesting regions are not effectively isolated from the foundation. To address these issues, researchers are proposing a strategy that benefits neighborhood energy highlights utilizing an irregular versatility calculation and earlier information on a Chartbook opportunity map. In terms of precision and robustness, this method outperforms the conventional RW [53]. Previous data have been shown to increase phase accuracy in prostate MRI [54] and to facilitate spontaneous boundary separation of the colonic wall in CT colonography (CTC) [55].

Finally, misusing data from publicly available sources is a problem for just a few applications. Computer-aided design (CAD) diagnostics using huge information and in-depth learning has been accomplished through the development and implementation of a clinical imaging dataset. The proposed clinical picture can keep up a thoracic CT picture and its demonstrative subtleties adequately and in a manner intended for the diagnosis of a pulmonary nodule [56].

## 5 Proposed methodology

Identifying and classifying breast cancer at the cell level is considered to be a more challenging task. Since the morphological features and other cell highlights of malignant growth cells are unique about typical healthy cells, it is conceivable to characterize disease cells and ordinary cells based on features. For pattern recognition, AI procedures such as the least square support vector machine (LS-SVM) were used. It has yet to be determined how they are used to isolate cancer cells from diagnostic results.

The alternative techniques have been developed by using different AI strategies to characterize malignant growth and typical cells from the given image. It incorporates the use of texture features derived from cell images of MCF-7, MDA-MB-231 breast cancer cell lines, and MCF-10A, a human general breast cancer cell line. By applying pattern recognition techniques to various standard cell images, it is possible to effectively segment cell images, remove texture-based characteristics, and eventually identify breast cancer and typical healthy and affected cells.

Fig. 1 shows the cognitive-based proposed model to classify breast images. In this approach, during training phase the neural network was trained with a large number of breast cancer datasets including both healthy and cancer-affected people. The training dataset includes CT and MRI scan based breast

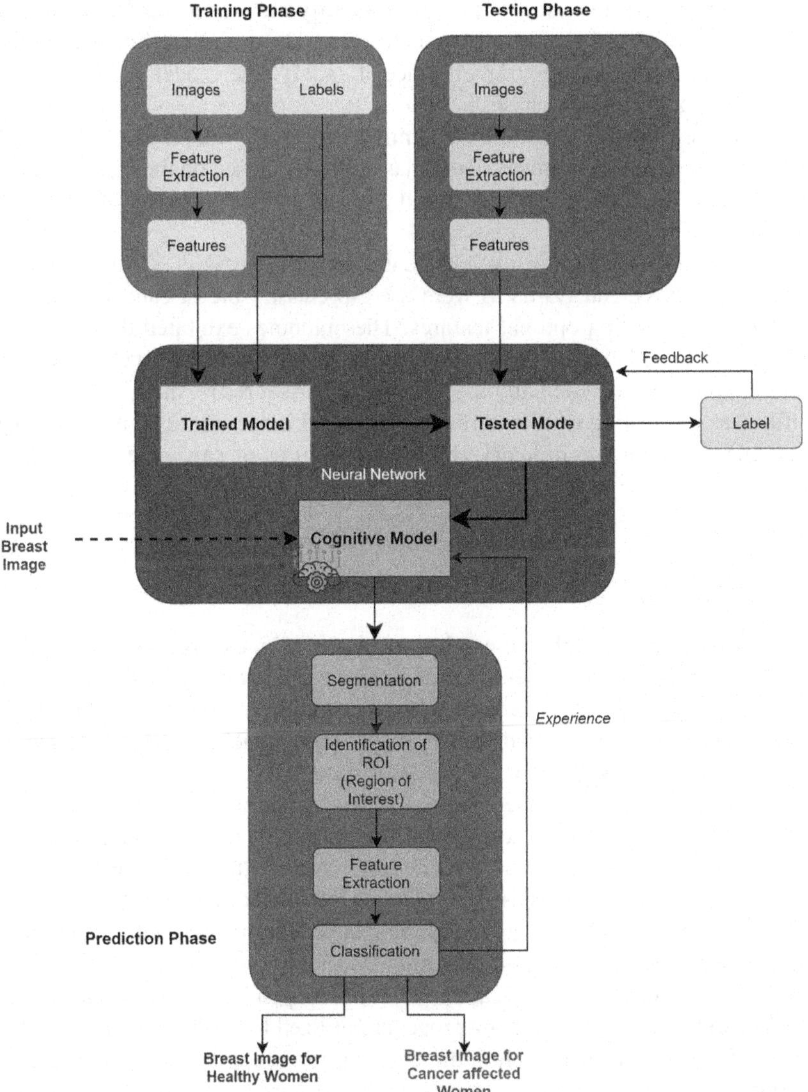


**FIG. 1** Proposed cognitive model-based approach.

images and all other associated parameters. In this phase, the model is properly trained with associated labels. The performance as well as accuracy is based on the number of training datasets used during training.

Based on training, the model was allowed to next phase called testing phase. At this stage, the model was evaluated by testing the accuracy based on applying images from predefined datasets. Suppose, if the model failed to meet the required accuracy level, it is necessary to modify the architecture of the neural network by altering the number of hidden layers. The procedure will be repeated until it meets the accuracy level. Once it satisfy, the model is allowed for evaluation or prediction phase.

In the evaluation phase, the cognitive model has the ability to classify whether the given input image is nonmass or mass. Based on the classification, the model is again improved based on experience obtained from each prediction.

AI techniques including artificial neural networks (ANNs), SVMs, k-nearest neighbor (KNN), and LS-SVM were used to classify breast cancer from segmented images using optimal features. The outcomes exhibited that LS-SVM with linear kernel classifier and radial basis function had the most classification rate of above 90% among all other approaches. As a result, the LS-SVM classifier was discovered to be an effective prepared model capable of classifying malignant growth and ordinary cells using features of cell images in a short period of time.

## 5.1 Workflow

The main objectives of this research were to use an image processing algorithm and/or an AI approach to identify breast cancer and nonmalignancy cells in the obtained image. An image segmentation technique was used to segment the image and obtain the desired ROI from the image background. Fig. 2 shows the workflow of cognitive-based proposed model.

To separate cells from the image context, morphological activities and gradient operations were used to segment the image. To differentiate segmented cells from the background of the images, color contrast must be used. The image's gradient value was used to calculate the transformation. The histogram values, texture properties, and wavelet-based texture highlights from each image were extracted after segmentation. MATLAB software was responsible for image segmentation and feature extraction depending on location.

The extraction of features is a procedure utilized for gathering different features of images and reduction in dimensionality. The different texture feature extraction strategies such as Tamura texture features, ChIP Histogram-based texture features, and wavelet-based texture features were used to obtain features from each sectioned image. All the obtained features are combined to make the feature dataset after extracting individual features from the segmented image. Based on suitable image processing or machine learning algorithms, such as principal component analysis (PCA), the combined feature dataset was reduced. These reduced feature datasets were taken care of with different classifiers to separate malignant growth and normal class. Different classifiers, such as KNN, ANN, SVM, and LS-SVM, were used to differentiate between malignant and normal cells.

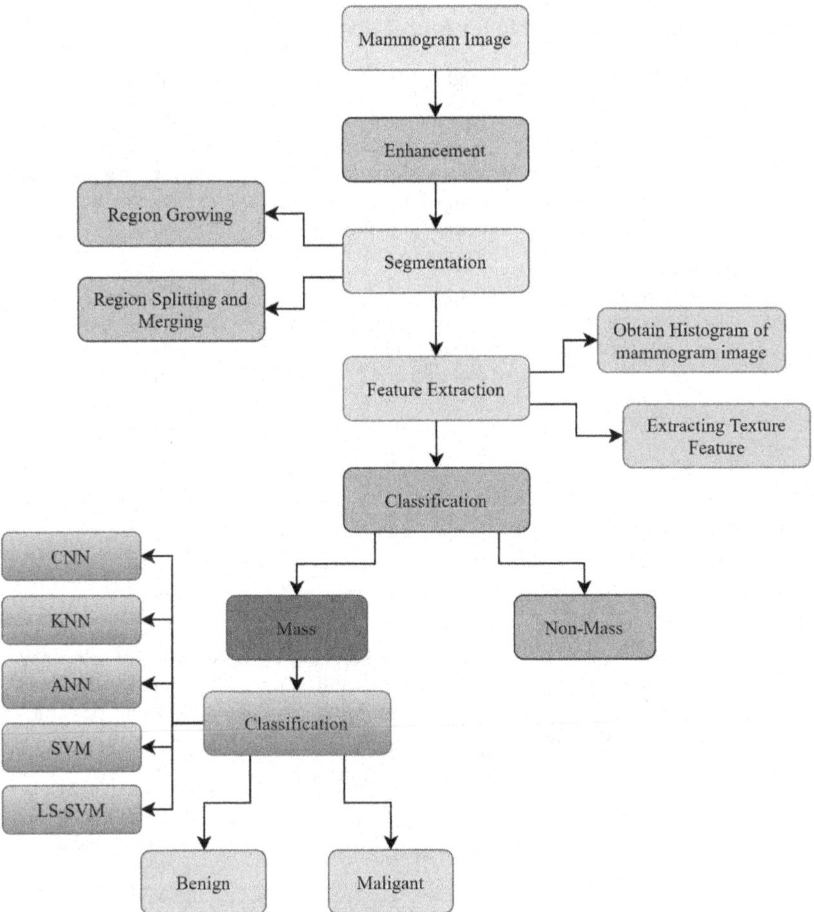


FIG. 2 Workflow of proposed model.

## 6 Algorithms used

Table 2 shows the various image processing algorithms used to diagnose breast cancer. There are several other algorithms also used in practice. But, the choice of an algorithm suitable for the particular application is based on certain features associated with this technique and the advantages of each algorithm.

## 7 Results and discussion

Fig. 3 shows the results of processed breast cancer images obtained from CT scans by using the Weiner and Clahe filter. Fig. 3A shows the original breast image captured by CT. Fig. 3B illustrates the spectrum of the original breast image. The corresponding binary image (black and white) is shown in

**TABLE 2 Algorithms suitable for cancer diagnosis.**

| S. No. | Algorithm | Highlights | Advantages |
|---|---|---|---|
| 1 | Automated Classification | Uses BC histopathology image examination and specifically to the computerized grouping of benign or malignant images for CAD analysis | Precision goes from 80% to 85% indicating opportunity to get better is left |
| 2 | Canny Edge Detection and Backpropagation | For breast cancer diagnosis, this technique utilizes thermal image processing | The Levenberg-Marquardt (LM) calculation was chosen because it produces the quickest convergence and the lowest mean square error (MSE), particularly for a smaller network with all neurons exchanging information |
| 3 | Radial Basis Function Networks and Back Propagation networks | Based on severity, the abnormality classification was done by ANNs.<br>The mean difference, the difference in variance, and Kurtosis are the parameters to be considered. | • An abnormality may be analyzed with the canny detector and snake transforms<br>• For example, ANNs, radial base feature networks, and backpropagation networks may be used for the classification of anomalies and detection of severity |
| 4 | Blob Detection Algorithms | Different blob identification techniques were examined. | • Different blob identification techniques were examined<br>• Derivation from the review says three techniques are effective in clinical image processing. They are LOG (Laplacian of Gaussian), DOG (Difference of Gaussian), and DOH (Determinant of Hassian) |

**TABLE 2** Algorithms suitable for cancer diagnosis—cont'd

| S. No. | Algorithm | Highlights | Advantages |
|---|---|---|---|
| 5 | Cross-validation Method | To bring another automated model for forecasting breast cancer risk shortly to the test | Using three sets of "earlier" full-field digital mammography screening studies, the correlation between improvements in mammographic image features and risk for the occurrence of near-term breast cancer was predicted easily |
| 6 | Dual-Mesh Method | The dual-mesh method was utilized in electrical impedance tomography. | For tank experiments with inclusion depths and radial offsets of less than 3 and 1.5 mm, the center of mass errors were less than 0.47 mm |
| 7 | PCA | An unsupervised, nonparametric statistical technique is fundamentally utilized for dimensionality decrease in AI. | • Improves the performance of an algorithm<br>• Visualization can be much improved<br>• Overfitting may be reduced<br>• Removes feature similarity<br>• Independent variables become less interpretable |

Fig. 3C. The ROI part may be obtained by the segmentation concept, which is shown in Fig. 3D. Fig. 3E describes the image after deleting the background portion. The required portion of the breast is shown in Fig. 3F. Fig. 3G and H show the response of breast image after applying through Weiner filter and Clahe filter. Based on the response obtained from each filter, it is easy to diagnosis of breast cancer.

Fig. 4 shows the results of processed breast cancer images obtained from positron emission tomography (PET) scans by using the Weiner and Clahe filter.

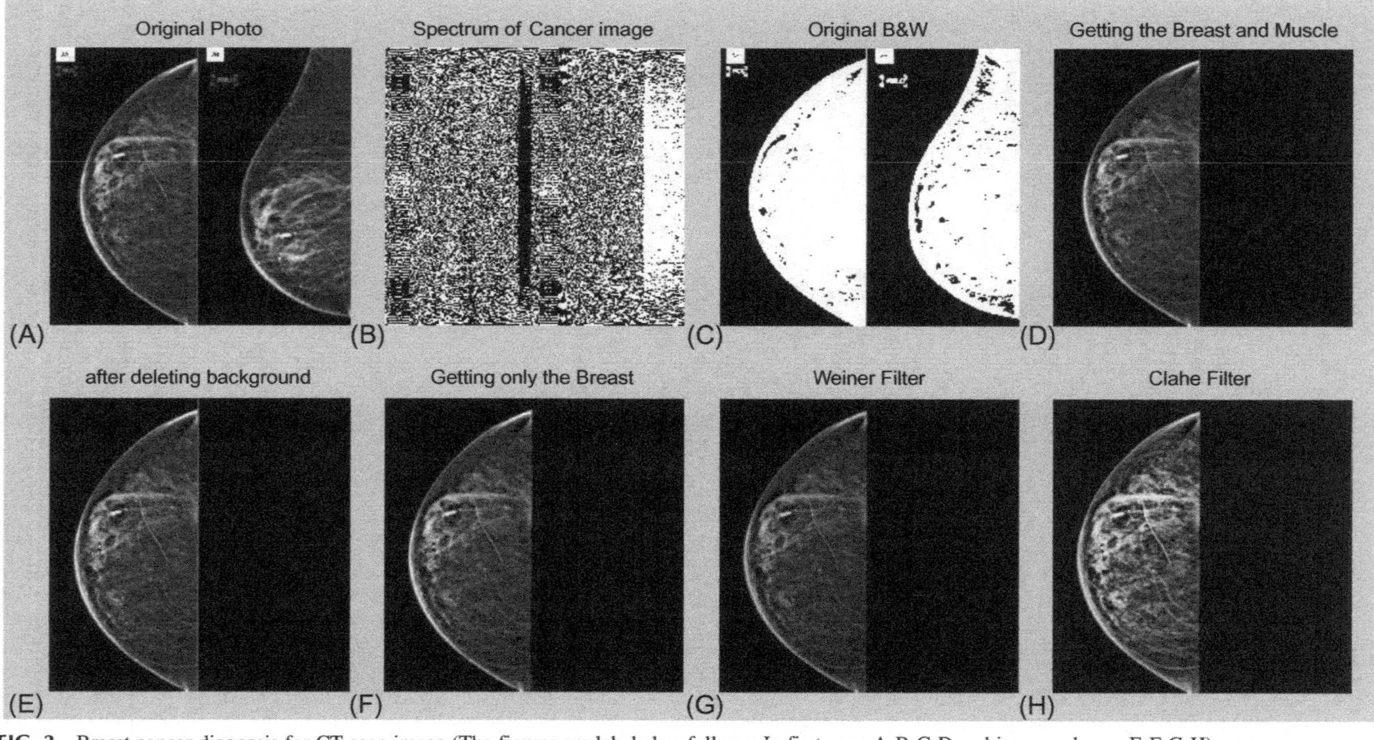


**FIG. 3** Breast cancer diagnosis for CT scan image (The figures are labeled as follows: In first row: A-B-C-D and in second row: E-F-G-H).

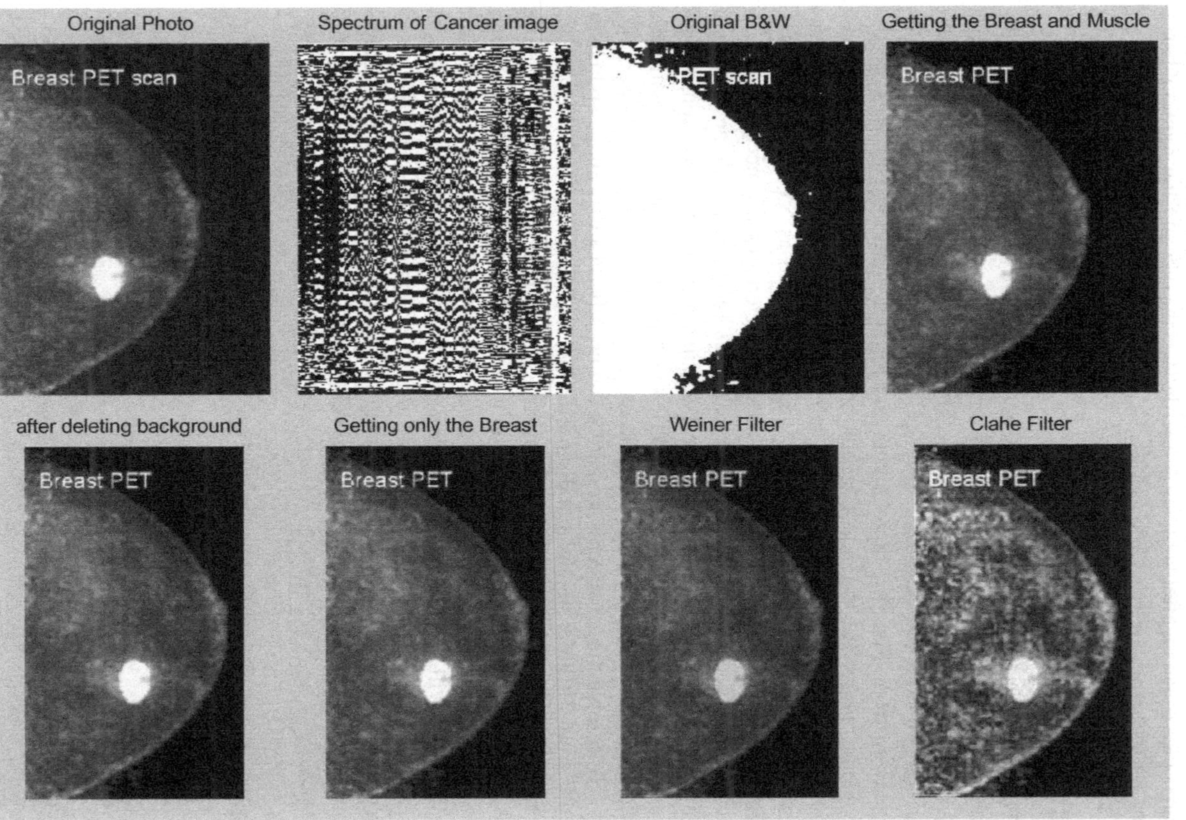


**FIG. 4** Breast cancer diagnosis for PET scan image.

Thus, the cognitive models analyze the input mammogram image based on knowledge base obtained from both training and testing phase. The model decides the appropriate technique needed to classify the breast image based on details obtained after analysis. It also decides the type of filter required based on pretrained model.

## 8 Conclusion

The morphological characteristics of refined breast cancer cell lines are the most realistic method of reproducing healthy human breast cells. The characteristics of the cells have not changed for individual people since they were developed from human breast cancer cell lines. The characteristics of the cells obtained from damaged breast tissue and isolated from the cell lines are the same as before. The diagnostic technique was successfully performed to characterize the malignancy and typical cells from refined cell images in current examination procedures. Various AI classifiers such as SVM, KNN, ANN, and LS-SVM have effectively named these characteristics as cancerous and typical cells. The refined breast cancer cell lines provided all of the classified images. As a result, the morphological features of these cells are confined to breast cells. Despite the fact, that different types of malignant growth cells can be diagnosed using the same process.

To resolve these concerns, researchers must rely on a vast image archive of cells from different organs and disease forms. It is important to correctly distinguish/diagnose a condition like breast cancer in the early stages whether you want to get treated or prevent complications later on. On the off chance that we accomplish over 95% exactness by the utilization of cognitive strategies, this reality will upgrade the discovery and conclusion of the infection and thus make it ready for a treatment at a prior stage. This may decrease the hours required in distinguishing and examining the malignant growth cells in numerous other existing techniques and forestall the demise in malignancy like deadly illness.

## References

[1] MedicineNet. Website: www.medicinenet.com.

[2] D. Pandey, Xiaoxia, H. Wang, M.Y. Su, J.-H. Chen, J. Wu, Y. Zhang, Automatic and fast segmentation of breast region-of-interest (ROI) and density in MRIs, Heliyon 4 (2018), e01042.

[3] J. Ferlay, D.M. Parkin, E. Steliarova-Foucher, Estimates of cancer incidence and mortality in Europe in 2008, Eur. J. Cancer 46 (4) (2010) 765–781.

[4] F. Lalloo, D.G. Evans, Familial breast cancer, Clin. Genet. 82 (2) (2012) 105–114.

[5] C.E. DeSantis, S.A. Fedewa, A.G. Sauer, J.L. Kramer, R.A. Smith, A. Jemal, Breast cancer statistics, 2015: convergence of incidence rates between black and white women, CA Cancer J. Clin. 66 (2016) 31–42.

[6] H. Weedon-Fekjaer, P.R. Romundstad, L.J. Vatten, Modern mammography screening and breast cancer mortality: population study, BMJ 348 (2014) g3701.

[7] R. Mann, C.K. Kuhl, K. Kinkel, C. Boetes, Breast MRI: guidelines from European society of breast imaging, Eur. Radiol. 18 (2008) 1307–1318.

[8] S.G. Orel, M.D. Schnall, MR imaging of the breast for the detection, diagnosis, and staging of breast cancer, Radiology 220 (2001) 13–30.

[9] Y. Zheng, S. Baloch, S. Englander, M.D. Schnall, S. Shen, Segmentation and classification of breast tumor using dynamic contrast-enhanced MR images, MICCAI 4792 (2007) 393–401. 18044593.

[10] X.X. Yin, S. Hadjiloucas, J.H. Chen, Y. Zhang, J.L. Wu, M.Y. Su, Tensor based multichannel reconstruction for breast tumours identification from DCE-MRIs, PLoS One 12 (3) (2017), e0172111.

[11] X.X. Yin, B.W.H. Ng, Q. Yang, A. Pitman, K. Ramamohanarao, D. Abbott, Anatomical landmark localization in breast dynamic contrast-enhanced MR imaging, Comput. Methods Prog. Biomed. 108 (2) (2012) 629–643.

[12] N. Saidin, H.A.M. Sakim, U.K. Ngah, I.L. Shuaib, Segmentation of breast regions in mammogram based on density: a review, Int. J. Comput. Sci. 9 (4) (2012) 108–116.

[13] A. Eng, Z. Gallant, J. Shepherd, Digital mammographic density and breast cancer risk: a case–control study of six alternative density assessment methods, Breast Cancer Res. 16 (5) (2014) 439.

[14] J. Yao, J. Chen, C. Chow, Breast tumor analysis in dynamic contrast enhanced MRI using texture features and wavelet transform, IEEE J. Sel. Top. Signal Process. 3 (1) (2009) 94–100.

[15] K. Ganesan, U.R. Acharya, C. Chua, L.C. Min, K.T. Abraham, Pectoral muscle segmentation: a review, Comput. Methods Prog. Biomed. 110 (1) (2013) 48–57.

[16] B. Zheng, J.H. Sumkin, M.L. Zuley, X. Wang, A.H. Klym, D. Gur, Bilateral mammographic density asymmetry and breast cancer risk: a preliminary assessment, Eur. J. Radiol. 80 (11) (2012) 3222–3228.

[17] G. Ertas, H.O. Gulcur, O. Osman, O.N. Ucan, M. Tunaci, M. Dursun, Breast MR segmentation and lesion detection with cellular neural networks and 3D template matching, Comput. Biol. Med. 38 (1) (2008) 116–126.

[18] N. Just, Improving tumour heterogeneity MRI assessment with histograms, Br. J. Cancer 111 (12) (2014) 2205–2213.

[19] A.Q. Al-Faris, U.K. Ngah, N.A.M. Isa, I.L. Shuaib, Computer-aided segmentation system for breast MRI tumour using modified automatic seeded region growing (BMRI-MASRG), J. Digit. Imaging 27 (2014) 133–144.

[20] B. Keller, D. Nathan, Y. Wang, et al., Adaptive multi-cluster fuzzy c-means segmentation of breast parenchymal tissue in digital mammography, in: Medical Image Computing and Computer-Assisted Intervention–MICCAI, vol. 6893, 2011, pp. 562–569.

[21] Y. Cao, X. Hao, X. Zhu, S. Xia, An adaptive region growing algorithm for breast masses in mammograms, Front. Electr. Electron. Eng. 5 (2) (2010) 128–136.

[22] L. Wang, K. Filippatos, O. Friman, H.K. Hahn, Fully automated segmentation of the pectoralis muscle boundary in breast MR images, Proc. SPIE 7963 (2011) 796309.

[23] F. Khalvati, C. Gallego-Ortiz, S. Balasingham, A.L. Martel, Automated segmentation of breast in 3-D MR images using a robust atlas, IEEE Trans. Med. Imaging 34 (2015) 116–125.

[24] A. Gubern-Merida, M. Kallenberg, R.M. Mann, R. Marti, N. Karssemeijer, Breast segmentation and density estimation in breast mri: a fully automatic framework, IEEE J. Biomed. Health Inform. 19 (1) (2015) 349–357.

[25] J. Milenkovic, O. Chambers, M.M. Marolt, J.F. Tasic, Automated breast-region segmentation in the axial breast MR images, Comput. Biol. 62 (2015) 55–62.

[26] P.T. Fwu, J.H. Chen, Y. Li, S. Chan, M.Y. Su, Quantification of regional breast density in four quadrants using 3D MRI–a pilot study, Transl. Oncol. 8 (4) (2015) 250–257.

[27] Q. Yang, J. Zhang, G. Shao, C. Zhang, B. Zheng, Computer-aided diagnosis of breast DCE-MRI images using bilateral asymmetry of contrast enhancement between two breasts, J. Digit. Imaging 27 (1) (2014) 152–160.

[28] J.H. Hipwell, V. Vavourakis, L. Han, T. Mertzanidou, B. Eiblen, D.J. Hawkes, A review of biomechanically informed breast image registration, Phys. Med. Biol. 61 (2) (2016) R1.

[29] R. Azmi, N. Norozi, R. Anbiaee, L. Salehi, A. Amirzadi, IMPST: a new interactive self-training approach to segmentation suspicious lesions in breast MRI, J. Med. Sign. Sens. 1 (2) (2011) 138–148. 22606669.

[30] M.J. Yaffe, Mammographic density. Measurement of mammographic density, Breast Cancer Res. 10 (3) (2008) 209.

[31] J.J. Heine, M.J. Carston, C.G. Scott, et al., An automated approach for estimation of breast density, Cancer Epidemiol. Biomark. Prev. 17 (2008) 3090–3097.

[32] F. Habte, S. Budhiraja, S. Keren, In situ study of the impact of inter-and intra-reader variability on region of interest (ROI) analysis in preclinical molecular imaging, Am. J. Nucl. Med. Mol. Imaging 3 (2013) 175. 23526701.

[33] C.H. Wei, Y. Li, P.J. Huang, C.Y. Gwo, S.E. Harms, Estimation of breast density: an adaptive moment preserving method for segmentation of fibroglandular tissue in breast magnetic resonance images, Eur. J. Radiol. 81 (4) (2012) e618–e624.

[34] S. Wu, S. Weinstein, D. Kontos, Atlas-based probabilistic fibroglandular tissue segmentation in breast MRI, in: medical image computing and computer-assisted intervention, MICCAI (2012) 437–445.

[35] L.W. Lu, T.K. Nishino, R.F. Johnson, et al., Comparison of breast tissue measurements using magnetic resonance imaging, digital mammography and a mathematical algorithm, Phys. Med. Biol. 57 (21) (2012) 6903–6927.

[36] Y. Wang, G. Morrell, M.E. Heibrun, A. Payne, D.L. Parker, 3D multi-parametric breast MRI segmentation using hierarchical support vector machine with coil sensitivity correction, Acad. Radiol. 20 (2) (2013) 137–147.

[37] J.A. Rosado-Toro, T. Barr, J.P. Galons, et al., Automated breast segmentation of fat and water mr images using dynamic programming, Acad. Radiol. 22 (2) (2015) 139–148.

[38] D. Pandey, X. Yin, H. Wang, Y. Zhang, Accurate vessel segmentation using maximum entropy incorporating line detection and phase-preserving denoising, Comput. Vis. Image Underst. 155 (2017) 162–172.

[39] A Comprehensive Guide to Breast Cancer. Website: https://www.healthline.com/health/breast-cancer#awareness.

[40] A. Andreopoulos, J.K. Tsotsos, 50 years of object recognition: directions forward, Comput. Vis. Image Underst. 117 (2013) 827–891.

[41] S. Aditya, Y. Yang, C. Baral, Y. Aloimonos, C. Fermuller, Image understanding using vision and reasoning through scene description graph, Comput. Vis. Image Underst. (2017) 1–13.

[42] A. Clarke, L.K. Tyler, Understanding what we see: how we derive meaning from vision, Trends Cogn. Sci. 19 (11) (2015) 677–687.

[43] M. Ivasic-Kos, I. Ipsic, S. Ribaric, A knowledge-based multi-layered image annotation system, Expert Syst. Appl. 42 (2015) 9539–9553.

[44] Y.Y.M. Hu, L.Z.F. Shen, H.T. Shen, X. Li, Robust web image annotation via exploring multi-facet and structural knowledge, IEEE Trans. Image Process. 26 (10) (2017) 4871–4884.

[45] P. Qian, K. Zhao, Y. Jian, K.-H. Su, Z. Deng, S. Wang, R.F. Muzic Jr., Knowledge-leveraged transfer fuzzy C-Means for texture image segmentation with self-adaptive cluster prototype matching, Knowl. Based Syst. 130 (2017) 33–50.

[46] L. Onofri, P. Soda, M. Pechenizkiy, G. Iannello, A survey on using domain and contextual knowledge for human activity recognition in video streams, Expert Syst. Appl. 63 (2016) 97–111.

[47] Y. Zhu, D. Gordon, E. Kolve, D. Fox, L. Fei-Fei, A. Gupta, R. Mottaghi, A. Farhadi, Visual Semantic Planning Using Deep Successor Representations, IEEE International Conference on Computer Vision, Venice, 2017.

[48] N. Bicocchi, D. Fontana, F. Zambonelli, Improving activity recognition via satellite imagery and commonsense knowledge, in: 25th International Workshop on Database and Expert Systems Applications, Munich, 2014.

[49] F. Kromp, I. Ambros, T. Weiss, D. Bogen, H. Dodig, M. Berneder, T. Gerber, S. Taschner-Mandl, P. Ambros, A. Hanbury, Machine learning framework incorporating expert knowledge in tissue image annotation, in: 23rd International Conference on Pattern Recognition (ICPR), Cancun, 2016.

[50] J.T. Rayz, V.L. Rayz, V. Raskin, Cognitive imaging: using knowledge representation for reliable segmentation of MR angiography data, cognitive informatics & cognitive computing (ICCICC), in: 2017 IEEE 16th International Conference on, Oxford, 2017.

[51] H. Zhang, H. Han, Z. Liang, Y. Hu, Y. Liu, W. Moore, Extracting information from previous full-dose CT scan for knowledge-based Bayesian reconstruction of current low-dose CT images, IEEE Trans. Med. Imaging 35 (3) (2016) 860–870.

[52] A. Li, C. Li, X. Wang, S. Eberl, D.D. Feng, M. Fulham, in: Automated segmentation of prostate MR images using prior knowledge enhanced random walker, International Conference on Digital Image Computing: Techniques and Applications (DICTA), Tasmania, 2013.

[53] M.L.S.C.d. Andrade, E. Skeika, S.B.K. Aires, Segmentation of the prostate gland in images using prior knowledge and level set method, in: 2017 Workshop in computer vision, Natal, 2017.

[54] K.N. Manjunath, K.G. Prabhu, P.C. Siddalingaswamy, A knowledge based approach for colon segmentation in CT colonography images, in: IEEE International Conference on Signal and Image Processing Applications (ICSIPA), Kuala Lumpur, 2015.

[55] C. Zhang, F. Sun, M. Zhang, W. Liu, Q. Yu, Design and implementation of a medical image knowledge base for pulmonary nodules diagnosis, in: 3rd IEEE International Conference on Computer and Communications, Chengdu, 2017.

[56] I. Marin, N. Goga, A. Vasilateanu, I.-B. Pavaloiu, Integrated platform for extracting dental knowledge imaging and 3D modeling, in: 6th IEEE International Conference on E-Health and Bioengineering, Sinaia, 2017.

Chapter 11

# Groundnut leaves and their disease, deficiency, and toxicity classification using a machine learning approach

**K.R. Anu Bama and S. Suja Priyadharsini**
*Anna University Regional Campus-Tirunelveli, Tirunelveli, TN, India*

## 1 Introduction

Agriculture is the prime occupation of India. The automatic detection of plant diseases and deficiencies has turned into difficulty and is an important topic in the agricultural area. Computer vision helps analyze the visual input from an image and produces a description to interact with the world. Computer vision and image processing plays a vital role in the agricultural field, such as weed detection, fruit grading, and so on [1]. The automatic identification of leaves may have benefits while monitoring large field areas of crops. It can also automatically detect the disease from the symptoms that appear in the plant leaves. Common technological applications like human–computer interaction, virtual environment, robotics and multimedia, image processing, and speech processing are possible in the field of agriculture. Better crop yield needs to be ensured in future for the growing population around the world. This is achieved through the early detection of diseases, deficiencies, and toxicities in the crop.

Plant disease classification is a critical step, which can be useful in the early detection of pests, insects, controlling diseases, increasing productivity, and more. For this image processing techniques are used for fast, accurate, and appropriate classification of diseases. Farmers recognize the disease, deficiency, or toxicity manually with the foregoing symptoms of plants, and with the help of experts, the actual disease, deficiency, or toxicity is identified, but not with the naked eye, which is time-consuming. The wrong judgment of disease by the farmers may lead to the imprecise or enormous use of pesticides, which may damage the plants and their production. The scope of the work is

**Cognitive Systems and Signal Processing in Image Processing. https://doi.org/10.1016/B978-0-12-824410-4.00003-9**

to identify the type of crop using leaf images and to help the farmers identify whether the crop is affected by disease, deficiency, or toxicity.

In the proposed work, real-time images of groundnut crop leaves are included for analysis apart from the images available in the PlantVillage dataset. Toxicity identification in groundnut crop using leaf images is carried out along with disease and deficiency identification in groundnut crop and also for few other crops available in the PlantVillage dataset.

## 1.1 Groundnut crop

Groundnut or peanut (*Arachis hypogaea*) is a species in the legume or "bean" family that ranks 6th among the oilseed crop and 13th among the food crops in the world. It is an annual herbaceous plant, and it grows 30–50 cm tall. India is the second-largest producer of groundnuts in the world. The different varieties of Indian groundnuts are Bold or Runner, Java or Spanish, and Red Natal. The main groundnut varieties in India are Kadiri-2, Kadiri-3, BG-1, BG-2, Kuber, GAUG-1, GAUG-10, PG-1, T-28, T-64, Chandra, Chithra, Kaushal, Parkash, and Amber. The varieties in Tamil Nadu include TMV-7, TMV-8, TMV-10, M-13, and Kaushal [2].

Groundnut is the major oilseed crop in India, and it plays a major role in bridging the vegetable oil defect in the country. In India, groundnuts are available throughout the year because they are harvested in the two-crop cycle in March and October. Groundnuts are protein-rich crops in India, which grow mostly in rain-fed conditions. Groundnut kernels, such as oil pressing, seeds, green material, and straw, are used as animal feed, and oilcake and fertilizer are used as industrial raw material [3].

## 1.2 Major diseases

The major diseases that affect the groundnut crop are bacterial, viral, and fungal diseases. The major diseases of the groundnut plant are early and late leaf spot, groundnut rust, Alternaria leaf spot, anthracnose, spider mites, Web-Bloch.

## 1.3 Major deficiencies

The major deficiencies found in the groundnut crop are phosphorous, zinc, manganese, boron, and iron deficiencies.

## 1.4 Disease, deficiency, and toxicity management

One of the important factors contributing to low yield in groundnut plant is due to disease attack mentioned in this section:

(i) Early leaf spots

The leaves are dark brown in color on the upper surface where most sporulation occurs and a lighter shade of brown on the lower surface leaflet. Symptoms include the appearance of light to dark brown center and a yellow halo.

**(ii)** Late leaf spots

Lesions are usually circular to subcircular in shape with a diameter of about 1–6 mm. It is dark brown or black in color.

**(iii)** Groundnut rust

Groundnut rust can be recognized by orange-colored pustules, which appear on the lower leaf set surface, and it ruptures to expose the messes of reddish-brown spores. The pustules are usually circular in shape and range from 0.5 to 1.4 mm in diameter.

**(iv)** Alternaria leaf spot

Lesions become necrotic and brown in color, and they are round to irregular in shape.

**(v)** Anthracnose

Lesions enlarge rapidly, become irregular in shape, and cover the entire leaflet and extend.

**(vi)** Spider mites

Leaves are stippled with yellow and may appear bronzed. Mites may be visible as tiny moving dots on the webs or on the underside of leaves.

**(vii)** Web-Bloch

Circular lesions are with red-brown margins and light brown or tan centers on leaves.

**(viii)** Phosphorous deficiency

Older leaves turn into purplish color.

**(ix)** Manganese deficiency

The symptom is dark green veins with yellow areas on the leaf.

**(x)** Zinc deficiency

Zinc deficiency results in stunted growth. Due to the deficiency, the young leaves are smaller than normal.

**(xi)** Toxicity

In groundnut, the aflatoxin production in kernels is produced due to the presence of fungus in soil and air. This occurs at every stage from pre-harvest to storage.

## 1.5 Lack of accurate detection

Visual observation by experts has been conducted to diagnose plant disease. However, there is a risk for error due to subjective perception. Various spectroscopic and imaging techniques [3] have been studied for detecting plant diseases. However, they require precise instruments and bulky sensors, which lead to high cost and low efficiency. In recent years, due to the popularization of digital cameras and other electronic devices, automatic plant disease diagnosis through machine learning techniques has been widely applied as a satisfactory alternative.

The proposed work concentrates on the automatic identification of the type of crop, plant disease, deficiency, and toxicity and to analyze the effectiveness of different machine learning algorithms in the identification of the same.

## 2 Literature review

Several methods have been proposed by researchers for classification of plant diseases. They have their own merits and demerits.

In this section, a brief review of some important contributions from the existing literature is presented. Sabrol and Kumar [4] proposed an effective algorithm for the plant leaf disease detection. They applied the Laplacian filter to sharpen images. The Otsu and local entropy segmentation techniques are applied to the leaf image. The gray-level Cooccurrence matrix (GLCM) and spatial gray-level dependence matrix (SGDM) features are extracted. The novel method based on adaptive neuro-fuzzy inference system architecture is proposed. The various diseases in tomato and brinjal have been classified. The algorithm shows the higher recognition accuracy of about 98%. Merchant et al. [5] has evaluated the mango leaf nutrient deficiencies using machine learning techniques. After preprocessing, features are extracted and subjected to $k$-means clustering technique for nutrient deficiency identification. The extracted features include the red, green, blue (RGB) values and the texture of the leaves. This work detected the precise deficiency in the plant. Bhimte and Thool [6] proposed an algorithm that detects the leaf spot in cotton. They have used segmentation and clustering for image processing and a support vector machine (SVM) classifier for classification of healthy and unhealthy leaves. They have proposed an efficient algorithm that works on 98% accuracy. However, the major drawback of SVMs is that they were originally developed to solve binary classification problem. Multiclass classifiers are typically constructed by combining several binary classifiers. Rudraraju and VineelaSravya [7] have presented the deep neural network-based (NN-based) detection of cashew plant diseases. The proposed work is made-out of the KNN algorithm and the classifier used is the fuzzy C-means. This work perceives three distinct sort of plant sicknesses out of solid leaves. Before preprocessing, the acquired image is converted into a grayscale picture. The leaf image is then clustered and classified. Kaur et al. [8] have used SVMs for detecting and classifying various soybean diseases through image processing. In the preprocessing step, a background removal technique is applied on the image in order to remove the background from the image. Then the background-removed images are further processed for image segmentation, and lab space conversion is done. Different segmented images were used for extracting features such as color, shape, size, and texture from the images. At last, these extracted features were used as inputs to the classifier. Ramakrishnan and Nisha [9] suggested the backpropagation algorithm for groundnut leaf disease detection. Four different types of diseases are classified. The RGB image is converted into HSV (hue, saturation, value).

The SGDM feature is extracted from the leaves. The next step includes the plane separation. An accuracy of about 97.4% is achieved.

From the existing work it is observed that several work have been carried out to in crop disease identification and few in deficiency identification. The main objective of this proposed work is to identify the type of crop using leaf images and further identification of diseases, deficiencies, and toxicities of the crops by processing the image of the affected leaf and classification using machine learning techniques individually. The proposed method includes identification of toxicity in groundnut crop along with disease and deficiency identification in groundnut crop and in crops such as corn, paddy, bell pepper, pomegranate, potato, and tomato using leaf images. In this work machine learning techniques, such as support vector machine (SVM), random forest (RF), decision tree (DT), k-nearest neighbor (KNN), and neural network (NN), were employed.

## 3 Methodology

This section describes the recognition of leaves using image processing via machine learning algorithms. The input image is captured using normal mobile camera.

The block diagram of the proposed workflow is shown in Fig. 1. The proposed methodology for leaf disease detection and classification using image processing consists of the following steps:

- Acquisition of the image
- Preprocessing of the acquired image
- Image segmentation
- Feature extraction of the segmented image
- Classification

The initial step of the proposed work is preprocessing, which is followed by segmentation and extraction of features, such as shape, size, color, and texture of different leaf samples. Features like shape and size include region properties. The color feature includes the RGB and HSV color spaces.

Texture features are found using the GLCM method. The k-means segmentation is used to cluster the regions [6]. Apart from these attributes, the features are extracted from the affected area of the leaf. The classification is performed by the classifier. Initially, the image of the leaf is subjected to the median filter,

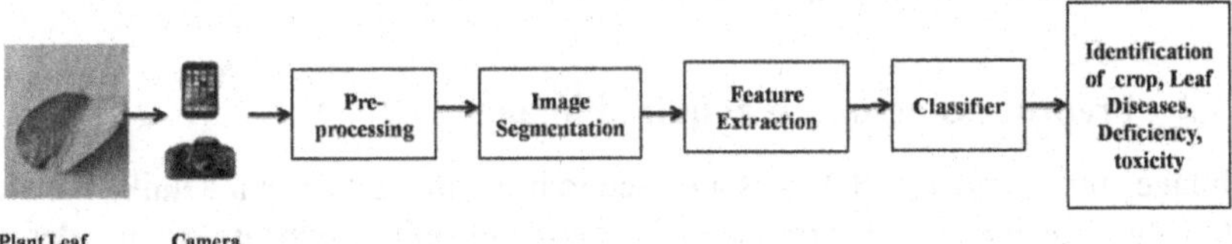


FIG. 1 Block diagram of the proposed work.

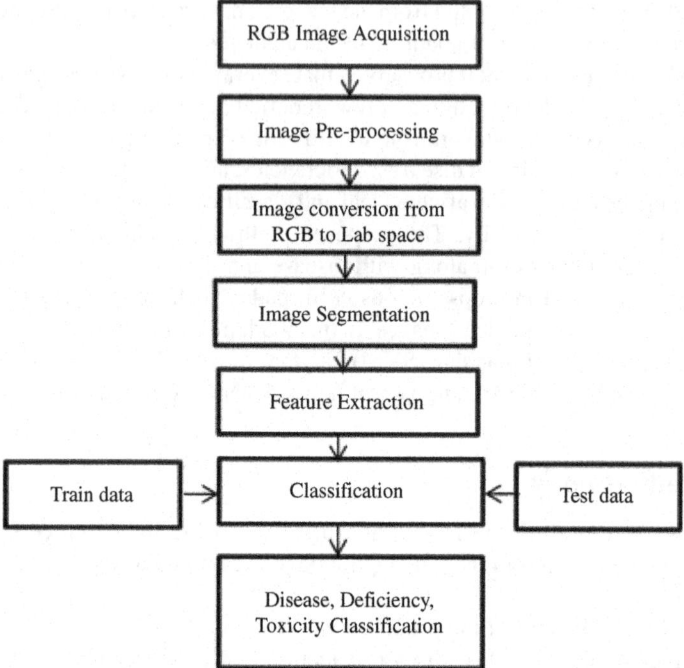


**FIG. 2** Workflow of image processing using machine learning algorithm.

which removes the noise. Fig. 2 shows the workflow of image processing using the machine learning algorithm.

## 3.1 Image dataset

The images of groundnut leaves collected from the field of the Maruthakulam area, Tirunelveli, Tamil Nadu, are shown in Figs. 3–10.

## 3.2 Image acquisition

The groundnut leaf images are captured using a camera with a resolution of 20 megapixels. The images are captured in a white background under fixed focal length and normal illumination conditions. Further, the images are collected from the PlantVillage dataset for validation.

## 3.3 Preprocessing of the acquired image

Image enhancement techniques are used to bring to light certain details that are hidden in the image. The preprocessing steps are applied to the image in order to improve the quality of the images.

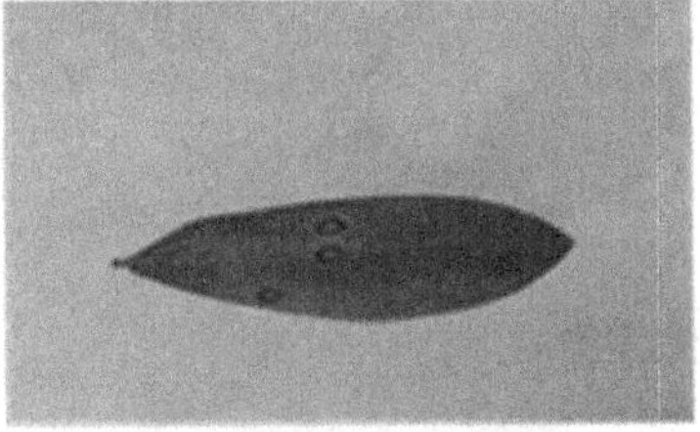
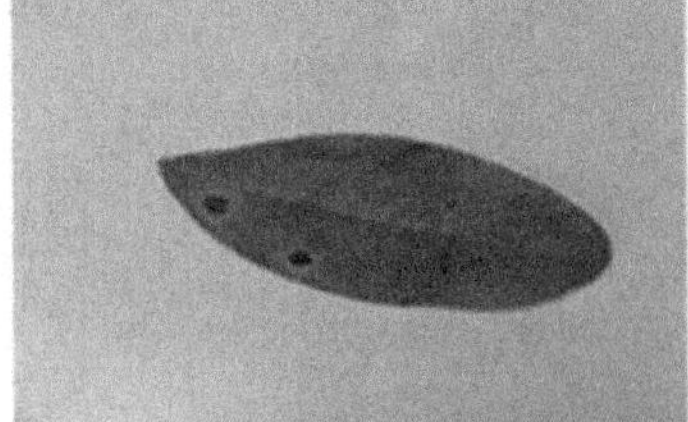

FIG. 3 Sample images of early leaf spot.

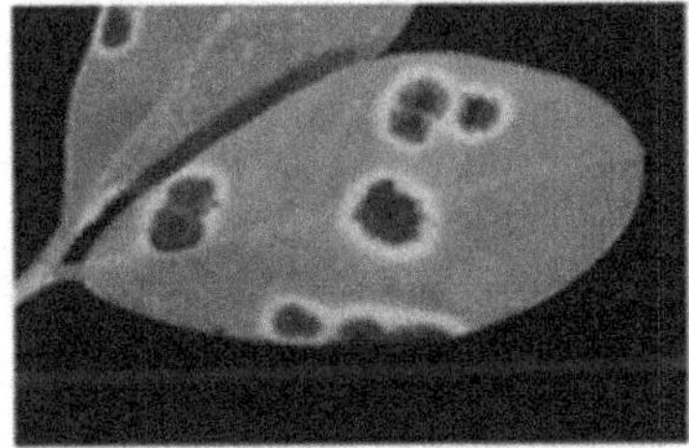

FIG. 4 Sample images of late leaf spot.

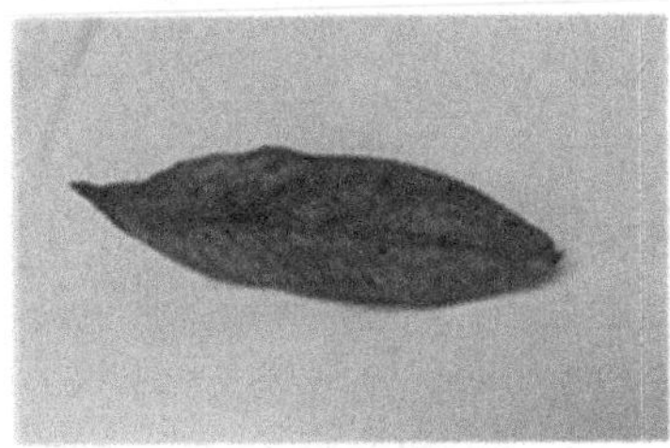
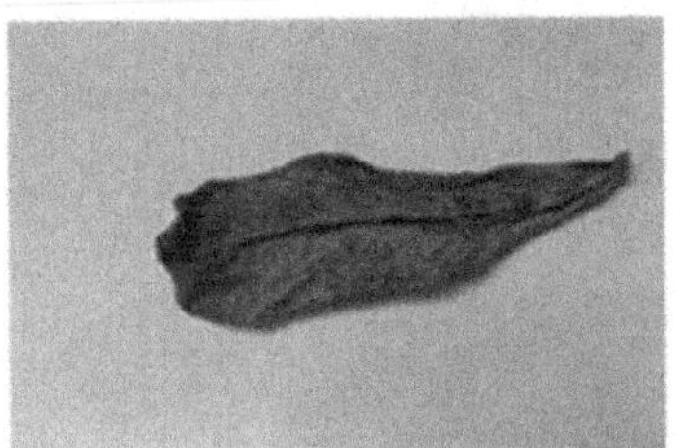

FIG. 5 Sample images of rust.

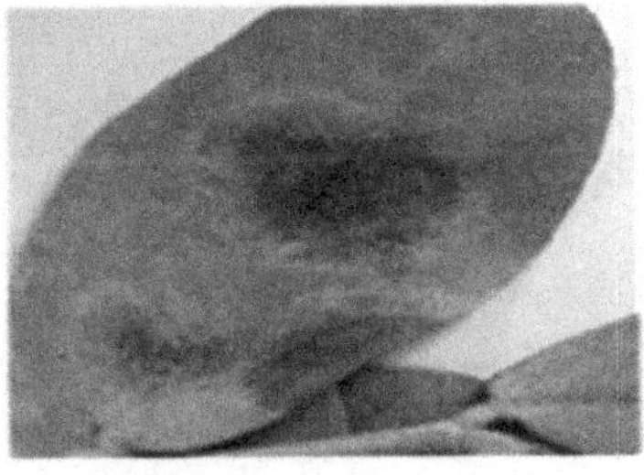
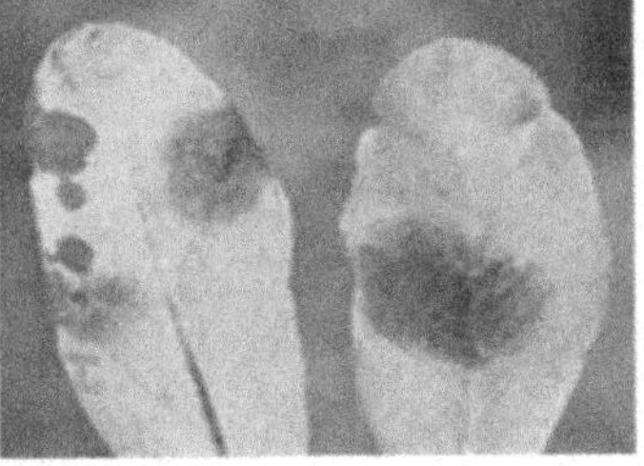

FIG. 6 Sample images of Web-Bloch.

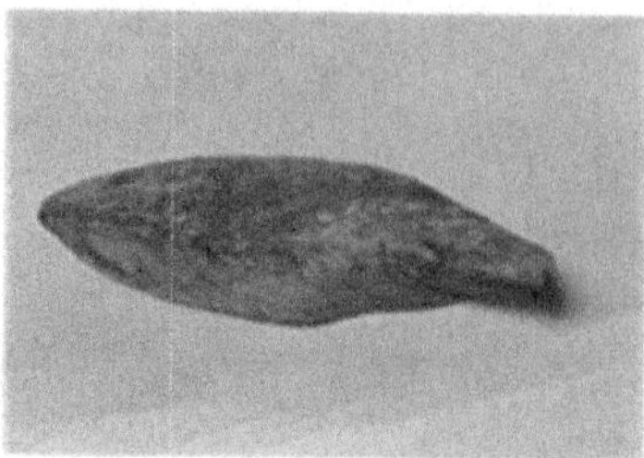

FIG. 7 Sample images of spider mites.

FIG. 8 Sample images of deficiency.

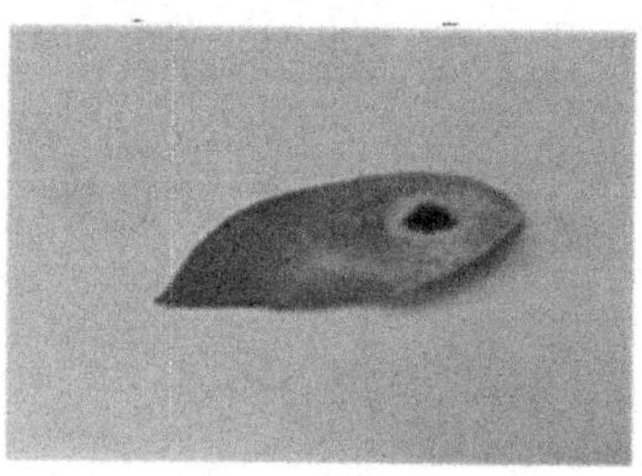
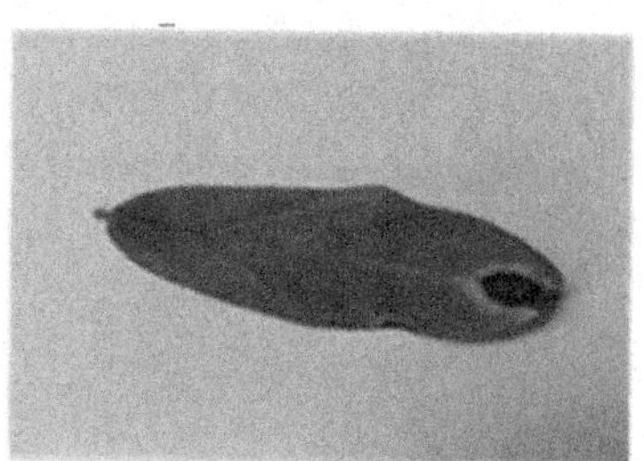

FIG. 9 Sample images of Alternaria leaf.

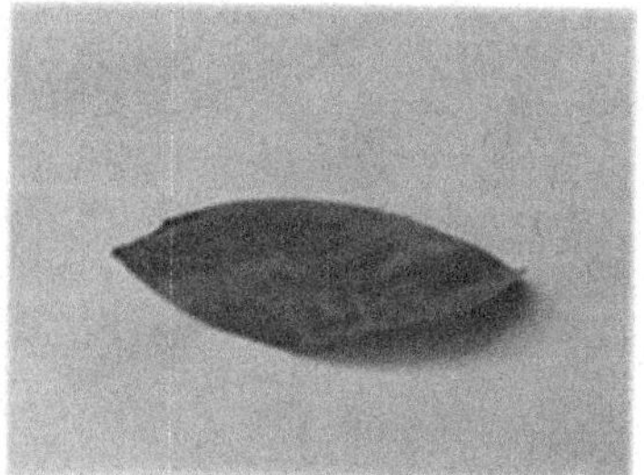

FIG. 10 Sample images of healthy groundnut.

The preprocessing technique helps to extract useful information in an image. Some images obtained from the camera might possess shade. Due to variation in outdoor lighting conditions, some regions are brighter and some are darker than the mean value for the whole image. This phenomenon causes an inaccuracy in the system. Precise tuning of the camera is done to minimize this effect. The images taken in real-time may contain scratches and more. Thus a median filter has been used to remove such artifacts. The images acquired from the camera are 2000 × 2000 pixels. The images are then reduced to a suitable size for feature extraction.

Initially, the region of interest is selected manually, and then binary mask and its complements are computed. In order to remove the irrelevant background, the original image is added to its complement. Finally, extra white spaces are cropped and the background elimination process is completed. In the proposed work, conversion of color space from a device-dependent RGB model into a device-independent model is carried out. The proposed system employs L*a*b* (L* signifies the lightness, a* and b* are the chromaticity layers) color space. The segmentation module is accomplished on the "a*b*" channel as two-channel color representation decreases the processing time. Also, L*a*b* is more suitable as it provides good segmentation results when compared to other color models [10].

## 3.4 Image segmentation

Digital image segmentation is a technique that divides a digital image into multiple pieces. It is typically used to recognize the objects and identify various similar and dissimilar regions from the digital images. Various segmentation methods are available to analyze and identify different regions from digital images.

Usually, many methods are employed to segment the image, but identification of segments by assigning each pixel is not achieved perfectly. The imperfection occurs due to the pixel property that belongs to two or more regions. Another reason for not achieving the classification perfectly is because of the oversegmentation and undersegmentation. A pixel belonging to one object can also belong to another object. Hence clustering technique is employed.

## 3.5 Clustering technique

Clustering is a technique by which a group of similar pixels of an object are grouped and clustered into an object while dissimilar pixels are neglected from the clustering [11]. More than one cluster can be created. This cluster can also be grouped together to recognize the type of new object. Therefore, the disease, deficiency, and toxicity on the leaves are identified by using the clustering technique. In the present work, a k-means clustering algorithm is used for clustering. The k-means clustering flow chart is given in Fig. 11.

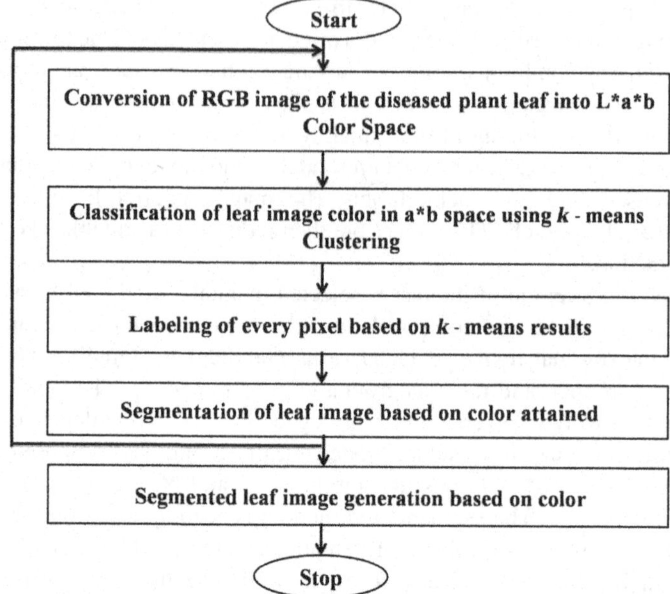


**FIG. 11** Process chart for k-means clustering.

### 3.5.1 K-means clustering algorithm

K-means clustering is used to classify the pixels on leaf present in a* and b* color space by grouping based on the colors into three clusters as background, foreground, and diseased part. K-means labels every pixel in the segmented image with cluster index, that is, segmented images. In k-means algorithm, clusters completely depend on the initially selected cluster centroids. The basic steps for the k-means clustering algorithm are as follows:

1. For a set of data points $X_1$ ....$X_n$, k clusters and centroids are initialized.
2. Position centroids $C_1$...$C_k$ at random locations for k number of clusters. Clusters are allocated such as the cluster are nearest to the centers.
3. The Euclidean distance d is calculated between the center and each pixel in the image by,
   $C_k(a) = \frac{1}{n_k}\sum_{x_i \to C_k} x(a)$, for $a = 1,2....$d.
   where $n_k$ represents the number of data points in the $k$th cluster.
4. For every cluster recompute the cluster center by finding the mean.
5. Reiterate the process until no more change occur in the cluster.
6. Reshape the cluster pixels into images [6].

In this work, each leaf is divided into three clusters, namely Cluster 1, Cluster 2, Cluster 3. The rules are framed after closely observing the formed clusters [6].

### 3.6 Feature extraction

Feature extraction is one of the important steps in image processing. Features extracted from the segmented images are used for classification. Features impart different information that help understand the computational work related to a particular application.

A variety of leaf features based on texture are exploited by means of gray level cooccurrence matrix (GLCM) for disease, deficiency, and toxicity identification. GLCM methodology considers the spatial relationship of pixels for determining second-order statistical feature extraction for analyzing the texture [6].

The texture features such as contrast, correlation, dissimilarity, energy, entropy, homogeneity, mean, variance, standard deviation, skewness, kurtosis, and smoothness are employed in this proposed work and are calculated as per Eqs. (1)–(12).

$$\text{Contrast} = \sum_{i,j=0}^{N=1} P_{i,j}(i-j)^2 \tag{1}$$

$$\text{Correlation} = \sum_{i,j=0}^{N-1} P_{i,j}\frac{(i-\mu)(j-\mu)}{\sigma^2} \tag{2}$$

$$\text{Dissimilarity} = \sum_{i,j=0}^{N-1} |i-j|.P(i.j) \tag{3}$$

$$\text{Energy} = \sum_{i,j=0}^{N-1} (P_{i,j})^2 \tag{4}$$

$$\text{Entropy} = \sum_{i,j=0}^{N-1} -\ln(\mathrm{P}_{\mathrm{i,j}})\mathrm{P}_{\mathrm{i,j}} \tag{5}$$

$$\text{Homogeneity} = \sum_{i,j=0}^{N-1} \frac{P_{i,j}}{1+(i-j)^2} \tag{6}$$

$$\text{Mean} = \sum_{i,j=0}^{N-1} i(P_{i,j}) \tag{7}$$

$$\text{Variance}\,\sigma^2 = \sum_{i,j=0}^{N-1} P_{i,j}(i-\mu)^2 \tag{8}$$

$$\text{Standard deviation } \sigma = \sqrt{\sum_{i,j=0}^{N-1} P_{i,j}(i-\mu)^2} \tag{9}$$

$$\text{Skewness } S = \sum_{i,j=0}^{N} [(P(i,j) - \mu)/\sigma]^2 \tag{10}$$

$$\text{Kurtosis } K = \left\{ \sum_{i,j=0}^{N} [(P(i,j) - \mu)/\sigma]^4 \right\} - 3 \tag{11}$$

$$\text{Smoothness} = 1 - \frac{1}{1+\sigma^2} \tag{12}$$

where

$P(i, j)$: GLCM value on element $(i, j)$.
$N$: Number of gray levels used in quantization process.
$\mu$: GLCM mean.
$\sigma^2$: The variance of the intensities of all reference pixels in the relationship that contributed to the GLCM [6].

Contrast is defined as a measure of the intensity of a pixel and its neighbor over the image. Correlation is a measure of similarity between two images. Dissimilarity is the variation of gray-level pixel pairs. Energy can be defined as the measure of the extent of pixel pair repetitions. Entropy is the randomness of gray-level pixel pairs. Homogeneity is the quality of being homogeneous. Skewness is the measure of the asymmetry of the gray levels near mean. Kurtosis is the measure of the shape of the probability distribution. Smoothness helps quantify mutually related pixels and group of pixels of an image [12, 13]. Thus 12 texture features are extracted in the proposed work.

The color feature extraction involves color space selection. A color space is a multidimensional space. An example of a color space is RGB, in which each pixel is a function of a three-element vector, with color intensities of the three primary colors, namely red (R), green (G), and blue (B). The primary step in the extraction of the RGB features is the removal of RGB components from the original color image. Followed by the computation of the mean, standard deviation, and variance from the extracted RGB components using the Eqs. (13)–(15) [14].

$$\mu = \frac{1}{N}\sum_{i=1}^{N} xi \frac{x1 + x2 + \ldots xn}{N} \tag{13}$$

where $N$ is the total number of pixels, and xi is the ith pixel value.

$$\text{Standard deviation}\ \sigma = \frac{1}{N}\sum_{i=1}^{N}\sqrt{(x-\mu)2} \tag{14}$$

$$\text{Variance} = \sigma x \sigma \tag{15}$$

Maximum element from the given input color (RGB) image is calculated using Eq. (16).

$$\max 1 = \max(\text{image}), \max 2 = \max(\max 1) \tag{16}$$

Eq. (16) returns the row vector containing maximum element from each column, similarly finding the minimum element from the whole matrix using Eq. (17).

$$\min 1 = \min(\text{image}), \min 2 = \min(\min 1) \tag{17}$$

The HSV color model is also extracted from the leaf image. The hue, saturation, and intensity components are extracted from the RGB components. RGB color space can be transformed to HSV color space using the following equations.

The hue component is found by using Eqs. (18–19)

$$H = \begin{cases} \theta, & \text{if } B < G \\ 360' - \theta, & \text{if } B \geq G \end{cases} \tag{18}$$

where

$$\theta = \cos^{-1}\left(\frac{1/2[(R-G)+(R-B)]}{[(R-G)\wedge 2+(R-B)(G-B)]\wedge\left(\frac{1}{2}\right)}\right) \tag{19}$$

The saturation component is calculated by using Eq. (20).

$$S = 1 - \frac{3}{R+G+B}[\min(R,G,B)] \tag{20}$$

The value component is estimated by using Eq. (21).

$$V = \max(R,G,B) \tag{21}$$

Thus 18 color features are extracted from the images, which include the mean, maximum and minimum values of RGB and HSV color spaces [14].

In addition to the previously mentioned features, size and shape features, such as area, perimeter, major axis, minor axis, centroid, convex area, convex hull, major axis length, minor axis length, solidity, eccentricity, and major minor area, are extracted.

## 3.7 Classification

Based on the features extracted, the values are classified and identified. For classification purpose, the machine learning techniques are used individually and their performances are compared. The proposed method attempts to identify the crop type, deficiency, toxicity, healthy leaves, and diseases such as leaf blight, rust, spider mites, Web-Bloch, Alternaria, anthracnose, brown spot, bacterial blight, early blight, late blight, mosaic virus, curl virus and more. In total, 42 features are extracted from the leaves. Among them, 12 are texture features, 12 are size and shape, and 18 are color information features.

The five classifiers used in this proposed method are:

- SVM classifier;
- RF classifier;
- KNN classifier;
- DT classifier; and
- NN classifier.

### 3.7.1 *Support vector machine classifier*

The SVM algorithm is a supervised learning model, and it is used for classification and regression analysis. The SVM classifier is suitable for both high dimensional problems and small datasets. By screening training input vector in an n-dimensional space, SVM classifiers create a hyperplane in the space, which can be employed for classification that has the highest distance to the closest training data point of any class (functional margin). The margin is computed by constructing two parallel hyperplanes, one on every side of the isolating hyperplane, which is pushed up in opposition to the two datasets. The objective of this classifier is to find out to which class a new data point belongs based on data points associated to one of the two classes [14]. A multiclass SVM intends to allocate labels to instances by using SVMs. Such labels are drawn from a finite set of different elements. In a multiclass SVM, the single multiclass problem is reduced into multiple binary classification problem.

In the proposed work, classification parameters, such as numerical tolerance and iteration limit is set as 0.0015 and 155. The cost function is 1.80. The regression loss is set to be 0.5. The kernel function used is radial basis function.

### 3.7.2 *Random forest classifier*

A RF algorithm is a supervised algorithm. It is an ensemble-based algorithm, which is used to classify the unlabeled data. It can be used both for classification and regression problems. The RF algorithm selects observations and features at random to create several DTs and then, finally, averages the results. The algorithm constructs multiple DTs and combines them together to get a more accurate prediction. In this algorithm, the number of trees is created to form a forest. The forest with more trees produces high classification accuracy results. But a large number of trees makes the algorithm slow [15]. The number of trees set in the proposed work is 15.

### 3.7.3 K-nearest neighbor classifier

KNN is a simple classifier used for diverse classification problems. The advantage of KNN is that it does not require any earlier knowledge of training [16]. In the training phase, no learning is performed. The training data is used in the testing phase. In instances in which the unknown class is subjected for evaluation, the KNN algorithm computes its K closest neighbors and allocates the class among those neighbors. The training vectors, each with class label, are stored in the training phase. In the classification phase, the test point (test vectors) K is categorized by allocating a label, which is the most frequent among the K training samples nearest to that test point. The algorithm compares the input (test) feature vector with a library of reference vectors, and the test vectors are labeled with the nearest class of feature vector in the library. KNN algorithm use only K and distance metric to tune and attain high classification accuracy. The choice of K and distance metric plays a crucial role in computing the nearest distance. In the proposed work, the number of neighbors is selected as 5 so as to attain high accuracy and Euclidean distance as the distance metric [17].

### 3.7.4 Decision tree classifier

DTs are a type of supervised machine learning where the data is continuously split according to a certain parameter. Entropy is the measure of the amount of uncertainty or randomness in data. Let it be denoted by H(S) for a finite set S. Information gain is the effective change in entropy after deciding on a particular attribute x denoted by IG (S, x) for a set S. Ross Quinlan developed ID3 (Iterative Dichotomiser 3) DT algorithm. Only categorical type features can be used in ID3 DT. ID3 is an information gain-based algorithm. The information gain obtained from training data is used to construct the DTs, which in turn classifies the test data. The training dataset, which consists of objects and different attributes, is used as the input to the DT. Initially, the class entropy and entropy of each attributes are computed, and then the information gain is computed for all the attributes. The attribute with the highest information gain is believed to be the most informative attribute, and it is selected as the root node. This process is continued until all the attributes are in the tree [18]. In the proposed work, the number of instance and maximum tree depth is set as 3 and 90, respectively.

### 3.7.5 Neural network classifier

A NN consists of units called neurons, and they are arranged in a sequence of layers, each of which connects to the layers on either side. The input units receive various forms of information from the outside as input, and the network will attempt to learn about it. The units on the opposite side of the network are known as output units, the output nodes are the ones that respond according to the information learned. In between the input units and output units are one or more layers of hidden units. The majority of NNs are fully connected, so that each hidden unit and every output unit is connected to every unit in the layers on either side. The signal passing from one unit and another unit are weighted, and these weights are tuned during the training phase to fine-tune to the specific problem at hand [19].

In the proposed work, neurons in the hidden layer are 300, activation function is ReLu, the regularization parameter is set as 0.0001, and the maximum number of iterations is 250.

# 4 Results and discussion

In this work, the images of groundnut leaf are captured from a field in Maruthakulam, Tirunelveli District, Tamilnadu, and the images of the PlantVillage database [20] are subjected for evaluation. The images of healthy and diseased leaves of corn, paddy, bell pepper, potato, and tomato are obtained from PlantVillage database. The images of the groundnut leaf are captured using a mobile camera.

In this work, initially, crop identification is performed by using leaf image, followed by identification of disease, deficiency, and toxicity using the affected leaf.

Using image processing algorithm, the color, shape, size, and texture features of the leaf image are extracted.

## 4.1 Experimental results

The experimental result of a sample image is shown in Fig. 12.

Fig. 12 depicts the affected leaf, histogram equalization, black and white image, grayscale image, clustered image, cluster index image, and image in RGB and HSV color space.

## 4.2 Performance evaluation

The performance evaluation of the proposed work is evaluated by computing the statistical parameters, such as sensitivity (Se), specificity (Sp), classification accuracy (Ac), precision, and F1 score.

### *4.2.1 Classification matrix*

The classification matrix (CM) is found by using Eq. (22).

$$\mathrm{CM} = \begin{bmatrix} \mathrm{TP}\,\mathrm{FP} \\ \mathrm{FN}\,\mathrm{TN} \end{bmatrix} \tag{22}$$

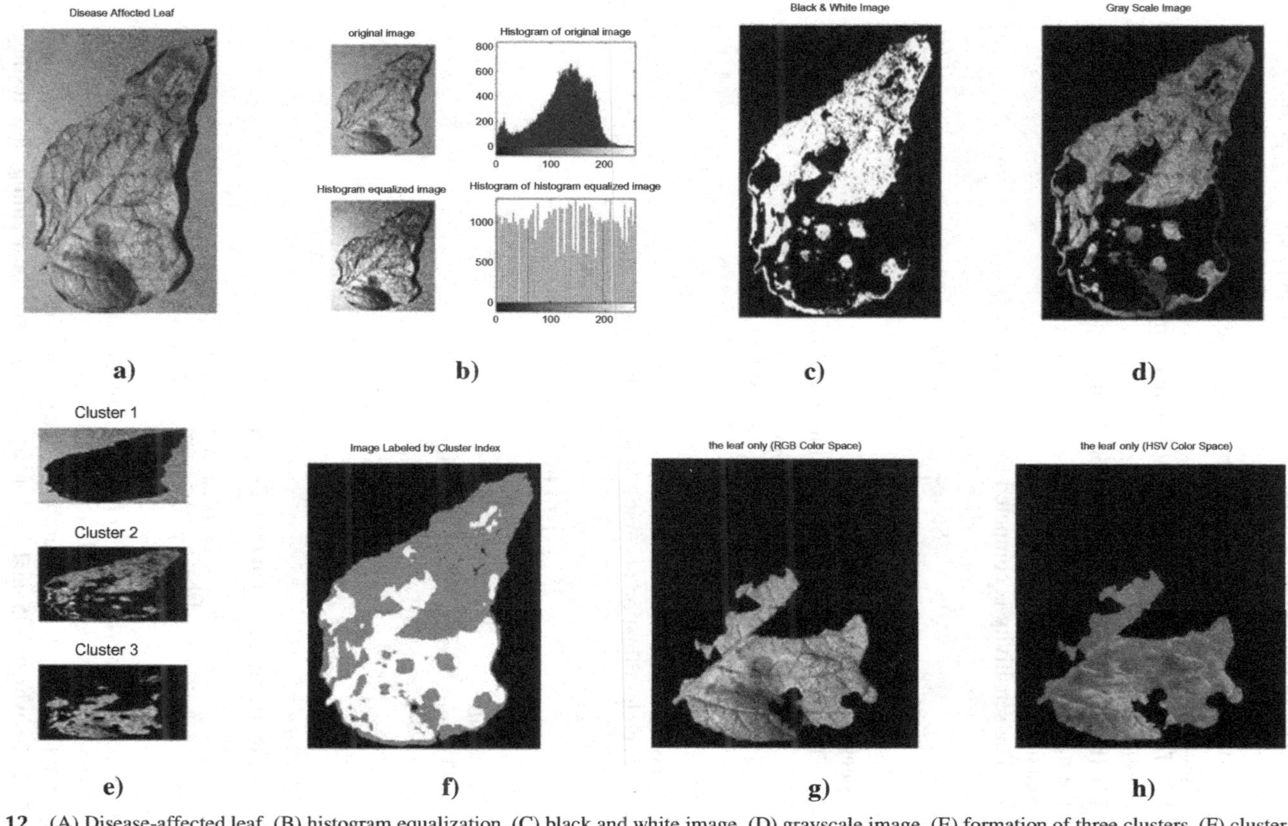


**FIG. 12** (A) Disease-affected leaf, (B) histogram equalization, (C) black and white image, (D) grayscale image, (E) formation of three clusters, (F) cluster index, (G) RGB color space, and (H) HSV color space.

where

**TP (true positives)**: is an outcome where the model correctly predicts the positive class.
**TN (true negatives)**: is an outcome where the model correctly predicts the negative class.
**FP (false positives)**: is an outcome where the model incorrectly predicts the positive class.
**FN (false negatives)**: is an outcome where the model incorrectly predicts the negative class.

**Sensitivity (Se)**

The sensitivity is computed by using Eq. (23)

$$\mathrm{Se} = \frac{TP}{TP + FN} \times 100 \tag{23}$$

**Specificity (Sp)**

The specificity is found by using Eq. (24)

$$Sp = \frac{TN}{FP + TN} \times 100 \tag{24}$$

**Classification accuracy (Ac)**

The classification accuracy is found by using Eq. (25)

$$\mathrm{Ac} = \frac{\mathrm{TP} + \mathrm{TN}}{\mathrm{TP} + \mathrm{FP} + \mathrm{TN} + \mathrm{FN}} \times 100 \tag{25}$$

**Precision (P)**

The precision is found by using Eq. (26).

$$\mathrm{P} = \frac{\mathrm{TP}}{\mathrm{TP} + \mathrm{FP}} \times 100 \tag{26}$$

**F1 score**

The F1 score is found by using Eq. (27).

$$\mathrm{F1} = \frac{(\mathrm{Precision} \times \mathrm{Sensitivity})}{\mathrm{Precision} + \mathrm{Sensitivity}} \times 2 \tag{27}$$

The performance evaluation in terms of classification accuracy for crop identification using leaves for individual classifier with respect to individual crop is tabulated in Table 1. Total number of image samples considered for evaluation is 660, in which 495 and 165 images are used for training and testing, respectively.

**TABLE 1** Performance evaluation in terms of classification accuracy for identification of different types of crop leaves.

| | Classifiers | | | | |
|---|---|---|---|---|---|
| Type of crop | *S VM* | *DT* | *RF* | *KNN* | *NN* |
| Corn | 100% | 100% | 100% | 100% | 100% |
| Paddy | 100% | 100% | 100% | 100% | 100% |
| Bell pepper | 100% | 100% | 100% | 100% | 100% |
| Pomegranate | 100% | 100% | 99.37% | 100% | 99.37% |
| Potato | 100% | 100% | 99.37% | 100% | 99.37% |
| Tomato | 100% | 100% | 100% | 100% | 100% |
| Groundnut | 100% | 100% | 100% | 100% | 100% |

**TABLE 2** Overall performance evaluation of different classifiers in the identification of crops from different types of leaves.

| Classifier | Accuracy | Sensitivity | Specificity | Precision | F1 Score |
|---|---|---|---|---|---|
| SVM | 100% | 100% | 100% | 100% | 100% |
| RF | 99.8% | 99.2% | 99.8% | 99.2% | 99.2% |
| DT | 100% | 100% | 100% | 100% | 100% |
| KNN | 100% | 100% | 100% | 100% | 100% |
| NN | 99.8% | 99.2% | 99.8% | 99.2% | 99.2% |

**TABLE 3** Performance evaluation in terms of classification accuracy for identification of various types of diseases, deficiencies and toxicity.

| | Classifiers | | | | |
|---|---|---|---|---|---|
| Name of the disease | *SVM* | *DT* | *RF* | *KNN* | *NN* |
| Corn Cercospora | 100% | 100% | 100% | 100% | 99.69% |
| Corn Healthy | 100% | 100% | 100% | 100% | 99.84% |
| Corn Rust | 100% | 100% | 100% | 100% | 99.24% |
| Paddy Leaf Blight | 100% | 100% | 99.84% | 100% | 99.84% |
| Paddy Brown spot | 100% | 100% | 100% | 100% | 100% |

*Continued*

**TABLE 3** Performance evaluation in terms of classification accuracy for identification of various types of diseases, deficiencies and toxicity—cont'd

| Name of the disease | Classifiers | | | | |
|---|---|---|---|---|---|
| | *SVM* | *DT* | *RF* | *KNN* | *NN* |
| Bell Pepper Bacterial spot | 100% | 100% | 100% | 100% | 99.24% |
| Bell Pepper Healthy | 99.84% | 100% | 100% | 100% | 99.39% |
| Pomegranate Alternaria | 100% | 100% | 100% | 100% | 99.39% |
| Pomegranate Anthracnose | 100% | 100% | 100% | 100% | 99.69% |
| Pomegranate Bacterial Blight | 100% | 100% | 100% | 100% | 99.54% |
| Pomegranate Leaf Spot | 100% | 100% | 100% | 100% | 99.54% |
| Pomegranate Healthy | 100% | 100% | 100% | 100% | 99.84% |
| Potato Early Blight | 100% | 100% | 100% | 100% | 99.24% |
| Potato Healthy | 100% | 100% | 100% | 100% | 99.54% |
| Potato Late Blight | 99.69% | 100% | 99.84% | 100% | 99.54% |
| Tomato Target Spot | 99.69% | 100% | 99.84% | 100% | 98.63% |
| Tomato Mosaic Virus | 100% | 100% | 100% | 100% | 99.24% |
| Tomato Curl Virus | 100% | 100% | 100% | 100% | 100% |
| Tomato Bacterial Spot | 100% | 100% | 99.84% | 100% | 99.54% |
| Tomato Early Blight | 100% | 100% | 100% | 100% | 99.39% |
| Tomato Healthy | 100% | 100% | 100% | 100% | 99.24% |
| Tomato Late Blight | 100% | 100% | 100% | 100% | 99.39% |
| Tomato Leaf Mold | 100% | 100% | 100% | 100% | 98.78% |
| Tomato Septoria Spot | 100% | 100% | 100% | 100% | 99.39% |
| Tomato Spider Mites | 100% | 100% | 100% | 100% | 99.54% |
| Groundnut Alternaria | 98.48% | 98.6% | 98.63% | 98.6% | 98.33% |
| Groundnut Deficiency | 99.54% | 99.8% | 99.84% | 99.8% | 99.84% |
| Groundnut Healthy | 99.39% | 99.8% | 99.84% | 99.8% | 99.54% |
| Groundnut Rust | 98.63% | 98.6% | 98.63% | 98.6% | 98.18% |
| Groundnut Spider Mites | 99.84% | 100% | 100% | 100% | 99.54% |
| Groundnut Toxicity | 99.69% | 100% | 100% | 100% | 99.69% |
| Groundnut Web-Bloch | 99.84% | 100% | 100% | 100% | 98.93% |
| Groundnut Leaf Blight | 100% | 100% | 100% | 100% | 99.84% |
| **Average** | **99.84%** | **99.9%** | **99.88%** | **99.9%** | **99.44%** |

**TABLE 4** Overall performance evaluation of different classifiers for identification of various types of diseases, deficiencies and toxicity.

| Classifier | Accuracy | Sensitivity | Specificity | Precision | F1 Score |
|---|---|---|---|---|---|
| SVM | 99.84% | 97.54% | 99.88% | 96.35% | 96.94% |
| RF | 99.88% | 98.18% | 99.94% | 98.18% | 98.18% |
| DT | 99.9% | 98.48% | 99.95% | 98.48% | 99.21% |
| KNN | 99.9% | 98.48% | 99.95% | 98.48% | 99.21% |
| NN | 99.44% | 90% | 99.71% | 90.68% | 94.98% |

The performance measures, such as accuracy, sensitivity, specificity, precision, and F1 score of different classifiers such as SVM, RF, DT, KNN, and NN in the identification of crops from different types of leaves, are tabulated in the Table 2.

The performance evaluation in terms of classification accuracy for identification of different types of disease in crops, such as corn, paddy, potato, bell pepper, pomegranate, and tomato from PlantVillage database, and identification of different types of disease, deficiency, and toxicity in real-time groundnut leaf images captured in the field is tabulated in the Table 3.

The overall performance evaluation of the classifiers in identification of different types of disease in crops, such as corn, paddy, potato, and tomato from PlantVillage database, and identification of different types of disease, deficiency, and toxicity in real-time groundnut leaf images captured in the field is tabulated in Table 4.

From the results it is evident that all the methods show high levels of accuracy in classification of various diseases, deficiencies, and toxicity in leaves. The highest classification accuracy was attributed to DT and KNN classifiers. The highest classification accuracy corresponds to the ability of properly recognizing the correct class, which corresponds to DT and KNN classifiers with sensitivity value of 99.9% after which RF, SVM, and NN performs well.

## 5 Conclusion

In the proposed work, initially the type of the crop is identified from the image of its leaf followed by the identification of the affected leaf, which may be due to disease, deficiency, or toxicity. The work employs image processing techniques along with machine learning algorithms for identification and classification of crop type and disease, deficiency, or toxicity. This work concentrates on identification and classification of disease, deficiency, and toxicity in groundnut crop. The groundnut leaf samples are collected from the field area in Maruthakulam of Tirunelveli District, Tamil Nadu, India. In addition, the work is validated using crop leaf dataset collected from the PlantVillage dataset. Initially preprocessing of the image is performed. Further color image segmentation and k-means clustering are performed. The features, such as shape, size, color, and texture, are extracted from the image of the leaf. The shape and size features include the area, perimeter, convex hull, major, and minor axis. The color features are extracted from RGB and HSV color spaces. The texture features are the GLCM features. In addition, the affected area is calculated from the segmented image. The classifiers used for the classification of the leaf are the SVM, RF, DT, KNN, and NN. The overall classification accuracy yielded by SVM, RF, DT, KNN, and NN in classifying the crop types is 100%, 99.8%, 100%, 100%, and 99.8%, respectively, using machine learning. Furthermore, the classification accuracy yielded by the classifiers in classifying the diseases, deficiencies, and toxicities is 99.84% by SVM, 99.88% by RF, 99.9% by DT, 99.9% by KNN, and 99.44% by NN. From the results it is evident that all the classifiers employed in this work, that is, SVM, RF, DT, KNN, and NN, perform well in crop identification and disease, deficiency, and toxicity identification using leaf images. But machine learning algorithms are suitable only where limited numbers of training and testing datasets are used, and hence deep learning can be used for the work that involves more categories of disease, deficiency, and toxicity identification with a large number of training and testing datasets.

## Acknowledgment

The authors thank Dr. K. Eraivan Arutkani Aiyanathan, Professor and Dean, and Dr. B. Jeberlin Prabina, Associate Professor, Department of Soil Science of Agricultural College and Research Institute, Killikulam for their support and guidance toward this work.

## References

[1] A. Anup Vibhute, S.K. Bodhe, Applications of image processing in agriculture: a survey, Int. J. Comput. Appl. 52 (2) (2012) 34–40.

[2] http://agritech.tnau.ac.in/agriculture/oilseeds_groundnut.html.

[3] A. Antonin Skoch, F. Jiru, J. Bunke, Spectroscopic imaging: basic principles, Eur. J. Radiol. 67 (2) (2008) 230–239.

[4] H. Sabrol, S. Kumar, Plant leaf disease detection using adaptive neuro-fuzzy classification, advances in intelligent systems and computing, Springer Nature 943 (2020) 434–443, https://doi.org/10.1007/978-3-030-17795-9_32.

[5] M. Merchant, V. Paradkar, M.S. Khannaand Gokhale, Mango leaf deficiency detection using digital image processing and machine learning, in: 3rd International Conference for Convergence in Technology (I2CT), IEEE, 2018, pp. 1–3.

[6] N.R. Bhimte, V.R. Thool, Diseases detection of cotton leaf spot using image processing and SVM classifier, in: Second International Conference on Intelligent Computing and Control Systems (ICICCS), IEEE, 2018, pp. 340–344.

[7] P. Rudraraju, Y. VineelaSravya, Deep neural networks based disease detection in family of cashew plants by leaf image classification, Int. J. Eng. Sci. Invent. 7 (6) (2017) 60–65.

[8] S. Kaur, S. Pandey, S. Goel, Semi-automatic leaf disease detection and classification system for soybean culture, IET Image Process. 12 (6) (2018) 1038–1048.

[9] M. Ramakrishnan, S.A. Nisha, Groundnut leaf disease detection and classification by using back propagation algorithm, in: International Conference on Communications and Signal Processing (ICCSP), IEEE, 2015. 0964-0968.

[10] S. Kaur, S. Pandey, S. Goel, Semi-automatic leaf disease detection and classification system for soybean culture, IET Image Process. 12 (6) (2018) 1038–1048.

[11] M. Lalitha, M. Kiruthiga, C. Loganathan, A survey on image segmentation through clustering algorithm, Int. J. Sci. Res. 2 (2) (2013) 348–358.

[12] S. Shyni Carmel Mary, S. Sasikala, An expert system of MRI spinal cord tumor types using GLCM features for classification techniques, Int. J. Sci. Technol. 5 (2) (2019) 20–34.

[13] P. Brynolfsson, D. Nilsson, T. Torheim, T. Asklund, C.T. Karlsson, J. Trygg, T. Nyholm, A. Garpebring, Haralick texture features from apparent diffusion coefficient (ADC) MRI images depend on imaging and preprocessing parameters, Sci. Rep. 7 (1) (2017) 1–11, https://doi.org/10.1038/s41598-017-04151-4.

[14] D. Pujari, R. Yakkundimath, A.S. Byadgi, SVM and ANN based classification of plant diseases using feature reduction technique, Int. J. Interactive Multimedia Artif. Intell. 3 (7) (2016) 6–14.

[15] https://builtin.com/data-science/random-forest-algorithm.

[16] M.E. Hossain, F. Hossain, M.A. Rahaman, A color and texture based approach for the detection and classification of plant leaf disease using KNN classifier, in: International Conference on Electrical, Computer and Communication Engineering (ECCE), Cox'sBazar, Bangladesh, 2019, pp. 1–6, https://doi.org/10.1109/ECACE.2019.8679247.

[17] I. Saini, D. Singh, A. Khosla, QRS detection using K-nearest neighbor algorithm (KNN) and evaluation on standard ECG databases, J. Adv. Res. 4 (2013) 331–344.

[18] I.D. Mienye, Y. Sun, Z. Wang, Prediction performance of improved decision tree-based algorithms: a review, Proc. Manuf. 35 (2019) 698–703.

[19] https://www.explainthatstuff.com/introduction-to-neural-networks.html.

[20] https://www.kaggle.com/emmarex/plantdisease.

Chapter 12

# EEG-based computer-aided diagnosis of autism spectrum disorder

A. Sivasangari[a], Kishore Sonti[b], Grace Prince Kanmani[b], Sindhu[b], and D. Deepa[c]

*[a]Department of IT, Sathyabama Institute of Science and Technology, Chennai, India, [b]Sathyabama Institute of Science and Technology, Chennai, India, [c]Department of CSE, Sathyabama Institute of Science and Technology, Chennai, India*

## 1 Introduction

EEG-based computer-aided design (CAD) system for autism spectrum disorder (ASD) is a neurons disorder that includes many brain problems. An electroencephalogram (EEG) is a test method used to detect activity in the brain using small, metal discs that are attached to the scalp. Human brain cells will communicate via electrical impulses that are active all the time, even when sleeping. They are recorded in EEG as wavy lines. An EEG is used to determine each change in brain activity that might be diagnosing a brain disorder, especially epilepsy or any other seizure disorder. An EEG is also helpful for diagnosing or treating many disorders like brain tumor, stroke, sleep disorder, brain damage due to head injury, inflammation of the brain, and more.

An EEG is one of the main diagnostic tests for epilepsy. An EEG can also play a role in diagnosing other brain disorders. Some of the things that we can expect will happen during an EEG are: (1) An expert estimates your head and denotes your scalp with an extraordinary pencil to show where to connect the cathodes. Those spots on your scalp may be cleaned with a lumpy cream to improve the nature of the recording. (2) A technician attaches discs (electrodes) to your scalp utilizing a unique case. In some cases, a flexible cap fitted with electrodes is utilized, all things being equal. The anodes are connected with wires to an instrument that enhances the cerebrum waves and records them on PC equipment. Once the terminals are set up, an EEG normally takes as long as an hour. (3) Testing for specific conditions expect you to rest during the test. All things considered, the test can be longer. You unwind in an agreeable

**Cognitive Systems and Signal Processing in Image Processing. https://doi.org/10.1016/B978-0-12-824410-4.00010-6**

situation with your eyes shut during the test. At different occasions, the professional may request that you open and close your eyes, play out a couple of straightforward estimations, peruse a section, look at an image, inhale profoundly for a couple of moments, or look at a glimmering light. (5) Video is regularly recorded during the EEG. Your body movements are caught by a camcorder while the EEG records your cerebrum waves. This joined account can enable your primary care physician to analyze and treat your condition. ASD affects neuron characteristics and causes behavioral impairments in social communication and interactions.

ASD symptoms and severity are very unique. The most common symptom include difficulty in understanding facial expressions, delayed speech, and poor comprehension skills. These kinds of symptoms start from early childhood, usually within the first 3 years. One of the report of the Centers for Disease Control identifies that having siblings or parents with ASD are general risk factors of ASD. The main observation behind this literature is the lack of a defined automated methodology approach for ASD diagnosis. To help concentrate on robotized ASD grouping, it is critical to investigate different strategies alongside the indicative cycles.

This chapter investigates and breaks down the strategies for EEG preparation, including extraction and order, which empowers to computerize the indicative cycle. In addition, this chapter distinguishes the current restrictions and challenges and recommends future examination bearings. Subsequently, the analysts and experts can use the recommended strategies and address the impediments over the span of the conceivable exploration territory. The ASD diagnosis is divided into four methodology phases like: (1) Internet of Things-connected (IoT-connected) sensor from EEG data collection; (2) preprocessing from collected sensor data; (3) feature extraction; and (4) classification of ASD. Under EEG information assortment we have examined EEG metadata and difficulties because of its variety. The preparation stage examines various methods for commotion evacuation, information change, and famous EEG handling apparatuses.

Usually utilized EEG-based highlights for ASD characterization include extraction strategies, and highlight determination methods are talked about under the element extraction stage. The order stage states diverse artificial intelligence (AI) calculations and distinctive assessment measurements. Medically introverted people frequently experience issues communicating or controlling feelings and have helpless eye-to-eye connection, among different indications.

The predominance of chemical imbalance is expanding worldwide, representing a need to address this worry. Current indicative frameworks have specific constraints; consequently, a few people go undiscovered or the analysis is deferred. In this examination, a successful chemical imbalance indicative framework utilizing EEG signals, which are produced from electrical action in the cerebrum, was created and described.

The frameworks have numerous applications in the clinical field, for example, for electronic health records frameworks, hospital information systems, and

CAD frameworks. Computer system can be utilized by clinical specialists to analyze certain problems via consequently dissecting clinical pictures or physiological signs recorded from patients using EEG signals. Clinical analysis is frequently a difficult undertaking that requires purposeful exertion and ability from clinical specialists. With advances and improvements in signal preparing and AI strategies, computer-based frameworks have gotten ready to perform more complex assignments, including EEG signal examination. These programmed systems would at last spare time and improve worldwide determination precision.

Investigating the signs of brain irregularity may give some insight to cerebrum conditions and pathologies. EEG, which catches signals from the human brain, can possibly be utilized for mind movement and condition investigation. EEG has been utilized for quite a while as a demonstrative apparatus for epilepsy; as of late, analysts have used EEG for ASD determination purposes. Alzheimer's and other neurological issues are among focuses of EEG-based investigation applications. Regardless of their low spatial goal, EEG chronicles have a few preferences, for example, high temporal resolution and simplicity, lower costs, and wider availability.

The remainder of this chapter is organized as follows. Section 3 describes the proposed methods, including feature extraction and classification techniques. Section 4 provides the performance evaluation. Section 5 provides our main conclusions.

## 2 Related work

Ridha et al. [1] in their paper have worked on discrete wavelet transform (DWT), entropy (En), and artificial neural network (ANN) for EEG analysis of autism-affected children to decompose EEG signals into approximation and details coefficients to obtain EEG subbands. Shannon entropy values computed are used to construct the feature vector from each band. Classification of EEG for autistic spectrum was done using ANN.

In the work presented by Sheikhani et al., 21 electrodes were used to record the dataset with both earlobes chosen as common referential electrodes. Data was extracted from two groups: 10 (9 boys and 1 girl) ASD and 7 (4 boys and 3 girls) non-ASD children. EEG signals were extracted using short-time Fourier transform (STFT) technique and given as an input to k-nearest neighbor (KNN) classifier, which gave an accuracy up to 82.4% [2].

In a paper published by the same authors later [3], they refined the method and used larger data to increase the accuracy to 96.4%. Ahmadlou et al. [4] measured investigated complexity and dynamical changes in ASD brain by measuring fractal dimension on a group of 9 ASD and 8 non-ASD children. A radial basis function classifier presented a 90% accuracy.

Later, the same group used [5] visibility graph and fuzzy synchronization likelihood (fuzzy SL) for ASD diagnosis and also enhanced probabilistic neural network classifier, both the proposed methods exhibited an accuracy of 95.5% [6]. Fan et al. [7] utilized a 14-channel EEG neuroheadset to furnish spectral features of EEG signals during day-to-day emotions to train a group of classification models. Seven classification techniques Bayes network, naïve Bayes, support vector machine (SVM), multilayer perceptron, KNN, random forest, and decision tree classifier were utilized to achieve the classification accuracy between 75% and 85%.

Bosl et al. [8] reported an accuracy of 80% in boys and 90% in girls by using a 64-channel Sensor Net System and Net Station software, which is amplified, filtered, and sampled. Mean square error (MMSE) for feature vector and KNN, SVM, and naïve Bayesian classification algorithms are applied to classify typical signal and autistic signal.

In Alhaddad et al. [9] time and frequency domains were used as feature extraction techniques and Fisher linear discriminant for classification with an accuracy up to 90% by collecting dataset from 12 children: 8 (5 boys and 3 girls) with ASD and 4 (all of them are boys) with non-ASD. Alhaddad [10] for autism disorders diagnosis and gave a 80.27% accuracy, which is lower than previous work. Later Alsaggaf [11] and Kamel used the same dataset and processing techniques used by another paper. Dilantha [12] and their team classified ASD using both thermographic and EEG data. Features extracted were mean, standard deviation, and entropy values of the EEG signals and mean temperature values of regions of interest in facial thermographic images. Naïve Bayes, random forest, logistic regression, and multilayer perceptron classification algorithms are utilized. The blending of EEG and thermographic features gives an accuracy of 94% with both logistic regression and multilayer perceptron classifiers.

In the work by Hemalatha et al. [13] neuromax32 picks the brain waves of the normal and autism children. The features like mean, variance, standard deviation, kurtosis, skewness, and entropy are extracted, analyzed, and classified by KNN and NBC classifiers.

Brihadiswaran et al. [14] conducted a survey of major EEG-based ASD classification approaches from 2010 to 2018, which adopt machine learning and explored different techniques and tools used for preprocessing, feature extraction and feature selection techniques, classification models, and measures for evaluating the model. It summarizes the ASD classification approaches and discusses the existing challenges, limitations, and future directions.

Ibrahim et al. [15] have worked on feature extraction and classification techniques to assist in the diagnosis of both epilepsy and ASD. Decomposition of EEG subbands is done using a DWT. Shannon entropy and largest Lyapunov exponent measures complexity and chaoticity in the EEG recording along with standard deviation and band power. A cross-correlation approach is also used to measure synchronization between EEG channels that reveals abnormalities.

In the work reported by Hanh [16], higher-order spectra bispectrum converts preprocessed signals to two-dimensional (2D) images. Extracted nonlinear features are reduced using locality sensitivity discriminant analysis. Significant features were selected from the condensed feature set using students' $t$-test, and were then input to different classifiers. The probabilistic neural network classifier achieved the highest accuracy of 98.70% with just five features.

Mamata et al. [17] presented an overview of recent studies in the semiautomatic or fully automatic CAD of ASD and compares the parameters visualized as methods applied, classes considered, features used, criteria of assessment, and results obtained. KNN classifies ASD and TC subjects for sMRI and fMRI.

In the paper published by Tawhid et al. [18], they proposed a simple and performance-oriented decision support system that preprocesses raw EEG data by re-referencing, filtering and normalization and converted to 2D images using a STFT. Principal component analysis helps in extraction, and extracted features are fed to SVM classifier for classification. The system gave a 95.25% accuracy.

Abdolzadegan et al. [19], proposed an approach that uses linear and nonlinear features for describing the EEG signal. Artifact removal and robustness is done using density-based clustering. KNN and SVM classifiers are used for classification. The classification accuracy SVM is 90.57%, while for KNN it is 72.77%.

The paper published by Sinha et al., presents a system that uses prerecorded EEG signal, preprocesses it using a digital filter, and extracts features in time and frequency domain using DWT. Neural networks, SVM, KNN, subspace KNN, and linear discriminant analysis classifies the extracted features. It showed subspace KNN provides the best accuracy of 92.8% for time-domain features.

Nur Alisa Ali et al. [20], used a deep learning algorithm for EEG classification. They performed classification using a multilayer perceptron network. It gave more accurate and effective results. Laxmi Raja and Mohana Priya [21] proposed the AR feature extraction algorithms. Cascade forward back propagation neural network model and Elman neural network (ENN) identifies the combination for high accuracy. Network- and subject-based classification are performed on the dataset. AR Burg and ENN combination were found to have the highest classification accuracy rate of 95.63%. In an existing system not much proposed in delta, theta model in EEG signal. This paper proposed a Shannon entropy model for alpha, beta, delta, and theta waves with clear output presented with IoT cloud-based services in EEG signals.

## 3 Proposed work

The research work on EEG signals done by the investigators has prompted us to develop a device that would be cost effective and easily wearable. The EEG signal is the prime marker for detecting neurological diseases, and it is especially used in the diagnosis of autism disorder. Certain EEG-based seizure prediction devices use an EEG cap and many electrodes placed on it. The numerous wires hanging from the cap would make the patient very uncomfortable, and it cannot be worn for a very long period of time. Hence it has been planned to design and test a device that has a minimum of two and a maximum of four electrodes placed on the head with a portable EEG device that does the processing. The patient data will also be made available at the hospital for the review and treatment of the autism patient. Fig. 1 shows the EEG signal.

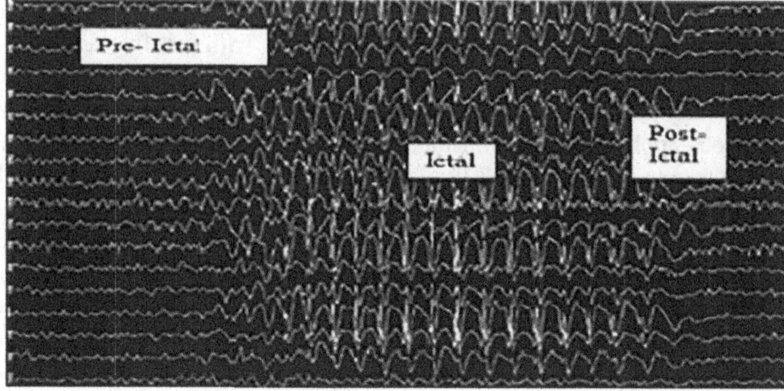


FIG. 1 EEG signal.

The EEG signals are highly random signals, and it can be strenuous to analyze and classify normal and abnormal signals. Though autism-affected signals have different characteristics from the normal signal, an automated system still needs training to extract the maximum number of features from the signal. Usually 21 electrodes are placed in an arrangement of 10–20 on the scalp to obtain EEG of the brain. If this type of electrode has to be placed throughout the day for measuring the brain activity, it would be inconvenient and uncomfortable for the patient even when it is in the form of a cap. Numerous wires would reduce mobility of the patient to the maximum. Another type of device that has only four electrodes is also available. The EEG signal analysis with lesser number electrodes is a challenging task for accurate prediction or detection of disorder. It becomes more demanding when the patient is mobile because the EEG signals vary for different mental and physical activities. Fig. 2 shows the EEG processing unit.

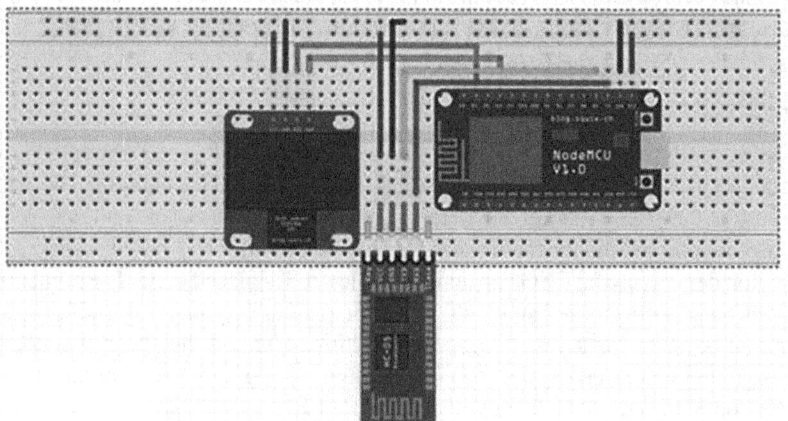


FIG. 2 Circuit diagram of EEG processing unit.

**FIG. 3** Brain wave sensor and NODEMCU.

Fig. 3 shows the prototype of an automated autism detection unit. In the proposed system, features from all the three domains will be extracted to explore how each feature of the EEG signal changes with respect to the occurrence of autism. A wearable device will be designed that would contain a minimum number of electrodes to accurately predict and detect the autistic or normal. The signal processing unit will be miniaturized and made like a pocket device so that it would not affect the social stigma of the patient. This device would be used for chronic patients where the occurrence of autism is more frequent. The device will be powered by GPS and GSM facility. This device will enable the patients to be safe, and it would also help them get immediate medical attention.

We propose to develop a wearable device that can monitor the EEG signals, which can be acquired using dry surface electrodes placed on the optimized location of the scalp. The EEG signals are acquired using scalp electrodes. The magnitude of EEG signals varies from 5 to 500 μV, and the frequency varies from 1 to 100 Hz. Since the signal is of very low amplitude, it has to be amplified using an instrumentation amplifier. Low pass, high pass, and notch filters are used to remove noise and artifacts. A post amplifier will be used to enhance the signal further. Then the analog EEG signal is converted to digital signals using an analog to digital converter and sent to the processor, which would process the data and classify it into normal or autistic signals. Features will be extracted from the EEG signal for classification.

Wavelet packet transform provides more information about the signal than wavelet transform. The EEG signals are decomposed based on Shannon entropy, and hence no information of the signal is lost as in wavelet transform. The signal is split into approximation and decimation coefficients at each and every stage of the decomposition. In this work, Daubechies 6 wavelet is used as the mother wavelet and four levels of decomposition is done. The decomposition is based on Shannon's entropy. Fig. 4 shows the four-level classification of EEG signal.

The four-level wavelet packet decomposition produces 16 terminal nodes. To study the spectral information of the signal, the color spectral map is used.

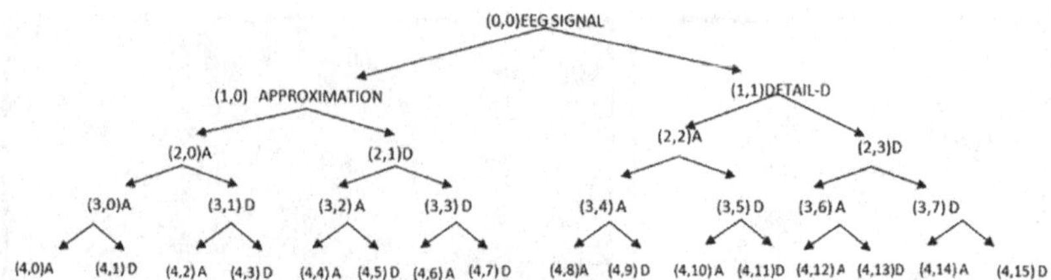


**FIG. 4** Four-level wavelet packet decomposition.

The wavelet packet transform is done for alpha, beta, delta, and theta waves. We developed a classifier model for predicting autism from EEG signals using random forest. The current dataset consists of the following labels: F, N, O, S, and Z. N was identified to represent normal data and S to represent severe (epilepsy) data. Each folder consists of a hundred text files of individual patient data. Feature extraction was carried out only from N and S labels as 0 and 1, respectively (Fig. 5).

The following features were extracted:

**(1)** Skewness—Lack measure of the lack of symmetry or the asymmetry of an *EEG* signal data set
**(2)** Kurtosis—Outlier
**(3)** Hjorth—Signal slope descriptor
**(4)** Bin power
**(5)** Spectral entropy—Amount of repeatability or predictability in the waveform patterns of an EEG signal
**(6)** Mobility
**(7)** Complexity

The random forest method is suitable for high-dimensional data and runs very fast. It consists of a collection of decision trees that could act as a single classifier with several variables. Several subsets of training data are supplied to each tree to produce the most stable tree classification. In terms of ANN based on detecting ASD diagnosed by detecting individual in eye-tracking data. Here each eye-tracking record is presented as text sequence, then data is transformed using a natural language processing method data. This kind of applied classification is called sequence learning.

## 4 Performance analysis

EEG proves to be a very good biomarker for the detection of autism. The EEG signals are successful in identifying autism in kids as early as 3 months of age [a]. The EEG waves can be classified into alpha, beta, gamma, delta, and theta based on the frequency ranges. The alpha wave has a frequency range of 8–16 Hz. The beta wave has a frequency of 16–32 Hz, the gamma wave has a frequency of 32–64 Hz. The delta and theta waves possess very low ranges of

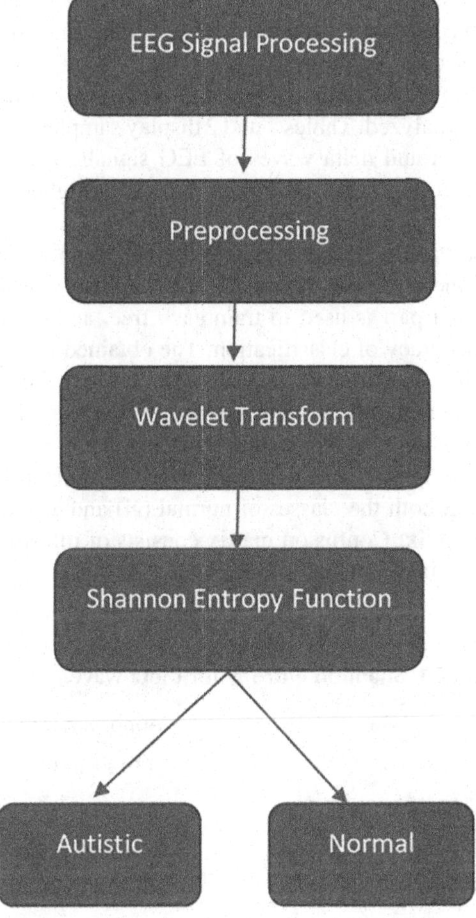


**FIG. 5** EEG signal processing.

frequency. Delta waves are merely visible and have a frequency of 0–3 Hz, and the theta wave has a frequency of 4–7 Hz. The delta and theta waveforms are said to have slowly varying signals. For patients with autism, the spectral component of theta and delta waves seem to be higher than that of a normal person. The EEG signals of an autistic patient have the characteristics of absence epileptic EEG[b]. Studies have revealed that around 61% of persons who are autistic have epileptic form discharges though they have no history of epileptic seizure[c]. In this work, the EEG signal is split into four bands of frequencies using wavelet transform. Fast Fourier transform of the signal is taken. The levels are fixed, and the signals are decomposed into alpha, beta, delta, and theta waves. The Shannon entropy of delta and theta waves are calculated for delta and theta waves for normal and abnormal EEG signals. If the value of entropy is higher, it specifies the presence of more frequency components in the signal, and it also reflects the chaotic nature of the waveform. EEG signals are collected through the dataset and preprocessed based on the continuously segments that were selected from the beginning of each of the EEG recordings for each patient will be taken and analyzed. Tables 1 and 2 display samples of entropy of normal and abnormal theta and delta waves of EEG signals. It can be seen that for abnormal wave forms, the entropy values are higher than the normal EEG waves.

Hence entropy can be taken as one of the features for classification of the EEG signal for the detection of autism. The original dataset is divided into two parts. The first part is used to train each tree, and the other part is used to evaluate the accuracy of classification. The obtained route of traversal from the root node to the leaf node is applied as the new instance for classification. Random forest method produced better results compared to other machine learning algorithms in terms of accuracy (Table 3).

The total dataset is obtained from normal and autistic conditions people dataset—100 from both the classes of normal (N) and autistic conditions.

**Confusion matrix**: Confusion matrix consists of information about actual and predicted classifications performed by a classifier.

**TABLE 1** Shannon entropy for theta wave.

| Normal EEG | Abnormal EEG |
|---|---|
| −1.0859e+07 | −2.1301e+09 |
| −1.9126e+07 | −2.1806e+09 |
| −1.1809e+07 | −8.6215e+08 |
| −9.2627e+06 | −5.3521e+08 |

**TABLE 2** Shannon entropy for delta wave.

| Normal EEG | Abnormal EEG |
|---|---|
| −9.4031e+06 | −2.9809e+09 |
| −1.3552e+07 | −3.0561e+09 |
| −5.2075e+07 | −1.1872e+09 |
| −2.8126e+07 | −2.6619e+08 |

**TABLE 3** Prediction results for different classifiers for epilepsy data.

| | PREDICTION | | | | | |
|---|---|---|---|---|---|---|
| SL. no. | Validation Data (n) | True Positives | False Positive | False Negative | True Negative | Accuracy Score |
| Random Forest | 60 | 30 | 0 | 2 | 28 | 96.66 |
| Decision Tree | 60 | 30 | 0 | 3 | 27 | 95 |
| Logistic Regression | 60 | 25 | 5 | 2 | 28 | 88.33 |
| Naïve Bayes | 60 | 30 | 0 | 29 | 1 | 51.66 |

| | Predicted positive | Predicted negative |
|---|---|---|
| Actual positive | True positive (TP) | False negative (FN) |
| Actual negative | False Positive (FP) | True negative (TN) |

The following figures describe the Confusion matrices for classifiers used for classification of EEG signals into seizure and nonseizure (Fig. 6).

In confusion matrix analysis, performance parameters are compared with classifiers. Random forest gave better accuracy than other classifiers. A low-cost, comport device transfers data to the cloud storage. This device could offer a substantial improvement in quality of life for patients, enabling them to avoid seizure-related injuries. The EEG signal can be used as a marker for early detection and detection of the autism disorder. The wearable device will have electrodes placed on the scalp that would be connected to a miniaturized signal processing device. It detects the autistic with a higher true positive rate compared to traditional methods. The signal processing unit will be miniaturized and made like a pocket device so that it would

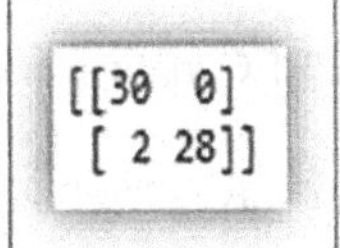


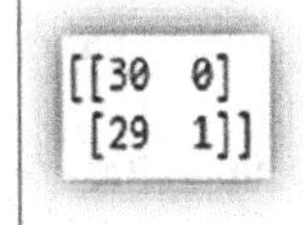


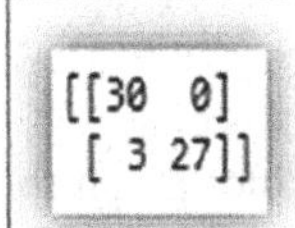


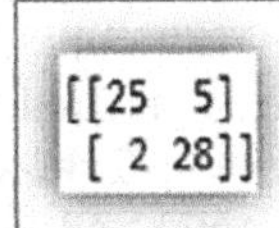


**FIG. 6** Confusion matrix: (A) random forest; (B) naïve Bayes; (C) decision tree; (D) logistic regression.

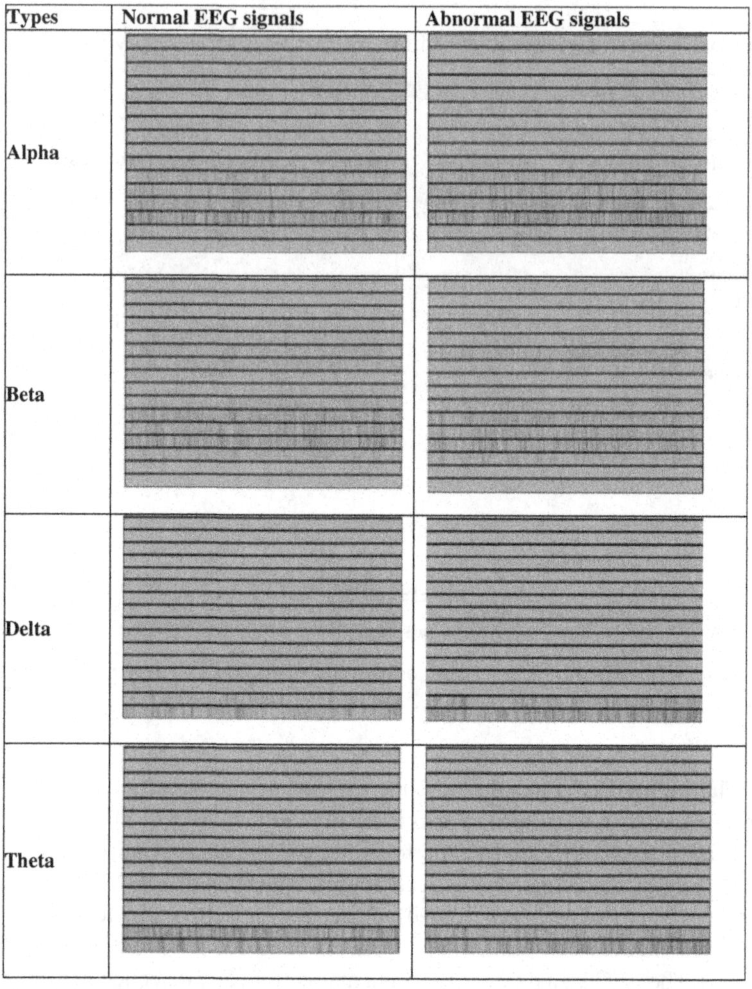

| Types | Normal EEG signals | Abnormal EEG signals |
|---|---|---|
| Alpha | | |
| Beta | | |
| Delta | | |
| Theta | | |

**FIG. 7** Color graph for alpha, beta, delta, and theta waves for normal and abnormal signals.

not affect the social stigma of the patient. This device would be used for chronic epileptic patients where the occurrence of seizure is more frequent. A wearable, lightweight, miniaturized device that is easy to wear for longer period of time are the unique features of the epilepsy detection device.

Cloud-based services are used to collect and analyze the EEG data from EEG electrodes at real time.

Fig. 7 shows the color graph for alpha, beta, delta, and theta waves for both normal and abnormal signals. The higher frequency components are represented in darker shades of pink. The frequency variation of low to high is shown from *blue* to *pink* (*gray to light gray in print version*) in the color graph. The

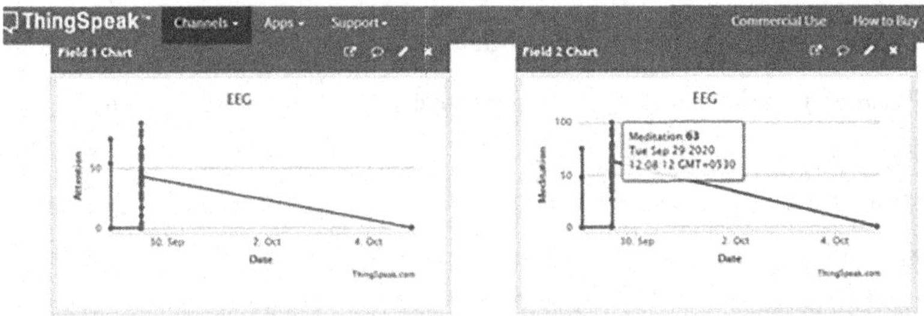


**FIG. 8** EEG data on IoT cloud.

alpha waves are seen in the 2nd to 6th band of the color graph. Each band represents the terminal node. Beta waves are seen from 3rd to 12th band of the color graph. Delta and theta waves are seen in the first two bands of the color graph. The EEG of autism patients have higher low-frequency components. Hence it is observed that the lowest band has more *pink* (*gray color in print version*) shades for abnormal EEG when compared to the normal EEG. Hence the visualization of shades of *pink* (*gray color in print version*) signifies that a lower frequency component is present for abnormal EEG (Fig. 8).

This study proves that constructive features can be derived to classify the EEG signals, which would aid in the early diagnosis of autism. The statistical analysis of delta and theta wave forms is done, and eight statistical parameters are considered for this analysis. They are mean, median, standard deviation, median absolute deviation, mean absolute deviation, L1 Norm, L2 Norm, and maximum Norm. Table 4 shows the samples of these statistical parameters of delta waveforms for a few samples of normal and abnormal signals. It is observed that the mean and median values of normal and abnormal signals overlap. Hence these parameters will not be useful for classification of autism using EEG. Similarly, L1 Norm also cannot be used since the values of normal and abnormal signals overlap each other. Statistical parameters, such as standard deviation, median absolute deviation, mean absolute deviation, L1 Norm, L2 Norm, and maximum Norm show marked difference between normal and abnormal EEG signals. Hence these parameters can be used as features for classification of the signal. Similarly, Table 5 also shows the parameters of theta waves.

## 5 Conclusion

We designed a wearable device that derived the features from EEG signal and uploaded all the information to the cloud storage. The EEG signals are decomposed based on Shannon entropy signal and split into approximation and decimation coefficients at each and every stage of the decomposition. Hence entropy can be taken as one of the features for classification of the EEG signal for detection of autism display samples of entropy of normal and abnormal theta and delta wave of EEG signals. It can be seen that the abnormal wave forms, the

**TABLE 4** Statistical parameters of delta wave.

| Parameters | Normal | | Abnormal | |
|---|---|---|---|---|
| *Samples* | *N1* | *N2* | *A1* | *A2* |
| Mean | −0.019 | 0.0065 | 0.10 | 0.014 |
| Median | 0.068 | −0.38 | −2.55 | 0.19 |
| Standard deviation | 13.72 | 17.75 | 108.6 | 139.2 |
| Median absolute deviation | 7.923 | 9.31 | 67.74 | 86.86 |
| Mean absolute deviation | 10.42 | 12.94 | 84.34 | 108.9 |
| L1 norm | 4.27e+04 | 5.3e+04 | 3.455e+05 | 4.46e+05 |
| L2 norm | 878 | 1136 | 6951 | 8911 |
| Maximum norm | 57.7 | 74.65 | 390.8 | 427.3 |

**TABLE 5** Statistical parameters of Theta wave.

| Parameters | Normal | | Abnormal | |
|---|---|---|---|---|
| *Samples* | *N1* | *N2* | *A1* | *A2* |
| Mean | 0.005 | −0.006 | 0.17 | 0.058 |
| Median | 0.31 | 0.051 | −1.615 | 0.38 |
| standard deviation | 16.74 | 20.95 | 192.9 | 127.1 |
| Median absolute deviation | 10.22 | 11.11 | 115.9 | 61.73 |
| Mean absolute deviation | 12.79 | 15.09 | 146.6 | 90.62 |
| L1 norm | 5.24e+04 | 6.18e+04 | 6.00e+05 | 3.71e+05 |
| L2 norm | 1071 | 1341 | 1.23e+04 | 8133 |
| Maximum norm | 70.06 | 141 | 753.5 | 612.6 |

entropy values, are higher than the normal EEG waves. The Shannon entropy of delta and theta waves are calculated for normal and abnormal EEG signals. If the value of entropy is higher, it specifies the presence of more frequency components in the signal, and it also reflects the chaotic nature of the waveform. In confusion matrix analysis, performance parameters are compared with classifiers. Random forest gave better accuracy than other classifiers. A low-cost, compact device transfers data to the cloud storage. This device could offer a substantial improvement in quality of life for patients, enabling them to avoid seizure-related injuries.

## References


[1] R. Djemal, K. AlSharabi, S. Ibrahim, A. Alsuwailem, EEG-based computer aided diagnosis of autism spectrum disorder using wavelet, entropy, and ANN, Biomed. Res. Int. 2 (2017) 1–9.

[2] A. Sheikhani, H. Behnam, M.R. Mohammade, M. Noroozian, P. Golabi, Connectivity analysis of quantitative Electroencephalogram background activity in Autism disorders with short time Fourier transform and Coherence values, in: Proceedings of the 1st International Congress on Image and Signal Processing (CISP '08), pp. 207–212, IEEE, Hainan, China, May 2008. View at: Publisher Site | Google Scholar3.

[3] A. Sheikhani, H. Behnam, M.R. Mohammadi, M. Noroozian, M. Mohamamadi, Detection of abnormalities for diagnosing of children with autism disorders using of quantitative electroencephalography analysis, J. Med. Syst. 36 (2) (2012) 957–963.

[4] M. Ahmadlou, H. Adeli, A. Adeli, Fractality and a wavelet-chaos-neural network methodology for EEG-based diagnosis of autistic spectrum disorder, J. Clin. Neurophysiol. 27 (5) (2010) 328–333.

[5] M. Ahmadlou, H. Adeli, A. Adeli, Improved visibility graph fractality with application for the diagnosis of autism spectrum disorder, Physica A Stat. Mech. Appl. 391 (20) (2012) 4720–4726.

[6] M. Ahmadlou, H. Adeli, A. Adeli, Fuzzy synchronization likelihood-wavelet methodology for diagnosis of autism spectrum disorder, J. Neurosci. Methods 211 (2) (2012) 203–209.

[7] J. Fan, J.W. Wade, D. Bian, et al., A Step towards EEG-based brain computer interface for autism intervention, in: Proceedings of the 37th Annual International Conference of the IEEE Engineering in Medicine and Biology Society (EMBC'15), pp. 3767–3770, IEEE, Milan, Italy, August 2015.

[8] W. Bosl, A. Tierney, H. Tager-Flusberg, C. Nelson, EEG complexity as a biomarker for autism spectrum disorder risk, BMC Med. 9 (2011) 18.

[9] M.J. Alhaddad, M.I. Kamel, H.M. Malibary, et al., Diagnosis autism by fisher linear discriminant analysis FLDA via EEG, J. BioSci. Biotechnol. 4 (2) (2012) 45–54.

[10] M. Ahmadlou, H. Adeli, Electroencephalograms in diagnosis of autism, in: V.B. Patel, V.R. Preedy, C.R. Martin (Eds.), Comprehensive Guide to Autism, Springer, New York, NY, USA, 2014, pp. 327–343.

[11] E.A. Alsaggaf, M.I. Kamel, Using EEGs to diagnose autism disorder by classification algorithm, Life Sci. J. 11 (6) (2014) 305–308. 40.

[12] D. Haputhanthri, G. Brihadiswaran, S. Gunathilaka, D. Meedeniya, S. Jayarathna, M. Jaime, C. Harshaw, Integration of facial thermography in EEG-based classification of ASD, Int. J. Autom. Comput. 17 (2020) 837–854.

[13] K. Hemalatha, P.P. Janarthanan, E. Rakshana, R. Naveen Kumar, K. Raj Kumar, Electroencephalography for autism spectrum disorder diagnosis, IJSTR 9 (3) (2020) 3400–3402.

[14] G. Brihadiswaran, D. Haputhanthri, S. Gunathilaka, D. Meedeniya, S. Jayarathna, EEG-based processing and classification methodologies for autism spectrum disorder: a review, J. Comput. Sci. 15 (8) (2019) 1161–1183.

[15] I. Sutrisno, R. Djemal, A. Alsuwailem, Electroencephalography (EEG) signal processing for epilepsy and autism spectrum disorder diagnosis, Biocybern. Biomed. Eng. 38 (1) (2018) 16–26.

[16] T.-H. Pham, J. Vicnesh, J.K.E. Wei, S.L. Oh, N. Arunkumar, E.W. Abdulhay, E.J. Ciaccio, U. R. Acharya, Autism spectrum disorder diagnostic system using HOS bispectrum with EEG signals, Int. J. Environ. Res. Public Health 17 (2020) 97.

[17] M.V. Lohar, S.S. Chorage, Detection of autism spectrum disorder (ASD) using machine learning techniques: a review, Int. J. Future Gener. Commun. Netw. 13 (1) (2020) 426–438.

[18] M.N.A. Tawhid, S. Siuly, H. Wang, Diagnosis of autism spectrum disorder from EEG using a time–frequency spectrogram image-based approach, Electron. Lett. 56 (2020) 3.

[19] D. Abdolzadegan, M.H. Moattar, M. Ghoshuni, A robust method for early diagnosis of autism spectrum disorder from EEG signals based on feature selection and DBSCAN method, Biocybern Biomed Eng. 40 (1) (2020) 482–493. T. Sinha, M.V. Munot, R. Sreemathy, An efficient approach for detection of autism spectrum disorder using electroencephalography signal, IETE J. Res. (2019).

[20] N.A. Ali, A.R. Syafeeza, A.S. Jaafar, M.K.M.F. Alif, Autism spectrum disorder classification on electroencephalogram signal using deep learning algorithm', IAES Int. J. Artif. Intell. 9 (1) (2020) 91.

[21] M. Laxmi Raja, M. Priya, Neural network based classification of EEG signals for diagnosis of autism spectrum disorder, Int. J. Pharm. Bio. Sci. 8 (2) (2017) 1020–1026.

Chapter 13

# Toward improving the accuracy in the diagnosis of schizophrenia using functional magnetic resonance imaging (fMRI)

**M. Kaviya Elakkiya and Dejey**

*Department of Computer Science and Engineering, Anna University Regional Campus—Tirunelveli, Tirunelveli, Tamil Nadu, India*

## 1 Introduction

Early diagnosis of any mental illness is still an exacting problem. The research efforts are growing to develop diagnostic tools that may aid practitioners in predicting disorders with maximum accuracy. As the diagnosis of a mental disorder relies primarily on the subjective decision of the medical practitioner, it is vital to provide objective evidence to assist doctors in the clinical results.

Developmental disorder is a severe chronic disability that interrupts the accomplishment of developmental tasks, such as attention, memory, communication, social interaction, and motor skills in children. These conditions may either impact day-to-day activities or last throughout the lifetime of an individual. Some of the developmental disorders are autism spectrum disorder (ASD) or autism, attention deficit hyperactivity disorder (ADHD), intellectual disability, vision impairment, hearing loss, and speech disorder [1].

Autism is a developmental disorder that impairs the ability to communicate and interact. Schizophrenia is a mental disorder that affects the thoughts, behaviors, and social interactions of an individual. The schizophrenic subject may experience hallucinations and delusions whereas autistic subjects may not. The axial view of normal and schizophrenic subject is shown in Fig. 1.

The symptoms of schizophrenia may be either positive or negative. Extra experiences or abnormal experiences, such as hallucinations and delusions, are referred as positive symptoms. Missing experiences, such as lack of enjoyment in everyday life, loss of interest in social activities, and disruption in

Cognitive Systems and Signal Processing in Image Processing. https://doi.org/10.1016/B978-0-12-824410-4.00004-0

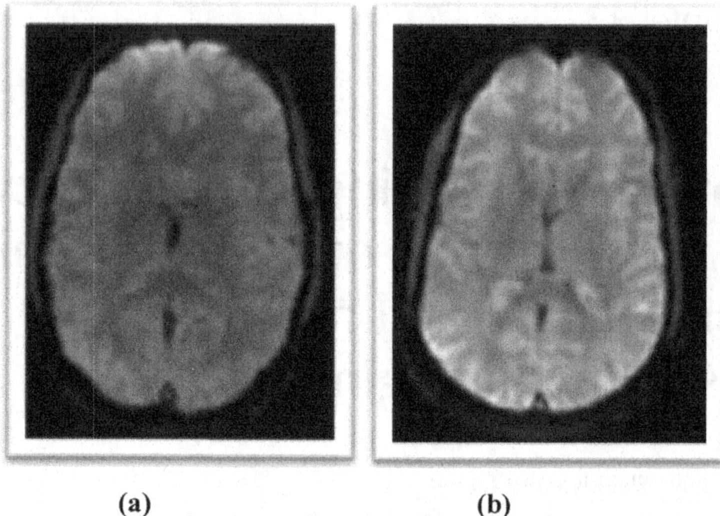


**FIG. 1** Sample axial view of fMRI from NAMIC database: (A) normal subject; and (B) schizophrenic subject

normal emotions, are negative symptoms. Schizophrenic subjects have some cooccurring disorders. The most common cooccurring disorders include anxiety, depression, and alcoholism.

An individual with schizophrenia is affected by false beliefs that are unreal, seeing or hearing that does not exist, ineffective communication, disorganized or abnormal motor behavior, and lack of ability to function normally [2]. The diagnosis of schizophrenia depends on the clinicians' decision by ruling out other disorders with similar symptoms (medical data), observing the appearance and behavior to check mental status (mental health data), and examining family history (family data). Schizophrenia is incurable, but it can be treated with medication and psychological treatment. The risk to live independently is higher if schizophrenia remains untreated. It is difficult to identify schizophrenia correctly because of the following:

- There is no medical test to confirm schizophrenia.
- Subjective finding may add risk to the diagnosis and treatment of schizophrenia.
- Other mental disorders have similar symptoms of schizophrenia.
- Boundaries between schizophrenia and other psychotic disorders are ill-defined.

A computer-aided diagnosis (CAD) system for schizophrenia must be developed for the prognosis, diagnosis, and treatment of schizophrenia. Suicide is one of the major causes of death for schizophrenic subjects. Therefore, if schizophrenia is identified at the onset of illness, then the life of a person may be saved. A computer-based schizophrenia diagnostic system may be helpful for accurate diagnosis and effective treatment. Functional magnetic resonance imaging (fMRI) has reported abnormalities in schizophrenic subjects in various tasks, namely motor tasks, attention, working memory, emotions, word fluency, and decision making [3].

The contributions of the proposed work are listed as follows:

- Group analysis of principal component analysis (PCA) and independent component analysis (ICA) are performed to handle high-dimensional fMRI data.
- Modified volume local binary pattern (MVLBP) is applied on three-dimensional (3D) brain images.
- A two-sample t-test is used to select histogram bins.
- Classification is done based on the texture of independent components (ICs).
- Three classifiers such as linear discriminant analysis (LDA), nearest neighbor (NN), and support vector machine (SVM) are used for effective classification.
- The results of three different classifiers are analyzed by varying the number of ICs and different types of three classifiers.

The rest of the chapter is organized as follows. Section 2 outlines the literature works about the CAD system of schizophrenia and research gaps of the same. Section 3 elaborates the complete view of the proposed system. Section 4 presents briefly about implementation results and comparison of the performance measures with different classifiers. Section 5 discusses conclusion and future work.

## 2 Literature review

Neuroimaging techniques have gained more importance in the diagnosis of schizophrenia in recent years, of which, fMRI scans rather than magnetoencephalography (MEG) and positron emission tomography have been used widely in recent works to identify schizophrenic subjects [4–12]. Researchers have done some experiments intensively with the ultimate aim of developing a computerized diagnostic system for schizophrenia [4–12]. Furthermore, the literature review is done for feature extraction, feature selection, and classification to detect schizophrenia [4–12]. Research work that have been done so far related to the diagnosis of schizophrenia are summarized as follows.

Pouyan and Shahamat [9] have initiated a new method for the classification of subjects into schizophrenia and control using fMRI. Realignment, normalization, and smoothing is carried out in the preprocessing step using SPM8. The number of fMRI time points is minimized using PCA. ICA is used to estimate ICs of PCA results. Local binary pattern (LBP) is used to extract features of the ICs. Genetic algorithm is employed to choose a set of features with large discrimination power. LDA is utilized to extort features that maximize the ratio of between-class and within-class variability. Euclidean distance-based classifier and majority vote method are used to classify a test subject into schizophrenia or control group. Leave-one-out cross-validation (LOOCV) method is used to assess the performance.

Pouyan and Shahamat [4] have proposed a texture-based method for the classification of schizophrenia. Preprocessing is done using SPM8 (statistical parametric mapping) software, which includes realignment and normalization. PCA is used to reduce the number of time series. ICA is used for the estimation of ICs. FastICA is applied to the fMRI data. ICs are sorted based on their variance. MVLBP is applied on the estimated ICs for feature extraction. A two-sample t-test is used to select two different bins with maximum discrimination power. Finally, each subject is represented using 10*2 features according to 10 ICs. The three different classifiers, such as LDA, NN, and SVM, are used for classification. The evaluation measures, such as accuracy, sensitivity, specificity, and precision, are calculated. An accuracy of 94% and 100% is obtained using the combination of three classifiers while predicting healthy and schizophrenic subjects, respectively.

Juneja et al. [7] have presented the combination of single value decomposition (SVD) and multivariate feature extraction method for the diagnosis of schizophrenia using fMRI. Realignment, slice time correction, spatial normalization, subsampling, and spatial smoothing are performed in the preprocessing step with the help of SPM8. Generalized linear model (GLM) and ICA are used to obtain 3D spatial maps from original 4D fMRI data. Group spatial ICA is performed using group ICA of fMRI Toolbox (GIFT). Spatial clustering, SVD, and novel hybrid multivariate forward feature selection methods are used for three-phase dimensionality reduction. Discriminative brain regions are also identified in terms of the ratio of selection. SVM classifier is used to build a decision model with LOOCV scheme. The classification accuracy of 92.6% is attained for IC score-maps corresponding to the 5th and 8th ICs of Dataset 1 (D1), and 94% is reached corresponding to the 5th and 13th ICs of Dataset 2 (D2).

Juneja et al. [5] have demonstrated fMRI-based CAD of schizophrenia using fuzzy kernel feature extraction and hybrid feature selection. The preprocessing step includes realignment, slice time correction, de-noising, subsampling, normalization, and smoothing method and is implemented using SPM8. The de-noising method is based on artifact suppressed dictionary learning. The subsampled fMRI is normalized into MNI space using EPI template. The normalized fMRI is then smoothed using full width at half maximum Gaussian kernel. GLM and ICA are used independently to generate 3D spatial maps from fMRI data. ICs are represented using spatial scores (Z-score), which are termed as IC score-maps. The features are constructed using nonzero valued voxels of β-maps and IC score-maps. Using fuzzy kernel PCA, 116 features are extracted. The discriminative and uncorrelated features are selected using hybrid filter. The relevant features are selected using wrapper. The discriminative regions are represented using selection ratio (SR). SVM is used for classification with LOOCV. Classification accuracy, sensitivity, and specificity are utilized to estimate the performance. The classification accuracy of 95.6% and 96.0% is obtained for D1 and D2, respectively.

Algunaid et al. [8] have preferred graph-theoretic features for the identification of the schizophrenia patient using resting-state fMRI (R-fMRI). Noise reduction, normalization, and smoothing methods are implemented for preprocessing, using data processing and analysis for brain imaging tool. Automated anatomical labeling atlas is used to parcellate the brain into 90 anatomical regions of interest (ROIs). The average fMRI signal for each region is computed. Pearson's correlation matrix is calculated to form $90 \times 90$ region connectivity matrix. A weighted undirected graph is constructed, and graph measures such as local and global measures are computed. Feature vector has 364 feature values. Feature selection methods, namely Welch's t-test, Fisher score, multivariate minimal redundancy maximal relevance, Bhattacharyya, Wilcoxon sum-rank test, entropy, relief, $l_0$-norm, and feature selection via concave minimization (FSV) are used to select the most discriminant features. SVM classifier is used for classification, and the local graph measures outperformed the global graph measures during classification. The detection results are found to be 82.85%, 91.43%, and 95% using Welch's t-test, $l_0$-norm, and FSV.

Sartipi et al. [6] have suggested a system for the diagnosis of schizophrenia from R-fMRI data using Ripplet transform and orthogonal locality preserving projection (OLPP). R-fMRI is preprocessed using SPM8 for realignment and normalization. OLPP is used to reduce the number of time points in the normalized R-fMRI. The number of ICs is estimated using ICA. Feature extraction is done by applying orthogonal Ripplet-II transform. A two-sample t-test is used to find the most discriminative features. The selected features are reduced by applying OLPP. A test subject is classified into the NC (Normal Control) or SZ (Schizophrenia) and the Probability of Correct Classification (PCC) is achieved as 1 using linear SVM.

Based on the literature survey, some of the research gaps are identified in the following list.

- Due to lack of large samples, poor generalizability is created in the computer-aided system of schizophrenia.
- Preprocessing has to be done effectively to produce artifact-free fMRI data.
- Proper feature selection method should be employed in order to handle extremely high-dimensional fMRI data.
- Suitable classifier with appropriate kernel function must be implemented to gain maximal accuracy rate.
- Nonlinear classifier has to be used to achieve maximum accuracy.

The proposed system is developed to address certain challenges previously mentioned.

# 3 Methodology

The overall view of the proposed system is shown in Fig. 2. Section 3.1 describes the fMRI database and fMRI acquisition in detail. Section 3.2 explains the procedures to be carried to filter fMRI for further processing. Section 3.3 narrates about dimensionality reduction and PCA. ICA is discussed in Section 3.4. Section 3.5 illustrates feature extraction and MVLBP. Feature selection and a two-sample t-test are reported in Section 3.6. The process of classifying schizophrenic subjects from normal subjects is detailed in Section 3.7.

## 3.1 Database

The publicly available National Alliance for Medical Imaging Computing (NAMIC) database has a collection of 12 medical image datasets for the analysis and visualization of medical image data. NAMIC: Brain Multimodality dataset is used for the proposed work [4, 6, 13].

### *3.1.1 Subject*

NAMIC: Brain Multimodality dataset is comprised of totally 20 cases, of which 10 are normal controls and 10 are schizophrenic subjects. Each case contains 10 files, which includes structural MRI (sMRI), diffusion tensor imaging (DTI), and R-fMRI, namely, weighted T1 scan, weighted T2 scan, label map of the ICC based on T2, fMRI scan, raw DTI scan, DWI scan after noise filtering, eddy current, and head motion correction, grayscale image with skull, and dura-matter stripped, and FreeSurfer segmentation of the t1w image. Only R-fMRI scans are used in the proposed work. However, R-fMRI scans for case01017 and case01073 do not exist in the dataset [4, 6, 13].

### *3.1.2 fMRI and acquisition of fMRI*

fMRI, a functional neuroimaging technique, has become a predominant tool for clinical research to furnish information about psychiatric disorders, such as schizophrenia, major depressive disorder, bipolar disorder, obsessive-compulsive disorder, posttraumatic stress disorder, and Alzheimer's disease. fMRI measures neural activation through changes in oxidation and blood flow noninvasively. Blood oxygenation level-dependent (BOLD) and arterial spin labeling are the most commonly used fMRI types in psychiatric neuroimaging. BOLD fMRI is preferred due to greater sensitivity and high temporal resolution [14].

R-fMRI is a supplementary echo planar imaging BOLD (EPI BOLD) sequence that needs Brain Wave software, available only with 8-channel coil. It is a 10-minute long sequence. It contains 200 repetitions of a high resolution EPI scan. All the subjects are instructed to close their eyes and rest during fMRI acquisition [4, 13].

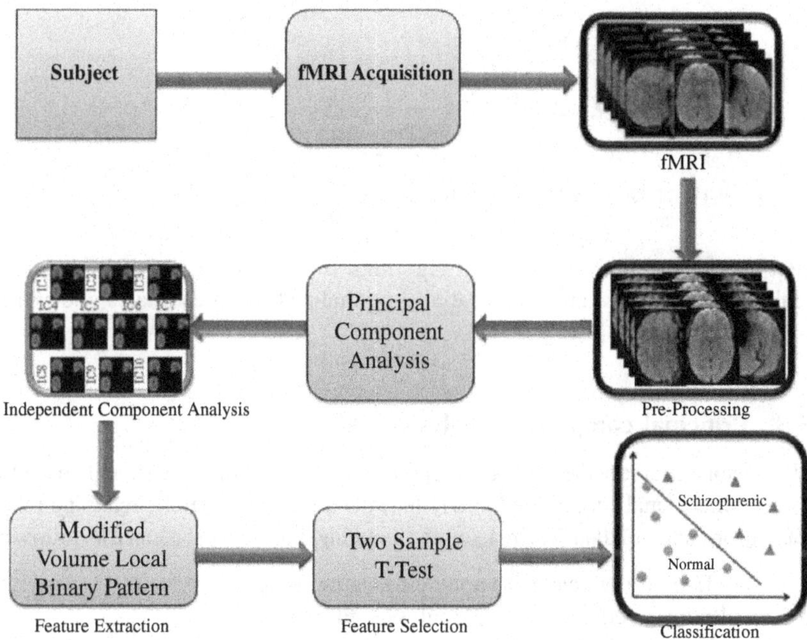


**FIG. 2** Overall view of the proposed system

## 3.2 Preprocessing

Preprocessing is the primary aspect of image processing because it improves the image quality. It is the method of removing noise, unmated data, or eliminating variations that arise during the acquisition of an image without evading essential information.

fMRI data are very noisy. The sources of noise in fMRI data are thermal, system, subject, and task-related noise. Thermal and system noise occur owing to the properties of the scanner. Subject and task-related noise are related to the subjects under study. Thermal noise refers to the thermal motion of the electrons in the sampled tissue and in the electronic components of the scanner. System Noise is caused by magnetic resonance hardware fluctuations that are a problem with radiofrequency coils and signal drift. Subject and task-related noise occur due to head movement and performing an experimental task [14]. Noisy fMRI should be preprocessed inevitably to reach maximum prediction accuracy.

Several open source and commercial software are available for the examination of fMRI data. Yet, statistical parametric mapping is used to preprocess fMRI data in the proposed work because it is used by most of the researchers and hinges on MATLAB [4–9, 15]. Preprocessing steps are applied to fMRI data for transforming them into a form appropriate for statistical analysis. Fig. 3 indicates the steps involved in preprocessing. Realignment is the first preprocessing

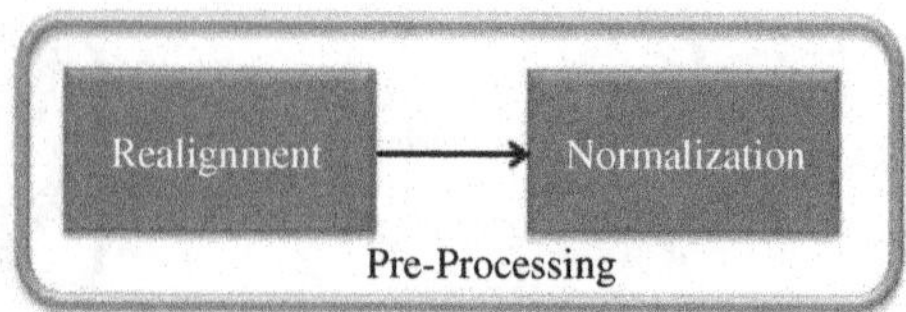


**FIG. 3** Steps in preprocessing with the proposed system

step in which a motion correction algorithm is applied to the fMRI data. The realigned fMRI data are then spatially normalized using estimates and write normalize function [16].

### 3.3 Principal component analysis

Dimensionality reduction denotes mapping of data in high-dimensional space to lower dimensional space in order to reduce the dimension, thereby retaining relevant information of data. The reasons for reducing dimension are stated as follows:

- To reduce storage capacity and computation time.
- To eliminate redundant, meaningless, and noisy data.
- Visualizing high-dimensional data is challenging.
- To simply the classification process and improve accuracy.

PCA [4, 7, 9] is one of the dimensionality reduction techniques that take less computation time [17]. As PCA is computationally challenging for a very large dataset, group PCA is used to handle very large fMRI datasets [18]. PCA and group PCA are implemented using the GIFT package in the presented work. The temporal dimension is reduced using PCA for each subject in an individual phase. The reduced data of individual subjects are concatenated, and the dimension of the aggregate data is minimized to the desired number of components using group PCA in the group stage [7].

### 3.4 Independent component analysis

ICA [4–6, 9] is a blind source separation method that separates linear mixtures of unknown source signals. Single spatial, temporal, and subject-specific modes are used for the group and multigroup analysis of fMRI data. Spatial ICA is the most common ICA approach to fMRI data because fMRI assumes that each image over time is composed of linear combination of T spatial IC images with associated time courses whereas temporal ICA is used by EEG and MEG [19].

During fMRI acquisition, subjects are instructed to do experimental and control tasks in an alternating time second. ICA is used to extract signals of interest and not of interest without any prior information about the task. Group analysis of fMRI is important to study specific conditions within or between groups of

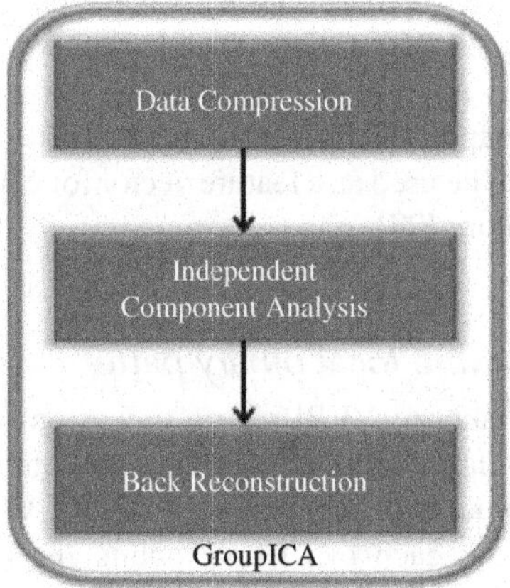


**FIG. 4** Three levels in group ICA

subjects. Group ICA [5, 7] is performed at three levels, such as data compression, ICA, and back reconstruction using the GIFT package, as shown in Fig. 4 [20].

Spatial ICA is used to get 3D spatial maps of fMRI data. Group spatial ICA is performed in two stages, which are individual stage and group stage. ICs are calculated using group spatial ICA with the help of GIFT tool. The number of ICs is evaluated using minimum description length (MDL) [7]. As FastICA is the best ICA algorithm for biomedical signal processing [4], group PCA is performed on reduced group data using the FastICA algorithm [4]. Group ICA generates ICs and corresponding ICA time course for each subject [7].

## 3.5 Feature extraction

Feature extraction is the process of transformation of original high-dimensional raw data to a more meaningful representation of numerical features in a lower dimensional space by preserving the information in the original dataset and to produce a compact feature set [7, 21]. Feature extraction is the first step in texture analysis.

fMRI data are abundant, noisy, and highly correlated both spatially and temporally [15]. Texture analysis is used to assess the spatial heterogeneity of ROIs in medical images [22]. Texture analysis is aimed at providing complete quantitative analysis of heterogeneity with the assessment of voxels in fMRI.

### *3.5.1 Local binary pattern*

LBP is a texture descriptor used for the property of high discrimination power. LBP labels each pixel in an image by comparing the gray level with the neighboring pixels and then assigning a binary number. A value of unity is assigned to the neighbors with gray level greater than the center pixel in a predefined patch otherwise a value of zero. A binary number is then obtained and assigned to the center pixel. The original LBP operator considers a 3 × 3 patch so the surrounding pixels form a binary number of 8 digits. After all the pixels in an image are labeled, LBP feature map, and a histogram that consists of 256 bins is obtained. The LBP histogram can be used as a feature vector for classification where each bin represents one feature [23].

### 3.5.2 Modified volume local binary pattern

Volume local binary pattern (VLBP) is an extension of the LBP descriptor, which is used for 3D data. Original VLBP deals with textures in 3D planes $X, Y, T$ where $T$ is the motion during the time. In fMRI, VLBP is used to describe the brain volume data in each fMRI time points and motion does not exist. Hence, MVLBP is introduced in which $T$ dimension is replaced with $Z$ dimension. $Z$ dimension is formed using the brain slices in each fMRI time points. Modified VLBP is depicted in Fig. 5.

Modified VLBP is defined as follows:

$$\begin{aligned} B = \big(&C\big(v_{x,y,z-1}, v_c\big), C\big(v_{x+1,y,z-1}, v_c\big), C\big(v_{x,y-1,z-1}, v_c\big), \\ &C\big(v_{x-1,y,z-1}, v_c\big), C\big(v_{x,y+1,z-1}, v_c\big), \\ &C\big(v_{x+1,y,z}, v_c\big), C\big(v_{x,y-1,z}, v_c\big), C\big(v_{x-1,y,z}, v_c\big), \\ &C\big(v_{x,y+1,z}, v_c\big), C\big(v_{x+1,y,z+1}, v_c\big), C\big(v_{x,y-1,z+1}, v_c\big), \\ &C\big(v_{x-1,y,z+1}, v_c\big), C\big(v_{x,y+1,z+1}, v_c\big), C\big(v_{x,y,z+1}, v_c\big)\big) \end{aligned} \tag{1}$$

where $B$ is a binary array obtained by comparison of the voxel value $v_c$ at the center position $x$, $y$, $z$ and the voxel values of its neighbors, and $C(v, v_c)$ is defined as follows:

$$C(v, v_c) = \begin{cases} 1, v \geq v_c \\ 0, v < v_c \end{cases} \tag{2}$$

Finally, for labeling the center voxel $v_c$ using MVLBP, a binomial weighting factor $2^P$ is assigned to each element of $B$, and VLBP code is calculated as follows:

$$\text{MVLBP}(v_c) = \sum_{p=0}^{p-1} B_p 2^P \tag{13.3}$$

where $P$ is the number of elements in array $B$. After computation of the VLBP codes for all voxels, the histogram of these codes is extracted and considered as the feature vector, and there will exist $2^P$ possible histogram bins for any fMRI time points [4].

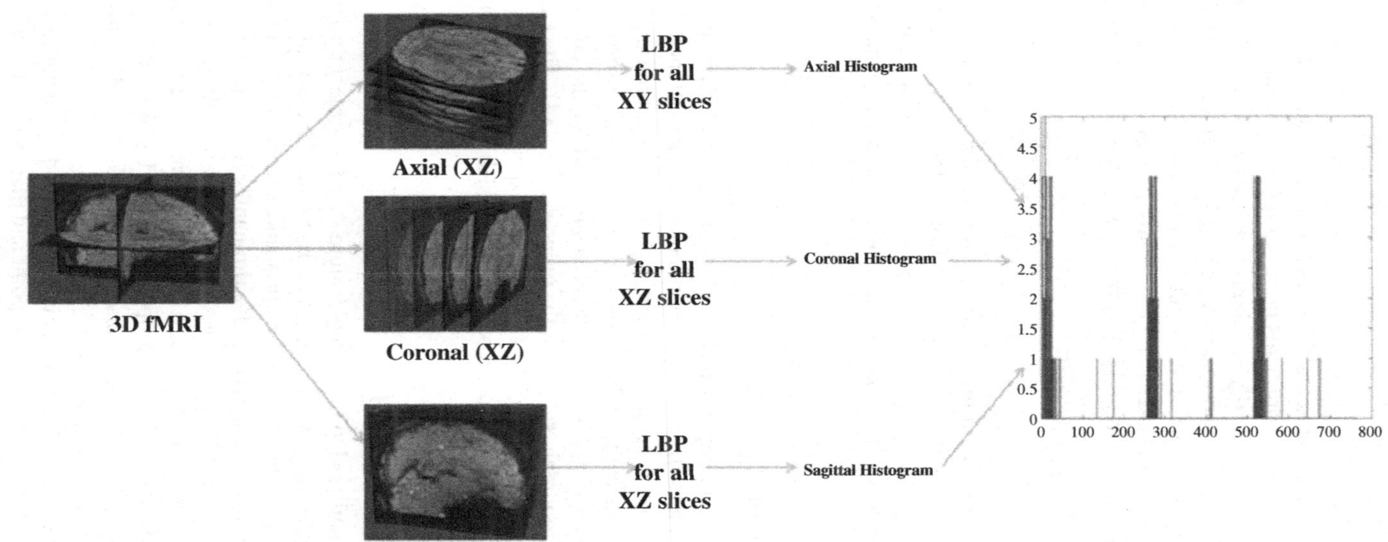


**FIG. 5** Process involved in MVLBP

## 3.6 Feature selection

Feature selection is the process of finding the best set of features from the extracted features. Feature selection is essential because high computational complexity and overfitting problems occur with the use of all features [17].

The feature vector is actually very high dimensional as a result of employing MVLBP to fMRI data. A two-sample t-test is used to select remarkable histogram bins [4]. A two-sample t-test is a statistical method that calculates the ratio of the means of the two classes $i$ and $j$ to identify whether they are statistically different from each other or not [17]. A two-sample t-test is defined as follows:

$$\text{Two sample } T-\text{test}, t = \frac{\mu_n - \mu_s}{\sqrt{{}^{v_n}/_{\eta_n} + {}^{v_s}/_{\eta_s}}} \tag{4}$$

where $\mu$ denotes the mean of the sample, $v$ indicates the variance of the sample, $\eta$ represents the number of samples in each class, $n$ stands for normal group, and $s$ refers to schizophrenic group. The greater $t$ statistic means a greater difference between the two classes and more discriminative features that can separate two classes [17].

## 3.7 Classification

Classification is a technique that learns how to predict a category or assign a class label to examples from the problem domain using machine learning algorithms. Classification is applied in segment analysis, ad targeting, spam detection, risk assessment, medical diagnosis, and image classification [24, 25]. LDA classifier, NN classifier, and SVM classifier are used for the classification of normal and schizophrenic subject in the proposed work [4]. The classification process is applied for all ICs of fMRI data of corresponding test subjects. In the present work, the ICs of schizophrenic subjects are labeled as 1 and normal subjects as −1.

### *3.7.1 LDA, NN, and SVM*

LDA classifier is utilized to find a new feature space to project the data in order to maximize classes' separability and thereby predict the class label of test feature. Diagonal linear discriminant, pseudo linear discriminant, quadratic discriminant, diagonal quadratic discriminant, and pseudo quadratic discriminant are some of the variants of LDA classifier. Linear discriminant is the most commonly used types. Except for quadratic discriminant, all other discriminant types are used in the proposed work. LDA is used for linear classification of data whereas quadratic discriminant analysis (QDA) is applied for nonlinear classification of data.

The principle behind NN classifier is to find a predefined number of training samples closest in distance to the new point and then predict the label from the training samples. NN classifier is often implemented in the classification process where the decision boundary is irregular [26]. The distance may be of any measure namely euclidean, city block, chebychev, cosine, hamming, jaccard, mahalanobis, minkowski, standard euclidean, and spearman, but euclidean distance is used generally. All distance types are used in the proposed work except mahalanobis distance.

SVM is a supervised machine learning approach in which a particular set of input data is used for training to produce a desired output. The different types of SVM are linear SVM, RBF or Gaussian SVM, and Polynomial SVM. Linear SVM is the default type of SVM.

### *3.7.2 Performance evaluation*

The performance of the system is evaluated using various metrics, such as accuracy, sensitivity, specificity, precision, and error. The dataset contains ground truth that is used to make an assessment against accuracy. Accuracy approximates the overall performance of the algorithm in terms of true class labeling. Accuracy is computed as given in Eq. (5).

$$\text{Accuracy} = \frac{(\text{TP} + \text{TN})}{\text{TP} + \text{FP} + \text{TN} + \text{FN}} \tag{5}$$

where TP is the number of true positives, FP is the number of false positives, TN is the number of true negatives, and FN is the number of false negatives. Sensitivity measures the probability of the true label that is being truthful. Sensitivity is also defined as a true positive ratio or bit ratio or recall. Sensitivity is calculated as specified in Eq. (6).

$$\text{Sensitivity} = \frac{\text{TP}}{\text{TP} + \text{TN}} \tag{6}$$

Specificity measures the probability of the negative label that is being truthful. Specificity is also known as the false positive rate or false alarm rate. Specificity is measured as stated in Eq. (13.7).

$$\text{Specificity} = \frac{\text{TN}}{\text{TN} + \text{FP}} \tag{13.7}$$

Precision is the probability that a positive prediction is correct. Precision is also called the predictive value. Precision is computed as prescribed in Eq. (13.8).

$$\text{Precision} = \frac{\text{TP}}{\text{TP} + \text{FP}} \tag{13.8}$$

All evaluations are prone to error. Error refers to the uncertainty of the result. The error is calculated as mentioned in Eq. (13.9).

$$\text{Error} = \frac{(\text{FP} + \text{FN})}{\text{TP} + \text{TN} + \text{FP} + \text{FN}} \tag{13.9}$$

The performance of the proposed system is evaluated using three different classifiers namely LDA, euclidean distance NN, and linear SVM based on the prediction of the classification label on the test subject.

## 4 Results and discussion

In the NAMIC Brain Multimodality dataset, fMRI scans of all subjects are acquired with 200 repetitions of a high resolution (128 × 128 × 39) EPI scan. Each repetition consists of 39 slices. An example of a normal subject (case01019) with one repetition containing 39 slices is shown in Fig. 6. All the fMRI data are preprocessed using SPM12 tool. The fMRI data are spatially aligned to make the effect of the subject movement error-free during scanning in the first preprocessing step, realignment, or motion correction. The realigned fMRI data, as shown in Fig. 7, are spatially normalized into a standard space in the second preprocessing step, normalization, as shown in Fig. 8. The dimensions of the preprocessed fMRI data are 79 × 95 × 79, but the number of repetitions remains 200. Subject-specific group PCA is applied, which not only maps the fMRI data to new space but also reduces the number of repetitions

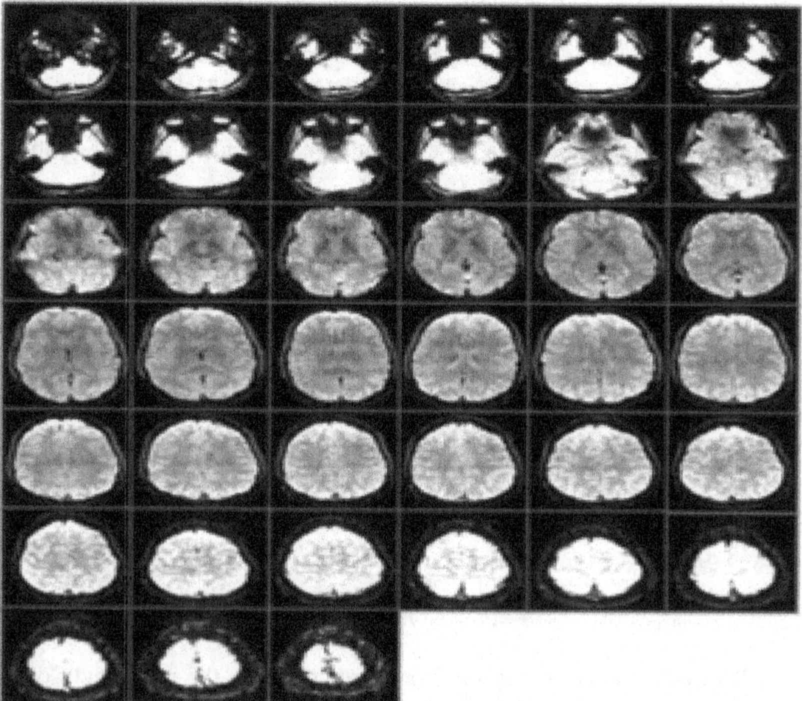

**FIG. 6** Thirty-nine slices of raw fMRI data of a normal subject from NAMIC dataset.

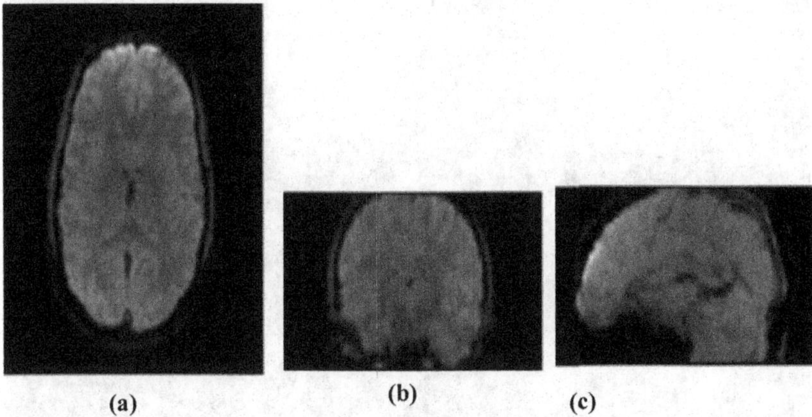


FIG. 7 (A) Axial, (B) coronal, and (C) sagittal view of realigned fMRI data of a normal subject.

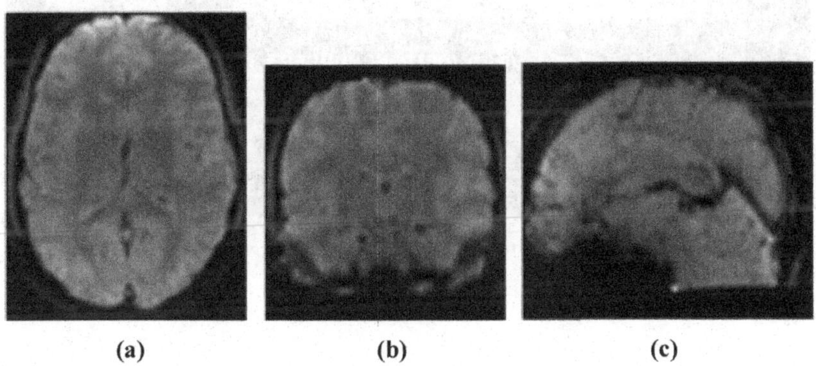


FIG. 8 (A) Axial, (B) coronal, and (C) sagittal view of normalized fMRI data of a normal subject.

to 10. A variance maximization preprocessing step is used in group ICA. Standard group ICA is used for extracting 10 ICs and then GICA back reconstruction is used to reconstruct subject spatial maps and time courses, as shown in Fig. 9. The extracted 10 ICs are sorted based on variance. A modified version of VLBP is applied on the sorted ICs, which extracts histogram of those ICs to provide significant features for the diagnosis of schizophrenia, as shown in Fig. 10. MVLBP is implemented with 8 neighbors, L2 normalization, and linear interpolation. Two different histogram bins with maximum discrimination power are selected using a two-sample t-test. All the ICs of the test subjects are classified separately using LDA, euclidean NN, and linear SVM classifiers individually. The performance metrics used for the diagnosis of schizophrenia are accuracy, sensitivity, specificity, precision, and error. The classification accuracy of 60%, 40%, 80%, and 70% of IC1, IC6, IC7, and IC10 is obtained for normal subjects

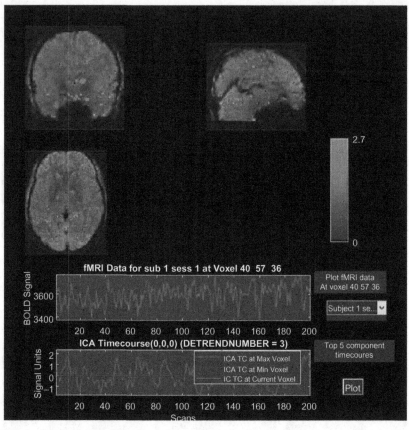

FIG. 9 Output of group ICA of a normal subject.

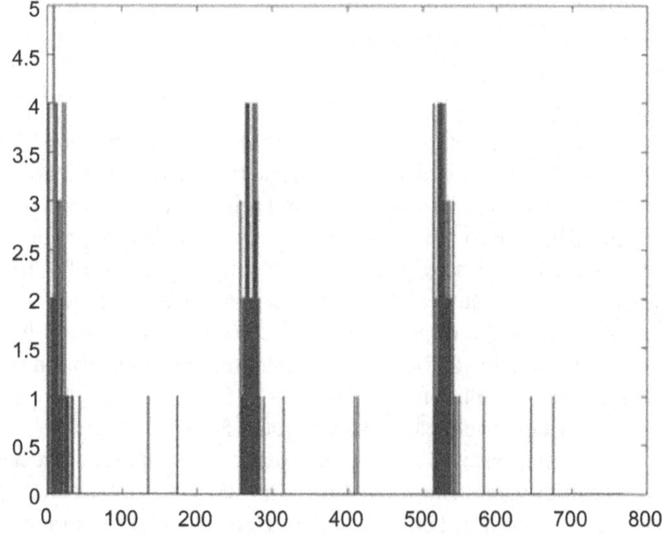


FIG. 10 Output of MVLBP of a normal subject.

and 50%, 50%, 75%, 75% of IC1, IC6, IC7, and IC10 is obtained for schizophrenic subjects using LDA classifier. The classification accuracy of 50%, 40%, 70%, and 70% of IC1, IC6, IC7, and IC10 is attained for normal subjects and 75%, 62.5%, 75%, 62.5% of IC1, IC6, IC7, and IC10 are attained for schizophrenic subjects using euclidean NN classifier. The classification accuracy of 100%, 100%, 100%, and 90% of IC1, IC6, IC7, and IC10 is predicted for normal subjects and 0%, 0%, 0%, and 0% of IC1, IC6, IC7, and IC10 is predicted for schizophrenic subjects using linear SVM classifier.

## 4.1 Performance evaluation by varying the number of ICs

The performance of the system is evaluated by the varying number of ICs from 10 to 40, and the results are summarized in the following sections. The NAMIC database consists of 10 normal subjects, namely, case01019, case01020, case01025, case01026, case01029, case01033, case01034, case01035, case01041, and case01104, and 8 schizophrenic subjects, namely, case01011, case01015, case01018, case01028, case01039, case01042, case01044, and case01045.

### *4.1.1 Using LDA classifier*

The performance of the system is evaluated with 10 ICs using LDA classifier and the results of the same are tabulated in Table 1. From Table 1, it is understood that an accuracy of 80%, 70% with IC7, and IC10 is obtained for normal subjects and 75%, with IC7, and IC10 is obtained for schizophrenic subjects using LDA classifier.

With 20 ICs, the accuracy with IC12, IC15, and IC17 is 80% for normal subjects and the accuracy with IC12, IC13, IC15, and IC19 is 62.5% for schizophrenic subjects. With 30 ICs, the accuracy with IC21, IC22, IC26, and IC27 is 80% for normal subjects and the accuracy with IC21, and IC23 is 62.5% for schizophrenic subjects. With 40 ICs, the accuracy with IC35 is 90% for normal subjects and the accuracy with IC35 is 62.5% for schizophrenic subjects.

**TABLE 1** Accuracy reported with the first 10 ICs using LDA classifier.

| | Accuracy | | | | | | | | | |
|---|---|---|---|---|---|---|---|---|---|---|
| **Subject type** | *IC1* | *IC2* | *IC3* | *IC4* | *IC5* | *IC6* | *IC7* | *IC8* | *IC9* | *IC10* |
| Normal | 60 | 50 | 60 | 60 | 50 | 40 | 80 | 40 | 50 | 70 |
| Schizophrenic | 37.5 | 50 | 12.5 | 50 | 62.5 | 50 | 75 | 25 | 37.5 | 75 |

**TABLE 2** Accuracy reported with the first 10 ICs using NN classifier

| | Accuracy | | | | | | | | | |
|---|---|---|---|---|---|---|---|---|---|---|
| **Subject type** | *IC1* | *IC2* | *IC3* | *IC4* | *IC5* | *IC6* | *IC7* | *IC8* | *IC9* | *IC10* |
| Normal | 50 | 70 | 40 | 50 | 70 | 40 | 60 | 80 | 60 | 70 |
| Schizophrenic | 75 | 37.5 | 37.5 | 37.5 | 50 | 62.5 | 75 | 25 | 12.5 | 62.5 |

### *4.1.2 Using NN classifier*

The performance of the system is evaluated with 10 ICs using euclidean NN classifier, and the results of the same are tabulated in Table 2. From Table 2, it is concluded that an accuracy of 80%, with IC8 is attained for normal subjects and 75% with IC1, and IC7 is attained for schizophrenic subjects using euclidean NN classifier.

With 20 ICs, the accuracy with IC19 is 90% for normal subjects and the accuracy with IC12, IC13, IC15, and IC20 is 62.5% for schizophrenic subjects. With 30 ICs, the accuracy with IC24 is 90% for normal subjects and the accuracy with IC23, IC24, IC25, and IC27 is 50% for schizophrenic subjects. With 40 ICs, the accuracy with IC38 is 100% for normal subjects and the accuracy with IC31, IC32, IC34, IC35, IC37, and IC38 is 50% for schizophrenic subjects.

### *4.1.3 Using SVM classifier*

The performance of the system is evaluated with 10 ICs using linear SVM classifier, and the results of the same are tabulated in Table 3. From Table 3, it is inferred that except for IC10, all other ICs for normal subjects are predicted correctly, but none of the schizophrenic subjects with IC1, IC6, IC7, and IC10 is predicted correctly using linear SVM. With 20, 30, and 40 ICs, the accuracy with all ICs is 100% for normal subjects, but the accuracy with all ICs is 0% for schizophrenic subjects.

## 4.2 Performance evaluation using different types of LDA, NN, and SVM

The performance of the proposed system is evaluated with 10 ICs using various types of three different classifiers, such as LDA, NN, and SVM. By comparing

**TABLE 3** Accuracy reported with the first 10 ICs using SVM classifier.

| | Accuracy | | | | | | | | | |
|---|---|---|---|---|---|---|---|---|---|---|
| **Subject type** | *IC1* | *IC2* | *IC3* | *IC4* | *IC5* | *IC6* | *IC7* | *IC8* | *IC9* | *IC10* |
| Normal | 100 | 100 | 100 | 100 | 100 | 100 | 100 | 100 | 100 | 90 |
| Schizophrenic | 0 | 0 | 0 | 0 | 0 | 0 | 0 | 0 | 0 | 0 |

the accuracy of different types of LDA, NN, and SVM, only the ICs, which show maximum accuracy under each type of those three classifiers are considered. Finally, only the best ICs, namely, IC1, IC6, IC7, and IC10, that predict the maximum number of test subjects correctly are chosen for the proposed work.

### 4.2.1 Performance evaluation using LDA classifier with different types of discriminants

The performance of the proposed system is evaluated using LDA classifier with different types of discriminants, namely, diagonal linear, pseudo linear, diagonal quadratic linear, and pseudo quadratic linear, as shown in Fig. 11. An accuracy of 70%, 60%, 80%, and 70% for IC1, IC6, IC7, and IC10 is acquired, respectively, for normal subjects and 75%, 87.5%, 75%, and 75% for IC1, IC6, IC7, and IC10 is acquired, respectively, for schizophrenic subjects using a diagonal linear discriminant classifier. An accuracy of 60%, 60%, 60%, and 70% for IC1, IC6, IC7, and IC10 is acquired, respectively, for normal subjects and 37.5%, 37.5%, 62.5%, and 62.5% for IC1, IC6, IC7, and IC10 is acquired, respectively, for schizophrenic subjects using a pseudo linear discriminant

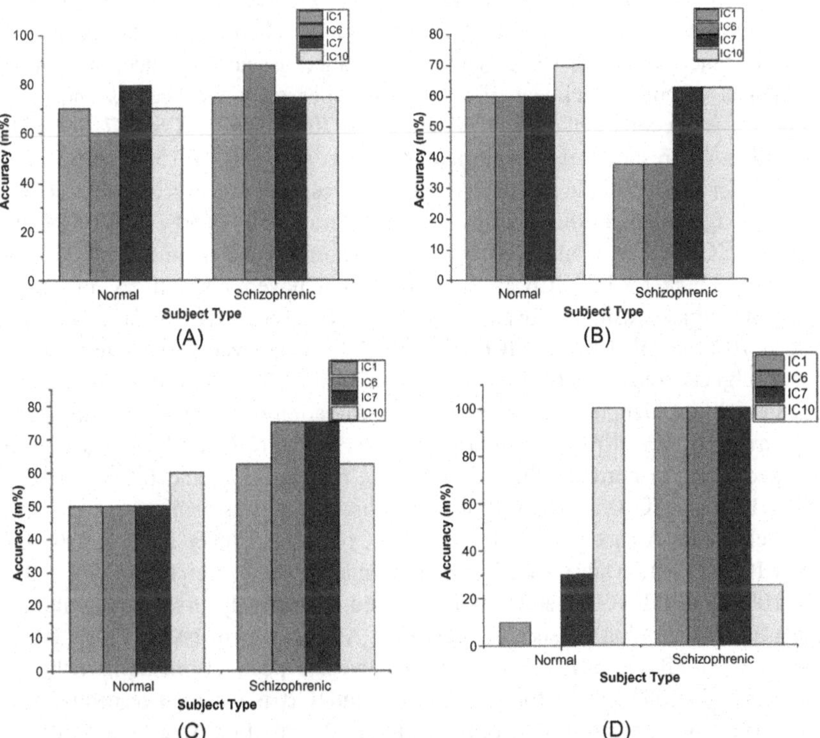


**FIG. 11** Accuracy of the proposed system using LDA classifier for different discriminants plotted for Normal and Schizophrenic subjects: (A) diagonal linear discriminant; (B) pseudo linear discriminant; (C) diagonal quadratic discriminant; and (D) pseudo quadratic discriminant

classifier. An accuracy of 50%, 50%, 50%, and 60% for IC1, IC6, IC7, and IC10 is acquired, respectively, for normal subjects and 62.5%, 75%, 75%, and 62.5% for IC1, IC6, IC7, and IC10 is acquired, respectively, for schizophrenic subjects using a diagonal quadratic discriminant classifier. An accuracy of 10%, 0%, 30%, and 100% for IC1, IC6, IC7, and IC10 is acquired, respectively, for normal subjects, and 100%, 100%, 100%, and 25% for IC1, IC6, IC7, and IC10 is acquired, respectively, for schizophrenic subjects using a pseudo quadratic discriminant classifier.

From Fig. 11, it is assumed that the maximum accuracy of 100% is acquired for normal subjects with IC10 and the maximum accuracy of 100% is acquired for schizophrenic subjects with IC1, IC6, and IC7 using a pseudo quadratic discriminant classifier. In addition, an accuracy of 80% is acquired for normal subjects with IC7 and an accuracy of 87.5% is acquired for schizophrenic subjects with IC6 using a diagonal linear discriminant classifier.

### *4.2.2 Performance analysis using NN classifier with various distance measures*

The performance of the proposed system is analyzed using NN classifier with various distance measures, such as city block distance, chebychev distance, correlation distance, cosine distance, hamming distance, jaccard distance, minkowski distance, standard euclidean distance, and spearman distance, as shown in Fig. 12. An accuracy of 50%, 40%, 60%, and 70% for IC1, IC6, IC7, and IC10 is achieved, respectively, in normal subjects, and 75%, 62.5%, 62.5%, and 62.5% for IC1, IC6, IC7, and IC10 is achieved, respectively, in schizophrenic subjects using a city block distance NN classifier. An accuracy of 50%, 80%, 90%, and 40% for IC1, IC6, IC7, and IC10 is achieved in normal subjects, and 87.5%, 62.5%, 50%, and 50% for IC1, IC6, IC7, and IC10 is achieved, respectively, in schizophrenic subjects using chebychev distance NN classifier. An accuracy of 40%, 50%, 70%, and 50% for IC1, IC6, IC7, and IC10 is achieved, respectively, in normal subjects, and 75%, 62.5%, 75%, and 62.5% for IC1, IC6, IC7, and IC10 is achieved in schizophrenic subjects using correlation distance NN classifier. An accuracy of 50%, 40%, 70%, and 70% for IC1, IC6, IC7, and IC10 is achieved, respectively, in normal subjects, and 75%, 62.5%, 75%, and 62.5% for IC1, IC6, IC7, and IC10 is achieved in schizophrenic subjects using cosine distance NN classifier. An accuracy of 100%, 100%, 100%, and 100% for IC1, IC6, IC7, and IC10 is achieved, respectively, in normal subjects, and 12.5%, 25%, 0%, and 0% for IC1, IC6, IC7, and IC10 is achieved, respectively, in schizophrenic subjects using hamming distance NN classifier. An accuracy of 100%, 100%, 100%, and 100% for IC1, IC6, IC7, and IC10 is achieved, respectively, in normal subjects, and 25%, 0%, 0%, and 0% for IC1, IC6, IC7, and IC10 is achieved, respectively, in schizophrenic subjects using jaccard distance NN classifier. An accuracy of 50%,

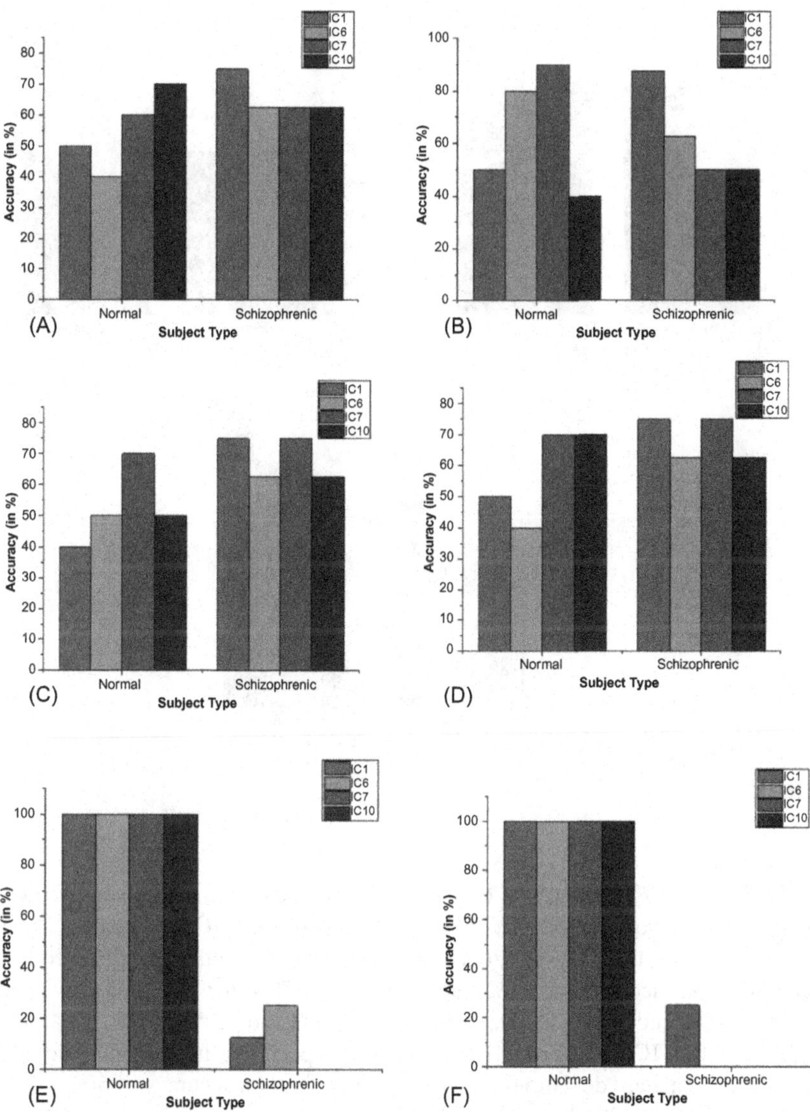


**FIG. 12** Accuracy of the proposed system using NN classifier with different distance measures plotted for Normal and Schizophrenic subjects: (A) city block distance; (B) chebychev distance; (C) correlation distance; (D) cosine distance; (E) hamming distance; (F) jaccard distance; (G) minkowski distance; (H) standard euclidean; (I) spearman distance.

*(Continued)*

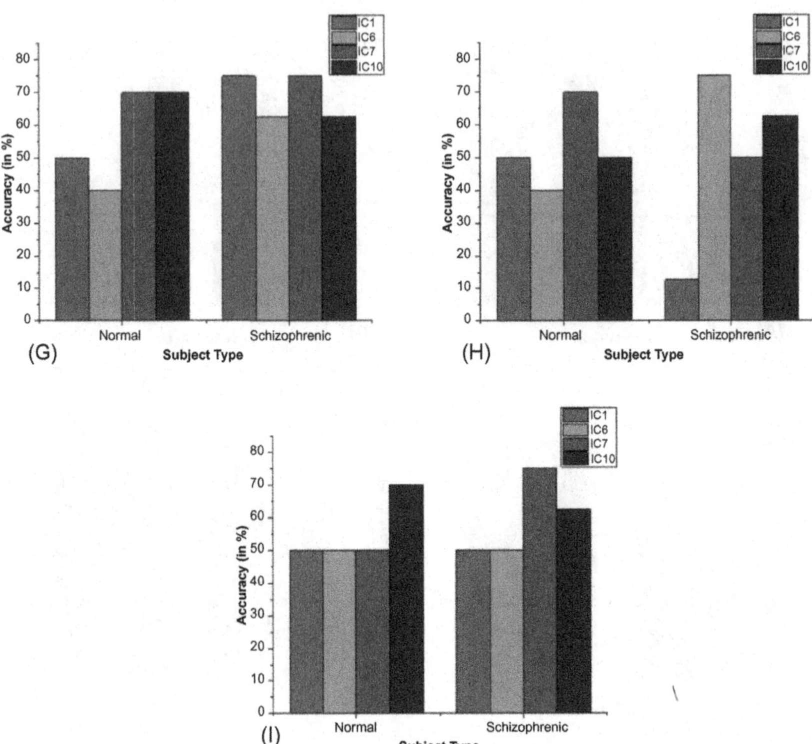


FIG. 12—CONT'D

40%, 70%, and 70% for IC1, IC6, IC7, and IC10 is achieved, respectively, in normal subjects, and 75%, 62.5%, 75%, and 62.5% for IC1, IC6, IC7, and IC10 is achieved, respectively, in schizophrenic subjects using minkowski distance NN classifier. An accuracy of 50%, 40%, 70%, and 50% for IC1, IC6, IC7, and IC10 is achieved, respectively, in normal subjects and 12.5%, 75%, 50%, and 62.5% for IC1, IC6, IC7, and IC10 is achieved, respectively, in schizophrenic subjects using standard deviation distance NN classifier. An accuracy of 50%, 50%, 50%, and 70% for IC1, IC6, IC7, and IC10 is achieved, respectively, in normal subjects, and 50%, 50%, 75%, and 62.5% for IC1, IC6, IC7, and IC10 is achieved, respectively, in schizophrenic subjects using spearman distance NN classifier.

From Fig. 12, it is evident that the maximum accuracy of 100% is achieved in normal subjects with IC1, IC6, IC7, and IC10 using hamming and jaccard distance NN classifier, respectively. Besides this, an accuracy of 90% for IC7 is achieved in normal subjects and 87.5% of IC1 is achieved in schizophrenic subjects using chebychev distance NN classifier.

### 4.2.3 Performance estimation using SVM classifier with other types of kernels

The performance of the proposed system is estimated using SVM classifier with other types of kernel like RBF and polynomial, as shown in Fig. 13. An accuracy of 100%, 100%, 100%, and 100% for IC1, IC6, IC7, and IC10 is obtained, respectively, in normal subjects, and 0%, 0%, 0%, and 0% for IC1, IC6, IC7, and IC10 is obtained, respectively, for schizophrenic subjects using SVM with RBF kernel. An accuracy of 60%, 60%, 60%, and 80% for IC1, IC6, IC7, and IC10 is obtained, respectively, in normal subjects, and 75%, 75%, 25%, and 75% for IC1, IC6, IC7, and IC10 is obtained, respectively, in schizophrenic subjects using SVM with polynomial kernel.

From Fig. 13, it is observed that the maximum accuracy of 100% is obtained in normal subjects with IC1, IC6, IC7, and IC10 using SVM with RBF kernel, and the maximum accuracy of 75% is obtained in schizophrenic subjects with IC1, IC6, and IC10 using SVM with polynomial kernel.

## 4.3 Discussion

From Sections 4.1.1, 4.1.2, and 4.1.3, it is inferred that the accuracy is 90% with IC35 for normal subjects and 75% with IC7, and IC10 for schizophrenic subjects while using LDA as a classifier. Accuracy is 100% with IC38 for normal subjects and 75% with IC1, and IC7 for schizophrenic subjects while using NN classifier. When using linear SVM with all the ICs, the accuracy is 100% for normal subjects and 0% for schizophrenic subjects using linear SVM.

Also, the highest accuracy of 100% is recorded in normal subjects using pseudo quadratic discriminant with IC10, hamming and jaccard distance NN classifier with IC1, IC6, IC7, IC10, and RBF with SVM classifier with IC1,

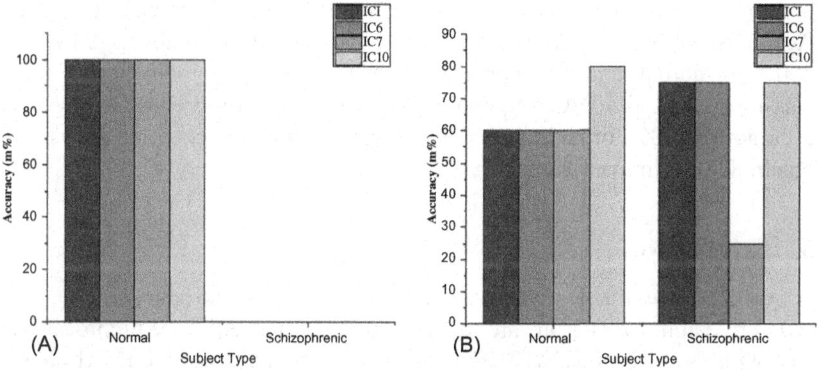


**FIG. 13** Accuracy of the proposed system using SVM classifier with different kernel functions plotted for Normal and Schizophrenic subjects: (A) RBF; (B) polynomial.

IC6, IC7, and IC10. And the highest accuracy of 100% is noted for schizophrenic subjects using pseudo quadratic discriminant with IC1, IC6, and IC7. Finally, it is concluded that IC1, IC6, IC7, IC10, and IC38 are the best ICs to aid in the classification process. Also, the pseudo quadratic discriminant classifier was found to be suitable for the classification of normal and schizophrenic subjects. The benefits of pseudo quadratic discriminant classifiers are summarized as follows:

- The covariance matrices can differ among classes.
- The inversion of the covariance matrix is done using pseudo inverse [27].

### *4.3.1 Comparison with the existing system*

VLBP have been applied only for video sequences in the literature. MVLBP [4] is used for feature extraction by replacing T dimension with Z dimension in the proposed system. Group PCA is used for dimensionality reduction. Group ICA is used for the extraction of ICs. Only linear classifiers are used for classification in most of the existing research work. But nonlinear classifiers, such as QDA, NN, and SVM with nonlinear kernel functions are used in the proposed work to improve classification accuracy. With respect to LDA classifier, pseudo quadratic discriminant, a variant of QDA classifier is used in the proposed work, which results in 100% accuracy for both normal and schizophrenic subjects. The classification accuracy of 100% is achieved in normal subjects with the help of hamming and jaccard distance NN classifier individually in the current research. By applying the chebychev distance NN classifier, 87.5% accuracy is obtained for schizophrenic subject in the proposed research. Nonlinear SVM with RBF kernel is employed in the present work, which attains 100% accuracy for normal subjects. Nonlinear SVM with polynomial kernel is applied in the proposed system, which records 75% accuracy for schizophrenic subjects.

While comparing the results with the existing system [4], the classification accuracy is improved using the pseudo quadratic discriminant classifier. According to the existing system, the classification accuracy is 94% and 100% for normal and schizophrenic subjects using the combination of three classifiers such as LDA, NN, and SVM. But the proposed work achieves an accuracy of 100% for both normal and schizophrenic subjects using the pseudo quadratic discriminant classifier.

## 5 Conclusion

A new feature extraction method known as MVLBP is introduced in the proposed research. fMRI scans are realigned and normalized in the preprocessing step with the help of SPM12. The number of time points in the fMRI data is reduced using group PCA. Afterwards, group ICA is carried out to extract ICs. In addition, the ICs are sorted based on variance. MVLBP is put forward for the extraction of the histogram of the ICs. Then, a two-sample t-test is employed for recognizing discriminative features. Three classifiers, LDA, NN, and SVM are used to diagnose schizophrenia for the purpose of classification. The performance measures, such as accuracy, sensitivity, specificity, precision, and error, are used for evaluating the proposed work. Several different types of the three classifiers are analyzed in the proposed work with the aim of achieving maximum accuracy. Additionally, the proposed work is investigated by increasing the number of ICs from 10 to 40. In the end, it is evident that the pseudo quadratic discriminant classifier is an appropriate choice for the classification of normal and schizophrenic subjects. Later, it is obvious that IC1, IC6, IC7, IC10, and IC38 are considered to be the perfect ICs to support classification process. The proposed work is found to be time consuming in the training phase.

The proposed system will be useful to diagnose schizophrenia accurately. In future, fMRI scans from various schizophrenia databases can be used. The proposed work may be extended to deep learning. The proposed work may be applied to other developmental disorders, such as ASD and ADHD.

## References


[1] UMC, Developmental Disorders, 2020. https://www.umc.edu/Research/Centers-and-Institutes/Centers/Center-for-Developmental-Disorders%20Research/Development%20Disorders/Overview.html. (Accessed 04 November 2020).

[2] M. Clinic, Schizophrenia Symptoms and Causes, 2020. https://www.mayoclinic.org/diseases-conditions/schizophrenia/symptoms-causes/syc-20354443. (Accessed 04 November 2020).

[3] E. Raquel Gur, C. Ruben Gur, Functional magnetic resonance imaging in schizophrenia, Dialogues Clin. Neurosci. 12 (3) (2010) 333–343.

[4] A. Pouyan, H. Shahamat, A texture-based method for Classification of Schizophrenia using fMRI data, Biocybern. Biomed. Eng. J. 35 (1) (2015) 45–53.

[5] A. Juneja, B. Rana, R.K. Agrawal, fMRI based computer aided diagnosis of schizophrenia using fuzzy kernel feature extraction and hybrid feature selection, Multimed. Tools Appl. 77 (2018) 3963–3989.

[6] S. Sartipi, H. Kalbkani, M.G. Shayesteh, Diagnosis of schizophrenia from R-fMRI data using Ripplet transform and OLPP, Multimed. Tools Appl. 79 (2020) 23401–23423.

[7] A. Juneja, B. Rana, R.K. Agrawal, A combination of single value decomposition and multivariate feature selection method for diagnosis of schizophrenia using fMRI, Biomed. Signal Process. Control 27 (2016) 122–133.

[8] F. Rami, H. Alqumaei, M.A. Rushdi, A. Inas, Schizophrenic patient identification using graph-theoretic features of resting-state fMRI data, Biomed. Signal Process. Control 43 (2018) 289–299.

[9] A. Pouyan, H. Shahamat, Feature selection using genetic algorithm for classification of schizophrenia using fMRI data, J. Artif. Intell. Data Mining 3 (1) (2015) 30–37.

[10] D. Chyzhyk, A. Savio, A.M. Grana, Computer aided diagnosis of schizophrenia on resting state fMRI data by ensembles of ELM, Neural Netw. 68 (2015) 23–33.

[11] L. Steardo, E.A. Carbone, R. Filippis, C. Pisanu, C. Segura-Garcia, A. Squassina, et al., Application of support vector machine on fMRI data as biomarkers in schizophrenia diagnosis: a systematic review, Front. Psychiatry 11 (2020) 1–9.

[12] D. Chyzhyk, A. Savio, A.M. Grana, Computer aided diagnosis of schizophrenia based on local-activity measures of resting-state fMRI, in: Proc. International Conference on Hybrid Artificial Intelligence Systems, 2014.

[13] MIDAS, 2020. http://insight-journal.org/midas/community/view/17. (Accessed 09 November 2020).

[14] M. Filippi, fMRI Techniques and Protocols, Humana Press, Italy, 2009.

[15] N. Lazar, The Statistical Analysis of Functional MRI Data, Springer, New York, 2008.

[16] S. Ulmer, O. Jansen, fMRI Basics and Clinical Applications, Springer, London, 2013.

[17] S. Velliangiri, S. Alagumuthukrishnan, S.I. Thankumar Joseph, A review of dimensionality reduction techniques for efficient computation, in: Proc. ICRTAC, 2019.

[18] M. Smith, A. Hyvarinen, G. Varoquax, L. Miller, F. Beckmann, Group PCA for very large fMRI datasets, NeuroImage 101 (2014) 738–749.

[19] D. Calhoun Vince, T. Adah, Multisubject independent component analysis of fMRI: a decade of intrinsic networks, default mode, and neurodiagnostic discovery, IEEE Rev. Biomed. Eng. 5 (2012) 60–73.

[20] Trendecenter, Group ICA/IVA of fMRI Toolbox (GIFT) Manual, 2020. https://trendscenter.org/trends/software/gift/docs/v4.0b_gica_manual.pdf. (Accessed 11 November 2020).

[21] MATLAB & Simulink, Feature Extraction, 2020. https://www.mathworks.com/discovery/feature-extraction.html. (Accessed 11 November 2020).

[22] Radiology Reference Article, Texture Analysis, 2020. https://radiopaedia.org/articles/texture-analysis. (Accessed 10 November 2020).

[23] A. Larooza, V. Bodi, D. Moratal, Texture Analysis in Magnetic Resonance Imaging: Review and Considerations for Future Applications, IntechOpen, 2016, https://doi.org/10.5772/64641.

[24] Machine Learning Mastery, 4 Types of Classification Tasks in Machine Learning, 2020. https://machinelearningmastery.com/types-of-classification-in-machine-learning/#:~:text=In%20machine%20learning%2C%20classification%20refers,one%20of%20the%20known%20characters. (Accessed 11 November 2020).

[25] Coursera, Machine Learning: Classification, 2020. https://www.coursera.org/learn/ml-classification. (Accessed 11 November 2020).

[26] Scikit-Learn, Nearest Neighbors—Scikit-Learn 0.23.0 Documentation, 2020. https://scikit-learn.org/stable/modules/neighbors.html. (Accessed 11 November 2020).

[27] Fit Discriminant Analysis Classifier – MATLAB Fitcdiscr, 2021. https://www.mathworks.com/help/stats/fitcdiscr.html#bt6d86x-1_sep_shared-DiscrimType. (Accessed 11 February 2021).

Chapter 14

# An artificial intelligence mediated integrated wearable device for diagnosis of cardio through remote monitoring

A. Sivasangari[a], R. Subhashini[a], S. Poonguzhali[b], Immanuel Rajkumar[b], J.S. Vimali[a], and D. Deepa[c]

*[a]Department of IT, Sathyabama Institute of Science and Technology, Chennai, India, [b]Department of ECE, Sathyabama Institute of Science and Technology, Chennai, India, [c]Department of CSE, Sathyabama Institute of Science and Technology, Chennai, India*

## 1 Introduction

Cardiovascular diseases, obstructive sleep apnea, and bipolar disorder are a group of disorders related to the heart or blood vessels. These diseases are frequent and the leading factor of death in the world. Early diagnosis and medical treatment will reduce the number of deaths due to cardiovascular disease. There is a need to design an early diagnostic system for reducing the death ratio. Myocardial infarction is the silent, rapid damage of cardiac muscles. Bipolar disorder is a chronic mental illness characterized by alternation of mood states from depression to hypomania. Heart rate variability is also used for diagnosing this disease.

Wearable devices play a vital role in remote health monitoring. Wearable devices and artificial intelligence (AI) facilitate the remote measurement and examination of patient data in real time. Wearable devices have progressed slowly in the form of clothing, watches, glasses, accessories, body attachments, and implanted devices. Wearable devices are becoming pervasive in an extensive range of applications, from healthcare to biomedical monitoring systems, which comprises of key enabling technologies, such as sensor technology, communication technology, and data analysis techniques. This enables efficient remote monitoring and cost-effective follow-up of patients. Wearable devices are noninvasive biosensors and real-time devices, which allow continuous monitoring of individuals and preliminary medical diagnosis.

**Cognitive Systems and Signal Processing in Image Processing. https://doi.org/10.1016/B978-0-12-824410-4.00008-8**

Wearable devices used for patient monitoring consist of three major components:

**(1)** sensing and data collection Internet of Things (IoT) device to collect physical and movement data;
**(2)** communication hardware and software to transmit data to a remote center or to the cloud; and
**(3)** data analysis techniques to extract insights from physiological and movement data.

Current developments in sensor technology, microelectronics, telecommunication, and data analysis techniques have enabled the development and deployment of wearable devices for patients' remote monitoring. Wearable sensors have diagnostic and monitoring applications. Their current capabilities include physiological, biochemical, and motion sensing. Physiological measures, such as heart rate, respiratory rate, blood pressure, blood oxygen saturation, and muscle activity, are the indicators of health status and have tremendous diagnostic value. Previously, constant monitoring of physiological parameters was probable only in the hospital environment, but nowadays, with advances in the field of wearable technology, the possibility of accurate, continuous, real-time monitoring of physiological signals is a reality.

One of the major hurdles in sensor technology is the size of the sensors. It has been resolved by the miniaturization of sensors and electronic circuits based on the use of microelectronics, which has played a key role in the development of wearable systems. Current advancements in the field of microelectronics have allowed researchers to develop miniature circuits entailing sensing capability, front-end amplification, microcontroller functions, and radio transmission. These standards have been developed by focusing on these parameters: (1) low cost, (2) small size of the transmitters and receivers, and (3) low power consumption. The newly developed IEEE 802.15.4a standard based on ultra-wideband (UWB) impulse radio provides low-power, low-cost, but high-data rate sensor network applications with the likelihood of highly accurate location estimation.

In a patient remote monitoring system, the data gathered using sensor networks has to be transmitted to a remote site, such as a hospital server for clinical analysis. This can be done by an information gateway, such as a mobile phone or personal computer, for transmitting the data from the sensor network to the remote server. For in-home monitoring, sensor data can be collected using a personal computer and communicated to the remote site over the Internet. By using the availability of 4G mobile telecommunication standards, health monitoring is possible when the patient is outside the home environment. Mobile telephony has had a major impact on the development of remote patient monitoring systems based on wearable sensors. Ubiquitous health monitoring and intervention applications are becoming possible due to the available significant computing power in pocket-sized devices. The Global Positioning System (GPS) integrated in mobile phones helps locate and monitor patients in case of an emergency. Since storage and computation has been pushed to the cloud, patient remote monitoring systems can become low-cost, platform-independent, rapidly deployable, and accessible from anywhere. Recently, wearable devices are driven by their own receiver and operating as a microcomputer, which allows the connection of all processes, processing, communication, and power supply. Wearable devices connect to other smart devices via Bluetooth, infrared, radio-frequency identification, and near-field communication technology. Together, this connectivity enables the wearable systems for remote and long-term monitoring of patients and elderly people in homes and communities. Applications in rehabilitation of remote monitoring systems depend on wearable and inertial sensors for movement detection and tracking. Inertial sensors include accelerometers and gyroscopes. Frequently, magnetometers are used in aggregation with them to improve motion tracking. Currently, movement sensors are inexpensive, small, and require very slight power, making them highly good-looking for patient monitoring applications. Wearable sensors are often combined with ambient sensors that monitor people in their home environment. The combination of wearable and ambient sensors is of great interest and has been incorporated in a variety of rehabilitation-related applications. For example, when monitoring older adults while deploying interventions to improve balance control and reduce falls, one would be attentive in using wearable sensors to trail motion and vital signs. Specifically designed data analysis procedures would then be used to sense falls via processing of motion and vital sign data. In this context, ambient sensors could be used in conjunction with wearable sensors to improve the accuracy of falls detection.

Assistive technologies for elder care are needed for both continuous and on-demand measurement of physiological and medical data to monitor and maintain an active and healthy lifestyle in old age and for independent living. Smart home devices, usually ambient, are used for indoor positioning systems, emphasizing on human activity recognition, as well as AI-based wearable biometric monitoring sensors are used to analyze the vital sign monitoring, blood pressure, and glucose. Wearables and smart home sensors are also used to enable multimodal fall detection, prevention, and risk assessment. Monitoring sensor devices are used to monitor the movement and activity of elderly people, especially those who are suffering from chronic and Parkinson's disease (PD). For monitoring of PD patients, the smart watches as a clinical tool can be used to analyze tremor and balance dysfunction with a gyroscope or accelerometer. People suffering from PD are in need of fall detection services, and elderly people who are in need of continuous monitoring are target users of the sensor device. PD is a communal and incapacitating pathology that is categorized by both motor and nonmotor symptoms and affects millions of people globally. The sensor devices are low cost, low power, unremarkable, and precise in their measurements for monitoring and dealing with the pathology. The purposes of wearable devices for PD applications are as follows: early diagnosis, tremor, body motion analysis, motor fluctuations (on-off phases), and home- and long-term monitoring. The AI-based sensors are used to observe the pathology at each stage of development, from the beginning of the disease to deliberate early symptoms, during disease evolution with analysis of the most common disorders, and including supervision of the most complicated situations (i.e., motor fluctuations and long-term remote monitoring).

This chapter proposes a smart healthcare system that can track a patient's basic health signs in real-time in an IoT setting. Patient conditions are communicated to medical personnel through a portal, where they can process and assess the patient's current situation. The prototype built is well-adapted for healthcare monitoring, as shown by the system's efficacy. Morphological operators applied for extracting the feature from the electrocardiogram (ECG) signal. A principal component analysis technique is applied for reducing unnecessary features. Automated backpropagation network (BPN) for efficient classification of medical data with high accuracy.

## 2 Related work

Partha et al. [1] discussed various machine learning techniques used for interventional cardiology decision-making aids and advanced interventional treatments. The absence of vast databases of carefully annotated images and videos, however, has been restricted across different medical disciplines, including intensive care. Interestingly, generative adversarial networks were used to compensate for this deficiency and to synthetically generate large, high-resolution image datasets, like angiograms and echocardiograms, which could be used to help train deep neural networks. According to Mounir et al. [2], it is technology that is just picking up, which needs to be generally known and cost-effective, for which certain suggestions are made, such as solar-powered batteries in the device for their ever fully working capability. However, they need to become common knowledge, to figure out their economics, and also to handle them effectively. There are difficulties or concerns associated with the devices that need to be tackled effectively, such as costs, general acceptance, efficient management, safety, and so on.

In [3] a phenotype-based classification with new analytical methods and high-computational capacity using multiomics, lifestyle, and environmental data may potentially change future clinical trials was proposed. Keys for unlocking big data research are data cleaning and data imputation. To date, the data on both wearables and genomic data that evoke long-term changes in behavior is negative or, at best, neutral. In big data analysis, bio banks and curated public databases can play an important role. While the proposed solution has already been clearly tested with many drawbacks, there is immense potential for big data analysis to enhance the cardiovascular quality of care and patient outcomes.

Johnson [4] provides clinicians with a guide on specific aspects of AI and machine learning, discusses selected cardiology implementations of these methods to date, and describes selected applications of these methods and how AI may be integrated into cardiovascular medicine in the future. In particular, the paper first discusses cardiology-relevant predictive modeling principles such as feature selection and common pitfalls, such as inappropriate dichotomization. Second, popular algorithms used in supervised learning are discussed, and selected applications in cardiology and associated disciplines are reviewed. Third, it discusses the emergence of deep learning and related techniques, collectively referred to as unsupervised learning, and offers contextual examples in general medicine as well as in cardiovascular medicine, and then explains how these techniques could be used to allow precision cardiology and improve patient outcomes. However, this work has a low accuracy for a new set of data.

In other studies [5–7], the sense of achieving home monitoring of older adults and subjects with chronic conditions and the integration of wearable and environmental sensors are addressed. They address potential work needed to advance the field toward the clinical application of wearable sensors and systems. Market developments in wearable electronics, commercial and emerging products, and manufacturing methods are discussed in other articles [8–10]. Also analyzed is real-time monitoring of vital signs using biosensors, drug delivery stimulus-responsive materials, and closed-loop theragnosis systems. In augmented, virtual, and mixed reality, communication modes, energy management, displays, conformity, and data protection, it covers potential challenges. The development and implementation of patient-oriented wearable technology in randomized clinical trials will promote the design of safe and efficient approaches. But the costs are high for the equipment used.

The authors of [11] proposed an IoT-based heart disease monitoring framework for ubiquitous healthcare service. This model tracks the patient's physical signs, such as blood pressure, ECG, SpO2, as well as appropriate environmental indicators and offers four separate modes of data transmission that balance the need for healthcare and the need for connectivity and computing services. To present an overview of the framework, we also implemented a prototype. A method of cardiac status prediction derived from IoT and machine learning that can collect required data from the human body using IoT devices (sensors) and transfer those data to the cloud where user authentication stores the data is been proposed by the authors [12].

Sološenko [13] proposed a system that uses a piece of equipment that incorporates PPG monitoring with ECG recordings to confirm atrial fibrillation (AF) would facilitate detection of the condition in daily life. However, PPG is not able to identify atrial activity (P wave) and cannot be used to diagnose AF; confirmation by ECG is still required.

Until machine learning algorithms are used to measure and predict the overall state of a patient's heart, the data collected from the human body must then be normalized. Wang et al. [14] reviewed the new advances in biocompatible optical devices. These optical devices can be categorized into waveguides, integrated implantable and wearable devices. The applications of these devices in photo medicine, including optical imaging, physiological signal detection, health monitoring, photothermal therapy (PTT), photodynamic therapy (PDT), and photobiomodulation (PBM), along with the newly emerging optogenetics, are reviewed.

A novel system for incorporating ensemble deep learning into edge-computing devices called HealthFog was proposed and implemented for a real-life application of automated heart disease analysis in [15]. HealthFog offers healthcare using IoT devices as a fog service and handles heart patient data effectively, which comes as user requests. FogBus, a fog-enabled cloud system, is used to deploy and measure the model's efficiency in terms of power consumption, network bandwidth, latency, jitter, correctness, and finishing time. In [16] the authors presented a resumed evolution of smart devices based on the prototypes developed over the years. Finally, we discuss likely market trends and future challenges for the emerging WHDs area.

Jamshidi et al. [17] proposed most recent challenges toward medical input reports and target networks that facilitate liable artificial neural network (ANN) during COVID-19. AI experts analyzed large datasets, training and applying a set of algorithms that help optimized solutions for the problems.

Lopez-Jimenez et al. [9] discussed the difference between the present and the future in terms of AI in cardiology. The future of AI in cardiology and in medicine, in general, is bright as the collaboration between investigators and clinicians continues to excel.

Research cap identified in this work are wearable devices developed as fitness bands and intelligence platforms to monitor motion activities, pulse rates, and heart rate using AI technology. AI's effect on wearable devices highlights the fact that smart technology is used to build devices that sense intelligence in body language and gestures. We can reliably predict the risk of heart failure worsening requiring hospitalization well before physicians and patients are aware that something is wrong.

## 3 Proposed work

A portable biomedical device is designed for people suffering from chronic diseases and to assist elderly people. This device comprises of heart beat (pulse), ECG sensors and phonocardiogram (PCG) sensor with high sensitivity. These sensors continuously read the pulse rate, ECG signals, and cardiac sounds. The measured ECG signal then a undergoes feature extraction phase where the required coordinates for disease classification were derived using Hilbert transform and principal component analysis (PCA). After extracting the essential features from the QRS complex of ECG, they were given as input to the ANN classifier, which is trained to diagnose the diseases from obtained features of ECG. The PCG signal is detected by PCG sensor, which represents various valve closures and openings along with murmurs. Z-transform is used finding the envelope of the PCG signal, which is considered to be effective information about heart sounds.

The coefficients are extracted from PCG signal by using linear predictive coding. The automated BPN classifier gives maximum accuracy of classification. Here the measured sensor data were sent to a mobile via Bluetooth and an android application in the mobile sends these input parameters to the cloud where all the previously mentioned processes were carried out. Finally, the classifier in the cloud provides the information about the diagnosed disease with all results to doctor and also to the patient caretaker. An alert message will be given under emergency condition. Thus, the emergency situation can be immediately serviced by the doctor from hospital itself. Fig. 1 shows the proposed workflow diagram.

An emergency telemedicine healthcare system was designed for supporting ECG signal and PCG signal monitoring and fall detection. This system detects the abnormality of the patient health. The ECG signal is processed to count the heartbeat for 1 min. The parameters of critical components (QRS) are obtained and processed. If any abnormality is detected in the ECG signal, SMS with a link consisting of patient details are sent to the doctor. This is mainly based on output obtained from sensors that are processed immediately. It helps take the appropriate protective measures by the doctor. It is a real-time system intended for use in telemedicine application. The applications of this device in photomedicine include optical imaging, physiological signal detection, health monitoring, PTT, PDT, and PBM.

Heart failure happens when the heart can no longer pump the blood properly throughout the body. This creates a backup of pressure in the small blood vessels of the lungs, which causes the vessels to leak the fluids. The proposed device has a pulse oximeter that measures a person's blood oxygenation level and their pulse rate. A healthy person should have oxygen saturation level (SPO2) at or above 96% and a resting heart rate from 60 to 100 beats per minute. A lower heart rate with low oxygen saturation may indicate lung

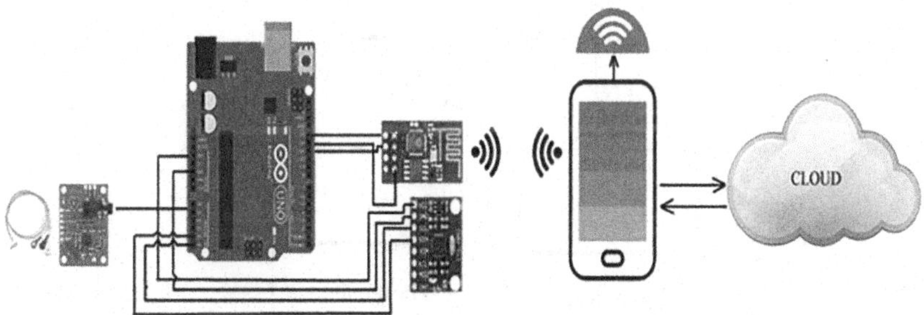


**FIG. 1** Proposed workflow diagram.

problems. Our proposed diagnostic device is designed to achieve the highest classification result with accuracy and sensitivity. Our proposed monitoring device monitors the movement and activity of elderly people, especially those who are suffering from chronic and PD. The people who are suffering from PD are in need of fall detection services, and elderly people who are in need of continuous monitoring are target users of the proposed device. The proposed automatic diagnostic system reduces the challenges of interpreting the visual subtle changes.

# 4 Feature extraction

## 4.1 ECG filtering

In the early stage of processing, the ECG signal is filtered. The QRS complex is improved by passing through a band pass filter. This procedure also removes the muscular noise. The baseline wanders, and higher order frequencies are removed by setting the band stop frequencies as 5–15 kHz. The ECG is a waveform that represents the electrical and muscular functions of the heart. It consists of five waves, such as P, Q, R, S, and T waves. The QRS complex waveform is the important waveform in ECG that represents the simultaneous activity of right and left ventricles. The doctor analyzes the heart rate analysis using QRS. The time and shape of QRS complex provides more information about the heart.

Fig. 2 shows the ECG signal with peak values. The QRS complex of ECG signal is shown in Fig. 2. The extraction of QRS signals is done by using morphological operators. Information on the shape of the signal is extracted by using the structuring element. It works on the basis of mathematical formulation and are simple to implement. A morphological operation is the interaction of a set or function that represent an object with another simpler set. The information of the signal is extracted by using the structural element. Several morphological operators, such as dilate, erode, open, and close, are performed in order to

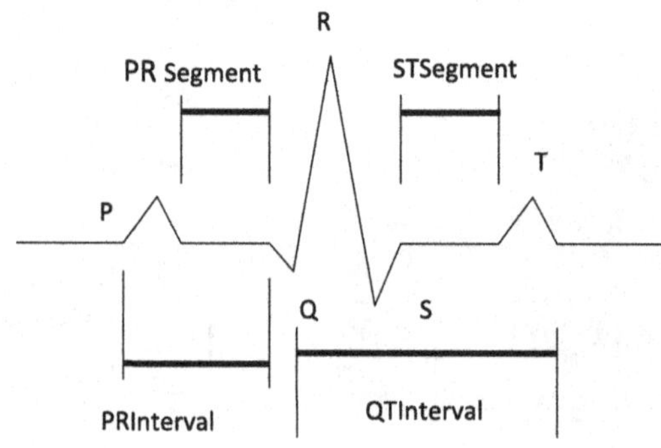


FIG. 2 ECG signal.

extract the QRS peaks of the signal. The dilation operation enlarges the input object, whereas the erode operator reduces or shrinks the input object. The open operator makes the edges or outline of the input object in an even fashion. The close operator fills the gap between the edges, and the tiny holes are excluded. The proposed work exploits dilate and erode operators. It performs the reduction of peak values and widening of the valleys in the ECG signal. The width of the peaks and valleys are determined by structuring element. The operators for signal *f*(*n*) and structuring element *g*(*n*) are described in the following:

$$\text{Dilation}: f(n) \oplus g(n) = \max\,[f(n-i) + g(i)] \tag{1}$$

$$\text{Erosion}: f(n)\, \Theta\, g(n) = \max\,[f(n-i) - g(i)] \tag{2}$$

The steps used to detect QRS Peaks as follows.

Step 1: Dilate and erode the input signal Sd and Sr, respectively.
Step 2: Calculate the average of Sd and Sr.
Step 3: Calculate the difference between the average and the input signal.
Step 4: Apply modulus operation to improve the quality of filtered ECG signal.
Step 5: Choose an adaptive threshold as the deciding function.

The adaptive threshold depends on the signal, so that it can adapt to the changing behavior of the signal. The threshold can be selected as given by:

$$\text{Th} = \begin{cases} 0.2M, & M < 2 \\ 0.4M, & 3 \le M \le 6 \\ 0.10M, & M > 6 \end{cases} \tag{3}$$

In Eq. (3), *M* is derived from the signal that is within the range of milli volts. Thus, the QRS peaks are detected. The peak values are quantized and converted into a binary string. Fig. 3 shows the feature extraction.

## 4.2 Principal component analysis

The PCA projects the data with highest variance by reducing it linear dimensionally. The required features of ECG data can be extracted by this technique.

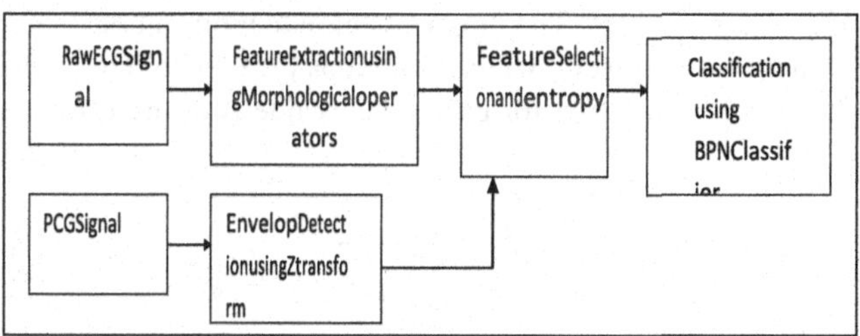


**FIG. 3** Feature extraction.

Let $Y(k)$ be signal segment of a heartbeat. It can be given as:

$$y(k) - \begin{bmatrix} y(1) \\ y(2) \\ \vdots \\ y(m) \end{bmatrix} \tag{4}$$

where,

$m$—no. of samples of heartbeat $y_1, y_2, y_3, \ldots, y_n$ – heartbeats.
$N$—observations of heartbeats.
Entire ensemble of heart beats is represented by $M \times N$ matrix $Y = [Y_1\, Y_2 \ldots Y_N]$

## 4.3 Steps in principal components analysis

**1.** Calculate mean vector. It can be calculated as

$$\frac{1}{M}\sum\nolimits_{i=0}^{M} y_i \tag{5}$$

**2.** Adjust data w.r.to mean as

$$y_{adj} = y_i - \bar{y} \tag{6}$$

$$y_{adj} = \left[y_{adj1}\, y_{adj2} \ldots y_{adjn}\right] \tag{7}$$

**3.** Covariance matrix can be calculated as follows $adj_2$

$$C = \frac{1}{M-1}\sum\nolimits_{i=1}^{M} (y_i - \bar{y})^{+}(y_i - \bar{y}) \tag{8}$$

**4.** Compute eigen vectors $e_i$ and eigen values $\lambda_i$

$$C \cdot e_i = \lambda_i \cdot e_{i,i} = 1,2,\ldots,N \tag{9}$$

**5.** Components were selected and featured vector form. The highest value eigen vector will become the principal component. Arrange eigen vectors from highest to lowest eigen values. This gives back the components in the order of significance. The dimensional reduction can be done by choosing $k$-principal component, which maintains the physiological information. The percent of variance $r_k$ for each eigen value is desired by:

$$r_k = \frac{\sum\nolimits_{i=1}^{k} \lambda_i}{\sum\nolimits_{i=1}^{N} \lambda_i} \tag{10}$$

The principal components having the variance greater than thresholds were chosen (i.e., 0.9 or 0.95):

$$\hat{\mathbf{r}}_k = \left(\hat{k} \geq th\right) \tag{11}$$

**6.** Deducing the new dataset. The input dataset for ANN is obtained as $\hat{r}$:

$$Y_{pca}(k) = \hat{r}_k^T \cdot Y_{adj}^T \tag{12}$$

Entropy value increases when the variability in the ECG signal rises. Variability in normal ECG signal is more as compared to the disease-affected person's ECG signal. The variation in the entropy features can be taken as longer duration in the ECG signal. Wavelet entropy is used for measuring the deviation. The wavelet transform ($E_w$) is a combination of the wavelet decomposition and to determine the extent of disorder. The bigger entropy value shows that variability in ECG signal.

$$E_w = \sum\nolimits_{n<0} E_n \ \ln E_n \tag{13}$$

$E_n$ denotes the probability distribution of ECG signal.

The PCG signal is detected by PCG sensor, which represents various valve closure and opening along with murmurs. Z-transform is used finding the envelope of the PCG signal, which is considered to be effective information about heart sounds. The coefficients are extracted from PCG signal by using linear predictive coding.

Cardiac conditions, such as arrhythmias and heart failures, exhibit very irregular heartbeats, and as a result, the entropy values obtained from these conditions may be higher than the normal ECG signals. Student $t$-tests can be applied to rank the extracted entropy features. It compares the mean values of the extracted entropies from normal ECG signals to disease-affected signals. Features are ranked accordingly to their corresponding $t$-values. Highly ranked features are feeding as an input to the classifiers one by one. The CHB-MIT dataset is used in this work. In stage 1, the extracted spectral and statistical features should be able to distinguish between normal and deviating cases. In stage 2, the proposed work uses PCA for feature dimension. $N$ vectors of $n$-dimensional features $Y_i = i = 1, \ldots, N$. In this case, $n$ represents the number of extracted features after applying wavelet transform of ECG signal and $N$ is the number of ECG data segments. We developed a classifier models for predicting heart disease from ECG and PPG signals using BPN. Fig. 4 shows the BPN structure.

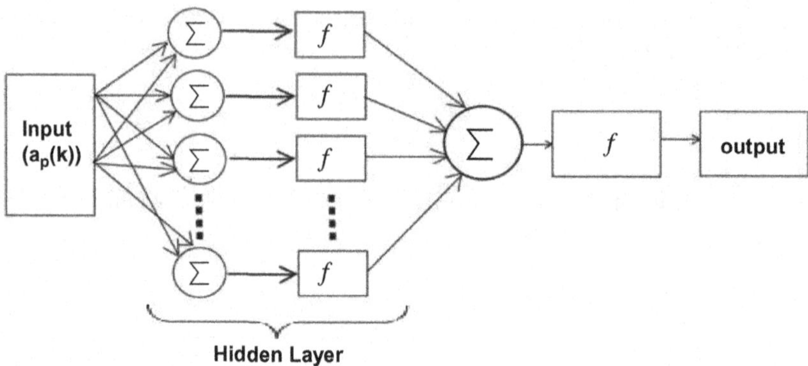


FIG. 4 BPN structure.

### 4.3.1 BPN classifier

By training the foregoing model with supervised and unsupervised methods, the highest number of disease classification with maximum accuracy can be achieved. It can be employed as a tool for distinguishing between a normal and an abnormal heart.

(i) Input function (signal input for input layer is set of extracted feature coefficient of ECG, PCG, and pulse oximeter information).
(ii) The hidden layer of neurons with a tangent sigmoid transfer function.
(iii) Output layer of neuron with linear transfer function.

Fig. 4 shows the BPN structure. The diagnosis result of the disease is sent to the doctor, patient, and caretaker as an SMS. This SMS consists of a link that connects to a website containing information about the patient's diagnosis report, and the patient can see the essential parameters required for verification such as pulse rate, ECG, and so on.

### 4.3.2 Convolutional neural network with Boltzman

This algorithm is a two-layer neural net that constitutes the building blocks of deep-belief networks. The first layer is called the visible or input layer, and the second is the hidden layer. The nodes are connected to each other across layers, but no two nodes of the same layer are linked. That is, there is no intralayer communication.

The signal input for the input layer is a set of extracted feature coefficients of ECG, PCG, and pulse oximeter information.

The hidden layer contains neurons with a tangent sigmoid transfer function.

### 4.3.3 Decision tree classifier

As the definition states, here the data is continuously split according to a certain parameter. In our proposed system, we use a set of extracted feature coefficients of ECG, PCG, and pulse oximeter information as split parameters.

### 4.3.4 K-SVD with MOD

K-singular value decomposition (K-SVD) is a dictionary learning algorithm. It is widely used for image and audio processing. We use this clustering algorithm in our proposed system for a better accuracy. This clusters the inputs based on the nearest neighbor.

### 4.3.5 Pan-Tomkinson algorithm

The Pan-Tompkins algorithm is the most widely used QRS complex detector for the monitoring of many cardiac diseases, including in arrhythmia detection. This method could provide good detection performance with high-quality clinical ECG signal data.

## 5 Performance analysis

The major features of the proposed method that help in enhancing the performance of the system are: compact size; easy to carry; transmission type: wireless via Bluetooth; uses three AG/AGCL disposable electrode; real-time transmission of ECG data; supported by mobile application. Fig. 5 shows the prototype model of proposed work.

The previous accuracy comparison chart clearly depicts in all the five tests that automated BPN provides the maximum efficiency, as seen in Fig. 6. Also, K-SVD with method of optimal directions (MOD) will give better accuracy just less than the automated BPN classifier. The contribution from the decision tree filter is not much more satisfactory compared with the other three classifiers. So the automated BPN classifier clearly showcases the dominance of better accuracy for its results.

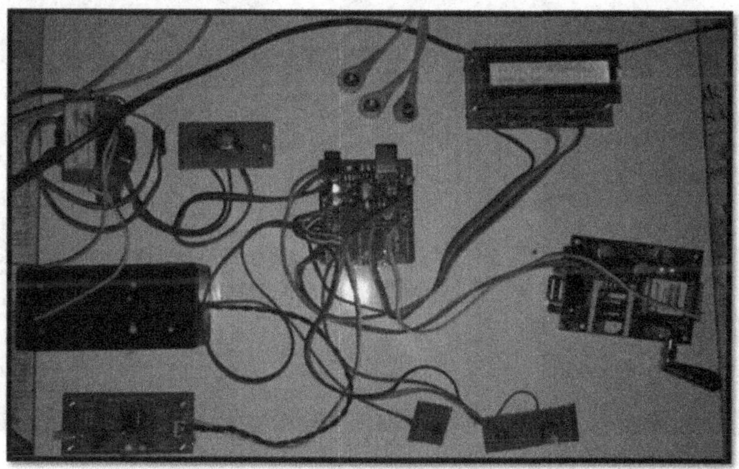

**FIG. 5** Prototype model.

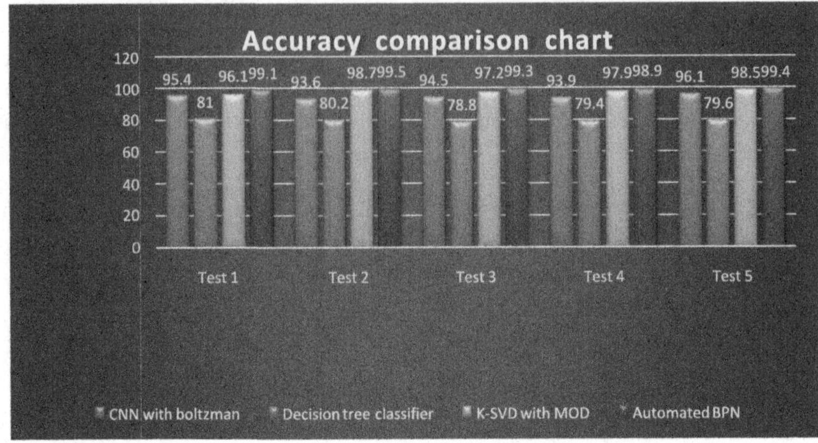


**FIG. 6** Accuracy analysis.

Fig. 7 clearly shows in all various tests that the automated BPN classifier provides maximum sensitivity, specificity, accuracy, TPR, and TNR compared with all other classifiers. In sensitivity, the automated BPN dominates all other evaluation parameters, especially automated BPN, with much clearer strikes in their dominating accuracy part of its classification. Real-time ECG and PPG signal information are obtained from sensor nodes. It will be sent to the remote server. The ECG and PPG datasets can be downloaded from CHB-MIT dataset. Training and testing data proportion is 70% and 30%.

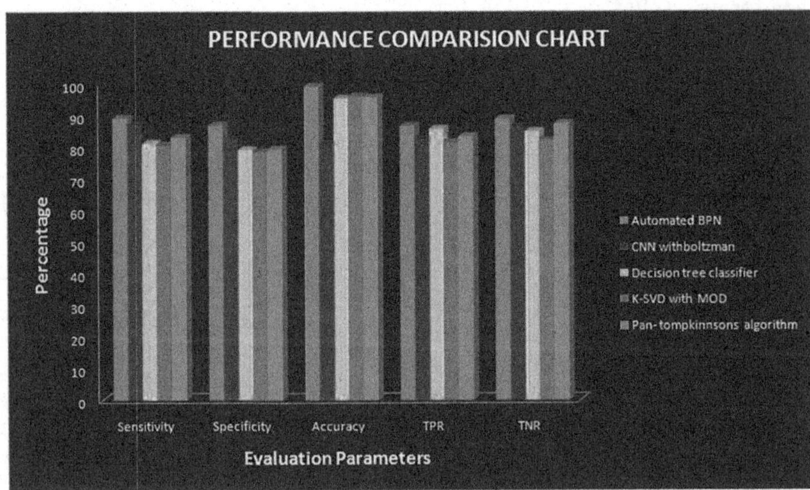


**FIG. 7** Performance evaluation.

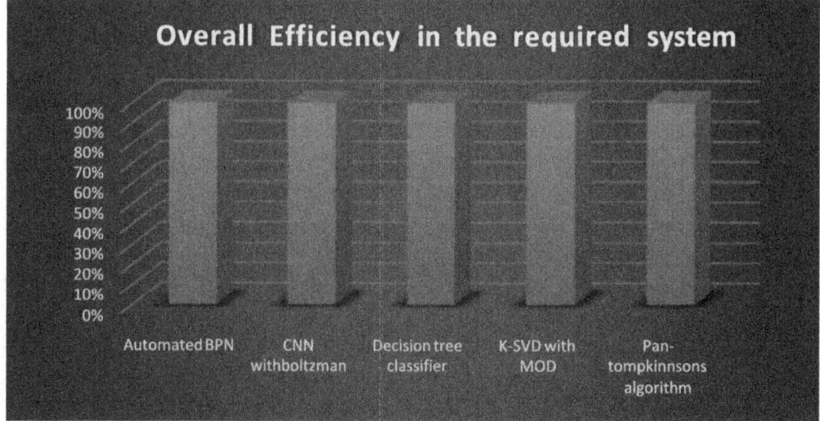


**FIG. 8** Efficiency analysis.

Fig. 8 shows the efficient analysis. The system thus developed provides optimized ambulatory, and ECG provides quick recovery from movement artifacts. It provides real-time heart function monitoring and verification of classified disease. The foregoing accuracy, specificity, and efficiency comparisons show that the automated BPN classifier used provides maximum efficiency based on all aspects. In considering the overall efficiency, the automated BPN classifier leads the other classifiers and has excellent domination over all other classifiers. Low-cost deployment is one acclaimed advantage of sensor networks. Limited processor bandwidth and small memory are two arguable constraints in sensor networks, which will disappear with the development of fabrication techniques. Depending upon the application, the densities of the WSN's may vary widely, ranging from very sparse to very dense. In these sensor nodes, the behavior is dynamic and highly adaptive, as the need to self-organize and conserve energy forces sensor nodes to adjust behavior constantly in response to their current level of activity. Sensor nodes will be deployed at a door field, such as a subway station. It is difficult for managers or operators to manage the network directly. Thus, the framework should provide an indirect, remote-controlled management system.

## 6 Conclusion

The proposed approach compares the existing systems and chooses the algorithm that gives better accuracy and efficiency. The emerging needs for immediate identification and treatment of diseases can be met with the proposed device and technology. Continuous monitoring of health can be carried out as the health data is sent to the cloud. This helps identify and detect sooner if the health condition goes low. The requirement of multispecialty hospitals at remote rural areas can be satisfied from hospitals and doctors living in an urban area with the proposed device. The sensors give good sensitivity of signal variations in the measured parameters, and the disease classifier AI technology enables the fast recognition of patient's medical issues, and quick response is given by doctor. If the patient needed to be treated at hospital, an ambulance can be sent to the patient's location using GPS. The cloud server in which all the measured data were stored and analyzed for diagnosis facilitates continuous monitoring of the patient's health condition. Thus, unnecessary serious conditions and death can be avoided.

## References

[1] P. Sardar, J.D. Abbott, A. Kundu, H.D. Aronow, J.F. Granada, J. Giri, Impact of artificial intelligence on interventional cardiology: from decision-making aid to advanced interventional procedure assistance, JACC Cardiovasc. Interv. 12 (14) (2019) 1293–1303. ISSN 1936-8798.

[2] M.M. El Khatib, G. Ahmed, Management of artificial intelligence enabled smart wearable devices for early diagnosis and continuous monitoring of CVDS, IJITEE 9 (1) (2019) 1211–1215.

[3] C. Krittanawong, K.W. Johnson, S.G. Hershman, W.H.W. Tang, Big data, artificial intelligence, and cardiovascular precision medicine, Expert Rev. Precis. Med. Drug Dev. 3 (5) (2018) 305–317.

[4] K.W. Johnson, J.T. Soto, B.S. Glicksberg, K. Shameer, R. Miotto, M. Ali, E. Ashley, J.T. Dudley, artificial intelligence in cardiology, JACC 71 (23) (2018) 2668–2679.

[5] S. Patel, H. Park, P. Bonato, et al., A review of wearable sensors and systems with application in rehabilitation, J. Neuroeng. Rehabil. 9 (2012) 21.

[6] D. Yadav, R.K. Garg, D. Chhabra, et al., Smart diagnostics devices through artificial intelligence and mechanobiological approaches, 3 Biotech 10 (2020) 351.

[7] S. Semaan, T.A. Dewland, G.H. Tison, G. Nah, E. Vittinghoff, M.J. Pletcher, J.E. Olgin, G.M. Marcus, Physical activity and atrial fibrillation: data from wearable fitness trackers, Heart Rhythm 17 (5 (Part B)) (2020) 842–846.

[8] A.K. Yetisen, J.L. Martinez-Hurtado, B. Ünal, A. Khademhosseini, H. Butt, Wearables in medicine, Adv. Mater. 30 (2018) 1706910.

[9] F. Lopez-Jimenez, Z. Attia, A.M. Arruda-Olson, R. Carter, Artificial intelligence in cardiology: present and future||, Mayo Clin. Proc. 95 (5) (2020) 1015–1039.

[10] E. Chen, J. Jiang, S. Rui, M. Gao, S. Zhu, J. Zhou, Y. Huo, A new smart wristband equipped with an artificial intelligence algorithm to detect atrial fibrillation, Heart Rhythm 17 (5 (Part B)) (2020) 847–853.

[11] C. Li, X. Hu, L. Zhang, The IoT-based heart disease monitoring system for pervasive healthcare service||, Proc. Comput. Sci. 112 (2017) 2328–2334.

[12] M.I.U. Zaman, S. Tabassum, M.S. Ullah, A. Rahaman, S. Nahar, A.K.M. Muzahidul Islam, Towards IoT and ML driven cardiac status prediction system, in: 2019 1st international conference on advances in science, engineering and robotics technology (ICASERT), Dhaka, Bangladesh, 2019, pp. 1–6, https://doi.org/10.1109/ICASERT.2019.8934639.

[13] A. Sološenko, A. Petrėnas, et al., Detection of atrial fibrillation using a wrist-worn device, Physiol. Meas. 40 (2019), 025003.

[14] J. Wang, J. Dong, Optical waveguides and integrated optical devices for medical diagnosis, health monitoring and light therapies, Sensors 20 (2020) 3981.

[15] S. Tuli, N. Basumatary, S.S. Gill, M. Kahani, R.C. Arya, G.S. Wander, R. Buyya, HealthFog: an ensemble deep learning based smart healthcare system for automatic diagnosis of heart diseases in integrated IoT and fog computing environments, Future Gener. Comp. Sys. 104 (2020) 187–200.
[16] D. Dias, J. Paulo Silva Cunha, Wearable health devices—vital sign monitoring, systems and technologies, Sensors 18 (2018) 2414.
[17] M. Jamshidi, A. Lalbakhsh, J. Talla, Z. Peroutka, F. Hadjilooei, P. Lalbakhsh, M. Jamshidi, L. La Spada, M. Mirmozafari, M. Dehghani, A. Sabet, Artificial intelligence and COVID-19: deep learning approaches for diagnosis and treatment, IEEE Access 8 (2020) 109581–109595.

Chapter 15

# Deep learning for accident avoidance in a hostile driving environment

**S. Selva Nidhyananthan, R. Newlin Shebiah, B. Vijaya Kumari, and K. Gopalakrishnan**

*Department of Electronics and Communication Engineering, Mepco Schlenk Engineering College, Sivakasi, Tamilnadu, India*

## 1 Introduction

Every day, more people die because of accidents due to road traffic. Much care must be taken to avoid such accidental death in crowded states like Bengaluru, Mumbai, Delhi, Pune, and Chennai. It is not a problem only for India but for the whole world. The main reason for this is lack of information regarding the vehicles and the obstacles on the road at a distant view. As a human, it is quite a hard task to handle. But, machines can handle it much better with efficient algorithms. Few of the existing solutions for the accident avoidance include: alarming the driver about the hindrances on the roadway; an obstacle-avoiding navigation system; a laser radar system for obstacle avoidance; and a sonar sensor-based system and spherical robots for accident avoidance. Though such methods are available, the vision-based intelligent vehicle control emerged during 1990s all over the world. Thanks to the advanced technology, today's high-end cars are equipped with an antilock braking system (ABS), electronic brakeforce distribution (EBD), supplemental restraint system air bags, immobilizer, parking sensors, and cruise control. These help avoid accidents to some extent. An Internet of Things-based (IoT-based) accident tracking and alerting system is also available in the literature. But, it needs to extract features and descriptors from the input images to implement the algorithm. It takes considerable time, and its computational complexity is comparatively higher.

Thus, the proposed approach overcomes these problems by using the more recent deep neural networks for segmentation, detection, and recognition of vehicles on the road.

**Cognitive Systems and Signal Processing in Image Processing. https://doi.org/10.1016/B978-0-12-824410-4.00002-7**

## 2 Literature review

For image recognition, many different approaches were introduced by the researchers over a long period. This chapter involves hostile driving environment database development, semantic segmentation of the images in the database, object detection in the segmented image, and object recognition so as to recognize the object present in the hostile environment scene so that brutal accidents can be avoided. The goal of computer vision is to understand the image with the objects present in it, its relation with other objects, and its properties [1]. In the literature, there are several methods based on graphical models [2], convolutional approaches [3], cascaded classifiers [4], and edge detection-based methods [5]. Exploiting depth information in the image also showed proven efficiency improvement for segmentation [6]. Recently, outstanding achievements were made in salient detection and semantic segmentation due to the deployment of deep neural networks (DNNs) [7–10]. With the popularity of deep learning [11, 12], semantic segmentation has achieved high accuracy and efficiency compared with the other conventional approaches. Semantic segmentation can be categorized into three heads: (1) region-based; (2) fully convolutional neural network-based (CNN-based) [13]; and (3) weekly supervised segmentation [14]. Recent developments in neural networks [15–19] led to a variety of deep learning architectures. Several deep network structures, such as GoogleNet [20], AlexNet [21], ZF Net [22], VGG Net [23], and ResNet [24], have been extensively incorporated to improve the performance. Region-based CNN (R-CNN) is unique in refining the closeness of candidate-bounding boxes to the region of interest [25] and to extract high-level deep features through deep neural architecture. SPP-net follows almost the same feature extraction, network tuning, classifier training, and bounding box fitting the same as R-CNN, therefore extraneous storage space is still required [26]. To overcome this, one study [27] introduced a novel CNN architecture called Fast R-CNN.

The ImageNet dataset [28] has been created with more than 14 million images with 20,000 categories. The pattern analysis, statistical modeling and computational learning visual object classes (PASCAL-VOC) is another standard dataset for objects [29]. The CIFAR-10 set and CIFAR-100 [30] set are derived from the Tiny Image Dataset, with the images being labeled more accurately. The STL-10 dataset [31] is derived from the ImageNet. SVHN (Street View House Number) [32] is a real-world image dataset consisting of numbers on natural scenes, more suited for machine learning and object recognition. NORB [33] database is envisioned for experiments in three-dimensional (3D) object recognition from shape. The 20 Newsgroup [34] dataset, as the name suggests, contains information about newsgroups. WordNet's structure [35] makes it a very useful tool for NLP. The Blog Authorship Corpus [36] dataset consists of blog posts collected from thousands of bloggers and was been gathered from blogger.com in August 2004. The Free Spoken Digit Dataset (FSDD) [37] is another dataset consisting of recording of spoken digits in. wav files.

AlexNet [38] is the first deep architecture introduced by Geoffrey Hinton and his colleagues. The VGG network [39] was introduced by the researchers at Visual Graphics Group at Oxford. GoogleNet [40] is a class of architecture designed by researchers at Google. ResNet (Residual Networks) [41] is one of the giant architectures that truly define how deep a deep learning architecture can be. ResNeXt [42] is said to be the current state-of-the-art technique for object recognition. R-CNN architecture [43] is said to be the most powerful of all the deep learning architectures that have been applied to the object detection problem. YOLO [44] is another state-of-the-art real-time system built on deep learning for solving image detection problems. The squeezeNet [45] architecture is another powerful architecture and is extremely useful in low bandwidth scenarios like mobile platforms. SegNet [46] is a deep learning architecture applied to solve image segmentation problem. GAN [47] is an entirely different breed of neural network architectures, in which a neural network is used to generate an entirely new image that is not present in the training dataset but is realistic enough to be in the dataset.

## 3 Research challenges and motivation

Accident avoidance in a hostile driving environment is a challenging task, and helping this through machine learning is still more challenging. In artificial intelligence, object recognition and detection still remains a major challenging task. It has been proved that neural network algorithms are better suited for object detection for the following reasons: neural networks are data-driven, self-adaptive algorithms; they require no prior knowledge of the data or underlying properties; they can approximate any function with arbitrary accuracy; and they can estimate the posterior probabilities, which provide the basis for establishing classification rule and performing statistical analysis. Though a number of effective solutions to intelligent transportation system problems have been proposed in past research, there are some shortcomings in the form of extracting best features, divergence, local minima, cost, computational complexity, and more. To overcome the limitations, our proposed method incorporates novelty contributions in deep learning architectures, such as usage mini-batch size faster computations, piecewise reduction of learning rate, optimally setting for convergence, and working with a database containing multichallenging image data.

## 4 Semantic segmentation

Semantic segmentation is one of the high-level tasks in computer vision that overlays the way for ample scene understanding. With the blessing of God, humans can easily understand the meaning of the image and locate the objects

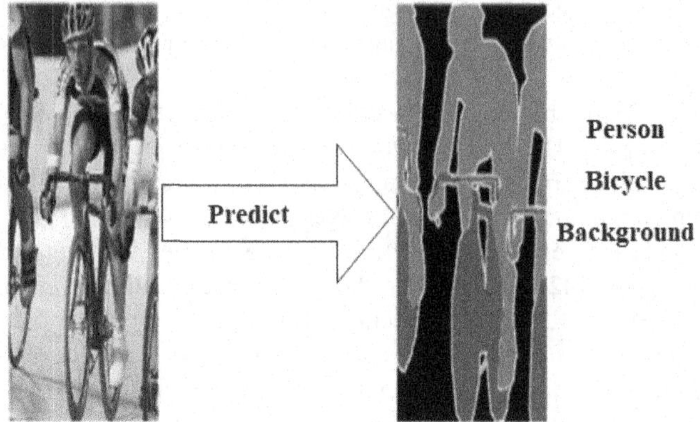


**FIG. 1** An example of semantic segmentation, where the goal is to predict class labels.

by just noticing the high-level semantic information, like geometry, shape, size, color, dimension, and so forth. Generally, semantic segmentation involves three steps: classification, localization/detection, and semantic segmentation. The classification stage provides the prediction about the whole object at first. In the second step, in addition to classes, some additional information like spatial location will be observed. In the third step, semantic segmentation is done by labeling pixels with reference to the enclosing pixels or region. In Fig. 1, the input image has three different classes, and each class is separated and labeled by using the semantic segmentation process.

## 5 Segmentation using deep learning architecture

A naïve approach toward constructing a neural network architecture for the segmentation task is simply to stack a number of convolutional layers (with same padding to preserve dimensions) and output a final segmentation map. This directly learns a mapping from the input image to its corresponding segmentation through the successive transformation of feature mappings; however, it is quite computationally expensive to preserve the full resolution throughout the network (Fig. 2).

For deep convolutional networks, earlier layers tend to learn low-level concepts while later layers develop more high-level (and specialized) feature mappings. In order to maintain expressiveness, we typically need to increase the number of feature maps (channels) as we get deeper in the network.

This did not necessarily pose a problem for the task of image classification, because for that task we only care about what the image contains (and not where it is located). Thus, we could alleviate computational burden by periodically downsampling our feature maps through pooling or strided convolutions

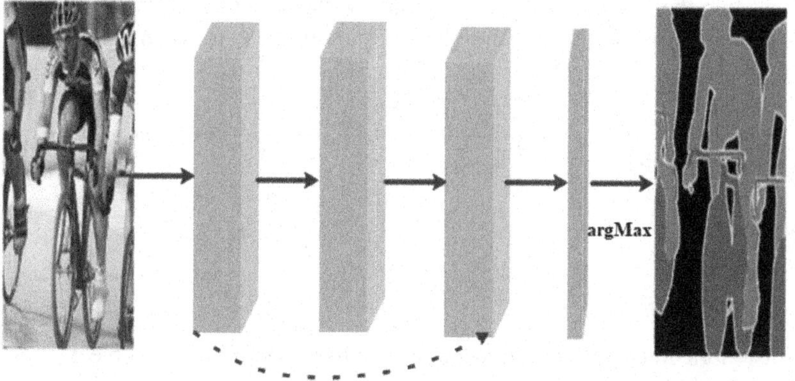


**FIG. 2** Deep architecture for semantic segmentation.

(i.e., compressing the spatial resolution) without concern. However, for image segmentation, we would like our model to produce a full-resolution semantic prediction.

One popular approach for an image segmentation model is to follow an encoder/decoder structure where we downsample the spatial resolution of the input, developing lower-resolution feature mappings that are learned to be highly efficient at discriminating between classes, and upsample the feature representations into a full-resolution segmentation map. Transpose convolutions are by far the most popular approach, as they allow for us to develop a learned upsampling. Whereas a typical convolution operation will take the dot product of the values currently in the filter's view and produce a single value for the corresponding output position, a transpose convolution essentially does the opposite. Convolution operation can be mathematically represented for a color image as:

$$I(x,y) * K(x,y) = \sum_{i=1}^{r}\sum_{j=1}^{c}\sum_{k=1}^{nc} K_{i,j,k} I_{x+i-1,y+j-1,k} \tag{1}$$

where $r$ and $c$ represents row and column respectively and $nc$ denotes number of channels for a color image, it is 3. The dimension of the resultant after convolution process can be obtained as:

$$\dim(I(x,y) * K(x,y)) = \begin{cases} \left\lfloor \frac{r+2p-f}{s} + 1 \right\rfloor, \left\lfloor \frac{c+2p-f}{s} + 1 \right\rfloor; \; s>0 \\ (r+2p-f, c+2p-f); \; s=0 \end{cases} \tag{2}$$

Here $p$ shows padding value and $s$ indicates striding value. For a transpose convolution, we take a single value from the low-resolution feature map and multiply all of the weights in our filter by this value, projecting those weighted values into the output feature map. Similarly, the dimensionality of the image after pooling operation can be predicted by using the expression:

$$\dim(pooling(I(x,y))) = \begin{cases} \left\lfloor \frac{r+2p-f}{s} + 1 \right\rfloor, \left\lfloor \frac{c+2p-f}{s} + 1 \right\rfloor, nc; \ s > 0 \\ (r+2p-f, c+2p-f), nc; \ s = 0 \end{cases} \tag{3}$$

## 6 Detection

Decision-theoretic and structural are the two basic approaches for object recognition. Based on quantitative representation and description of regions with vectors, objects are recognized in a decision-theoretic approach, whereas in a structural approach, it is based on a qualitative description using strings and trees. The proper arrangement of descriptors form a pattern of the object to be detected. An object class is constituted by set of patterns that have some common characteristics among them. Object classes are denoted as $O_1$, $O_2$, ..., $O_N$ where $N$ is the number of classes.

To gain knowledge on image understanding, it is necessary to classify different images and accurately estimate the location and size of objects contained in each image. This task is generally called object detection, which commonly consists of subtasks such as scene detection, object of interest detection, and skeleton detection. Object recognition by visual inspection is simple when the number of object classes is small, when the number of classes is more, and when each class has a greater number of images; it is advisable to use automation with algorithms for mapping patterns to their corresponding classes. The elements of the pattern vector depend on how the region of the image is described. The pattern vector would be a one-dimensional (1D) signal if the objects of the image are represented by its signature. In pattern representation, tree structuring results from tiered collation. In pattern matching, a query pattern is mapped to a class that has a similar pattern of objects. The quantitative measure to check the closeness of a query pattern with the predetermined pattern is the Euclidean distance measure. Other basic matching methods are correlation, statistical classifier, and Bayes classifier. Nonlinear classifiers with neural networks connect the processing elements in the same fashion as how neurons are connected in the brain. Perceptron was the starting network for two class classifications.

Perceptron is followed by multilayer feedforward neural networks, backpropagation networks, and self-organizing maps. Photos of road scenes are usually complex and contain multiple objects, including trees. Assigning a label with image classification models for text-based annotation and search can become tricky and uncertain. Object detection models are therefore suitable to identify objects of interest in an image. Compared to image classification, in object detection models, localization of the objects is obtained.

Usage of deep learning to object detection has kindled much research attention recently. Conventional object detection methods are built using derived features and trained architectures. Their performance easily stagnates when images have a large number of complex objects that need to be detected with a combination of low-level and high-level features. With the swift progress in CNN architectures, deeper features are introduced to address the shortcomings existing in conventional approaches. Different models behave differently in network architecture. Our focus is on typical generic object detection architectures, and we also briefly cover tasks, including salient object detection and vehicle detection. Experimental analyses are also presented to compare various methods and arrive at some useful conclusions. Inheriting from neural networks and artificial intelligence, the progress in these fields develops deeper neural network algorithms and will also have great impacts on object detection techniques.

Object detection is to determine where objects of interest are located in a given image and in which class each object belongs to. Put simply, the tasks involved in object detection are: (1) interest region selection, (2) representative feature extraction, and (3) object classification. Usually, binary naïve Bayes classifier, supported vector machine, AdaBoost and deformable part-based model are examples for object classifiers. Owing to the emergence of DNNs and with the introduction of R-CNN, a promising gain is obtained. DNNs have deeper architectures with the capacity to acquire more complex features than the surface ones.

## 6.1 Evolution of deep models for object detection

The history of neural networks started eight decades back, and the original idea was to mimic the human brain to solve complex problems. This field was picked up with the introduction of backpropagation algorithms. However, due to lack of accurate weight updation, learning parameter determination, bias setting, possibility of settling in local minima, and slow convergence compared with other machine vision mechanisms, neural networks went almost unnoticed in 2001. Deep learning has become popular since 2006 with an advancement in speech recognition, but the only limitation with deep learning is that to run the deep learning algorithms machines must have high-end GPU processor support. Training of DNN architectures becomes very efficient with the batch normalization (BN) technique.

## 6.2 Region-based network framework

The region-based framework at first matches the focus mechanism of the human brain by giving a coarse scan of the full image and then a fine focus on the region of interest. The R-CNN adopts a selective search method, which relies on bottom-up grouping and saliency points to provide better candidate boxes of random sizes swiftly and to reduce the search space in object detection. The scored regions are attuned with bounding box and filtered to produce final bounding boxes for conserved object locations. ResNet has a very deep network with around 150 layers by learning the residual representation of signal instead of signal representation learning. ResNet has a connection called shortcut connection to fit the input to the next layer from the previous layer without any alteration of the input. Even if there is a vanishing gradient at weight layers, we can still have the identity input x to transfer back to earlier layers. Skip connection in ResNet enables more accurate detection, localization, and classification tasks. To solve the vanishing problem, a shortcut connection is added to add the input x to the output after a few weight layers, as shown. Extreme deep ResNets are easy to construct and optimize, but the plain nets show higher training error for increased depth (Fig. 3).

Object detection is a regression and association task. First, to fine-tune the spatial precision, bounding box object candidates with an Intersection over Union (IoU) lesser than some threshold are discarded. Then, we use the IoU area whose value lies between 0 and 1. It corresponds the area of overlap to the area of union. It is also known as the Jaccard index. The higher the IoU, the better the predicted location of the object. It is obtained as:

$$IoU = \frac{Area\ of\ overlap}{Area\ of\ Union} \tag{4}$$

Usually, in binary classification, the precision-recall curve is obtained in terms of the average precision (AP) metric. The most generically used measure for object detection is the mean AP (mAP). It is simply the mean of the AP measured over all the classes. Precision can be calculated by:

$$precision = \frac{TP}{TP + FP} \tag{5}$$

where, TP is True Positive and FP is False Positive. The mAP is calculated as:

$$mAP = \frac{\sum_{i=1}^{T} AP(i)}{T} \tag{6}$$

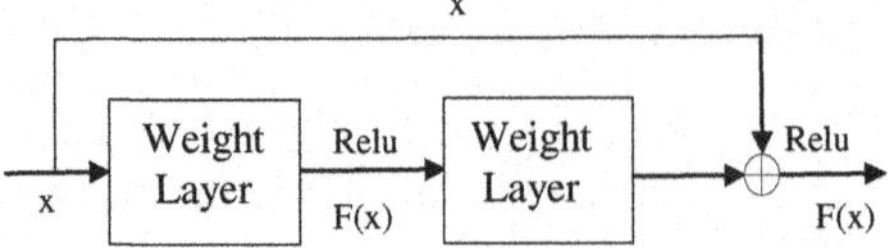


**FIG. 3** Residual network.

## 7 Object recognition

The key to get better at deep learning is practice on a variety of problems with different input data. Testing any newly arrived algorithms requires data. The major hurdles in deep learning at the start were the limited availability of labeled datasets. All the proprietary datasets are usually not released to the general public. Now, the datasets have been created by various research communities and made available for the public. The datasets can be divided into three categories: (1) image processing, (2) natural language processing, and (3) audio/speech processing. The most commonly used image processing datasets are: ImageNet, PASCAL-VOC, COCO, CIFAR-10 and CIFAR-100, STL-10, SVHN, MNIST, and NORB.

Even though numerous solutions to the accident avoidance in a hostile driving environment problem have been proposed in past research, our proposed algorithm adds academic value to this field by incorporating novelty contributions, such as using a mini-batch size of 8 to reduce memory usage while training instead to use batch and stochastic. Too large of a batch size will lead to poor generalization. When using the mini-batch, parameters are updated frequently and vectored implementation is used for faster computations piecewise, thereby reducing the learning rate by a factor of 0.3 every 10 epochs. This allows the network to achieve a higher learning rate while being able to find a solution quickly close to the local optimum, optimally set the validation patience to 4 to stop training early when the validation accuracy converges, and (iv) use the algorithm to validate its effectiveness for database containing multichallenging image data. Hence this study is so important to the field of accident avoidance problems.

## 8 Image processing dataset

The ImageNet dataset is one of the most popular datasets in deep learning research. This dataset is applicable for research works carried out in image classification, segmentation, and detection. In computer vision research, this dataset with more details has become the "standard" dataset for deep learning applications.

The PASCAL-VOC dataset contains 20 different classes. For testing network programs, this dataset is more suited than ImageNet because of its smaller size. COCO (Common Objects in Context) [48] is a new image recognition, segmentation, and captioning dataset, sponsored by Microsoft. This dataset has more than 3,28,000 images with 91 object groups. For semantic segmentation, this dataset is being used as a standard one as it has challenging images. The CIFAR-10 set has 10 different object classes with 6000 images each of these classes and comprises 60,000 images in total, and the CIFAR-100 set has 100 classes with 600 images for each class with resolution of $32 \times 32$.

The STL-10 dataset consists of both labeled and unlabeled images. It has 500 training images and 800 testing images for 10 classes, such as airplane, bird, car, cat, deer, dog, horse, monkey, ship, and truck.

SVHN dataset consists of more than 600,000 digital images. SVHN is obtained from house numbers in Google Street View images. The image resolution is 32 × 32. The MNIST database [49] of handwritten digits is a good database for learning techniques and pattern recognition methods on real-world data with minimal preprocessing. The training set has 60,000 samples and a test set of 10,000 samples. The digits have been size-normalized and centered in a fixed-size image of resolution 28 × 28.

NORB database contains images of 50 toys belonging to 5 generic categories: four-legged animals, human figures, airplanes, trucks, and cars. The objects were imaged by two cameras under 6 lighting conditions, 9 elevations (30–70 degrees), and 18 azimuths (0–340). The total number of image pairs is 50.

## 9 Natural language processing dataset

Twenty Newsgroup dataset is a collection of newsgroup documents and has become a popular dataset for experiments in text applications of machine learning techniques, such as text classification and text clustering. WordNet is a large database of English synsets. Nouns, verbs, adjectives, and adverbs are grouped into sets of cognitive synonyms, each expressing a distinct concept called synset. In Blog Authorship Corpus, each blog is provided as a separate file. Each blog contains a minimum of 200 occurrences of commonly used English words.

## 10 Audio/speech processing dataset

FSDD is an open dataset, so the hope is that it will keep growing as people keep contributing more samples. Free Music Archive is a dataset for music analysis. The dataset consists of full-length and HQ audio, precomputed features, and user-level metadata. It is an open dataset created for evaluating several tasks in MIR [50].

## 11 Deep learning architectures

To explore the tasks of computer vision, some advanced architectures are available for deep learning. The most important architectures and their descriptions are given here:

AlexNet is a simple and powerful network architecture, which is acting as cutting edge research in deep learning. AlexNet is a collection of simple three-layered architecture of a convolution layer with pooling and fully connected layers on the top. The significant points of this net are scaling and the usage of GPU. The training speed of CPU is 10 times less than the GPU. This is the secret behind this net.

The VGG network is of pyramidal shape. The layers at the bottom are wider and closer to the image, and the layers at the top are narrow and look like a pyramid. As per the image, VGG contains subsequent convolutional layers followed by pooling layers. The pooling layers are responsible for making the layers narrower.

GoogleNet was the winner of ImageNet 2014, where it proved to be a powerful model. In this architecture, during training, the feature extractors can be changed between the layers, and hence performance of this net is improved. It is the added feature of this net. This indirectly helps the network perform better.

ResNet consists of multiple subsequent residual modules, which are the basic building block of ResNet architecture. In simple words, a residual module has two options, either it can perform a set of functions on the input or it can skip this step altogether. Now similar to GoogleNet, these residual modules are stacked one over the other to form a complete end-to-end network. ResNeXt is a modified version of ResNet with the application of the concept of inception.

R-CNNs make use of the bounding box concept for identifying and then detecting the same. YOLO first divides the image into defined bounding boxes and then runs a recognition algorithm in parallel for all of these boxes to identify which object class they belong to. After identifying this class, it goes on to merging these boxes intelligently to form an optimal bounding box around the objects. All of this is done in parallel, so it can run in real time.

The squeezeNet architecture occupies only 4.9 MB of space, on the other hand, inception occupies approximately 100 MB. This drastic difference is brought up by a specialized structure called the fire module. SegNet consists of sequence of processing layers (encoders) followed by a corresponding set of decoders for a pixelwise classification. One key feature of SegNet is that it retains high frequency details in a segmented image as the pooling indices of encoder network is connected to pooling indices of decoder networks.

In this work, ResNet has been chosen to perform vehicle recognition, as it has an identity shortcut connection that skips one or more layers, which is computationally efficient.

## 12 Results and discussion

The chapter's argument is built on an appropriate base of theory, concepts, and ideas pertained to semantic segmentation, detection, recognition, and deep learning in the application of accident avoidance in a hostile driving environment using deep learning. The research is embodied with intellectual work on accident avoidance mechanisms and is well designed with the flow of sematic segmentation, detection, and recognition of the road scene image. The methods employed to accomplish accident avoidance in a hostile driving environment are appropriate, as advanced deep learning architectures are used with customized parameters to quickly recognize the road scene ahead to locate vehicles and pedestrians even in foggy, dull, and cluttered environments in order to ensure safe travel.

The database [51] addresses the need for experimental data to quantitatively evaluate emerging algorithms along with challenging conditions in recognition. Since this database data was captured from the perspective of a driving automobile, it is well-suited for experimenting with accident avoidance using advanced techniques. The vehicle driving scenario increases the heterogeneity of the observed object classes, which impose a good challenge for the technique undertaken. The images in the database have shadows (example: seq16E5_30 Hz), fog (example: seq01TP_30 Hz), and low contrast (example: seq16E5_15 Hz) captured at different times of the day, which all put constraints on the effectiveness of the algorithm used in detection and recognition.

The proposed algorithm is implemented with ResNet-101 architecture with Cambridge-driving Labeled Video Database (CamVid), ImageNet, and vehicle datasets. The performance of semantic segmentation using deep learning was evaluated on the CamVid [51], which is a collection of frames with 32 class semantic labels. Here, the original 32 classes are grouped into 11 classes: sky, building, pole, road, pavement, tree, sign symbol, fence, car, pedestrian and bicyclist. Then, vehicle detection has also been tested with the same dataset. For vehicle recognition, vehicle and ImageNet datasets were used for evaluation.

## 13 Semantic segmentation using deep learning

Some of the sample frames from the CamVid database and their corresponding ground truth images are shown in Fig. 4.

Semantic segmentation is implemented utilizing DeepLab v3+. DeepLab V3 uses ImageNet's pretrained ResNet-101 with atrous convolutions as its main feature extractor. The learning rate uses a piecewise schedule. The learning rate is reduced by a factor of 0.3 every 10 epochs. This allows the network to learn quickly with a higher initial learning rate while being able to find a solution close to the local optimum once the learning rate drops. The network is tested against the validation data for every epoch by setting the validation data parameter.

The validation patience is set to 4 to stop training early when the validation accuracy converges. This prevents the network from overfitting on the training dataset. A mini-batch size of 8 is used to reduce memory usage while training. Fig. 4 shows the input image, its corresponding ground truth, pixel visualization, and segmented output. The amount of overlap per class can be measured using the IoU metric (Table 1) (Fig. 5).

FIG. 4 Frames from CamVid database and their corresponding ground truth images.

TABLE 1 Image classes and their IoUs.

| Sl.No | Classes | IoU | Sl.No | Classes | IoU |
|---|---|---|---|---|---|
| 1 | Sky | 0.88745 | 7 | Sign Symbol | 0.55693 |
| 2 | Building | 0.71676 | 8 | Fence | 0 |
| 3 | Pole | 0.18163 | 9 | Car | 0.74902 |
| 4 | Road | 0.94817 | 10 | Pedestrian | 0.63721 |
| 5 | Pavement | 0.73218 | 11 | Bicyclist | 0 |
| 6 | Tree | 0.37543 | | | |

## 14 Vehicle detection using deep learning

Vehicle detection using deep learning is carried out with R-CNNs and fuses the bounding box characteristics with CNN features. Detection using R-CNN is a twofold approach where the liable region that contains the potential object is identified, and as the second stage, the detected object region is classified. Here, the feature extraction network is typically a pretrained ResNet-101 architecture. The first subnetwork is a region proposal network trained to classify objects from the background, and the second subnetwork is trained to classify the detected objects alone (car, pedestrian, etc.).

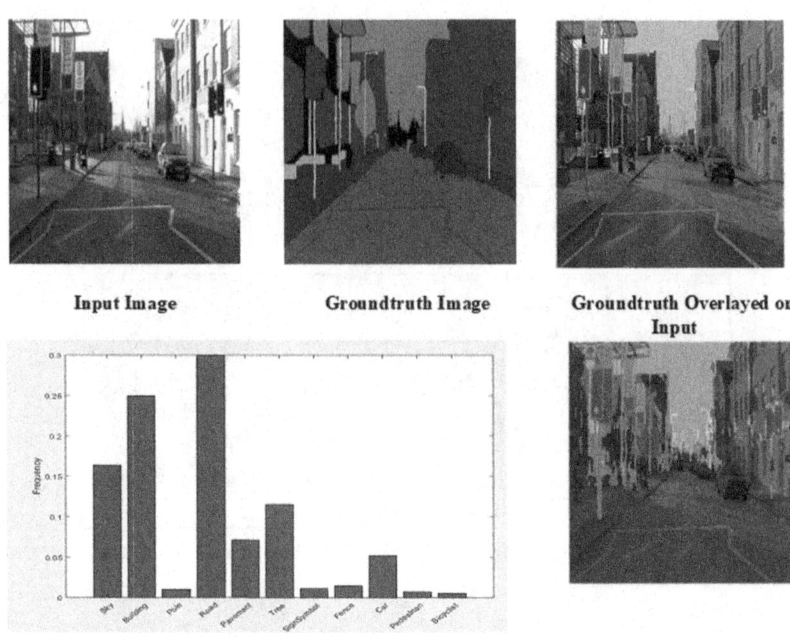


Visualization of pixel count by class

Segmented Output

**FIG. 5** Images for stages from input image to segmented image.

**FIG. 6** Input and output images of vehicle segmentation.

For training, mini-batch size property is set to 1 to effectively detect vehicles of varying size. If the object that needs to be detected is of the same size, then the mini-batch size can be greater than 1. Fig. 6. shows the test images and the corresponding detected output.

## 15 Vehicle recognition using deep learning

Vehicle recognition has attracted the attention of people in recent years. In the literature, vehicle recognition based on Harris cornermethod, Gabor transform with cascade classifier, LBP features, Fast Haar features, and polygon Haar features, among others, already existed. Currently, with the development of deep CNN (DCNN) and deep belief network (DBN), the previously mentioned deep networks were invented and showed better performance for vehicle recognition. CNN is an end-to-end system, in which the input is a raw image, while the output is a prediction through the distinctive features extracted via intermediate layers.

The dataset for vehicle classification (Fig. 7) consists of four classes of vehicles: (1) truck; (2) two-wheeler (bicycle and motorcycle) (3) bus and car; and

FIG. 7 Sample images for vehicle recognition.

(4) pickup truck with 6131 images under each category. In this example, images from a vehicle dataset [52] are classified into categories using a multiclass linear support vector machine (SVM) trained with CNN features extracted from the images.

The detailed description of AlexNet architecture used for vehicle classification is explained as follows:

The AlexNet network operates with three-channel images of size $224 \times 224 \times 3$ with max pooling and ReLU activations when subsampling. The filters used for convolutions are either $11 \times 11$) $5 \times 5$, or $3 \times 3$. The first layer of AlexNet was a convolutional layer that accepts a $224 \times 224 \times 3$ image tensor as its input, performs convolution operation using 96 $11 \times 11$ images, and produces output tensor of $55 \times 55 \times 96$. The second layer was a max pooling layer that accepts output from the first layer and performs a zero-padded subsampling operation using a $3 \times 3$ kernel with a stride of two and produces a $27 \times 27 \times 96$ output tensor. The third layer of AlexNet was another convolutional layer that accepted output from the layer S2, a $27 \times 27 \times 96$ tensor, as its input. It performed a convolution operation using 256 $5 \times 5$ kernels with a stride of one, and a padding of two. This operation produced a $27 \times 27 \times 256$ output tensor that was then passed through a ReLU activation function and then on to the next layer. The fourth layer is a max pooling layer accepts input of size $27 \times 27 \times 256$ that produced output tensor of $13 \times 13 \times 256$.

The fifth layer of AlexNet was another convolutional layer that accepts a $13 \times 13 \times 256$ tensor and produced a $13 \times 13 \times 384$ output tensor. The sixth layer of AlexNet was another convolutional layer that accepted output from the layer C5, a $13 \times 13 \times 384$ tensor, as its input. It performed the same convolution operation as layer C5, which led to the same output size. The seventh layer of AlexNet was another convolutional layer that accepts a $13 \times 13 \times 384$ tensor from the layer C6 as its input. It performed a convolution operation using 256 $3 \times 3$ kernels with a stride and padding of 1. This produced a $13 \times 13 \times 256$ output tensor. The eighth layer of AlexNet was a max pooling layer that accepted a $13 \times 13 \times 256$ tensor from the C7 layer as its input. It performed a zero-padded subsampling operation using a $3 \times 3$ window region with a stride of two, similar to layer S2 and S4. This produced a $6 \times 6 \times 256$ output tensor that was then passed through a ReLU activation function and then on to the next layer. The ninth layer of AlexNet was a fully connected layer that accepted a flattened $6 \times 6 \times 256$ tensor from the S8 layer as its input. It performed a weighted sum operation with an added bias term. This produced a $4096 \times 1$ output tensor that was then passed through a ReLU activation function and on to the next layer. The tenth layer of AlexNet was another fully connected layer that accepted a $4096 \times 1$ tensor from the F9 layer as its input. The eleventh and final layer of the network was also a fully connected layer that accepted a $4096 \times 1$ tensor from the F10 layer as its input. It performed the same operation as layer F9, and F10 and produced a $1000 \times 1$ output tensor that was then passed through a softmax activation function. The layer contained 4,097,000 trainable parameters, which totaled 62,378,344 trainable parameters overall. The output of the softmax activation function contained the predictions of the network.

In transfer learning, the last three layers of the pretrained network net are configured for 1000 classes. These three layers must be fine-tuned for the new classification problem. Extract all layers, except the last three, from the pretrained network. Transfer the layers to the new classification task by replacing the last three layers with a fully connected layer, a softmax layer, and a classification output layer. Specify the options of the new fully connected layer according to the new data. Set the fully connected layer to have the same size as the number of classes in the new data.

The final layer is the classification layer, and its properties depend on the classification task. The higher level features are better suited for recognition tasks because they combine all the primitive features into a richer image representation.

Table 2 shows the confusion matrix with the features extracted from AlexNet and classified using SVM.

Table 3 shows the confusion matrix from a tailored architecture with convolution, max pooling, and activation layers.

ResNet helps to avoid vanishing gradient problem to some extent. Not only that, it also encourages feature reuse, making the network highly parameter-efficient. ResNet architecture has repetitive short networks. So, the results obtained are not affected even while leaving out some of the layers. The recognition results from Tables 2–3 describe that the accuracy obtained is 92.1%, which does not change the test, and training ratios are changed. And the results obtained are comparable with SVMs, which is a machine learning approach. It is much higher than KNN classifier. As deep learning deals with huge data, accuracy seems to improve more than in the existing techniques. Though it takes a long time for training, in the test phase, it is comparatively quicker with good results. It is also observed that the accuracy obtained is slightly less while experimented with road images containing multiple vehicles.

This chapter demonstrates an adequate understanding of relevant literature in the fields of deep learning, object recognition, and intelligent transportation systems and cites an appropriate range of literature sources from the year 1986, to cover the fundamentals, to 2021 to incorporate emerging techniques in the research field. It seems that a few related works are included in the chapter. More recently published papers are discussed in the introduction section and also compared to the proposed method.

Due to the lack of a public database, limited research has been identified on this topic. Since most studies were based on private datasets that cannot be accessed, their results are somewhat incomparable. However, we still listed the results here. Yun [53] achieved a detection rate of 89% for crash detection. RTADS [54] reported a detection rate of 92%. Singh [55] reported a detection

**TABLE 2** Confusion matrix of vehicle classification using transfer learning.

| | Trucks | Two Wheelers | Bus | Car |
|---|---|---|---|---|
| **Trucks** | **99.78** | 0.11 | 0.00 | 0.11 |
| **Two Wheelers** | 0.78 | **98.45** | 0.00 | 0.78 |
| **Bus** | 0.99 | 0.66 | **93.15** | 5.19 |
| **Car** | 0.42 | 0.53 | 4.24 | **94.81** |
| **Average Accuracy = 96.54%** | | | | |

**TABLE 3** Confusion matrix of vehicle classification with a tailored convolutional neural network.

| | Trucks | Two Wheelers | Bus | Car |
|---|---|---|---|---|
| **Trucks** | **91.20** | 1.34 | 4.22 | 3.24 |
| **Two Wheelers** | 1.10 | **96.03** | 0.49 | 2.38 |
| **Bus** | 3.18 | 0.24 | **95.66** | 0.92 |
| **Car** | 6.11 | 5.25 | 3.12 | **85.52** |
| **Average Accuracy = 92.10%** | | | | |

rate of 77.5%. Chen Wang [56] reported a detection rate of 92.5%. JongBae Kim [57] reported a detection rate of 86.82%. Comparatively, our proposed method is simple and gives better results.

## 16 Conclusion and future work

With the advent of DNNs, an algorithm has been developed to avoid accidents in hostile driving environments. The performance of the task of object detection and recognition has been elevated with DNN. Deep learning for object detection and recognition involves semantic segmentation, detection, and recognition. In this work, vehicles are segmented in Cambridge-driving Labeled Video Database images. Semantic segmentation is implemented utilizing DeepLab v3+, which uses ImageNet's pretrained ResNet-101 with atrous convolutions as its main feature extractor. Vehicle detection using deep learning is carried out with R-CNNs. In vehicle recognition, images from a vehicle dataset are classified into categories using a multiclass linear SVM trained with CNN features extracted from the images and obtained an average accuracy of 92.10%, which is higher compared to classification using conventional methods. In future, the accuracy can further be improved by using VGG-16 Net, which may yield higher accuracy with minimal storage and faster computations.

## References


[1] C. Lawrence Zitnick, R. Vedantam, D. Parikh, Adopting abstract images for semantic scene understanding, IEEE Trans. Pattern Anal. Mach. Intell. 38 (4) (2016).

[2] J. Tighe, S. Lazebnik, Superparsing, Int. J. Comput. Vision 101 (2) (2013) 329–349.

[3] Y. LeCun, L. Bottou, Y. Bengio, P. Haffner, Gradient-based learning applied to document recognition, in: Intelligent Signal Processing, IEEE Press, Piscataway, NJ, USA, 2001, pp. 306–351.

[4] M. Fink, P. Perona, Mutual boosting for contextual inference, Proc. Adv. Neural Inf. Process. Syst. (2004) 9–16.

[5] J. Canny, A computational approach to edge detection, IEEE Trans. Pattern Anal. Mach. Intell. PAMI-8 (6) (1986) 679–698.

[6] Y. Cao, C. Shen, H.T. Shen, Exploiting depth from single monocular images for object detection and semantic segmentation, IEEE Trans. Image Process. 26 (2) (2017).

[7] Q. Hou, et al., Deeply supervised salient object detection with short connections, Proc. IEEE Int. Conf. Comput. Vis. Pattern Recognit. (2017) 5300–5309.

[8] P. Hu, B. Shuai, J. Liu, G. Wang, Deep level sets for salient object detection, Proc. IEEE Int. Conf. Comput. Vis. Pattern Recognit. (2017) 540–549.

[9] J. Kuen, Z. Wang, G. Wang, Recurrent attentional networks for saliency detection, Proc. IEEE Int. Conf. Comput. Vis. Pattern Recognit. (2016) 3668–3677.

[10] G. Lee, Y.-W. Tai, J. Kim, Deep saliency with encoded low level distance map and high level features, Proc. IEEE Int. Conf. Comput. Vis. Pattern Recognit. (2016) 660–668.

[11] L.-C. Chen, G. Papandreou, I. Kokkinos, K. Murphy, A.L. Yuille, Semantic image segmentation with deep convolutional nets and fully connected CRFs, arXiv 1412 (2014) 7062.

[12] J. Dai, K. He, J. Sun, Convolutional feature masking for joint object and stuff segmentation, Proc. IEEE Int. Conf. Comput. Vis. (2015) 3992–4000.

[13] J. Long, E. Shelhamer, T. Darrell, Fully convolutional networks for semantic segmentation, in: Proceedings of the IEEE Conference on Computer Vision and Pattern Recognition, 2015, pp. 3431–3440.
[14] Y. Wei, X. Liang, Y. Chen, X. Shen, M.-M. Cheng, J. Feng, Y. Zhao, S. Yan, A simple to complex framework for weakly-supervised semantic segmentation, IEEE Trans. Pattern Anal. Mach. Intell. 39 (11) (2017).
[15] A. Krizhevsky, I. Sutskever, G.E. Hinton, Imagenet classification with deep convolutional neural networks, in: NIPS, 2012.
[16] Z. Yang, R. Nevatia, A multi-scale cascade fully convolutional network face detector, in: ICPR, 2016.
[17] A. Dundar, J. Jin, B. Martini, E. Culurciello, Embedded streaming deep neural networks accelerator with applications, IEEE Trans. Neural Netw. & Learning Syst. 28 (7) (2017) 1572–1583.
[18] R.J. Cintra, S. Duffner, C. Garcia, A. Leite, Low-complexity approximate convolutional neural networks, IEEE Trans. Neural Netw. Learning Syst. 99 (2018) 1–12.
[19] [19] S. Ren, K. He, R. Girshick, X. Zhang, J. Sun, Object detection networks on convolutional feature maps, IEEE Trans. Pattern Anal. Mach. Intell. 39 (7) (2017) 1476–1481.
[20] C. Szegedy, W. Liu, Y. Jia, P. Sermanet, S. Reed, D. Anguelov, D. Erhan, V. Vanhoucke, A. Rabinovich, Going deeper with convolutions, in: CVPR, 2015.
[21] A. Krizhevsky, I. Sutskever, G.E. Hinton, Imagenet classification with deep convolutional neural networks, in: NIPS, 2012.
[22] M.D. Zeiler, R. Fergus, Visualizing and understanding convolutional networks, in: ECCV, 2014.
[23] G. Li, Y. Yu, Visual saliency detection based on multiscale deep cnn features, IEEE Trans. Image Process. 25 (11) (2016) 5012–5024.
[24] K. He, X. Zhang, S. Ren, J. Sun, Deep residual learning for image recognition, in: IEEE Conference on Computer Vision and Pattern Recognition (CVPR), Las Vegas, NV, 2016, 2016, pp. 770–778, https://doi.org/10.1109/CVPR.2016.90.
[25] R. Girshick, J. Donahue, T. Darrell, J. Malik, Rich feature hierarchies for accurate object detection and semantic segmentation, in: CVPR, 2014.
[26] K. He, X. Zhang, S. Ren, J. Sun, Spatial pyramid pooling in deep convolutional networks for visual recognition, IEEE Trans. Pattern Anal. Mach. Intell. 37 (9) (2015) 1904–1916.
[27] R. Girshick, Fast r-CNN, in: ICCV, 2015.
[28] J. Deng, W. Dong, R. Socher, L.-J. Li, K. Li, L. FeiFei, ImageNet: A large-scale hierarchical image database, in: CVPR, 2009.
[29] M. Everingham, L. Van Gool, C.K.I. Williams, J. Winn, A. Zisserman, The PASCAL Visual Object Classes Challenge 2007 (VOC2007) Results, 2007.
[30] A. Krizhevsky, Learning Multiple Layers of Features from Tiny Images, 2009.
[31] A. Coates, H. Lee, A.Y. Ng, An analysis of single layer networks in unsupervised feature learning, AISTATS (2011).
[32] Y. Netzer, T. Wang, A. Coates, A. Bissacco, B. Wu, A.Y. Ng, Reading Digits in Natural Images with Unsupervised Feature Learning NIPS Workshop on Deep Learning and Unsupervised Feature Learning, 2011.
[33] F.J. LeCun, L.B. Huang, Learning methods for generic object recognition with invariance to pose and lighting, in: CVPR, 2004.
[34] A. Conneau, H. Schwenk, L. Barrault, Y. Lecun, Very Deep Convolutional Networks for Text Classification, arXiv:1606.01781, 2016.
[35] V.B. Mititelu, Wordnets: state of the art and perspectives. Case study: the romanian wordnet, in: Proceedings of Recent Advances in Natural Language Processing, 2011, pp. 672–677.

[36] S. Ruder, P. Ghaffari, J.G. Breslin, Character-level and Multi-channel Convolutional Neural Networks for Large-scale Authorship Attribution, arXiv: 1609.06686, 2016.

[37] J. Lee, T. Kim, J. Park, J. Nam, Raw Waveform-based Audio Classification Using Sample-level CNN Architectures, arXiv: 1712.00866, 2017.

[38] A. Krizhevsky, I. Sutskever, G.E. Hinton, ImageNet classification with deep convolutional neural networks, Commun. ACM 60 (6) (2017) 84–90.

[39] K. Simonyan, A. Zisserman, Verydeepconvolutionalnetworksforlarge-Scaleimagerecognition, arXiv:1409.1556v6, 2015.

[40] C. Szegedy, W. Liu, Y. Jia, P. Sermanet, S. Reed, D. Anguelov, D. Erhan, V. Vanhoucke, A. Rabinovich, Going Deeper with Convolutions, arXiv:1409.4842v1, 2014.

[41] K. He, X. Zhang, S. Ren, J. Sun, Deep Residual Learning for Image Recognition, arXiv:1512.03385v1, 2015.

[42] S. Xie, R. Girshick, P. Dollar, Z. Tu, K. He, Aggregatedresidual transformations for deep neural networks, in: CVPR, 2017.

[43] R. Girshick, J. Donahue, T. Darrell, J. Malik, Rich Feature Hierarchies for Accurate Object Detection and Semantic Segmentation, arXiv:1311.2524v5, 2014.

[44] J. Redmon, S. Divvala, R. Girshick, A. Farhadi, You only look once: unified, real-time object detection, in: Proceedings of IEEE Conference, 2015.

[45] F.N. Iandola, S. Han, M.W. Moskewicz, K. Ashraf, W.J. Dally, K. Keutzer, SqueezeNet: AlexNet-Level Accuracy with 50x Fewer Parameters and <0.5MB Model Size, arXiv:1602.07360, 2016.

[46] V. Badrinarayanan, A. Kendall, R. Cipolla, SegNet: A Deep Convolutional Encoder-Decoder Architecture for Image Segmentation, arXiv:1511.00561, 2016.

[47] I.J. Goodfellow, J. Pouget-Abadie, M. Mirza, B. Xu, D. Warde-Farley, S. Ozair, A. Courville, Y. Bengio, Generative Adversarial Networks, arXiv:1406.2661, 2014.

[48] T.Y. Lin, et al., Microsoft COCO: Common Objects in Context. Computer Vision—ECCV 2014, Springer International Publishing, 2014, pp. 740–755.

[49] Y. LeCun, L. Bottou, Y. Bengio, P. Haffner, Gradient-based learning applied to document recognition, Proc. IEEE 86 (11) (1998) 2278–2324.

[50] M. Defferrard, S.P. Mohanty, S.F. Carroll, M. Salathé, Learning to Recognize Musical Genre from Audio, arXiv:1803.05337, 2018.

[51] G.J. Brostow, J. Fauqueur, R. Cipolla, Semantic object classes in video: a high-definition ground truth database, Pattern Recogn. Lett. 30 (2) (2009) 88–97.

[52] Z. Luo, F.B. Charron, C. Lemaire, J. Konrad, S. Li, A. Mishra, A. Achkar, J. Eichel, P-M Jodoin MIO-TCD: A New Benchmark Dataset for Vehicle Classification and Localization in Press at IEEE Transactions on Image Processing, 2018.

[53] K. Yun, H. Jeong, K.M. Yi, S.W. Kim, J.Y. Choi, Motion interaction field for accident detection in traffic surveillance vid-eo, in: 2014 22nd International Conference on Pattern Recognition, 3062–3067, IEEE, Stockholm, Sweden, 2014.

[54] H. Tan, J. Zhang, J. Feng, F. Li, Vehicle speed measure-ment for accident scene investigation, in: 2010 IEEE 7th Inter-national Conference on E-Business Engineering, 389–392, IEEE, Shanghai, China, 2010.

[55] D. Singh, C.K. Mohan, Deep spatio-temporal representa-tion for detection of road accidents using stacked autoencoder, IEEE Trans. Intell. Transp. Syst. 20 (3) (2019) 879–887.

[56] C. Wang, Y. Dai, W. Zhou, Y. Geng, A vision-based video crash detection framework for mixed traffic flow environment considering low-visibility condition, J. Adv. Transp. 2020 (2020), 9194028. 11 https://doi.org/10.1155/2020/9194028.

[57] J.B. Kim, Vehicle detection using deep learning tech-nique in tunnel road environments, Symmetry (2020), https://doi.org/10.3390/sym12122012.

Chapter 16

# Risk analysis of coronavirus patients who have underlying chronic cancer

**V. Kakulapati**
*Sreenidhi Institute of Science and Technology, Hyderabad, Telangana, India*

## 1 Introduction

The data collection needed for insights [1], the responses, and the guidelines to tackle and resolve the COVID-19 pandemic use advanced analytics and artificial intelligence (AI) from days to minutes and better-than-anticipated precision. Analytics will take things to another level by offering a more in-depth view of movements and behaviors in humans, thereby enabling insightful predictions. By implementing response protocols as a question of national emergencies, telco analysis will undoubtedly be used along with big data and AI to contain, mitigate, and finally solve the global issue sooner and more precisely.

Emerging data published by the US Centers for Disease Control and Prevention (CDC) on March 31 confirms the elevated incidence of COVID-19 chronic illness for Americans with severe medical problems, consistent with earlier Chinese and Italian studies.

- About 71% of those hospitalized for COVID-19 have at least one underlying condition, and of those admitted for critical attention due to COVID-19, approximately 78% had at least one autoimmune illness.
- Approximately 27% among those hospitalized for intensive care for COVID-19 have one or more risk factors.
- Diabetes, lung disease, and heart disease were the most frequently recorded complications in persons with COVID-19.

Individuals with existing health issues, including fever, cough, or shortness of breath, who have COVID-19 symptoms should contact their healthcare provider immediately, the CDC wrote in a recent report.

**Cognitive Systems and Signal Processing in Image Processing. https://doi.org/10.1016/B978-0-12-824410-4.00001-5**

The prevalence of COVID-19 has been higher in patients with cancer [2]. Hematological and lung malignancies and metastatic conditions are associated with an ongoing rise in cancer patients' risk. Solid tumor patients tend to experience an elevated risk, particularly in the first year of diagnosis, which is dependent on a diagnosis of >5 years ago [3]. Active diseases face a substantially higher risk of serious COVID-19 [IV] [4, 5] for all malignancies. Consequently, the rising prevalence and seriousness of COVID-19 are observations centered on noncomparative retrospective studies of cancer patients, in contrast to patients without cancer. Accurate prevalence data and detailed analyses differ significantly.

The influence of certain underlying medical conditions and whether they strengthen the risk of complications due to COVID-19 is currently reducing. Depending on what we presently know, there is potential for COVID-19 chronic disease in adults with disabilities under exceptional reasons. There is an emerging concern of specific chronic health issues, like leukemia, and COVID-19. COVID-19 identifies as a severe illness: inpatient, intensive care unit (ICU) entry, sedation or artificial breathing, or demise [6].

Assessments for SARS-CoV-2 are conducted using the nucleic-acid amplification procedure for cancer patients with low respiratory symptoms (e.g., fever or cough) and exposure to COVID-19. The potential causes for these patients' complaints are analyzed. Patients will screen by obstetric or immunosuppressive therapy performed in symptomatic or asymptomatic manner. Although some hospitals provide SARS-CoV-2 examinations to all patients with lung cancer (regardless of the existence of symptoms), this practice is variable.

The primary concern of coronaviruses is mainly affecting the respiratory system of human beings. Seventh in the family of coronaviruses infecting humans is COVID-19. COVID-19 alone remains a microorganism, and the role of novel SARS-CoV-2 coronaviruses in cancer is not very well studied. Impairments, such as hypertension and malignancy, are similar to other extreme acute respiratory outbreaks (SARS-CoV, MERS-CoV) and are predisposed to adverse side effects in COVID-19 cases [7–10]. One of China's quite severe comorbidities that raises the risk for COVID-19 was the scientific literature concerning 1590 positive COVID-19 patients [11].

There is a small amount of knowledge accessible to investigators from cancer patients at high risk affected by SARS-CoV-2 contamination. It is clear that the patients who have established or undergone cancer-related therapies are more likely to become sicker by contracting COVID-19 infection during chemotherapy, radiotherapy, stem cell transplantation, or CAR-T cell therapy [12, 13]. With improved testing availabilities, better immunosuppressive drug regimes, and possibly reduced dose levels, cancer patients undergoing antitumor treatments are subject to more robust tests for COVID-19 infections.

## 2 Related work

Knowledge bases of the effect of COVID-19 on victims and survivors of cancer are inadequate. Preliminary evidence from China and Italy reported that COVID-19 cases had a high prevalence in the hospital [14, 15]. The number of reports made during the COVID-19 pandemic lockdown to a significant British cancer organization illustrates the entirely reasonable fear of cancer patients undergoing therapy and remediation. The fact that patients with cancer have an increased chance for COVID-19 transformation is not yet noticeable. However, they are seriously immune from cancer and their treatment [16]. They are very vulnerable to adverse outcomes [17]. According to a report, 18 out of 1590 COVID-19 patients have a cancer history. The risk of ICU mechanical ventilation or COVID-19 death was highest in cancer patients [14]. The uncertainty is characterizing by patients who underwent cancer treatment or chemo 1 month before admission. Cancer treatment is a known pathogen causing, but the perplexed inflammatory system it develops may trigger a less severe hypersensitivity reaction, which is advantageous for cancer survivors.

Cancer survivors can be essential to accurately diagnose COVID-19 complications as pathogen characteristics frequently resemble cancer and toxic reactions associated with treatment [18, 19]. This could trigger a slow or missing identification of COVID-19, leading to problems and epidemic complications and thus life-threatening interventions [20]. COVID-19 can also be a limitation to the proper and ethical treatment of a perceived ease of cancer. The pandemic causes a major program reconfiguration of both curative and palliative oncology, which results in fewer clinical visits because of social distancing [21], delays in screening, and improvements in therapy, which inevitably have significant effects on the death and morbidity associated with cancer. There is currently no decisive evidence that cytotoxic drugs were prescribed to cancer patients treated with COVID-19 patients in a recent methodological review [22].

A few investigations were compatible but did not compare the significant increase of pneumonia by many cancer patients [23, 24] with research results from this domain. The effects of influenza cancer patients are investigating, and a slight amount of death variation was notice classified according to the type of hematologic, nonhematologic cancer activity. Some investigations disclose that patients with hematologic cancer are more likely than patients with nonhematological cancer to contaminate and affect adults or fatality risk.

Research findings using administrative statistics in South Korean practices led to flu claims among breast cancer survivors and pediatric cancer survivors [25]. Many researchers have investigated the susceptibility to respiratory infectious disease with some severity. Consequently, a substantial percentage of hematopoietic gene therapy patients had an infectious disease due to transplantation, but no clinical trial or knowledge was supporting the intensity of clinical infection [26]. It is unclear how COVID-19 impacts patients and victims. Previous reports from China and Italy indicated that COVID-19 hospitalized patients with leukemia histories were overexpressed [14, 15].

## 3 About COVID-19 with chronic diseases

The following recovery plan tends to be undertaken if a patient has an essential health condition:

- Continue personal medications without appealing to a patient healthcare provider, and do not change your treatment schedule.
- Get pharmaceutical and nonprescription pharmaceutical drugs available for at least 30 days. Talk with a health insurance manager, insurer, and pharmacist as needed to limit the pharmacy visits by receiving an additional stock (i.e., longer than 30 days) of prescription drugs.
- Do not postpone receiving emergency treatment due to COVID-19 for an essential medical condition. Contingency infection control plans are available in emergency rooms to shield you from COVID-19 if you need care.
- If you have questions or feel ill and suspect a COVID-19 infection, call your health care professional. Call 911 immediately if you need medical assistance.
- Contact your local health facility or health department if you do not have a health care provider.

The chance of acute COVID-19 viral infection is intensified by leukemia. It is usually inappropriate if a compromised immune system elevates the threat.
**Procedures to follow:**

- Communicate patient-perceived risk relying on diagnosis, recovery, and population-level transmission to patient health care providers or care team.
- Never stop taking medications or change in recovery schedule without communicating.
- Take steps to make sure the prescriptions are supplied for at least 30 days.
- Do not postpone surgery or urgent care that saves lives.
- If you have concerns about your diagnosis or medication, consider the patient vulnerable to COVID-19 or any other issues; call your primary care provider or health care team.
- Consult the appropriate health care service or hospital facility for more information on cancer prevention.

Patients infected by cancer with COVID-19 could experience diagnostic clinical complications and disease severity. The effectiveness of the anticancer medicine and cancer treatments hinder SARS-CoV-2 recovery. The patient at risk for cancer has continuing diagnostic, point, and treatment issues related to the deterioration of COVID-19 in noninfected patients. Appropriate and adequate utilization of existing health care services and analysis by government agencies of the COVID-19 cancer recommendations are giving elsewhere [27] to reduce the disparity between physical distance and cancer care implementation.

- Are cancer patients at high risk [28]?

  It is not currently clear whether or not cancer survivors are at an increased risk for contracting COVID-19. Irrespective of chronic disease, the risk of transmission of the epidemic is quite massive. Nevertheless, those cancer survivors are at an increased risk for developing the outbreak because they are immunodeficient. The epidemic is so significant that it may not yet be investigating thoroughly. There is substantial evidence that if a person with cancer has been with infected COVID-19, more severe complications can arising from the infection.
- COVID-19 is more severe in cancer patients.

  The immune system of the body, particularly under chemotherapy, is significantly weaker. Patients are more likely to have complications once they have an infection, like pneumonia. There are a few other reasons that individualize the likelihood of a person living with cancer having a more severe case. They include the perspectives of the patients and specific types of cancer, their therapy, and their immunodeficiency.
- Is it the same in all cancer patients?

  No. As such, in many cases, immune system are similar, or not entirely different, to a standard patient, in very few patients there is sustainability, such as in those who have been in regression for years. The immunological processes have been widely perverse and extremely unpredictable in patients undergoing chemotherapy within the first few months of diagnosis.
- Are the COVID-19 symptoms similar in cancer patients?

  The information gathering is small, but we assume the symptoms are probably the same at the moment. COVID-19 people experience moderate to severe symptoms of lung infections, such as:
  - fever;
  - fatigue;
  - hunger impairment or dehydration; and
  - shortness of breath.
- What should a cancer patient with COVID-19 do?

  Consult your oncologists, discuss symptoms, the location of the treatment course, whether the symptoms are linked to illness or cancer treatment, whether you require an emergency department, and the services the health team provides.

  The next step will be tailoring.
- Will the cancer patients be protected from COVID-19?
  - Physicians prescribe having similar medical recommendations and procedures.
  - Regularly washing hands with soap for 20 seconds.

- Use sanitizer containing at least 60% alcohol when soap and water are not available.
- Avoid rubbing the eyes, nose, or mouth.
- Avoid contact with others, particularly ill people.
- Cover the mouth and nose with a tissue while coughing or sneezing and discard tissue.
- Utilize standard professional carpet cleaning and spray or wipe to clean and disinfect frequently handled objects and environments.
- Proper social isolation.

- **When are cancer patients safe**

  A COVID-19 leukemia investigation team has been formulating healthcare facilities to deal with potential issues and recommend safe immunotherapy in this unprecedented period. A daily interactive meeting is conducted with clinicians, nursing staff, management, and so forth to communicate methodologies and circulate alternative suggestions in all hospitals and at all levels. The method integration was functional. There are effective strategies that we are inclined to exchange among clinics and medical facilities if required. People are also following the CDC's direction, influencing all residents', clinicians', and nurses' health and well-being.

**COVID-19 prevalence in cancer patients**—The prevalence of COVID-19 in cancer patients differs. In people with cancer, COVID-19 cases are more prominent than in the typical community, even though not all results indicate this. Some studies demonstrate that the prevalence rates of COVID-19 are still very modest, approximately 1% and 4% in leukemia patients receiving effective therapy. For instance, few study results showed reduced infections in people with cancer:

- The contamination intensity once the implementation of regional and institutional protection measures was 0.4% in an Austrian analysis of 1016 people with cancer in a limited, many outpatients tertiary healthcare facility (88%) [29]. This was comparable in the Austrian community and lower than the nonhospitalized patients who had cancer.
- Investigations in China and Lombardy, Italy, indicated a significantly higher likelihood of leukemia infections in people with cancer than those in the regular community, at roughly 1% [30].

Other assessments, such as a Spain study suggesting an occurrence of approximately 4% [31] and an investigation from the US Veterans Affairs, have reported an elevated infection rate within people with cancer, indicating an intensity of about 8% [32]. A higher percentage of contamination was identified in black patients relative to white patient populations (15% vs 5.5%).

There were huge discrepancies in cancer prevalence among people with COVID-19. Studies from Wuhan, China, indicate that approximately 1%–2% of those with COVID-19 reported cancer [32]. In comparison, a higher prevalence of cancer in COVID-19 patients from New York City was recorded (6% had cancer in one study of 5700 hospitalizing COVID-19 patients). In Lombardy, Italy, an active or previous malignancy history is present at 8% of the patients admitted to the COVID-19 Intensive Care Department [33]. Twenty percent of COVID-19 deaths in patients all over Italy were reporting in a survey to have had cancer.

The population currently influenced by cancer and the COVID-19 community will categorically expand to multiple geographies and cohorts asymmetrically as the infection progress.

## 4 Experimental analysis

Influenza symptoms and death rates of patients who survive cancer are being monitored. Individuals were observed from the initial date until the earliest occurrence of the outcome, death without the development, or end of the study period. Follow-up was not censored at the end of data collection in CPRD GOLD because the principal analysis did not require postbaseline primary care data. Experts then implemented Cox's random effects models with a corresponding duration before the initial examination, initially only by homogeneity by comparing the maturity level. By changing to the prevalence of risk factors at the index date (for this analysis, obesity was classified at the cancer diagnosis date since weight measures in the year following cancer diagnosis may be unstable). We examined the cancer diagnosis by fitting a time-updated variable indicating the time of cancer survivorship (1 to $<5$, 5 to $<10$, and $\geq 10$ years since diagnosis, vs control group).

### 4.1 Method and data source

Our proposed machine learning COVID-19 detection involves many stages, as displayed in Fig. 1. The stages are briefly explaining here.

- Collect X-ray images of COVID-19 patients and healthy patients.
- Generate 1500 chest X-ray images.
- Provide feature selection on images applying machine learning algorithm of artificial neural network (ANN), grade boosting machine (GBM), and deep neural network (DNN).
- Divide dataset into two groups: training group and validation group.
- Evaluate the performance of algorithm on the validation dataset.

### 4.2 Dataset

A Kaggle dataset, which includes X-ray tests of COVID-19 patients, was used for this project. This datasets have been utilizing for trials with and without COVID-19 patients. The dataset is described in Table 1. It was using only

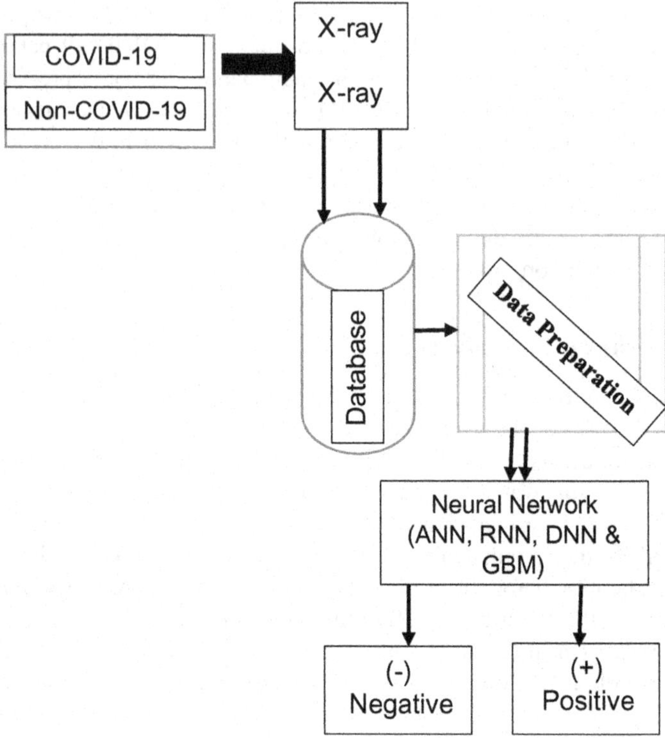


**FIG. 1** Propose machine learning diagnose system architecture.

**TABLE 1** Dataset.

| X-ray images | Frequency |
|---|---|
| COVID-19 | 60 |
| Healthy | 100 |
| **Total** | **160** |

the radiographs of both people—complete pictures for 160 of the sample. Data increase methods to control and convergence were also improving to achieve better results.

## 4.3 Evaluation metrics

Evaluation of the two proposed machine learning algorithms' reliability, metrics such as accuracy, recall, and area under curve (AUC) graph have been used.

These measures are assessing based on the true-positive, true-negative, false-negative, and false-positive.

$$Accuracy = \frac{(TP + TN)}{(TP + TN + FN + FP)}$$

$$Precision = \frac{TP}{(TP + FP)}$$

The reliability metric calculates the percentage of cases with the given dataset to identify accurately. If the accuracy is higher, most machine learning can do well.

Efficiency tests the accuracy, which is calculated as the percentage of optimistic projection, divided by the total.

It is reminiscent that the number of positive ones accurately identified as real positives and the number of actual positive ones separated is computed as completeness.

$$Recall = \frac{TP}{TP + FN}$$

$F$-measure is computed by merging precision and recall, which is substantial for a trial dataset involving an imbalance class.

$$F - measure = 2\frac{Precision * Recall}{(Precision + Recall)}$$

## 4.4 Implementation and result

The X-ray images were loaded for preprocessing, preparation, and cleaning to avoid data trawling. The orange application widgets were used for the training of the data and its validation. Sample of the data used (X-ray) images are shown in Figs. 2 and 3. The X-ray images had 1024 × 1024 pixels, while the train model was pretrained using images with 224 × 224 pixels.

The model design for diagnosing COVID-19 was based on ANN, RNN, DNN, and GMB, and these models were designed to detect COVID-19 using chest X-ray images. Orange application comes with an image analyzer that is very powerful and able to code to suit the kind of patterns needed within the image provided for training.

The detector for COVID-19 was trained and tested on collected dataset, 70% of which was for training and 30% was a remainder for testing. To reduce imbalance of data, class weight technique was applied. We adjusted weight inversely proportional to class frequencies in the input data. Both models were able to distinguish between dataset for higher classification accuracy.

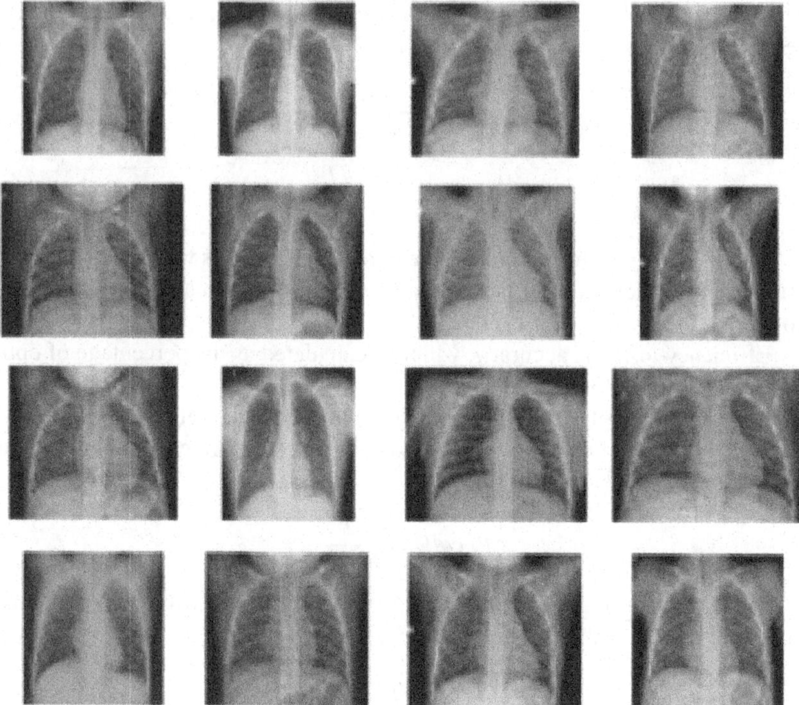

**FIG. 2** Normal X-ray images.

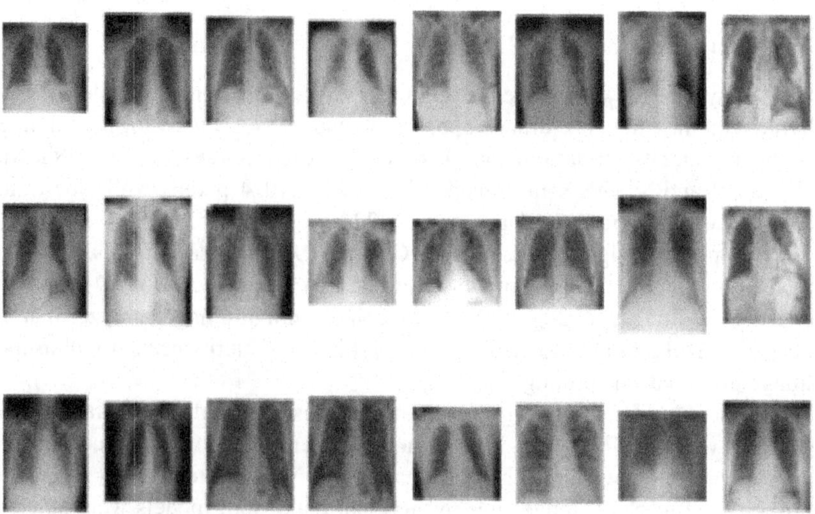

**FIG. 3** Abnormal X-ray images.

## 4.5 Result of the study

The result of the study was very encouraging in the field of diagnosing methods for COVID-19. Multiple epochs were applied to train the VGG16-based model of ANN, RNN, DNN, and GMB. The applied machine learning technique was effective. The prediction model for RNN was able to achieve a higher accuracy of 96.6% and *F*-measure of 94%; also the DNN was able to achieve an accuracy of 94.8% and *F*-measure of 92%, ANN too was able to achieve an accuracy of 93.9% and *F*-measure of 91%, and GBM was able to achieve an accuracy of 93.8% and *F*-measure of 94%. Figs. 4–7 show the performance of all the models and their classification accuracy.

# 5 Discussion

In this study we developed and tested a deep transfer learning of LSTN and RNN models to detect and classify chest X-ray images depicting COVID-19. All the proposed models obtained better result. Comparing our model accuracy and precision with other models, the RNN, COVID-19 prediction is best, obtaining 96.6% for accuracy and 96.4% for precision. A best training process was gained as the difference between the training and validation became closer. A robust COVID-19 detector was built as the *F*-measure improved to 0.97. The metrics of AUC was impressive as the model achieved 0.9. Fig. 8A–D shows the result of the metric AUC. Thus, the COVID-19 diagnosis model trained on the X-ray data provides superior performance metrics.

Using RNN proved highly sensitive, as can be seen from Fig. 8C. We recommend scientist working on COVID-19 to depend on systems with models built using RNN. It was followed by ANN, which was much closer with AUC (ROC) of 0.87. People with cancer diseases are very open for contracting COVID-19.

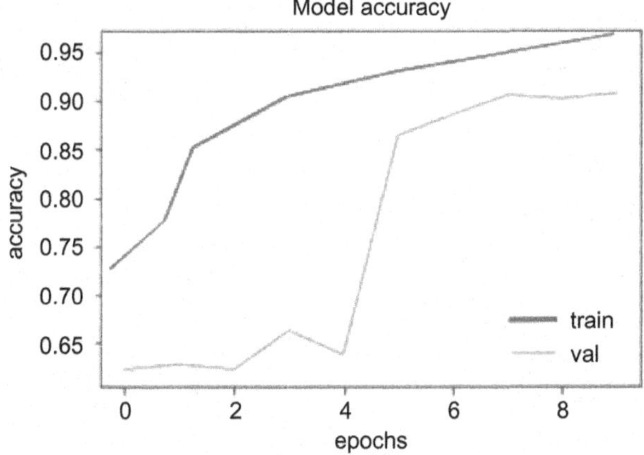


**FIG. 4** DNN training and validating accuracy.

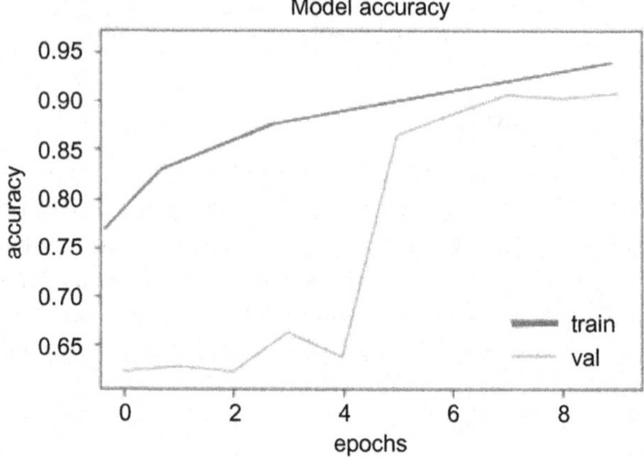


**FIG. 5** RNN training and validating accuracy.

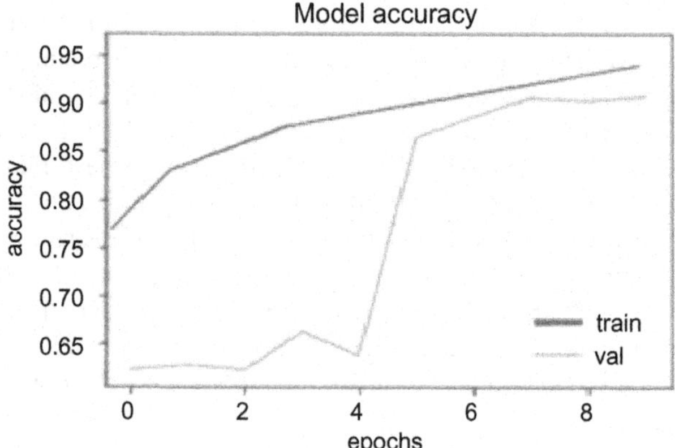


**FIG. 6** ANN training and validating accuracy.

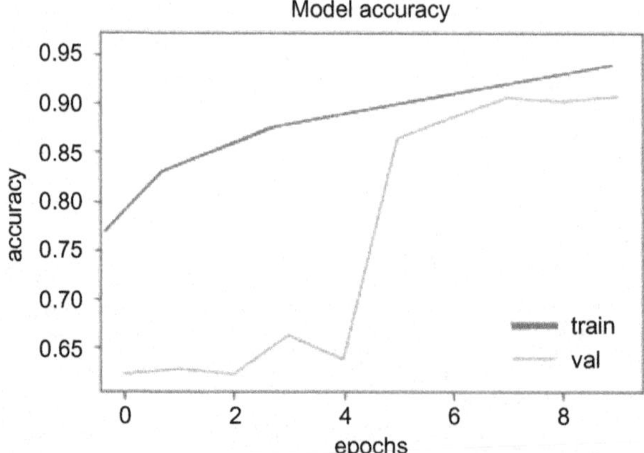


**FIG. 7** GMB training and validating accuracy.

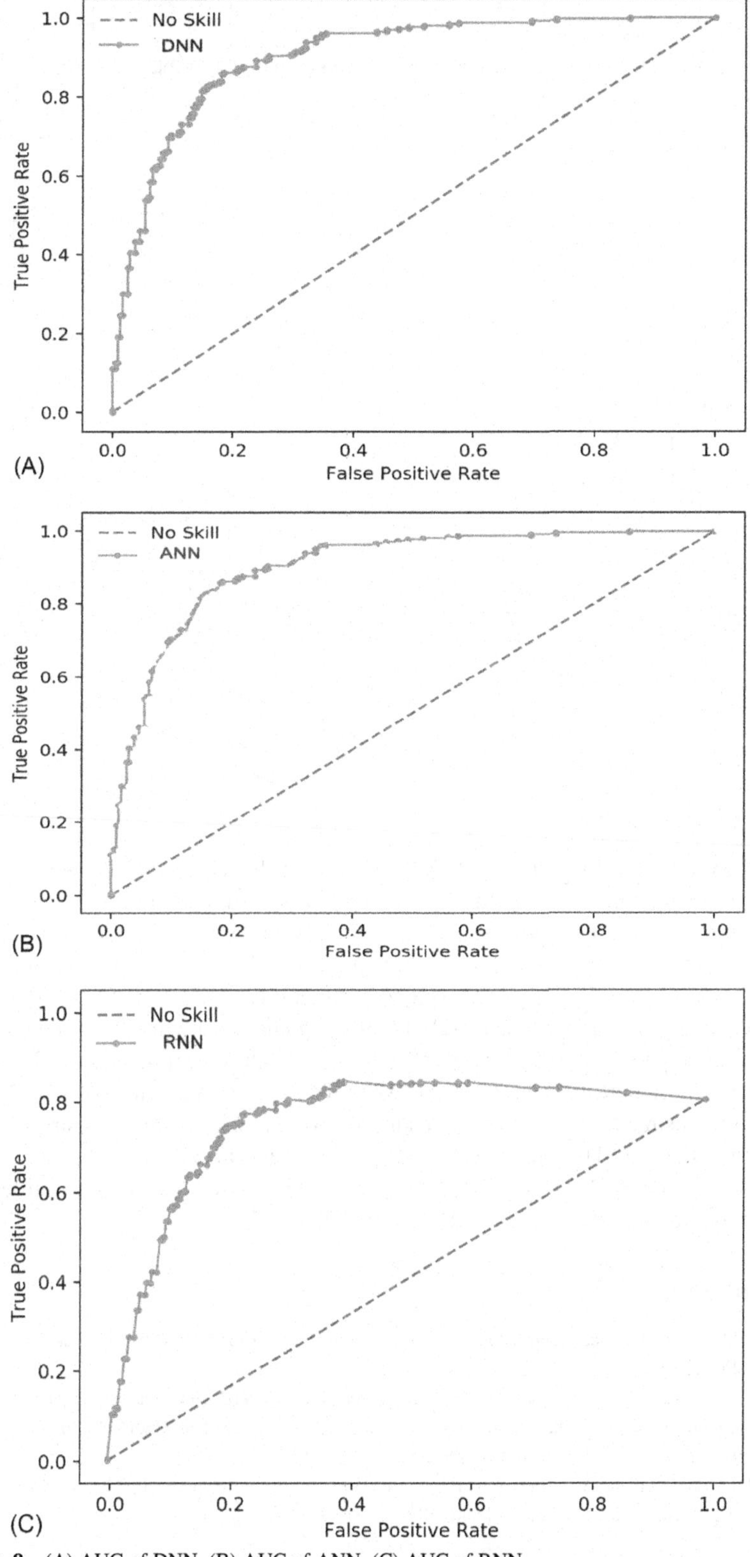


**FIG. 8** (A) AUC of DNN, (B) AUC of ANN, (C) AUC of RNN,

*(Continued)*

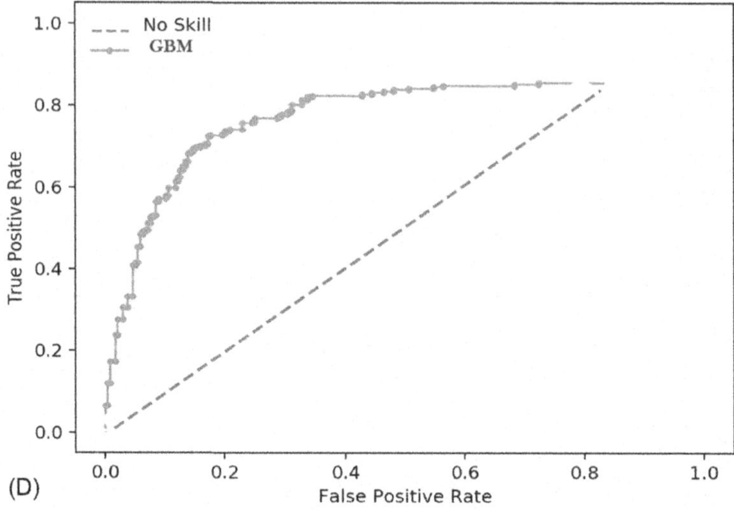


**FIG. 8, cont'd** (D) AUC of GBM.

## 6 Conclusion

The exponential increase of COVID-19 across the globe and the increasing number of deaths need urgent actions from all departments. Future forecasting of potential infections will enable authorities to battle the consequences effectively. In this study, a machine learning algorithm was used to propose a diagnosis system for COVID-19. A diagnosis model using CNN, RNN, DNN, and GBM was proposed to detect COVID-19 using chest X-ray images. The model was developed using a dataset from the Kaggle database to train and validate the effectiveness of the model. In future, we will consider diagnosing COVID-19 in RT-PCR using the VGG-16 version and compare their performance using a high volume dataset. The model with best performance in terms of precision and AUC was the RNN model. We therefore, recommended researchers and practitioners to use this model for detecting COVID-19.

## References

[1] https://www.teradata.com/Blogs/Advanced-Analytics-for-Coronavirus-Trends-Patterns-Predictions.

[2] M.M. Rüthrich, C. Giessen-Jung, S. Borgmann, et al., COVID-19 in cancer patients: clinical characteristics and outcome-an analysis of the LEOSS registry, Ann. Hematol. (2020), https://doi.org/10.1007/s00277-020-04328-4. Online ahead of print.

[3] E.J. Williamson, A.J. Walker, K. Bhaskaran, et al., Factors associated with COVID-19-related death using OpenSAFELY, Nature 584 (2020) 430–436.

[4] N.M. Kuderer, T.K. Choueiri, D.P. Shah, et al., Clinical impact of COVID-19 on patients with cancer (CCC19): a cohort study, Lancet 395 (2020) 1907–1918.

[5] F. Martín-Moro, J. Marquet, M. Piris, et al., Survival study of hospitalised patients with concurrent COVID-19 and haematological malignancies, Br. J. Haematol. 190 (2020) e16–e20.

[6] https://www.cdc.gov/coronavirus/2019-ncov/need-extra-precautions/people-with-medical-conditions.html#cancer.

[7] F.Y. Alqahtani, et al., Prevalence of comorbidities in cases of Middle East respiratory syndrome coronavirus: a retrospective study, Epidemiol. Infect. (2018), https://doi.org/10.1017/s0950268818002923.

[8] W.J. Guan, et al., Comorbidity and its impact on 1590 patients with COVID-19 in China: a nationwide analysis, Eur. Respir. J. (2020), https://doi.org/10.1183/13993003.00547-2020.

[9] A. Martinez, et al., Risk factors associated with severe outcomes in adult hospitalized patients according to influenza type and subtype, PLoS One 14 (1) (2019) e0210353.

[10] J. Mauskopf, et al., The burden of influenza complications in different high-risk groups: a targeted literature review, J. Med. Econ. 16 (2) (2013) 264–277.

[11] T.P. Hanna, G.A. Evans, C.M. Booth, Cancer, COVID-19 and the precautionary principle: prioritizing treatment during a global pandemic, Nat. Rev. Clin. Oncol. 17 (5) (2020) 268–270.

[12] W.H. Liang, et al., Clinical characteristics and outcomes of hospitalised patients with COVID-19 treated in Hubei (epicenter) and outside Hubei (non-epicenter): a nationwide analysis of China, Eur. Respir. J. (2020), https://doi.org/10.1183/13993003.00562-2020.

[13] K.K. Sahu, et al., Facing COVID-19 in the hematopoietic cell transplant setting: a new challenge for transplantation physicians, Blood Cells Mol. Dis. 83 (2020) 102439.

[14] W. Liang, W. Guan, R. Chen, W. Wang, J. Li, K. Xu, C. Li, Q. Ai, W. Lu, H. Liang, S. Li, J. He, Cancer patients in SARS-CoV-2 infection: a nationwide analysis in China, Lancet Oncol 21 (3) (2020) 335–337, https://doi.org/10.1016/S1470-2045(20)30096-6.

[15] D. Trapani, A. Marra, G. Curigliano, The experience on coronavirus disease 2019 and cancer from an oncology hub institution in Milan, Lombardy region, Eur. J. Cancer 132 (2020) 199–206, https://doi.org/10.1016/j.ejca.2020.04.017.

[16] Y. Xia, R. Jin, J. Zhao, W. Li, H. Shen, Risk of COVID-19 for patients with cancer, Lancet Oncol. 21 (4) (2020) e180, https://doi.org/10.1016/S1470-2045(20)30150-9.

[17] V. Jindal, K.K. Sahu, S. Gaikazian, A.D. Siddiqui, I. Jaiyesimi, Cancer treatment during COVID-19 pandemic, Med. Oncol. 37 (7) (2020) 58, https://doi.org/10.1007/s12032-020-01382-w.

[18] J. Spicer, C. Chamberlain, S. Papa, Provision of cancer care during the COVID-19 pandemice, Nat. Rev. Clin. Oncol. 17 (2020) 329–331, https://doi.org/10.1038/s41571-020-0370-6.

[19] B. Russell, C. Moss, A. Rigg, C. Hopkins, S. Papa, M. van Hemelrijck, Anosmia and ageusia are emerging as symptoms in patients with COVID-19: what does the current evidence say? Ecancermedicalscience 14 (2020) ed98, https://doi.org/10.3332/ecancer.2020.ed98.

[20] D. Schrag, D.L. Hershman, E. Basch, Oncology practice during the covid-19 pandemic, JAMA (2020), https://doi.org/10.1001/jama.2020.6236. Epub ahead of print.

[21] Cancer care goes virtual in response to COVID-19, Cancer Discov. 10 (2020) 755, https://doi.org/10.1158/2159-8290.CD-NB2020-027.

[22] B. Russell, C. Moss, G. George, A. Santaolalla, A. Cope, S. Papa, et al., Associations between immune-suppressive and stimulating drugs and novel Covid-19 – a systematic review of current evidence, Ecancer 14 (2020) 1022, https://doi.org/10.3332/ecancer.2020.1022.

[23] B. Hermann, et al., Influenza virus infections in patients with malignancies - characteristics and outcome of the season 2014/15. A survey conducted by the Infectious Diseases Working

Party (AGIHO) of the German Society of Haematology and Medical Oncology (DGHO), Eur. J. Clin. Microbiol. 36 (2017) 565–573.

[24] J. Heo, et al., Influenza among breast cancer survivors in South Korea: a nationwide population-based study, In Vivo (Athens, Greece) 31 (2017) 967–972.

[25] J. Heo, et al., Incidence of influenza among childhood cancer survivors in South Korea: a population-based retrospective analysis, In Vivo (Athens, Greece) 34 (2020) 929–933.

[26] G. Dyer, et al., A survey of infectious diseases and vaccination uptake in long-term hematopoietic stem cell transplant survivors in Australia, Transpl. Infect. Dis: Off. J. Transpl. Soc. 21 (2019) e13043.

[27] https://www.uptodate.com/contents/coronavirus-disease-2019-covid-19-risks-for-infection-clinical-presentation-testing-and-management-in-patients-with-cancer.

[28] https://www.cinj.org/patient-care/covid-19-what-cancer-patients-need-know.

[29] A.S. Berghoff, M. Gansterer, A.C. Bathke, et al., SARS-CoV-2 testing in patients with cancer treated at a tertiary care hospital during the COVID-19 pandemic, J. Clin. Oncol. 38 (2020) 3547.

[30] J. Yu, W. Ouyang, M.L.K. Chua, C. Xie, SARS-CoV-2 transmission in patients with cancer at a tertiary care hospital in Wuhan, China, JAMA Oncol. 6 (2020) 1108.

[31] A. Desai, S. Sachdeva, T. Parekh, R. Desai, COVID-19 and cancer: lessons from a pooled meta-analysis, JCO Glob. Oncol. 6 (2020) 557.

[32] A. Emami, F. Javanmardi, N. Pirbonyeh, A. Akbari, Prevalence of underlying diseases in hospitalized patients with COVID-19: a systematic review and meta-analysis, Arch. Acad. Emerg. Med. 8 (2020) e35.

[33] Y. Hu, J. Sun, Z. Dai, et al., Prevalence and severity of corona virus disease 2019 (COVID-19): A systematic review and meta-analysis, J. Clin. Virol. 127 (2020) 104371.

# Index

Note: Page numbers followed by "*f*" indicate figures and "*t*" indicate tables.

## C

# D

## H



## I



## J



## K



## L

## R



## S

Printed in the United States
by Baker & Taylor Publisher Services